APOCALYPSE IN
PARADISE

A Political, Religious and Social Expose

APOCALYPSE IN
PARADISE

Good and Evil, Volume IV

There was Mickey Mouse
And Donald Duck
And Snow White with her seven little Friends
All enjoying Make-believe

And so many other strange little Creatures
They are paired with a strange glaring form of music
All of the Creatures were jumping, mindlessly, up and down

⎯⎯⎯⎯

In this; the Fairyland of Fantasy
And Make believe?

ROBERT R. FIEDLER

iUniverse LLC
Bloomington

APOCALYPSE IN PARADISE
Good and Evil, Volume IV

iUniverse books may be ordered through booksellers or by contacting:

iUniverse LLC
1663 Liberty Drive
Bloomington, IN 47403
www.iuniverse.com
1-800-Authors (1-800-288-4677)

Because of the dynamic nature of the Internet, any web addresses or links contained in this book may have changed since publication and may no longer be valid. The views expressed in this work are solely those of the author and do not necessarily reflect the views of the publisher, and the publisher hereby disclaims any responsibility for them.

Any people depicted in stock imagery provided by Thinkstock are models, and such images are being used for illustrative purposes only.
Certain stock imagery © Thinkstock.

ISBN: 978-1-4917-1535-2 (sc)
ISBN: 978-1-4917-1612-0 (e)

Library of Congress Control Number: 2013920942

Printed in the United States of America.

iUniverse rev. date: 12/06/2013

CONTENTS

ILLUSTRATIONS

DEDICATION

This book is dedicated to those who seek the truth.
At times it can be a dangerous mission for some it has been fatal.
At most times the entire world is under some threat; all men cannot agree.
It is dedicated to the authors on the bibliography for what I have learned from them.

Certainly not everyone can know everything and there may be some incidents of error.
Such incidents are the result of lies that have been told and fabrications.
Much of what is learned as Historic reporting is often in correct.
Invention is evil when it is dishonest.
Much History is dishonest.

———

Also I dedicate this book to my deceased wife of 53 years.
She was the driving force of all that I have ever done since I was seventeen.
She was a truly wonderful and loving wife and a beautiful mother for our two children.

We had a wonderful life together.

I am and have been the happiest man in the World!

All this is because of my Geri.

Reality; Good and Evil Vol. IV

Apocalypse in Paradise

First, let us consider the good Gifts which we all enjoy

Space, Matter, Movement, Time and Light

All of these gifts are phenomenal and they are freely given

No matter when one is born these are always very special gifts

Every single human being has the same opportunity, the same gifts

Also those have the same responsibility

Additionally each has a responsibility to others

The virtues can and should be learned and practiced

We must apply Virtue to our existence and avoid all

SIN

One small infraction can destroy a lifetime of goodness

We should not corrupt others with our own personal Sins

**Some of the Virtues; Patience, Temperance,
Honesty and Truthfulness**

**Humility is a Cardinal Virtue upon
which many other Virtues rest**

A liar is the greatest enemy of Civilization and of all people

Believe this, it is the Truth

Always Consider Reality

As a complex

Multi-Faceted

Singularity

The Nature of Being
Can only be always a Singularity
A Civilization is always in a state of Flux; Changing

Is this for Real?

Or is this a Nightmare?

Are we living in Paradise?

Do you understand what this means, what it Implies?

In fact now is the Apocalypse of Present Existence

When we take our Children to some of the special events we are enthralled
Intellectually we are still in about the same place as they are
This is very Gentle however is certainly truthful

Is this a Catastrophe?

Not Well Understood

And keep in mind

Only very few are really aware

Their comments are unnoticed or they are simply denied!

HEAD OF CHRIST

This is of a Drawing I did which emphasizes the idea of photons moving in space. I consider this a very timely work which relates too much that is being done in Physics. The image is absolutely original and had come about in a definite and singular act within four hours: it is totally intuitive.

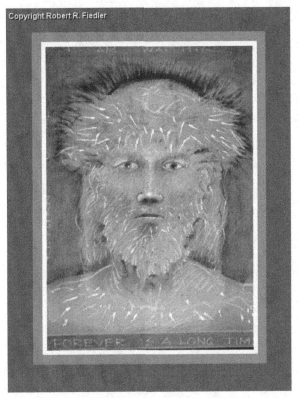

Head of Christ. This is a drawing which I have done.

A reproduction of this image, an eleven color printing, approximately 16" x 20" from a Limited-Edition printing of 250 is available for $35.00 plus $10.50 for shipping and handling. Checks are acceptable however they must clear before shipment. Therefore allow four weeks for delivery. All sales are final: no refunds and no returns. When you purchase this print you will own a very unique and very limited work of Fine Art. *(There are only a few left)*. The piece is unique and is timely relating to some of the most advanced work in optics and physics.

There does exist a prior printing of 1000 done as a promotional piece for;

Don Bosco, New Rochelle, New York.

PREFACE:
THE INDIVIDUAL

You have been told by some there are no Absolutes!
In fact there are many Absolutes there most certainly are billions of them!
Every single person is an absolutely singular human being, distinct from all others.

Recently it has been postulated that the DNA from the entire human race, past and present, would weigh less than a single aspirin. ***This is an important part of God's Plan.*** *The* name and the DNA are distinct: thus He will be able to identify every individual as such.[1] Hundreds of millions of individuals believe in God, <u>one way or another</u>. This, as a profound ***Idea***, ties in with the ***Time/Space*** phenomenon many associate only with Physics. Some Physicists are atheistic or are not certain if there is a God-Being; others are determinedly certain that **God** is not in the equation.[2] They are confused in their own knowledge of all that is. They prefer to concentrate on what they "imagine" and have discovered, as a part of reality. It is *their* Reality and they have used mathematics to explain what they do and what they have found in so doing.[3] Mathematics depends on a building of knowledge and is dependent upon the techniques employed and can be extended indefinitely with the discovery of new elements, or principles. Mathematicians have had profound consequence in the world of reality and are just now approaching "other" worlds as a consequence of a better understanding of time-space phenomenon. This, in fact, is related to ***Faith*** and ***Reason*** and allows, or provides, for much of what we do and for what we understand: also for what we cannot do and do not understand. Man seeks answers to questions and is often disappointed in the answers. Men, *"imagine"* much of which is simply not true; their thinking carries them inside and out of the sphere of ***Reality.*** They believe eventually they will figure out

---

[1]   **This understanding** gives phenomenal evidence of the ability of God the Father; nevertheless many do not recognize this is a fact and others simply discount it. In this instance we have "stumbled" upon one of God's miraculous inventions. He may very well refer to this when and if we face Him during the Last Judgment. Who knows? <u>*This presents an issue beyond human knowing and understanding.*</u>

[2]   **See our proof** that there must be a God and why this must be so (Chapter XIV). There must have been an omnipotence that had an **Idea** of reality. Without the word and the thought there would be no reality as we sense and know it to be. No one knows how the Universe came to be; there are many interesting Ideas however.

[3]   **Mathematics** is limited by its use of numbers, which are finite and by Symbols, which may be misinterpreted. When one deals with what is infinite and timeless, numbers will not suffice and the symbols are only abstractly indicative. So we cannot easily resolve the most important questions regarding issues about which we are only aware of a segment, a part, rather than a [the] totality.

what has happened, truthfully, in this Universe and exactly how it did happen. Humanity must wait and see?

It must be understood this work deals with the "Ultimate Question." **How far does Space extend so to support the total of Reality?** What, in fact, is Infinite Space? Infinite space is the ideal that the Western soul has always striven to find . . ." (Spengler, pg. 175)

ACKNOWLEDGEMENTS

First, I thank my immediate family for providing the love and patience necessary to raise a precocious son, especially my dad who had much of this figured out in 1938. He was a farm boy very intelligent: *the best man I ever knew.* Also my sister and my mom: later my wife the best of womanhood and her mother who raised four children alone. She was my hero! Also the good people I have met who have befriended me.

Especially I thank Oswald Spengler, Philosopher, Historian and Prophet: his monumental *Decline of the West,* in two volumes, no doubt obviates one of the best minds of the past several hundred years. He was a superlative Scholar and Writer. I also thank Eustice Mullins, with his book on *The Order* for his fine more current Historical research, in obviating what is wrong with the system and who made it the way it is: and why. Also I recently, five years ago, discovered the writings of Mathias Chang, a Chinese Catholic, *Future Fast Forward, The Zionist Anglo-American Empire Meltdown,* who has understandings that are current and have efficacy at this point in time. I also thank Francis Parker Yockey for his compelling book *Imperium.*

Additionally I thank Nesta Webster for her writing on *Revolution* and *World Revolution.* Both are classics on the subject with no holds barred. They should be required reading in our high Schools for insightful understanding of just what is a Revolution and why do we have "One" World Revolution. Who promotes this nonsense and how have they gained control, of our Civilization? I also thank E. C. Knuth, an engineer, for his *The Empire of the City,* a startling expose of the role of England in destroying America. They are still fighting the Revolutionary War and seem to be winning.

Also I thank Olivia Marie O'Grady for her book *The Beasts of the Apocalypse.* This is an insightful and well-documented work, which should reach a wider audience for the history and continuity of the assault on Christianity and Western Civilization. I thank Father Vincent P. Miceli, S. J. for his book *The Antichrist.* Much that is happening refers to the Antichrist and the Scriptures and Prophesies given by God. Not all believe this however some, in the future, will witness the power of He who made the World and the Heavens above. Special thanks, is extended to E. Michael Jones, Ph.D. for his *Degenerate Moderns* and others of his writing. He shows very clearly the outcome of the kind of thinking that has taken over our Civilization. We must change our ways or we are certainly doomed!

Also, I wish to thank Richard Gerber for his *Vibrational Medicine,* which obviates a profound and current understanding of the direction and methods of medical procedures.

And I wish to thank Bruce Cathie for his book *The Bridge to Infinity*, a most compelling work on the nature and function of Space.

Finally, I extend my gratitude to the many authors found on my bibliography at the end of the book. I am somewhat of a Renaissance man; the authors mentioned have helped me on the way.

This is a profound and mysterious
Introduction to an insightful encapsulation of Reality:
Time, Motion, History and how each one fits into the scheme of things!
Don't Forget God
THIS IS A GOOD READ FOR EVERYONE!

The book you are holding in your hand is an *absolute essential* for those who want to understand God, Reality and the World in which we live: as it is today.

This is no ordinary book; rather it is extraordinary in the range and diversity of the subject matter which covers a variety of disciplines. The focus of this work is as a continuation examining the fact; *Good* and *Evil* dominate the scene. It is written so you will understand the meaning of both the text and what is inferred by this most timely and explosive exposition. This is the author's seventh book. The others are also good bearing on the same type and extensiveness of subject matter!

This writing is a distillation of 65 years of careful and curious inquiry into a variety of subjects. The subjects are extraordinary and combine in ways generally not well understood. There is a brief, however compelling, mention of what is defined by this author as *Psychic Space.* This is the *inter-cranial space between the proximate neurons* in the brain tissue and extends to Infinity; that is, it extends to all of the Space outside the human body. There is interiorly bound and exteriorly infinite Psychic Space; each individual is very much affected by both forms of Space. *Space is a self defining Infinity*; no beginning, no end. It is now believed the inter-cranial space is where thinking occurs. An understanding of this, gives a somewhat obscure, however definite, tie-in between Reality and Holy Christian Scripture. This deals with the unknown; that which it is not possible to know. And some Scientists tell us there is only one two billionth part of matter in an atom. How do they know this? This infers almost all matter is mostly space. Can this be true?

There is much more to know than anyone is capable of knowing; thus as individuals, we have imperfect knowledge because *we lack the necessary information about all things.* One can imagine there is not sufficient time and no one can have sufficient Psychic Space to know all; Psychic Space refers to what is infinite, however limited in time in an unknown way by one's finite life span. Only God knows all there is to know. Who is God? As mentioned in other places, God is an Idea which is persistent. One wonder, how men like Stalin and Churchill could ever have become leaders and the destroyers of so many places and so many men.

There are trillions of thoughts which make up the infinite number of *thought clusters* that cause individuals to act. This is phenomenal! *Read what is written here with an open mind.* A closed mind is a dead one—death is forever! There is no valid reason to entertain the same ideas that have been ineffective and proven wrong over and over: Most of Marx's ideas, for example, are typical of this. Nevertheless, Marx's ravings are offered to students as a basic form of political thinking and action that is supposed to be compelling. *This is one fundamental reason for all of the confusion and ineptitude in contemporary Political Thinking.* Combine this with all of the lies and partly truthful thinking of the leader's and you have a very strange and destructive brew. This has been, and is, being pressed right now; Marx was a fool, somewhat a drunk, a womanizer who impregnated someone other than his wife; his illegitimate son was never welcome. Nevertheless, he imagined he could tell the *World* how to function. In fact he was a hypocrite! He had a profoundly vain and illusionary imagination; his personality was one of arrogance. What is written on Marx comes from many sources. I have attempted to simplify and make clear my understanding of the man and his ideas; *this is my understanding.* Vincent Miceli's book "The Antichrist" shows the effect of Marx's ideas on the world and the people. "The Antichrist", Vincent Miceli's @1981, ISBN 0-912141-02-6.

What is Reality? Is reality how you *"imagine"* it should be; How much of it is a contrived farce? Can one watch news on Television and *"believe or imagine"* they are being truthfully informed? Can one know what is true; can you assemble the information necessary to prove this? If you can you are unusual most could not do this, even if they could generally they do not. They will probably offend who they are addressing; remember the other person is always right. Such as this makes you *"automatically"* **WRONG.** This is part of a *"promoted"* understanding. This is part of a *"collective neurosis"* and is not easily altered; like six million Jews killed during the Second World War.[4] No one knows exactly how many Jews or others were killed by the war. Many died from old age; according to some there were about the same number of Jews before and after the War. This is a controversial and unholy Issue; but many are *"taught"* to believe this. Are you distracted by what is noise *"imagined as music"*? Do you read newspapers and some of the popular magazines for content and information? Are you enamored by all the talk shows and the stupid and silly Comedians? Do you like smutty entertainment: lots of breasts and thighs and pubic hair tempting you? Have you been educated or indoctrinated by our public education system? Will you spend one, two or three hundred dollars to see a football game? Would you if you could? Do you enjoy driving on the Freeways? Do you like the too big shopping centers with all the junk imported from other countries? Most is made for very little, marked up tremendously; you believe you are getting real value. Who takes the profit from this? Do you imagine the latest Style is something for you? Are you absolutely faithful to your wife and children, would you consider sleeping with another woman or another man? Are you a homosexual, a heterosexual or both?

---

[4]   The Internet has published evidence that refutes the idea of six million killed. Ten proofs against Six Million Jews murdered in 'Holocaust', translated from the Dutch: Reacties op "10 Bewijzen tegen 'Zes Miljoen' (# 29); The final end of the Myth.

"Six million murdered Jews in a "Holocaust" is a *Talmudic* topic, a Jewish religious metaphor for disaster, *distributed for centuries, without any concrete base.* The IMT at Nuremberg in 1945, re-enacted this number taken as 'evidence' from two bad "hearsay witnesses", whom supposed "spokesman" Eichmann called "phantasts". There was and is no justification for this now by historians called *'symbolic' number.* The religious character of it is confirmed by the current political and dogmatic Stalinist fixation and the rather inquisitorial persecution of critics in many Western countries."

"All this suffices to speak of this fixed quota as a religious myth. However, to deal for good with this Talmudic mantra, I give ***ten concrete proofs of the fallacy of this obligatory imposed and far too high number.*** Not because a lower number is less gruesome or sad, but simply because ***historical truth*** deserves primacy above myths." *(See Internet for what are the ten proofs; there is no forensic evidence apparent anywhere).*

See also "The Hoax of the Twentieth Century" by A. R. Butz, the Noontide Press. P. O. Box 76062, L. A. CA.

Have you ever been to a brothel? Was it gratifying, did you enjoy it or do your regret it? Remember everyone makes mistakes, perhaps one or two; sometimes many more. Are you addicted to follow *"Hollywood legends"* knowing what each actor is doing? Why? ***Humanness:*** We will consider the birth and becoming of humanness; and the effects of genetics on the development and continuation of the species. Nature is very prolific, is this necessary? In addition we will attempt to explain the existence of Infinite Space and Extant Matter. How can God be in all places at every moment given to eternity; forever? ***Is God as Space?*** We will consider some of the most recent discoveries in Physics and Psychology.

We will trace the becoming and pervasiveness of the Federal Reserve System to enslave the people to perpetual debt; *thus they unknowingly will support the Elite that hate them.*

We will explore the disaster of the recent Wars since the French Revolution, showing why and how we have come to be where we are. Who was killed? How much did all these murders cost? We will consider the brutal murder of the Russian monarchy in 1918. We will discuss why the other Russian monarchs were murdered; one by one part of a brutal unique take-over of a Nation. What happened to their wealth—gold, land and jewelry? Have they been accounted for; who now possess the remains of all their Treasures, gold, land and jewelry? Will we ever know? Was Russia a land of ignorant Bolsheviks or was the real Russia an impressive well administered nation. Have you ever seen the Art and architecture from the pre-revolutionary Russia? Is such as *this* the work of the primitive Asiatic as we were led to believe? *Russia was advertised badly. Nonsense has been fed to you for a century* by an indigent and irresponsible news service in the hand of Humanities and your enemy. Much of *"their news"* promotes the various other LIES. We will trace the forming and existence of the Federal Reserve System; discuss how and why. Do you remember a five-cent cup of coffee or coffee selling three pounds for thirty-nine Cents? In 1900 if one bought a beer they were given a free lunch: we realize this was a promotion. Can you imagine attending a movie for ten-cents for children or twenty-five cents for an adult? You have been told insistently there is no inflation; is this ignorance or simply cleverness? Who has all of the difference between what is and what was; all gone without any inflation. What about thirty third degree Masons: for example George Bush Sr. and Nikita Khrushev? They are, in fact, fraternal brothers; which oath will they really support? Why? You'll learn all you have to know about sex; simple as it is and why is it so pleasurable. Is a Democracy the best political system or is it simply a tool to console the people? The Ruric leaders of Russia, a Monarchy, ruled Russia for about six hundred years. They were followed by the Romanov's for about three hundred years; until they were murdered. Their currency was some of the best in the World; in 1917 it had a backing of 125% in gold. They maintained the highest standard for about nine hundred years; with a Monarchy. In our Democracy the currency has deteriorated to about 2% of what value it had since 1940. Why do the money lenders want to maintain and control our Democracy; it is a sham, destined to destruction, it will encourage the most-greedy men, money lenders, to control World Economics!

There is much more waiting for you than is listed above.
This is just a brief sample.

What is the meaning of life?

There is much more to life than economics.
Economics are fleeting and have only coincidental effect.
Bottom line profit for corporations should be considered as secondary.
Actually it should be considered much less than secondary: it is only temporary.
All this must be reasoned with the genuine and honest serving of the People in mind.
What is moral has become secondary and is often forgotten in the maelstrom.
This often happens, what is moral and decent is overlooked or confused;
As occurs when economics are the driving force of the Civilization,
This of course relates to the becoming of sinfully driven excess.
We have deemed success to be related to what is excessive.

The driving force then becomes the Sin of Greed.

Greed is A Mortal Sin; Believe, this!

One of the seven deadly Sins, it is deadly.

Don't be greedy!

Remember; in the end we are all dead.

―――ww・ぺ○ぉ○ぺ○・ww―――

Professor Emeritus; Robert Fiedler
January 20, 2013.

CHAPTER I

WHAT IS THE ESTABLISHMENT?

Every individual is aware of the **"ESTABLISHMENT"** however very few could tell you:

What is the Establishment?
A brief explanation follows!

To begin, the Establishment is a complex combination of entities coalescing to form a totality, a singularity, which is often very obscure, even to the most astute observers. It seems apparent control of economics gives a great advantage to those who are the controllers. And certain parts of the Establishment do control economics—*often quite secretly.* However even this is an evasive element, since the really big money (the billions spoken of) is difficult to follow, especially where Internationalism is being encouraged and where who to blame may be an issue.[5] For certain individuals, the Establishment provides a myriad of places where they can obscure their objectives. *Generally speaking,* most work for themselves or for an *"Idea"* they may believe in. This is precisely why, as understood by many observers, *"The Man without a country,"* that is the Zionist Jew and/or some others as well, have been very successful in Europe and now in the World. One can include many forms of liberal thinkers such as the Bolshevists and the Thirty-third Degree Masons, Socialists, Communists and Marxists. Harry Truman[6] and

---

[5] **Keep in mind Internationalism** *provides the greatest opportunity to promote and cover all forms of fraud and deceit in all manners of human negotiations.* All of the elements for criminal activity, secrecy, crime and deceit are, knowingly or unknowingly, built into the *Existing System.* When the presently controlled system of checks and balances has been completely removed as in a One World Order, what will exist will be a "Corrupt Colossus" of unimaginable proportions, which nobody will understand except the few that have determined the existence of such; a preposterous situation even those somewhat in control cannot be absolutely certain of outcomes. Many will be deceived. If and when the present System is destroyed, there will remain anarchy and despotism such as the World has not known or understood for a very long time. *Some may prefer this so to reduce the number of people in the World.* Without an understanding of God there will never be any truthfully significant Human understanding. The weakest amongst our numbers will be held captives, for a while, by the strong; however, innate sensibilities will function to begin the process of building a Group of Cultures that must, perhaps will, coalesce into an intelligently formed Civilization. In other words Humanity will once again attempt to live sensibly on this Planet. We are not certain what role a Divinity might assume [?]. And we are not certain how such Divinity might in fact act!

[6] **President Harry Truman** was chosen for that questionable honor the day after the bombing of Hiroshima and Nagasaki; one wonders why? "Some" considered this a very worthy accomplishment. These cities were two of the most Christian cities in Japan.

some others were chosen to be Thirty-third Degree Masons. Those have used the protections provided by the various Nations to further their own gains. Large scale is a Hallmark of what is called Internationalism. Nevertheless all those involved are now dead; one is exactly like the other; in darkness, cold and still.

Given the complexity of "now" Time;
It is more difficult to trace the "goings on" of any group!
The larger and more complex groups form
an evasive International entity.

The International characteristics of the Establishment may begin with a simple issue, which thereafter becomes threaded with interlocking issues affording protection in the accomplishment of that which **no decent or sane man would want.** And it is imperative one understands any leader is subject to the *idiosyncrasies of humanness* and is generally speaking primarily self-interested. Internationalism and the disparate information caused by such provide a perfect venue and the opportunity for the prevention and destruction of rational and cogent individual thought. It does this, even as most agree all is well; especially those concerned with governing the people.[7] **Many of those that govern** are not able to understand the Establishment except as a means to line their pockets, and to enlarge their own bank accounts.[8] This they do with impunity. They use the Establishment to acquire wealth and for this they *"turn the other cheek"* when questioned about it. The Rothschild Dynasty, The Rockefeller's the Sassoon's and more recently, George Soros, for example, represent what is being inferred: the worst form of economic intransigence.

They represent the World's most adept opportunists, using the World-wide venue they have helped to create, beginning with the slave trade and the Opium addiction of millions in China by the Sassoon's. The JEWISH Encyclopedia of 1905, states that Sassoon expanded his opium trade into China and Japan. He placed his eight sons in charge of the various major opium exchanges in China. According to the 1944 Jewish Encyclopedia: "He employed only Jews in his business and wherever he sent them he built synagogues and schools for them. He imported whole families of fellow Jews . . . and put them to work. Sassoon's sons were busy pushing their mind destroying drug in Canton, China. Between, 1830-1831 they had traffic of 18,956 chests of opium earning millions of dollars. Part of the profits went to Queen Victoria and the British

---

[7] **We the People** is the name given to the group of participants that have virtually nothing to say and little understanding concerning the governing process, which is given over to elected officials that *"presumably"* do not know what to do either. Some of the elected officials do not have a *motivational interest* in the governing process. For them the governing process has become the means of a vested interest: specifically and more seriously addressed by some appointed functionary. When an individual has created sufficient mischief, he will be replaced by another *seemingly different* functionary. Two heads, one body. Greenspan and Bernanke fit this description to a tee: before them there were others of the same persuasion. Most have been Zionists, as is well known; however one may not discuss this openly; it is wise to whisper when certain subjects come to the fore.

[8] **The hundreds of millions** in various bank accounts are generally safe because of the complexity and in some cases, unwillingness of law enforcement to pursue convictions. Some will be hampered, but only a few will face jail time or heavy fines.

2

government. In the year 1836 the trade increased to over 30,000 chests and drug addiction in coastal cities became endemic." *(See Internet, "Hong Kong founded as Sassoon Drug Center")*. Much of this profit went right to England, the great hope of liberal thinking.[9] As time and circumstance provide, they will continue to expand the effect of their political Ideas as well. This places a disinterested or uncaring population in a bad position. In fairness we mention that the Sassoon's also did much good for many people especially in India. *(See Internet for the details)*.

There are different types of Establishment Pressure. What is obvious, particularly in the realm of economics, for example, is the tremendous debt load, which is deliberately contracted,[10] as in the financing, of War—now even worse than ever ***Global Conflict?***[11] Just to get where the conflict is and back again requires billions in expenditures. This is justified as being good for business and to protect the people: it *"must be understood,"* such action *"with a bit of political encouragement"* is said to positively protect the country. Who could invade the United States? Perhaps a few Terrorists could invade us. The People are always told they are in danger. ***The Income Tax*** is another example, which everyone fears. Worse, however, it will continue and grow even more, in the future. This is part of Socialism where one has no defense unless they are well connected in the financial markets.[12] ***What is inferred***, such as fear of the effects of a shrinking supply of oil, is simply not a provable fact; which would be difficult to prove in any event. ***Apparently*** the earth did produce the oil. *It is quite likely that it will produce more in the future.* This seems as a natural process and should be well understood. One can certainly imagine that the oil was not produced by dead animals and disintegrated forests; rather the oil is probably a product (somehow) from the earth itself. *That is the earth creates the oil!*

---

[9]   **See Internet**, *"Hong Kong founded as Sassoon Drug Center".*

[10] **Cloward and Piven Strategy**: This is somewhat as they had imagined in their expose; in simplistic terms; "The strategy entails manufacturing a crisis and then implementing a solution that actually makes the crisis much worse and moreover, makes implementation of a real solution to the crisis next to impossible; and every solution to the crisis must invariably entail purposefully overwhelming federal government programs in an effort to cause those programs and the federal government to implode under its own weight"? They first outlined this plan in an article that was titled, *"The Weight of the Poor: A Strategy to End Poverty"* that was published in *"The Nation"* in May of 1966. See internet under **Cloward and Piven Strategy**. Their program had many flaws rewarding Evil and punishing Good.

[11] **We are informed** our leaders are attempting to figure out how to pay trillions, rather than billions, or millions as in the past. Do any of our leaders, so-called even comprehend how much is a trillion dollars $ 1,000,000,000,000? We think only a few may understand! *As long as we maintain a paradigm with the same factors, being a form of Humanism, millions will remain slaves to want and need, without being able to determine the nature of either.* As a routine, the people are given the questions and all of the answers on the same Television Program. One cannot have a stable government when inflation is chewing on the currency. We do have a serious inflation and have had it since 1900, even earlier to some extent.

[12] *As* **long as inflation persists** we are certain you will pay ever-higher taxes to cover these expenses. You will receive a nominal increase in salary; however it will fall short of *your* growing expenses and expectations. Some of the difference will be made up by cheapening the products; the rest will come from a lower standard of living for many in the impoverished population. *A lower standard of living for the middle class is the object of Socialist-Marxist-Collectivist thinking.* The really rich need not worry as they own whatever is worth owning.

The possibility of nuclear conflict, which may or may not happen, keeps millions in a state of anxiety.[13] Anxiety is further animated by the imposed need to keep in style with all the gimmicks and trends, to appear as being *"With It,"* keeping up with your neighbor.

What is true is that Pension funds and retirement accounts have shrunken considerably, due to the persistent inflation giving Individuals anxiety in imagining about their old age. Many spend more than they earn and save virtually nothing. If they had learned anything in school they would be able to count and to figure their plight decades before their retirement. The irony is *they are helping to drive themselves into a pit*. In some places housing prices are beyond reason a fact created by the illegitimate and risky forms of finance and the greed of the owners. In the last few years (2006-2012) housing prices have fallen however are now once again on the rise. Those who write the loans make millions all taken out from the projects. *There are probably too many labor saving devices.* Many, found work in the past doing simple things, however are now out of work by reason of so many technical and unnecessary *"Advancements"*. The number of women working has increased dramatically and they compete with the men for what was formerly a man's work. Rather they should make a home and care better and more for their children and for their husband; if they have one. Dad should give up on or limit the various sports, drinking, fishing and carousing. The demands for equality have created strange ways of thinking.

What happens in governments is mostly as a compromise. Our Democratic form of government appears to be adversarial: Democrats, the peoples' party, opposing Republicans, those that represent the moneyed interests, the rich, of this Nation. The Democrats have attracted the black population and many minorities for what they promise to give them free of charge. Everybody wants a free lunch; who do they imagine will pay for this? The two-party System is an *"Idea"* born in the past, which must be abandoned or the country, other countries as well, will be destroyed.[14] It appears the System will likely be replaced, by one or many *Cartels* that will hold the wealth and control the governing process and will determine who and how individuals must live, as did a King, or some other ruler in the past. Strangers will decide how everyone should behave and will assume an awesome authority over mankind. Military personnel from a far-away place will be called as the enforcers, thus to be able to shoot those in disagreement, with the imposed System, which has taught citizens to fear and to hate. The enforcers will, be

---

[13] **Anxiety** is necessary to keep the people in a constant state of worry over what will happen next. The debt issue is a wonderful tool for this, because it relates to the fact that individuals are generally greedy. In fact, the debt to which they refer is not what it is thought to be. The Debt is a means for a few to steal from the millions of honest persons. *The financial markets are so contrived they are simply preposterous.* All the various forms that have come into play are mostly or partly dishonest and they reward the thieves that manipulate the markets. This has developed instead of honest and forthright forms of accounting. Internationalism is a perfect cover for such manipulation.

[14] **The United Nations** and the one-World Type intend to destroy every nation, as such, and replace them with Socialist Districts. The United States is already portioned into ten districts. All will be ruled by the Talking Heads. The Talking Heads will be chosen from a wealthy group of speculators, industrialists, gangsters and frauds. Some of past noble strains will be amongst them, for example a Kennedy: those that agree in principal will be front runners, for effect, in the scheme of things. Wealth will be the real determining Factor. The little people will be taxed to pay for the incorrect thinking of "Leaders," who will appeal to Christian goodness as they shear the sheep.

well paid and commended for their allegiance to the ruling elite. The *"Idea"* of a One-World government provides the means for this to happen.[15] *This is also commonly known as the Corporate State,* which as a consequence will supplant all the forms of Government that now exist. Present forms of government have grown slowly *under the coercive influence of money and for somewhat other reasons.* Present forms are not perfect however they are a consequence of the *"melding of Tradition"* one way or another.[16] Many of our government solutions are under the control of "Czars" that have not been elected; rather they have been appointed by the President. Our President Obama believes himself to be a King; a real leader of men. This is absurd, really scary. *In fact his is a temporary appointment* whereabouts, if the System was honest, he should implement the will of the people; *the intelligent ones not the fools,* this is what our Democracy implies.

The people may be given to appear as they are participating; however this will be simply a part of the scam. For such recognition the People dance in the streets. When someone like President Obama can avoid many of the restraints placed on the President by our Constitution there is little hope for determining a proper course. The people must curtail their spending and prepare, at least somewhat, for their own future. We have been encouraged by clever advertising and expect more than is reasonable. Let's hope Obama is a one tern President:[17] in fact he should be impeached. If the President is found guilty, he should be dismissed from his Office. *As this is being written Obama (unfortunately) has been re-elected. He will have another four years in office. We will have to wait and see what may happen to our country.*

Too often deceit and fraud have determined guiding principles: *deceit, fraud and simply lying are the real problems.* Who will correct such problems? *Many men are scoundrels however their lies serve them well.* When the principals within the United Nations will steal food from those in great need one can understand the real nature of **Greed**. Starvation is the real problem for hundreds of millions. Simply stated to steal is dishonest and dishonorable; it is sinful. Economics, have determined much of the present "Scene". The present scene imposes upon Humanity and guarantees that eventually the system will collapse from the ignorance and ineptitude of the governed, that being *we the people,* and those elected and appointed, whom we imagine, *quite incorrectly,* are capable of governing the population. They are working for themselves and many for their own somewhat secret Political aspirations. One can imagine having the least amount of government would be best. Most institutions would function better if they were smaller; this is a difficult issue to deal with, however it must be considered. Everyone

---

[15] **The Idea** of a one-world government has been around since Greece and Rome; however; their world was much smaller. The *Idea* is appealing to those who have the most already, as a means of consolidation, and of those who have the least, as a means to acquire a free lunch. The *Idea* has racial implications as well. Caucasians have been recent leaders, however the Chinese pose the next group that will most likely ascend to leadership. Islam had a fling in past centuries; however are outnumbered by the Chinese, who have absorbed the technologies of the West very well and are able to do what the West has done in the recent past.

[16] **This is an important understanding:** the form and manner of law has grown in accord with those being governed. This is not perfect except it appears to be the most-reasonable way for this to happen.

[17] **As this is written** Obama has been elected to a second term. We must be patient we have not been able to be properly decisive.

imagines that big is better, which is simply not true. You will never get the best apple pie from a Corporation; never like your mother used to make in her kitchen when she stayed home.

The elements within the system are too large. Mistakes are always monumental and no one can be honestly blamed for the monumental failures. This is the significant problem with such Systems: the Bureaucracy has grown way too large and cannot and is not successfully managed. A system with no common Tradition or with a variety of Traditions cannot and will not work.

Warfare is a distraction for the population many of whose children are put into the conflict as the youthful and eager warriors, seen on television.[18] Youth are bribed with promises of a better tomorrow *(for those that survive)* and free tuition to a University. *In a State University they will be further indoctrinated into the socialist programs designed for them.* The fact that most youth are not capable of *"higher education"* escapes our leaders as they use the promise of a college education, a college education given to the intellectually inept. This is an election device to get votes from parents and the youth, first-time voters. In fact, most youth are too inexperienced to understand why they are voting. Some youth are brought home in a body bag or missing a limb or two, maybe an arm or only an eye, from the mines set for them. From there *(with their imagined college education)* they will join the corporate work force and buy an over-priced home in a community-like housing development, where all the buildings are made from the same plan, or a condominium where they will own just the space above the ground. We admit some personal touches may be evident. They will decorate their new dwelling so to appear like the ones owned by the rich and famous, sort of; for example someone like Tiger Woods a notable golfer, or Elizabeth Taylor a former movie Star: Ms. Taylor is deceased however we will continue to hear of her as long as some profit can be gained by the promoters. In fact with her many husbands one must feel sorry for her: with all her beauty, no one really loved her eternally.

Everyone cries crocodile tears however no one is certain which part of the Establishment is to blame. Who and where are these crocodiles? For the designers of our System this provides the necessary cover against some individual figuring out what is happening. They still talk about Hitler and the Nazis, even as their Establishment is set on the same socialistic framework, *old, out-dated and debilitating.* **Simply put it doesn't work.** There are men in this world who are cruel and will not compromise their strange values and ways of living. The naive youthful warriors will be used to eliminate such as those in a series of unending wars. We are in that phase just now, as this is written. *Our leaders, so imagined, will not tolerate individuals who deviate or challenge the system:* dissenters must be imprisoned, perhaps they will be killed, or converted to please the moneyed interests that rule.

Many Westerners no longer believe, "seriously", that each individual is a creature of God with body and soul destined for a possible eternal life hereafter: Heaven![19] There is much

---

[18] **The young warriors** are eager because they cannot understand the meaning of warfare at their young age. The men who placed them in that position do understand however they will not, generally speaking, be a part of the conflict.

[19] **Be sure to read the portion in this work on, "Who is God?"** (Chapter XIV). Much will be explained for you and you can take it from there. Pay attention to the elements dealing with Gothic Architecture and seek some of the related information which can be found on the Internet.

talk of religion, however the theology is missing or flawed. The flesh is weak and is involved in all manner of aberrant behavior; however we may not call a Sin by its rightful name: *Sin.* Consenting adult laws provide the necessary cover for all to do their own thing, whatever it may be! *We imagine a license to commit perverse or disgusting acts is a form of political freedom.* Everything in God's world is perfect. How has man been able to corrupt perfection so quickly?

The United Nations is seemingly an altruistic organization appealing to the sentiments of the population. The UN exudes an air of goodness; however the UN is always under the governance of a Socialist or Communist. Keep in mind Socialists and Communists pose a great threat to the *Catholic Church, which has given the West its tenor in theology, philosophy and eschatology, with many attendant accomplishments.* The United Nations, as an entity, becomes very religious, so-called, when there are floods and famines, and on a continuing basis reminds the world of all the ways the children suffer.[20] Admittedly, segments of the United Nations seemingly do many good things, which dissuade many from critical thinking concerning the politically destructive nature of that Socialist and Communistic System. The World will spin without the United Nations, which is one political device to gain acceptable control of the wealth and riches of this world. People are very different for reasons no one understands completely and few can explain. A People, given reasonable limitations, should be allowed their own space for survival—*social, geographic and intellectual.* Everyone wants a place to call his own. Small groups share this desire. Various movements of populations will provide sufficient opportunity for individuals to exist as part of a totality. These same individuals may possibly become *"One in being with the Father from whom all good things come". We are not yet there.*

Christ admonished his followers to go forth and teach all Nations. Some are doing this however they meet with organized and personally antagonistic subjects, whom are unyielding in their opposing faith or lack of faith. Many Moslems are notoriously anti-Christian: especially they are anti-Catholic. Many Missionaries have been murdered as was Christ when they try to convert some atheist or someone from another religion. Men who murder the missionaries and priests do not and are not intellectually equipped to understand what religion is. Missionaries build orphanages and schools and are effective in dealing with problems of starvation and loneliness. Missionaries take care of and love their enemy's children. Missionaries afford some support for children born illegitimately or for those whose fathers and mothers were killed in a senseless conflict. In addition some are simply seeking another Faith from their own. *There can be only one God omnipotent and eternal; this is a fact!* What kind of Faith will disavow or kill a dissenter from their faith? Such action as this prevents the individual from thinking for himself as God has intended.

Economic news is on all the stations broadcasting of such events. We hear who may have been robbed and how much was stolen. The real thieves working through the Establishment in government and finance are rarely caught. When some are caught they are often given a new position from which to continue in a nefarious pursuit. How about the ones who have stolen the country? Where are they? They are on their multi-million dollar yachts, or in some

---

[20] **Recently** individuals within the United Nations work-force have been found to be stealing the food intended for the starving. Presumably they would sell it for what could be gotten as payment for it. Who would do such a thing? Sin knows no boundaries.

lavish accommodation, somewhere, in full view, appearing splendid at that; however no one knows what they have done or are doing to maintain their opulent life style.[21] The leaders in the Establishment have all the right connections and the attendant financing with Wall Street and the various semi-criminal organizations designed to extract a bit from the accumulating wealth. They do very well. The accumulation of wealth is a matter of greater numbers and is tied to inflation which, generally speaking, is a silent nevertheless *persistent and certain form of theft.*

The problem which inflation presents has been long considered. It has not yet been solved. We will not solve inflation which appears to present great opportunity to the deceitful. We have heard spoken of a cancelling of debt obligations at the end of a number of years. Is this a good Idea? Probably not: those who are more compulsive would tend to go beyond reason in the hope their obligations would be cancelled; many have already gone beyond reason. In fact, the issuance of debt should be reduced. Instead, just the opposite is occurring: people are encouraged to go into greater debt and to pay later with cheaper money. This attitude is a consequence of Inflation. In fact the cost of carrying such obligations is generally greater than what one will save on the inflation, which figures into the equation. Additionally the item will be worn out or outdated before it is paid for. Style plays an important role as it works to encourage one to want what is new. Change the color or the cut and you will have what is "presumed" as a new style. Real style is nearly non-existent; note how the people are dressed, each tries to be more outrageous than the others. The thrift shops should be giving a clue to what is and is not necessary. However the population has been educated to prefer *"cheap newness,"* from China and India among other places, which presents another problem: actually several other problems involving, amongst other things, International Finance.

Leveling the playing field is a common cliché. No one with significant wealth wants this; they enjoy being where they are, which is certainly understandable. What we are seeing is a consequence of the compounding of interest, coupled with significant tax advantages favoring those who have amassed great wealth, no matter how this was accomplished. Many of the truly great fortunes were amassed using illegal or highly questionable means: slave trading (some Africans, the Jews and the Rothschild's), narcotics (the Sassoon's), and prostitution (organized crime). There was also direct theft and the result of evil genius and timing in which John D. Rockefeller and J. P. Morgan were involved. Governments gave unimaginable wealth to privileged individuals (the Railroad Barons and mining interests). Part of those same government gift-giving, involved huge tracts of land, stolen from the Indians and distributed to the favored few. *Some research suggests that 10% or less of the recipients got 90% of the land.* The Indians had no recourse in law contrived for the wealthy and no adequate defense; they were massacred. The favored few recipients became the elite of the present epoch. ***Seeing the situation honestly, some made their fortunes honestly, while many of our presumed elite benefitted from the consequence of simple theft and horrendous crimes:*** land and riches stolen from a defenseless people. I realize this is an over-simplification nevertheless there is much truth in the assertion. However what is past cannot be altered, it is History. Face the real truth without the embroidery.

---

[21] **Some numbers** are given in another section of this book. Pay attention so you know how much the really rich, in fact, have of wealth and power.

No nation will survive which depends only on Economics as the main event. This is especially true when one encourages inflation. There are many more things in life than acquiring the newest gadget for the home or the newest of anything, for that matter. The discount stores import from other lands, they incorporate and hope to sell here in America and get rich. Everyone has a gimmick. The stores are bursting with stuff, most of which is not needed. We have too many items from which to choose; however they are all about the same, except for the labels and the price. At this juncture of our discussion we will meet with the resistance of those with little intelligence who demand a wide range of selection. They overlook that the boxes are changed from one year to the next and the colors too. Often the presentation is worth more than the item. As part of the corporate hype, television is bursting with advertisements for various items from bubble gum to vaginal douche, from automobiles to thumb tacks.

Football and the various sporting events are important in gathering hoards together to watch the game between the million-dollars a minute commercials.[22] Recently Bret Favre has been the talk of the town for weeks; some continue to be discussed for many years, like Babe Ruth. This is the Establishment deciding you will spend your leisure time in a dome, watching football with a Budweiser or Miller in your hand. The beer, at $5.00 to $6.50 per can, isn't that good, but the game, some imagine, is awesome. Turn on your TV and watch how the people abandon common sense and discreet behavior. But they are having fun! Think how much money is made building the sports stadium and laying down acres of asphalt and concrete, ruining the environment, to park the thousands of cars, for just a couple of hours on certain occasions. There are other examples that are just as stupid and just as dumb! All this is as a consequence of the Establishment in place and thriving without any cognizance of the reality that has been created for those with just enough to buy a ticket. Some may take a loan against their next pay check to buy a ticket. This is a form of mass neurosis. Simply stated this is madness.

The Medical Profession has its own Establishment within the greater Establishment. Hospitals and Drug Companies participate in the greatest advertising spectacle in history. Doctors treat every form of disease and emotional problem and the optional surgery is mind boggling. People can have their bodies changed or do many things to their appearance to look like a Barbie Doll or simply to look different from what was genetically intended. When one contracts any form of disease they are immediately consumed by the system with paperwork and a list of drugs to be taken. Though generally intelligent and well meaning, Doctors must comply with the rules and dictates of the American Medical Association, or be placed on the list for malpractice.[23] In any event, they cannot cure most of the serious illnesses. They do succeed admirably where technology is the main event and where there are social implications, such as war injuries, which can be utilized for the purpose of propaganda; it is a form of advertising that attracts sympathy.

The major hospitals, in large cities provide a never-ending epic of construction and additions to the already too-large facilities. Presumably the patient is treated well however is so confused

---

[22] **Big name Corporations** spend a million dollars a minute for airtime at a spectacle involving an athletic event or any event where millions of individuals sit glued to a television screen, watching for what is imagined to be the next important event.

[23] **Interestingly;** for many years, in the beginning of that Institution, the AMA was headed by one who was not even a Doctor; however, he was a good businessman!

and so small in comparison to the place, one can imagine they are psychologically overpowered by the *spectacle of Healing.* Persons are wheeled from one department to another and tested for things which nobody truthfully understands. The bills mount and the big question is *what kind of insurance is in place? Can we bill enough patients to pay for the machine before it is obsolete?* Everything is so expensive; a single trip with any lengthy stay can bankrupt the suffering victim. The victim will die and the hospital will attach any assets that are available.

Someone I knew quite well had some welfare in the thirties, her husband had died and she was left with four small children. She was a wonderful mom and raised four children plus two orphans, scrubbing on her hands and knees. The orphans were her sister's children, he sister and husband had died, but the children *became a part of her family.* To her at that time a family meant more than anything else. One of her children, her only son, was retarded and couldn't work; she took care of him until just before she died. Her three daughters were beautiful young ladies, who married for a lifetime and had families of their own. When the lady died in 1970 the money from her estate was taken by the State of Wisconsin; all of it. She was billed for what she had forty years before her death. This is the country many have died for. Presently in this country some have millions, much of it from simple theft or some crooked deal for which they are rarely punished. However this saintly woman, after she died her children were robbed of her estate, every penny except for funeral expenses, by a government that spends billions promoting Evil, and most of this is wasted. Her estate was built one nickel at a time; she even bought and paid in full for the house that she lived in with her six children. This woman was my hero, her name was **Margaret Merz** she was my wonderful mother-in-law. I married her beautiful baby daughter, recently deceased; *the best wife in the world, my Geri.*

The major Retailers have assumed a gigantic position in the scheme of things. They are instrumental in destroying the West as they import cheap goods from the Far East. In doing so, they also impact employment in the West especially so for the less intelligent and the less capable. We are informed that about nine million jobs have left the United States since the election of President Obama in 2008; that's a lot of pay checks. We have put our own tailors out of business, destroyed our clothing and shoe industries and provided business for the Chinese in Hong Kong. The *"one size fits all"* (this was a clever gimmick) is born of the attempt to *manufacture for the lowest possible price.* One third of the population will have clothing that is too large and one third will have what is too small. Only one third will have something nearly close to a somewhat decent fit; about ten percent will have a decent fit.

Many marginally skilled individuals cannot find any work at all. What is left is satisfied by aliens, many are illegal; they will work for a bit less. This is even worse since many aliens send their money back to their families in another country. Certainly this will affect how American people live and whether or not they are inclined toward an elegant or slovenly presence. *(For more information, check out population statistics on the Internet for Detroit, Michigan).*

In 1950 one could buy a tailor-made suit from English woolen mills (Milwaukee, WI) for $55.00 pants and jacket, $10.00 extra for the vest. This required three trips to the tailor for measurements, preliminary fitting and finally the finished garment. Occasionally a fourth trip was necessary so to complete final adjustments. The suites always fit perfectly. All for $55.00, the price one pays today for a tee shirt with a print of an animal or something ugly on the front.[24] Our $55.00, 1950's suit was of excellent quality and would look good for years in the future. At present one is expected to buy new clothes every year. Formerly Style did not change every season and a good suit was a near-permanent investment. The only men now wearing the tailor-made $4,000.00 suits are over-paid athletes, hoodlums, politicians and some entertainers; as such they have more money than they can spend.

The L. L. Bean catalogue has merchandise almost exclusively imported—except for the maple syrup which is a product of New England. Check the items you buy for the place of manufacture; many are made in China and the far Eastern countries. You will probably buy cheap to save money so you can buy your over-priced football tickets. What's the difference how you look?

One can observe the same situation with many items, for example shoes, which are now made in other countries. Our shoemakers are becoming extinct except for very high-end merchandise. At one point in time we were buying 400,000,000 pair of shoes from China. We can now buy cheaper ones from other countries. Big name makers New Balance, Adidas, Nike and others are all involved; the situation is not improving, it is getting worse. This is one instance of Internationalism. Many people are wearing athletic shoes almost exclusively: die-cast soles with ugly colored plastic/poly tops, from $20.00 to $195.00 per pair—even more for some high end merchandise. These replace the beautifully crafted leather shoes that could be bought for $6.95 or $7.95 in 1940. We admit, some new styles may be as good even better than the old ones; however, compare the pricing, you will know what has happened; and you will understand.

There has been no inflation, so we are told.

We spend billions [trying] to defeat an imagined enemy on the other side of the globe, even as our own country and prosperity are being given away. Our leaders are either fools or traitors! We can blame our President Barack Hussein Obama for much of the present trouble; he will be responsible for some future trouble as well. President Obama likes to blame George Bush. We have so many enemies, so we are told, and we believe this, almost to the man. After each conflict good old Uncle Sam steps up to fix what he has broken, hoping to make friends of formerly presumed enemies, with lending and construction, rebuilding and increasing our own debt to the Bankers. When one kills the young men and the old, then destroys the house with bombs and fire, one cannot expect to have made a lasting friend. What one will have is a sworn enemy; somehow they will get revenge. Old enemies will often remain enemies behaving as friends until a better moment arrives. They are more-clever than we!

Opportunists thrive where there is so much to be fixed and we know that most *"Fixin"* is expensive; however we must do it right, whatever the cost. This is the Establishment talking and all good citizens, being good Democrats, like some imagine our President Obama, should listen. Why not make all countries just like this one, the United States of America? We are such

---

[24]   **This is a sign** of a drop in the importance of one's personal appearance. Not many care about how they look; most want simply to be comfortable. There remain a few who have not been captivated however that number is declining; pretty soon everyone will look like a slob. Everyone will be equal at the bottom of the tank.

good people (so we have been told). In fact what has made us good is being destroyed by greed, opportunism and perverted sex. The really good people are being ridiculed and prevented from correcting anything wrong. Just *"widen the landscape"* so to include all forms of wretchedness and evil. Never the less we cannot let a single one of our transgressions upon innocent Populations, remain without the necessary *"Fixin"*. The Establishment, that being an Anglo-Zionist Conspiracy has nearly ruined the country and will certainly do so if it is not encouraged to reinstating *our failing industries, our failing character and our failing morality.* Socialism, Communism and Anarchy are very real threats to this nation, especially when unemployment reaches disastrous levels. We are nearly there. The police are being trained for riot control even as the politicians create a situation certain to cause a riot. Camps are being built expecting some near-uncontrollable inmates.

Many people work in the food industries tending the garden, serving, preparing food, cleaning the premises, or stacking the dishwashers. Many of these same individuals are illegal aliens who will work for less than the wage paid to a citizen who may also earn pension, insurance and other benefits. Can one imagine what is happening to the wage scale? *The whole illegal alien scene has been developed by the Establishment and is encouraged by do-gooders who do not truthfully understand what is happening.* **They are ignorant of economics and the social sciences**, which is why we have what we have. Societal Problems are not scientific; they are products of ignorance and ineptitude, poor education and are emotional rather than objective and wise. *The social scientists are not scientists at all.* They encourage the programs of madness that have allowed and encouraged the present system to become as it has. The system is one of rigging deals, fraud and, in truth, thievery. It is what has become of the capitalistic system. It has become a System of Finance Capitalism **deformed by cheaters and liars** replacing Truthful Capitalism. Socialism and Communism will be no better; they will be much worse!

Subsidies and support encourage the birth of the illegitimate children and are a disgrace in a Christian nation. Actually they are a disgrace to any nation so inclined. One should not reward irresponsible and sinful behavior. Consenting adult laws must be reconsidered and a fair, firm punishment for overt sinfulness must be enacted. When a woman has two or three illegitimate children and no husband who supports them she should be sterilized. This would cut welfare costs substantially. When on mentioned this however they are reminded of God's will.

Consenting adult laws sanction and encourage unwholesome behaviors. Such behavior can certainly destroy lives: What's the solution?
If, two adults consent to what they do this does not make it proper.

Consider the cost of maintaining some of the worldly goods of the very rich who control the Establishment. *Imagine the cost* of owning a $50,000,000.00 luxury yacht. At 5% the carrying cost would be $2,500,000.00 per year. In addition is a crew of perhaps 10 at an average cost of perhaps $30,000.00 per year. This adds a total of $300,000.00. Then there is also upkeep and fuel. Who can imagine how much that would be? Consider the carrying costs and the crew the total would be $2,800,000.00. Divide this number by 12 and you have $233,333.00 per month plus operational costs, fuel and docking fees. Let's say about $250,000.00 per month, every month. Start with the carrying costs on a twenty million dollar residence $20,000,000.00. At 6% that comes to $1,200,000.00 per year or $100,000.00 per month. The total expenditures would be about $4,000,000.00 per year. We admit the numbers are hypothetical to make our point; however you will be able to find some circumstances just about equal to our assumption. _Become interested in values and what the really rich take for granted._ There is nothing wrong with being wealthy and there is nothing personal in what is written here. It is written to make obvious the absurdity of such numbers in a free country *"where all are imagined as being equal"* in the eyes of an Omnipotent God. The expense is very close to $11,000.00 per day.[25] Who do you think can afford this? The yacht is for occasionally entertaining friends and other thieves taking advantage of the World's ocean beauty; just a few are able to do that.[26] There is a summer resort and a winter ski chalet: who knows how much for this? And there is a condominium in Paris, one in Rome and a third one in New York: who knows how much this will cost? There are several high end automobiles and the wardrobe for the wife, also fine wines, $200.00 a bottle, more or less, and country club dues, theatre tickets and other miscellaneous expenses. Don't forget the food! There is a butler, a chauffeur, probably several maids, a gardener (perhaps several or many) and other expenses incurred as part of the ownership obligation. And there must be more than one attendant at each places of residence. One can imagine where this is going.

This extraordinary wealth is a product of our Establishment and no one wants to change what is, except for the poor, and they have very few, actually probably no choices at all. The great accumulated wealth from the past earns considerable interest from year to year which can be protected by means of a contrived form of law. _We call such protection a loophole._ One can take his wealth to another country and deposit it in an account without having all of the strings attached that would be a part of a more legitimate legal system. ***The system is just a part of the problem!*** What we are missing is honesty, veracity, ***humility*** and love, all of which are ***Virtues.*** ***Humility is the prime Virtue*** determining the becoming of many others. Socrates is credited with saying, ***"He is happiest who is satisfied with the smallest portion."*** Who, in fact, believes this? Our entire system is based on greed and covetousness: *Get the most you can.* With this attitude we are teaching our children to act as though having more than another makes one better. This is simply not true: _it is the worst form a lie can take._

> ***Money is an abstract denominator and must***
> ***be more carefully considered:***
> ***Money is always separate from the person's being.***
> ***Money is not as important as life.***

What system allows this to happen? We are speaking of fixed expenses for a yacht and one residence, high end of course. We are speaking of at least $333,000.00 per month just to live *"Like a King,"* actually somewhat better than most Kings have ever lived. This is a consequence of freedom from governmental interference whereabouts some are able to pyramid a simple idea into a fortune. Much of it is a consequence of the people's own misunderstanding of economics and finance and much is because those are *"sucked in"* to the system as they purchase various unnecessary and some necessary things for their survival. _Such is life, which cannot be denied_

---

[25] **Imagine this** and also imagine that some individuals live on the street and steal for food or eat garbage.

[26] **There may also be tax advantages** for the owner who presumably uses the boat as a form for entertaining guests. He may keep his mistress on board however this is not discussed in polite company. His spending is advertised to show how lucky he is; his sins remain a private affair.

except through the government's barrel of a gun, which we do not advocate. Such as this is difficult to control and should not be controlled too carefully except, perhaps, by a *"fair-minded and reasonable taxing system,"* which might be a bit cumbersome to administer; however with present technology this is certainly not impossible. One must conclude there will always be the Poor and the Rich. We cannot escape this; however we can make it better for the poor if they co-operate. Socialism is not an answer. It has never worked and it, *Socialism,* will never work.

The only thing that will work is goodness and self-respect and a decent restraint on having babies. No man should expect that another man will support his children. This is what happens when one combines lust with ignorance and stupidity: and this lust and ignorance is supported by welfare. *Goodness, self-respect and decency are largely learned behaviors.* They can be learned by almost everyone. Further, we must enforce meaningful laws against fornication out of wedlock. Instead we are in fact promoting the growth of the pornographic industry. Divorce should once again be made difficult, in spite of some objections. Importantly, young women should keep their pants on and their legs crossed. What about the men? The men should act with decent restraint. A child needs two natural parents *regardless of the political nonsense being pushed by lesbian and homosexual lobbies and promoted by the government* and the special interest groups that profit directly from the disasters, created in the public schools.

Some Kings were killed in battle or beheaded by their subjects. There was much risk in being a King. Consider what happened just one hundred years ago to Czar Nicholas, a Romanoff; even his wife, and five children *"murdered,"* for the good of the people, of course. Today, there is little risk in taking advantage of various loopholes or defrauding simple-minded people in the Stock Market. There are probably tax codes that provide a generous allowance for the *"rich and infamous"* making the *"Deal,"* even better than our numbers suggest. The structure and working of the Stock Market must be reconsidered. The Stock Market although advertised as the best place for your money is seemingly structured, in many ways, to defraud the people. Prices of stock go up and down as is intended by those who control pricing. This may or may not have been intentional; it was designed by those with imperfect knowledge; it does not work quite right. Some will benefit tremendously however they are the minority. This is a subject of its own, too broad to be covered at this time.

We do have laws which have been structured in reference to need and they are mostly good, but they must be enforced with conviction. We should cut the changes that have made them ineffective. It is not necessary to *"steal"* the wealth from the rich: maybe a 5% increase in the taxing structure as formulated would be sufficient; we cannot expect the wealthy alone to support all of the poor. The poor should be correctly educated so they can share in the prosperity of the Nation which is plentiful, for the knowledgeable. Fornication should be discouraged which calls upon a decent restraint in all segments of society, especially commercials that use sex as a ploy to sell a variety of products. Sex should be understood for its true value and programs should be implemented to encourage reasonable restraint. Decent, mature individuals do not require sex as an inducement or an encouragement to purchase a product. Intelligent individuals can restrain their sex dives. Sex is ***THE*** reward for a faithful and lasting marriage. *Any other form of sex is in reality a perversion encouraged for the attention and profits derived from its promotion.* There is nothing equal to a good mate, one who shares the sorrows and joys of life. Following is a line from a popular song from a few years back. Today's popular song lyrics are vulgar and silly compared to this as a philosophy, coupled with decency and a profound understanding of life.

> **"When the one that you love is in love with you, that's the greatest blessing by far:**
> **Yet you won't know how lucky you are."**
> *This is a song about a man and a woman, correctly understood, a mom and a dad.*

Most of today's popular musicians are without any real talent, they are money grubbing fools. They rely on the noise that is a product of the *"over-applied"* technology. They are fools except they don't know what a fool is. They will destroy the Civilization unless overcome by other forms: this is probably what will happen. What mature individual wants to watch some moron gyrating for the effect it has on the children and voyeurs within the audience? By this means we are encouraging a guttural response. A guttural response is anti-social and a form of perversion.

My mate, the mother of my children, my lover and best friend for sixty two years, has recently died; we were married for fifty three years. This is the greatest sorrow and sadness I have ever known. I have never slept with another woman and I never will. In respect to our relationship and friendship this is how it should be, ideally so. *I learned this from my father; he was the best of men.* Youth can be taught well and they should be taught restraint and to choose wisely so not to make a mistake early in their adulthood. Such manner of mistake is a permanent mark on the soul and the personality from which all manner of hardship ensues. *Youth should be taught sex is a sacred commitment.* In Catholic theology, marriage is a sacrament, one of seven: the others are baptism, communion, confirmation, extreme-unction, holy orders and Sainthood. The reader should consider such things carefully; they make obvious the most important understandings.

Individuals must be encouraged to accept life's responsibilities and make the best of their own circumstances. This too can be learned. Where possible, circumstances should be improved for the victims by the victims themselves. They should be encouraged to work as best they can with competent and dependable help. They must avoid all forms of drugs and narcotics! No good can come from pumping one's self with such material. Those who sell narcotics, if they are young should be punished publicly if they are adults they should be given a death sentence; such sentence should be quickly enforced. This would eliminate many repeat offenders and discourage new ones. Many pretend to be too Christian to enforce a death penalty however they are not too Christian to lye and to cheat and to fornicate indiscriminately, for erotic pleasure, with another man's wife or daughter.

We should withdraw from fighting all Foreign Wars, as George Washington suggested. Warfare is overcoming most nations advancing the Anglo-Zionist attempt to control the world.[27]

It is asserted by some, that 350 people control about one half of the wealth of the World. If true, this is outrageous! *We are certain no morally and ethically decent God would desire the present state of the unfair division of the World's riches.* All men should be treated fairly and the death of a presumed enemy should not be considered as merely collateral damage.

---

[27]   **Chang, Matthias,** *Future Fast Forward, The Zionist, Anglo-American Meltdown.* First American Edition, 2006, American Free Press, Washington D. C. 20063

The good and prosperous of this nation are captivated by political nonsense, commercialism and too much misinformation.

This, together with the imposition of the International Banks (including New York Investment Banks and the City of London), has been carefully planned so as to destroy the existing political and ethical structures now in place. It is a slow process however it is working quite well.

Our current President Obama is not willing or able, to do what is right: *he is bound by his own misinformation and the promises which he may have made to become President.* Most important, he is somewhat a vain man with personal desires that run contrary to the reality which he embraces. He may be a good man in some respects. However, in a Democracy, a President must understand and represent the will and understanding of the best of the majority that elected him; he may not allow personal musings to dictate policy. The majority that elected him was a slender one, not overwhelming. Thus, he must also be aware of the wishes of that very large plurality.

What we have is unfortunate: actually it represents for millions a great disaster. We will be punished for having been so blind?

※

Professor Emeritus, Robert Fiedler
Anno 1-16-2013

CHAPTER II

DESTINY

To begin one must realize Destiny manifests in many forms:
Destiny comes about in a variety of ways: it has different forms and manners of being.
Every individual person is determined to a special Destiny
which may be favorable or a disaster.

Destiny brings both sadness and joy: Exuberance and ultimately death!
Many individuals speak of Destiny without giving it any real or insightful consideration.

First and foremost there is a World-wide Destiny dealing with the great earth-shaking catastrophes and great migrations of people. Such form of Destiny affects every person in the World. Noah and the great flood, it is believed by millions, was one such example. The becoming of a new geological age is another, with the disappearance of various life forms. The great earthly Cataclysms, that have reformed oceans and mountain ranges into new continents is another. Some research is compelling and descriptive, however who in fact understands exactly what happened? And why did it happen? These calls into being the existence of a supernatural, mystical and or a holy presence: the presence many imagine as being the one God. The presence of God is a complex and mysterious subject: some of our most reliable prophetic evidence appears within the Christian Bible a book which many do not believe. Those not Christian have other Ideas about this which may or may not be correct. Our Mass Media has made the unbelievers to appear important and they are made to be extremely visible; this is a phenomenon, based on the control of that same mass media. Some control of the mass media is as a secret understanding expressed in the actions of many; who and how they are, is not clear. There is evidence of a messianic countenance in many who attempt to control the news: they slant it to favor their own philosophical and ideological disposition. Unbelievers are visible in all of their profound misunderstanding: this is dangerous for our Civilization. Many prominent people deny belief in the one God[28] or they have taken up some misconception as their "personal" Religion.[29]

---

[28] **The Christian God** is a singularity: this must be so since there can only be one omnipotent presence with the force and position of being at the top; the apex. (This is applied Logic.)

[29] **For example,** some female celebrities and Actors who not unlike a harlot or a lecher abandon their mate. This is sinful and difficult for the children and the deserted ones. One might certainly blame the other party however marriage was intended and is supposed to be sacred and everlasting. Ideally it is inviolate and eternal which is obviated by the children that may become of such union. *The child is the next step toward what is infinite.* The child who represents the future is more important than the parent who is given to the past. This should be easy to understand.

Earth-shaking Cataclysms such as exist are followed, in order of importance, by International, Continental, National, Tribal, familial and personal Destiny, each of which has distinguishing characteristics. The characteristics vary in scope and effectiveness depending upon the nature and extent of the domain being influenced. The domain follows a somewhat strange pattern in the Form that a given destiny has taken. Destiny does have a form and substance: the form is about how things occur, what are the procedures. The form has to do with how the people are involved: one way or another. The substance is that upon which all forms of Destiny are dependent.[30] The substance has to do with the workings of Destiny in a given situation. Destiny is impossible, to predict and is difficult for most to understand and near-impossible to alter. What is destined to happen, cannot be altered: it must happen: one way or another? Destiny is a time-space phenomenon of great significance. Accidents are related to and determined by time-space.

Destiny is a composite Entity; a physical and sociological amalgamate which has elements that no one understands truthfully: some imagine they understand;
This may be vain or is simply foolish.

Economic destiny is primarily communal however has various ways of reaching the individual: individuals exist as singular functioning aspects of a more complex and extended form of economic destiny. In a practical sense Destiny is formed and responds to various influences. For the individual economic destiny is very important however is often beyond understanding of the individual so involved. Economic destiny involves money as specie and things, objects or charges for service: this is a simplification however to simply mention them is sufficient for our purpose. Economic destiny relates to what one does and how or who one is. This form of destiny is often, however not always, a place for sin to emerge: *the primary sin is* **Greed** however **Covetousness**, and **Envy** may be a part of the equation as well and certainly **Vanity** which is a Cardinal Sin (Christ Jesus). These are difficult issues for ordinary, quite disinterested, individuals who are concerned with the trivia of the day rather than great scientific, philosophical or religious thinking: thus, such issues are generally avoided because they may not be within the view and grasp of most persons. There is a group that believes they must inherit the earth, they imagine that they are God's chosen people and they have been very clever in their dialogue. Sometimes they cheat the more honest people whom they exploit for money. Some have amassed vast fortunes which they will use to "buy up" the Civilization much of which is a product of Christian goodness. If they accomplish their purpose they will sublimate the human race to do their bidding. This is a very important part of our present Destiny. I don't believe this will happen however they have caused and will cause great mischief.

Particularly youth, we are told, are victims of Destiny they are often abandoned by those who conceived them, other times the parents have died or were killed then the child must fend, some way, for themselves. For a fortunate number there are charities and Religious Organizations that

---

[30] **Spengler, Oswald:** *the Decline of the West,* (Encapsulation). "The "prime symbol" affects everything in the Culture, manifesting itself in art, science, techniques and politics; Each Culture's symbol/soul expresses itself especially in its Art, and each Culture has an Art form that is most representative of its own symbol. In the Classical, they were sculpture and drama. In Western culture, after architecture in the Gothic era, the great representative form was music—actually the pluperfect expression of the Faustian soul, transcending as it does the limits of sight for the "limitless" world of sound."

may help them to grow and some will even prosper. Others will suffer for a lifetime; often that life is cut short by a Tragedy.

The personal destiny is most compelling on the individual and includes all manner of hardship misfortune and luck (so-called) which might befall the/any individual. A personal destiny is largely influenced by who one knows and who one associates with. One's friendships and associations will steer one in a direction compatible with the expectations of such relationship: the expectations are not always clearly understood. *This is a very important element where youth are concerned and can be very good or can be fatal.* The young do not know much, having been children for about eighteen years, and longer they are more vulnerable to outside influence.[31] Some youth are destined to great accomplishment and the advantages of wealth others are destined to poverty, anguish and despair: suffering and an early or untimely death. We wonder why some die in their first year whereas others live to be ninety five and older.

Amidst the population of the United States, other places as well, cheating is a way of life: so to speak. Apparently this is wide-spread especially where economics is concerned. We have all heard of the Ponzi Schemes that have been promoted drawing sometimes billions of dollars for the perpetrators. Generally this represents only a temporary gain in wealth. The Scheme eventually runs short of cash and will collapse. Such schemes work into the Destiny of the general population including everything from bankruptcy to suicide. The perpetrators are caught, tried and placed in jail however, that does not help the victims very much except a few might have some or all of their money returned. In addition, surprisingly there is much cheating in Education so to enable entrance into a University or ultimately to gain employment. *Recently it has been discovered that even some teachers cheat so to place students into a higher level on their exams.* The teachers appear to be better teachers when the students do well. Why not help your students; just a bit. One wonders if the cheaters are given the best positions and how they might act in such position. When one person is employed instead of another, this works into the Destiny of who are involved; all are affected one way or another. One can find many examples of such instances.

---

[31]   **This is perhaps why the voting age has been lowered** and some are thinking of making it 17 rather than 18. This is ridiculous. In fact the age should have been raised to perhaps twenty five and have some other restrictions as well. Perhaps those who vote should own property, upon which they would probably be paying too much in taxes. This alone would wake them up to a reality which they cannot understand at seventeen or eighteen years of age; the fact is many adults don't understand either. At such age they are not even adults: they are older children but they are still children. Perhaps married persons should have one vote for both; such vote could have double value. If the married individuals do not agree they would not vote: one vote in fact would nullify the other. Why bother? Politicians know that youth is not well informed except by what they have been encouraged to believe in the Public Schools. Public schools at present in America are places where youth is enticed or perhaps forced to think in certain ways: ways that will support the existing One World-Anglo-Zionist way of thinking. They are being prepared for serfdom. *They are expected to consume the amount of goods that will keep them from saving any money and most must stay in perpetual debt or the System will not work.* Ultimately it is hoped by those that promote a One World government that the population will be numbered and given limitations. The world it is hoped by these same lunatics will be as a large rabbit farm where the masters will live in splendor and the Goy will barely exist. There are already many that live in absolute luxury exploiting the System which they have caused to happen.

Ultimately whatever happens will very likely affect the average man most seriously. The truly wealthy have the advantage of money, property and various assets, free of encumbrance. They also depend on each other and have various ways of exploiting every opportunity: they are indeed economically fortunate. Never the less all such advantages are temporary. At present various forms of *Debt with attendant interest rates are strangling America, especially the lower and middle classes: other Nations are in a similar position as well.* Add to this the influx of foreign born workers taking the place of those born in this country: those who are not the most skilled and are therefore the most vulnerable. This is accomplished under the guise of Christian compassion even though the ruling elite often discount a belief in God from politics. This is just one form of hypocrisy we can name. Many are confused because they do not understand what a Religion is or who is God. Considering the United States of America the final blow, is all of the cheap and unnecessary imports that are flooding the country and you have a program guaranteed to create disaster and servitude: to destroy America.[32] Some authorities attempt to stop this practice and they are somewhat successful. The imports are advertised to appear very useful and individuals will sell their soul for the latest forms. This is part of the plan of those who have determined, with unreasonable expectation, to rule the World. They hope to create a world of the dependently impoverished who will work from day to day just to stay alive while the privileged will exist in luxury enjoying a Sultan's riches.[33] There are historical and biblical warnings of this however no one seems to understand the meaning of such proclamations.

America right now could possibly benefit from a form of Jubilee Year![34]

---

[32] **Some individuals** are working assiduously to do just that: to destroy America. They imagine America stands for freedom and opportunity which is only partly correct.

[33] **Right now** there is much talk about one's credit score. One is supposed to feel good if they can barrow enough to buy what they *"imagine"* they *"might"* need. Imagination is a great incentive to acquire more and more debt. The lenders know this and encourage it with vengeance. What is worse the economy of the nation depends on millions going into debt to keep the System expanding: just a little. At present millions of homes are "under water" they are worth less than is owed on the mortgage.

[34] **Jubilee Year:** "The Jubilee solution is radical in the sense of being "creative" and "out-of-the-box," but it actually avoids most of the objections we are facing.—For example, the Jubilee solution does not defraud any creditors or violate any contracts. In fact the Jubilee Year is based reliably on the idea of honoring all of them and paying them off.—Nor would the Jubilee solution cause, any inflation, as raising reserve ratios would soak up the potential extra liquidity, trapping it within the Banking System." Again quoting from the Boston.com article, we see that Rogoff, a fringe economist shares the same analysis as this concerning of our current economic problem: (and other fringe economists like Steve Keen).

It's an argument that Rogoff himself admits is "radical," and one he says he'd rather not be making. But as he sees it, **what's holding the country back from recovery is not just a lack of consumer confidence or suppressed demand, as in a normal recession, but an _immense overhang of debt_:** thanks to the collapse of the real-estate bubble, millions of American families owe so much to banks that they're focusing all their energy on paying down their debts instead of spending their money on new investments. Rogoff argues: **There will be no recovery until the painful process of working through that debt is behind us.**

The full article here http://articles.boston.com/2011-08-28/news/29938939_1_inflation-rate-financial-crisis-economy

Presently much of the great wealth may have been inherited however such wealth has the same effect as what may have been recently gained by honest and productive means: however, truly significant wealth (in the hundreds of millions and now even in the billions) is most likely a matter of inheritance.[35] The multi-million dollar yachts and various forms of accommodation are in the domain of the significantly wealthy: millionaires and now billionaires, with such individuals money is never scarce. To be one of them places one in a position similar to the position of past Princes, Kings: of true Nobility. As a matter of fact, with the advent and development of new technologies, the truly wealthy now have more than most Kings could ever have obtained in the past. They are, by worldly standards, truthfully fortunate. Unfortunately they are not always the best of people and when they are not they can inflict serious damage on other less fortunate individuals and on the World in general.[36] War, fought for profits to greed is the greatest obvious enemy. This is unfortunate however true. The best amongst them can be very helpful to others however this is perhaps not as likely as one might imagine.

A familial destiny can be very compelling on an individual and is a bit more complex however is very effective in consequences. Familial destiny often includes concerns of what are called Politics. Some families have had numerous members involved in the direction and control of the becoming of others.[37] Their influence is temporary however can be very influential. To

---

Jubilee Solution Summarized: Federal government issues electronic checks to pay off all debt. Simultaneously: raising banking reserve requirements by a proportionate amount to soak up the money. Viola, all debts paid, economy reset and primed to soar again. **It is really that simple.**

The only thing lacking is general knowledge of the plan and the political will.

[The people in charge of the government at present, who are the Rentire'/creditor class, don't care at all about anything but personal enrichment, which the current debt deflation is accomplishing marvelously by liquidating the assets of the masses into the hands of the creditors and cash-holders, i.e. themselves.]

[35] **Wealth can double or triple** in time due to the compounding of interest or earnings on principle. When one has considerable wealth to begin the effects are gargantuan and will ultimately consume most of the World's assets. We can see this happening with some of the great fortunes at present. Consider the government's cost of contracted debt. The interest on $1,000,000,000,000.00 (one trillion) for only one year at just 2% would be $20,000,000,000.00 (20 billion). The present debt is about $16,000,000,000,000.00. Some suggest it is much higher.

[36] **Many individuals** believe that, for example George Soros, to some extent fits into this category: however he is a newcomer and is not totally established in his undertakings. The most significant wealth has been accumulated over generations extending back into past centuries of opportunity. The Rothschild's and Rockefeller's, the Du Pont's and Windsor's all fit this category: historically to a more pertinent extent: some of them may do many good things as well. Nevertheless *their main objective is to maintain and increase their manner of good fortune.* At the present time it is believed that about 350 individuals own one half of the World's assets that are available for ownership. One cannot know if this is true or exactly how this may have come to be. This may be often done by means of the corporation and the various tax-lenience's available to the truly wealthy. One might imagine that the leniencies are a matter of collusion with the governments of this World. This is true because the significantly wealthy play an important part in financing the *"Election Colossus"* that we have created.

[37] **President Roosevelt** for example was related to a number of Presidents that preceded him. Furthermore the family was able to date their history back to the Acti in Rome which is somewhat over two thousand

be a President, or Senator or some other functionary places one in an advantaged position.[38] Politicians have devised all manner of subterfuge so to maintain their power and their wealth till death. In a Democracy this can be very dangerous for the people as the present circumstances suggest. This is especially true when the President does not follow the Law. In fact political domination is short lived and changes with the players. In our system we have created a two-party system, each party about equal in weight. By this means the people can be easily controlled by those that they elect to lead them. Many of our leaders seem to agree, often secretly, on a One-World form of government such beliefs are probably incorrect however effect much of what happens. Many are in direct opposition to the Constitution of the United States and the needs and desires of most individuals.[39] In such instance, to make their position more acceptable, our leaders call upon a false use and understanding of religious thought and moral issues that they, in fact, do not fully understand and, in fact, many such individuals do not believe them:[40] *Few people understand this which is unfortunate however true.* Religion is a very important and sustaining aspect of "Reality". However athletics has taken on a form of religious

---

years. He was not the man that he was advertised to be. President Roosevelt was a liar and a real and certainly most obvious insider; his fortune was alleged to have been $50,000,000.00. That is value in 1940; adjusted for inflation that would be about $500,000,000.00 today. There would also be interest added which in 65 years would be considerable. Where did all of this money go?

[38] **Interestingly, once elected** to a public office the job is almost certainly for a lifetime because of the notoriety that one achieves from being so involved and the fact that people support who they know. This is a well understood principle and, of course, the amount of money required for a campaign, limits participation for almost everyone. The exceptional ones are those who are very wealthy or are able to raise a great sum for the purpose of being elected. This type is probably working for their own interests using a powerful group, a group who they will work for if elected: they are generally opportunistic and are often classic hypocrites.

[39] **The Bilderburgers**, the Club of Rome, The Alta Vendetta, The League of Just men and some other groups are working toward this objective: a One-World government. Those do this so to better their own circumstances.

We cannot forget the Masons of the thirty-third degree who are found in all of the above organizations. Since the time of Adam Weishaupt in the mid eighteenth century his Ideas have been advanced by all those who believe they are destined to rule the world. Cecil Rhodes followed in his footsteps as did many other powerful men.

[40] **Religion** has been removed from the dialogue, especially Catholic Christian religion, because of the ignorance of the common man. See what I have written on who is God? (Chapter XIV). Beside this, there have been traitors within the church as well. Some such traitors have in the past and presently have some of the highest posts in the Church. The subject is beyond what is possible here. Primitive religions and barbarism are encouraged for the benefit of the people. Such as those confuse the individuals as they draw individuals away from important Western Catholicism (Universal thought) and the philosophy which supports the Western Civilization. There is virtually nothing of great Western Philosophy taught in many perhaps most of our schools: the Socialist/Marxist types have rendered *the curriculum to be one of comparing one bad Idea with another.* Our Institutions of higher learning are primarily concerned with job training and destroying those elements that distinguish one individual from another. Religion is being replaced by athletics and entertainment in the minds of the population: youth have vulgar and sinful rap music and the various clubs which attract them in the cities. Most recently there is a burgeoning of tattoo art which one can define as primitive, retrograde or atavistic: a step back toward the jungle. The changes are being encouraged by those that intend to rule all others: they will use force where necessary.

zeal and is most distracting for the average individual who waves a handkerchief and *"prays"* for his team to win. All of the adversities affecting the individual also affect the family in a variety of ways: one can imagine how this might happen.

Tribal destiny relates to Culture and to Civilization in various ways which relate to a somewhat National understanding of the same issues. The Tribe in some ways is a fledgling Nation and is open to some of the same tenants and restrictions as a Nation: religion and race may be important factors in this instance as well. Primitive Tribes have had more trouble in communicating their understandings because of a lack in linguistic skills: their means of communication are limited.[41] In many instances there are forms which might be considered as mysticism involved in the more primitive religions.[42] A sophisticated Westerner has some trouble in understanding the meaning of their taboos and habits. Various forms of religious thought were interwoven with such procedures thus making them more difficult to understand. At this junction Occultism and Mysticism were clearly in accord/disaccord with the perceived Reality. A difficult issue to contemplate it is impossible for modern man to understand.[43] The Catholic Missionaries, some others as well, attempt to bring an understanding of the true God where this may be possible. Interestingly one cannot have an exclusive Religion which is a somewhat childish notion promoted by who wants to destroy the effectiveness of Christianity. Religions are communal and are always a matter of the agreement of many individuals. It is imagined that what works well for one will work well for all.

This is the "**Will to Power, the will of the beast, the call of Satan:**" all is given to a crude and childish decorative form and is considered real cool by those that display them.

[41] **It is the belief of some** that the Primitive man is more in touch with the Spirit world and the plentiful and natural gifts of the earth: this may or may not be true. Primitive man is not educated in the language and the meaning of words: he is primitive and as such is not able to understand as is the modern educated being: although Modern Education is often defective or simply incorrect. To understand with certainty is difficult and beyond the abilities of many: at times most. Certainly, a civilized man without any instruction would have difficulties existing in a primitive setting. In this respect modern man would be at a disadvantage and might perish from the earth.

[42] "**Mysticism** (pronunciation (help info); from the Greek μυστικός, *mystikos*, an initiate of a mystery religion)[1] is the pursuit of communion with, identity with, or conscious awareness of an ultimate reality, divinity, spiritual truth, or God through direct experience, intuition, instinct or insight. Mysticism usually centers on practices intended to nurture those experiences. Mysticism may be dualistic, maintaining a distinction between the self and the divine, or may be non-dualistic. The feeling listed above is deliberately encouraged in simple minded people who do not think for themselves. Cannibalism was widespread in the past among humans throughout the world, continuing into the 19th century in some isolated **South Pacific** cultures; and, in a few cases in insular **Melanesia,** indigenous flesh-markets existed.[12] **Fiji** was once known as the 'Cannibal Isles'.[13] Cannibalism has been well documented around the world, from Fiji to the **Amazon Basin** to the Congo to Mori **New Zealand.**[14] **Neanderthals** are believed to have practiced cannibalism, [15] [16] and they may have been eaten by modern humans."[17]

[43] **There are some modern day criminal types** that have ingested the bodies of whom they have tortured and killed. They are rare however they do exist.

From an improper or incomplete understanding of Race and Religion grows all forms of incorrect and disjointed thinking and various habits and customs antagonistic to those outside of the Tribe or Nation: those of an imagined different Race.[44] No modern man can know how and what an Indian may have thought three or four hundred years ago: what we have are imaginings and metaphor based on a general misunderstanding of the people: such as those existing long ago. In fact the indigenous population had what some others wanted and others took this from them. This too is unfortunate however is true. Was this thievery? In the past the manners, habits and customs of the Tribe have been peculiar in one Tribe or another. In a modern setting this distinction has been generally eliminated. The Tribe was often headed by a Shaman, a Holy Man or a Tyrant. Tyrants do not necessarily sustain because Tyrants are human with the problems attendant thereto and because they do not have a consistent and dependable financial base as modern men find necessary. In a more modern setting the roll of money takes on a decidedly advantageous form. Much of the help given to assist the American Indians on their becoming part of the present has been wasted beside which it has made them dependent on that same help: many are found waiting for the next dole! In the mix there are always thieves that will steal as much as they can: one way or another.

In some countries the more primitive people are sold weapons, often out dated by the new stuff being produced in the *advanced nations*, and with such weapons they kill each other. Some consider this a necessary form of genocide to keep the population somewhat in check. Rather they should spend such funds to better the lives of their women and children. Presently some of the more primitive men are sold modern weapons from the more *"advanced"* countries and they carry on a form of barbarism very much like the more *"advanced"* nations. In some ways they are even more barbaric than the more *"advanced"* nations. Men learn by example: in the instances of killing and warfare this is unfortunate however true. One can understand that a primitive man will be impressed with the modern weaponry and may even enjoy killing his presumed enemies.[45] Some individuals may even consider ingesting them for a strange religious purpose: this has something to do with manhood we are told. Many such men, so called, consider them to be superior to their women whom they use and abuse for carnal pleasure. This is a difficult issue to consider: more difficult to correct. Personal behavior between a man and a woman cannot be truthfully understood because of the circumstances within which they may occur. When the boys reach ten or twelve many are conscripted and are taught to be like the other men in the Tribe: to hate and to kill. How might one correct this? Catholic fathers, attempt to teach their children to love and respect all others, which places them at a disadvantage when encountering a brutal or more primitive type man.

Nations are somewhat more complex and we hear much about one or another: there are the good guys or the bad guys. The definition changes in time when the attitude and understanding

---

[44] **Even in Ireland** a nation of seemingly intelligent people there is considerable antagonism between the Catholic and Protestant constituencies. They fail to understand what they imagine in respect to their Religious beliefs. Such antagonisms are encouraged by some who hope to gain some advantage by the turmoil.

[45] **There is probably a subtle relationship** between his understanding of cannibalism and his present disposition. It should be understood that whatever anyone does is permanently encoded in their psyche and is not lost. It probably will have some effect on what the person knows and does.

may be reversed in reference to the respect given by a rival or a friend. All modern Wars are fought between what are called Nations when in fact they are because of the Ideas and/or the Resources held by one adversary or another. *Ideas separate men they separate now from then teaching simple men to fly and Heroes (so called) how to die.* The Ideas drive the Culture and the Civilization: the morphing of thought forms is what produces invention. The inventions from the past are what form the technologies and means for the present. This is true of weaponry from the cross-bow to the howitzer or airplane: and now the man-less devices that can kill and maim "indiscriminately". The Present will be further reformed in the future: the formations will be considered advanced. Our military technologies are miraculous, they are awesome however would be unnecessary in a more decently formed World. At the present time the over-emphasis on ways of killing others, who are presumed enemies, is an ominous sign which will be met and administered by Destiny in future time. Nations have flags and various forms of superficial accoutrements' that provide comfort for the generally unknowing citizens.[46] The citizens are concerned with daily living and are not well informed about many of the most important Issues and elements in their existence. This has changed somewhat with Television however now <u>we are buried in trivia much of which is based on a false understanding emanating from the LIE</u>. At the present time there is a great deal of anxiety over the process of inflation which, if it continues, will destroy the value of the currency and create havoc on the system.[47] In spite of the preposterous claims even in a Democracy the individual citizen has no real power. The only power the citizen may have, for a short period, is when he/she is part of a mob on the street. All such mobs are illusions and are used for the effect they have on the moment. The vote of a single individual, a wise man, is almost always cancelled by another, perhaps a fool, who may have what are thought to be different Ideas. In our situation we place too much emphasis on one's *"doing their own thing"* when in fact there are some things that should be discouraged. This is precisely why the two parties System and Democracy have been encouraged by who wants to control the World. In fact the Ideas are generally generated and entertained by higher powers personal and financial in nature. At present money is the arbiter and sets the tenor: money calls the shots and delivers the blows.

---

[46]   **In America** when a child Hero is slain, (someone between the age of 17 and 25), the family is presented with a carefully folded flag. *Keep in mind most of our Heroes are just a bit beyond childhood.* The Flag is supposed to cover for the nonsense and ineptitude that caused his/her death. All the while the munitions makers, on their yachts, are counting their profits. Just imagine we take a youth, right from High School, and put him in the army providing him with the necessary misinformation to kill those he does not understand and cannot possibly know. Is this decent? Is this progress?

[47]   **"Some economists see moderate inflation** as a benefit, and so there are a variety of fiscal policy arguments which favor moderate inflation. The problem is Inflation does not remain as moderate: it is an expansive phenomenon. Central banks can affect inflation to a significant extent through setting the prime rate of lending and through other *financial* operations. This is due to the fact that most money in industrialized economies is based on debt, so controlling debt is thought to control the amount of money existing and to thus influence inflation. A government may find some level of inflation to be desirable, particularly in order to raise funds for War. "<u>Wakinfo: Inflation</u>". Thinking such as this is always a form of evil it is the presence of the Devil using an individual to accomplish the Devil's objective. Those involved see an opportunity to become wealthy: In fact this is one factor that encourages GREED a MORTAL SIN. No form of sinful excess is ever welcome.

Our present state of affairs is not good. Those in more advantaged positions have so many elements in their favor that they are bankrupting many in the middle and lower classes. This is a subtle transformation however is certain unless conditions are changed. (See foot note above on the Jubilee Year). This seems to be the only possible way to correct what is wrong. Our leaders will not like this because they are an important part of the problem created by those and others before them who were, as they are, possessive and uncaring, sinful and greedy. Sin, especially *GREED* will destroy all that good men have created. Other sins are dominant also however they do not have the same effect. One need only view the bombed-out cities from the past Century and they will certainly understand: or will they?

A Continental Destiny may involve several or many Nations, each with its own set of problems and aspirations and distinctly different people: it could involve the whole World. In the recent past perhaps one thousand years, Europe has been such a place. Europe is composed of a variety of Nations each with their own habits, manners, customs and language. At the beginning of this time-frame Europe was separated by mountains, rivers and natural barriers that provided for a separation of the various groups of people. One group did not often encroach on another because there were few people. With an increase in the population and modern methods of communication and rapid transportation this is no longer the case.[48]

Add to this that presently, as in the past Europe is being invaded by somewhat alien beings: particularly people who hold a different faith than Christianity. This happened before most notably during what were called the Crusades.[49] The two happenings are not the same however

---

[48] **According to Oswald Spengler,** after nearly 900 years of dominance, the Faustian era has reached its death throes. He writes, "The future of the West is not limitless tending upwards and onwards for all time . . . but a single phenomenon of history" (30). Like other modernists, he attacked the positivistic, Enlightenment myth of unending progress based on universal criteria. *Harbingers of this cultural decay were, among other things, atonal music, avant-garde art produced for oversensitive connoisseurs, manipulation of the public opinion by mass media, and imperialism.* Much like Goethe's *Faust* man becomes shackled by his insatiable quest for knowledge, "Faustian man has become the slave of his creation," particularly through the machine which enslaves both the worker and entrepreneur (412). *Our machines are monstrous and the individual is less and less required. A single man with a monster machine can do the work of ten, even a hundred and more. This is why our buildings all appear so sterile they are Artless because the hand of the man is missing in their construction.* For Spengler, "Caesar-ism" is another manifestation of this decline, as authority becomes increasingly concentrated in the hand of one person, for example in the hands of an inept President, and the modern institutions of the State begin to disintegrate (396). Even modern writers, such as Nietzsche and Ibsen, who "embraced the possibilities of a true philosophy," also "exhausted them" (35). *(Italics are from this author).*

[49] **The word "Crusade"** literally means "going to the Cross." Hence the idea at the time was to urge Christian warriors to go to Palestine and free Jerusalem and other holy places from Muslim domination. The first crusade was a grand success for the Christian armies; Jerusalem and other cities fell to the knights. The second crusade, however, ended in humiliation in 1148, when the armies of France and Germany failed to take Damascus. The third ended in 1192 in a compromise between English king Richard the Lion-Hearted of England and the Muslim leader Saladin, who granted access to Christians to the holy places. The fourth crusade led to the sacking of Constantinople, where a Latin Kingdom of Byzantium was set up in 1204 and lasted for about 60 years. The Children's Crusade of 1212 ended with

there are some similarities. Europe is imagined to be a primarily Christian society and the invasion is and was primarily by Moslems.[50] The two forms of faith are certainly destined to be in opposition each to the other. Generally speaking the Christian population has been taught tolerance for others different than themselves. However the more zealous Moslems are not this way, many are taught to hate who does not believe in Allah. This is presented as a form of indoctrination and is not truthful education. *This is certainly a very poor teaching and is childish*: it may also be considered as a form of nonsense however those who believe as a Moslem would be offended by such insinuation. **In fact many believe Mohammad was a Heretic!** It will be interesting to see how this plays out in the future: what Idea will prevail? The European birth rates are low and are not sufficient to replace the declining population. The Moslem birth rates, at present, are much higher and the Moslem population is increasing. Any mathematically literate person can figure out what will happen. Destiny might change this: we must wait and see. We are told that the Moslem birthrates are falling in Europe amongst the youthful and vital Moslems. This is probably a consequence of women being given more opportunity in the scheme of things. Time and Destiny will determine the consequences of this understanding and whether or not it was a truthful one. In any event Population is a Political as well as a Religious issue. *Keep in mind population and the understandings of a people are important factors in determining what will happen next.*

Finally we come to an International or World Destiny. This is what the controllers hope to control, especially the money and real property: minerals, food stuffs and precious metals. This is the most complex and at present has two few commonalities. There is some thinking that centers on reducing the World's population. War seems a solution for some; who do we shoot first? Those men and women planning this are deceitful liars and hypocrites always claiming to be working for the people. The great Force is the force of economic endeavor with population numbers adding greatly to the problems that are being generated.[51] And populations are increasing amongst the World's poor. However they also add to the potential for improvement if they were allowed and encouraged to do so. Also included will be greater profits for the opportunists. There are some that consider genocide as an appropriate solution. No honest Christian can consider this as legitimate: we are our brother's keeper. Christianity suggests by implication and by act that *"All men are created equal and that they are endowed with inalienable rights: those being to pursue life, liberty and happiness."* This is the part of Christianity that has deep seated political and social responsibility: more than many are willing to tolerate. Even some Christians are soft on this issue. A former Secretary of State, Madeleine Albright, who is not a Christian however who must certainly be influenced by some of the Christians around her, suggested that when we kill or murder five hundred thousand Iraqi children that this might or can be considered as *"collateral damage,"* what do you imagine their mother's might think of this? A statement like this certainly will breed a lot of hatred in the hearts of the mothers and the fathers, especially so amongst those that do not like us right now.

---

thousands of children being sold into slavery, lost, or killed. Other less disastrous but equally futile crusades occurred until nearly the end of the 13th century. The last Latin outpost in the Muslim world fell in **1291.**

50   **See (Chapter XIV)** for an understanding of "Proof of the Existence of God."

51   **As greater numbers of People** come into being the World will require more fruitful economic conditions and greater effort will go into food production and other human essentials.

Beyond the International or World is a Galactic Destiny that propels the stars and the planets, our sun and moon and many elements that we have not yet discovered. The longest known cycle within such destiny, of which we are aware, is about twenty-six thousand years. Man is inquisitive about this however cannot quite comprehend the existence of so much (?) time. He can imagine and he can interpolate and postulate however the Time element makes certain knowing difficult. All of the past is *"buried"* in Time.

Destiny and Economics
Destiny is a driving force in Economics

Most trauma and nearly all problems have some manner of economic connection. This is because money or some other thing, for example gold or silver, is or has been a necessary element in all commerce. People need food and things to simply exist. As the world is peopled by ever greater numbers of individuals this is a continuing concern; there must be an ongoing and continuous development and increase in the food supply. Food would be plentiful if and when Nations live in harmony. Men have devised various forms to expedite trade and have done quite well in this respect: generally speaking. However in the present there are many laws and methods of doing business not all of which are honest and decent. Many of our laws are corrupted by self-interest and linguistic flaws: they might therefore be interpreted differently than was intended. Our new laws often contradict common sense and many have become monstrous. They are often formulated to attend to a political objective overlooking what, in fact, a Law should be. Additionally, our Laws are being altered preparing for One World Government where it is imagined that a few super-rich or well connected politically will dominate all others.

This is not a good IDEA.

At present, in The United States, many of the main personal and social issues revolve around debt. This is a **consequence** of a System deliberately formed by a German Alien, Paul Moritz Warburg, German Banker, who came to the United States in 1902, joining *Kuhn Loeb & Co.* at a yearly salary of $500,000.00. Even today that would be a very respectable salary; <u>*imagine how much that was in 1902.*</u> He became a citizen in 1911. One hundred years ago, he promoted the Federal Reserve System into being to enslave the people to their own inability to exercise restraint and the use of common sense in making economic decisions. Most everyone in this Nation, other Nations as well, is somewhat **GREEDY** and is anxious to have the newest and best things. They have been taught in Public Schools to equate this with success and with progress.[52]

The mathematics involved in consumption and payment work silently however effectively, they are certain and persistent. Whatever one wants must be paid for in Time: TIME is an important factor! Time is especially important where compounding of interest is concerned. When one has extra resources, no matter how obtained, they can earn interest or can be invested and their holdings will thereby increase. There are billions of illegally and criminally earned funds within and entering the economic system. Much of what might be considered as surplus will find its

---

[52]   **The advertisements** for creams and lotions, bust enhancers and corsets, makeup and various fashion forms are an indication of the shallowness of America's women. All such advertisements are an appeal to Vanity: Vanity is a Cardinal Sin.

way to some form of criminal or anti-social element where it is used to exploit innocent people. Most people with great wealth are rewarded inordinately while others starve. This issue must be addressed before tens of millions more starve to death. *At present, our Nation and the World might derive great benefit **from the understanding** supportive of a Jubilee Year.*[53]

———w•o๑๙๏๏ฦ๏๏ѡ———

Professor Emeritus; Robert Fiedler
January 2013

---

[53] **Question:** What is the Jubilee?

Answer: The word "jubilee"—literally "ram's horn" in Hebrew—is defined in Leviticus 25:9 as the sabbatical year after seven cycles of seven (49) years. The fiftieth year was to be a time of celebration and rejoicing for the Israelites. The ram's horn was blown on the tenth day of the seventh month to start the 50th year of universal redemption. The Year of the Jubilee involved a year of release from indebtedness (Leviticus 25:23-38) and all types of bondage (vv. 39-55). All prisoners and captives were set free, all slaves were released, all debts were forgiven, and all property was returned to its original owners. In addition, all labor was to cease for one year and those bound by labor contracts were released from them. One of the benefits of the Jubilee was that both the land and the people were able to rest and be replenished.

Consider our Federal Reserve Banking System. The Federal Reserve is not Federal and it has no reserves. It was formulated to keep the population in debt and for the profitability for a select group of insiders. Paul Moritz Warburg who is said to have devised this monstrosity was in 1900 awarded a salary of five hundred thousand dollars a year $500,000.00 when he came to the United States. Compare that to the earnings of the average man of perhaps one thousand dollars for the same year. Even today that would be a pretty decent salary.

The Jubilee presents a beautiful picture of New Testament themes of redemption and forgiveness. Christ is the Redeemer who came to set free those who are slaves and prisoners to sin (Romans 8:2; Galatians 5:1, 3:22).

The debt of sin we owe to God was paid on the cross as Jesus died on our behalf (Colossians 2:13-14) and we are forgiven the debt forever. We are no longer in bondage, no longer slaves to sin, having been freed by Christ, and we can truly enter the rest God provides as we cease laboring to make ourselves acceptable to God by our own works (Hebrews 4:9-10). **Return to: Got Questions.org Home**

CHAPTER III

CIVILIZATION, A COMPLEX FORM
OF HUMAN EXTENSION

Seemingly, Human Acts are driven by Objectivity as well as Subjectivity
A Critique of human behavior

This is based upon a peculiar understanding of distinctly formed Thought Patterns.
Thoughts do form patterns and also series of patterns as those are enacted.
Smart people recognize this and are able to exploit it for profit.
Professor Robert R. Fiedler © April 5, 2002

Civilization, as understood, is comprised of a wonderful array in respect to what is objectively determined to be as Artifact and Implement. All that we have is an example of a technical and inventive bringing fourth in order as it were, the ideas of many men. As the Ideas combine and are refined we find ourselves benefiting from the curious combinations in thought forms and thinking thus bringing this Reality to a significantly identifiable level of understanding. The actualized past can be understood *as forming a complex objectively determined multiplicity, **a summation of Humanities existence.*** *The known, understood and remembered* past is what we have recorded as history. Some of this is as tangible Reality and some is a matter of the mind, Invention, Mythology or Metaphor.

This complex phenomenon is observed by all that are presently a witness to reality. What is Reality? It manifests as the *unfolding as well as enfolding **simultaneity of accommodation**,* which is of an involving and evolving nature. It is axiomatic that any complex reality as defined above is, as a totality, without precedent. There can only be one **NOW.** This is true because of the nature of Time and Movement in Space in reference to individual life, especially human life, which includes a sense of personal being, with all that this implies. All previous Civilizations underwent internal transformations, thus might be understood from a similar point of view, however none of which we are aware are/were as complex nor as extensive as the present one, which because of this profound Idiomatic is perhaps (actually, probably) doomed because of it. Precisely, the most significant elements given to function, in this present circumstance, are products of highly technical and deliberate thought, which reaches back in time for origins that are difficult to imagine. Presumably there was much disagreement and conflict in the past, which has been carried forward, *as Ideas about the past,* manifesting in what we observe presently. Such thought is based upon *precise mathematical and physical knowledge,* rapidly extended by the advent of increasingly sophisticated implementation, given to near-instant communication. Man stands at present, coincident with what we deem as profound advancement in the realm of human thought. It is evident that our implementations must be applied with carefully determined objectives in mind and with truthfully discerning insight. It is important to understand subjectivity *seated in an evil intent* can be absolutely fatal to humanity. Without "Divine Intervention" this is a certainty!

> *Right now this is what we have! A few presumptuous and arrogant fools are attempting to usurp the prerogative of all humanity. Their understanding and therefore their acts are based on ancient and cabalistic forms of misunderstanding; many reject Christ as being inferior.*

Individually, we are the beneficiaries of all circumstance. Certainly, at any time there have been fortunate individuals who have been gifted with a particularly generous circumstance, and this is true at the present moment as well. Presently, success is projected on the multitude as some form of entertainment, which may have questionable motivations, or a devious purpose. It should be apparent that entertainment is a combination of truth and fiction, blended for the purpose of gaining attention, so as to be able to sell tickets and products and performances. However it is certain that crucially important truths should eventually be generally known. However, the assimilation of truth for each individual may, in some instance, require many years. Actually, it is also quite certain (at least in the opinions of some) that extended investigations may be politically or otherwise *subjectively* pursued, with little or no meaning or justification, except to gain wealth for those most immediately involved and interested parties.

An interested party, in any event, is always *subjectively* involved and is to some degree, self centered or generally self-concerned: Those may be somewhat vain. However what is acted out or written may project, with well-reasoned intent (however, tacitly), a message behind the message. The message behind the message is often completely different, from what is imagined by the object of the effort. Importantly, Ideas advanced for consumption gain prominence, in their effectiveness, from any public exposure brought about by sensation. Music provides the most obvious sensation and can be very compelling (see Chapter XVI). Importantly, all variations of human behavior can be given to some manner of expressive form, artistic and/or theatrical. Monumental productions have been developed, as never before, which exploit both the actual performance together with an ideology, all as a business venture, *most often as a production for money.* This brings forth the notion that money corrupts, from the long past Roman Empire, thus is carried forth the notion of bread and Circuses.

With great emphasis on subjectivity and innuendo in solicitation of gaining acceptance, for what was heretofore considered inappropriate forms of behavior, *Mass Media has given great force to the moron, the pubescent and the politically well situated celebrity*. This has been accomplished mostly to the demise of profound understanding and to confuse the meaning of Virtue as being much opposed to Sin. *Vice* is projected as pleasure whereas *Virtue* is most often depicted to be a laughing matter, and especially is denigrated by the *silly and profane comedian.* The subjectively projected nonsense, which is so apparent in our environment, is certainly important in the mind formation and consolidation of both children and adults, too preoccupied with their own circumstance to give time to serious study. As such they can be easily victimized. They are immured without understanding what is, in fact, happening to them. Astoundingly, the salaries paid to media personalities is outrageous compared to those who, in fact, offer much more for truthfully reasoned and honestly pursued endeavor.

All forms of acting, rhetoric, versification, elocution and artistic production, involving use of language, have an element of *subjectivity,* which is forceful, as it is evident. Actually, *the imposition of one's self* is what makes any production or work of literary merit especially meaningful, given to *subjectively* peculiar understanding, however by innuendo much can be implied tacitly, which will affect the way the work is projected and understood, and ultimately its effect on others. Tangentially, this ultimate effect on others is what is crucial to our interest and calls forth, that is beacons, some attendant understanding. Thus, we mention the current interest in probing, with intent to stimulate and/or modify the individual, as well as the collective mind. Furthermore, one must consider the notion, formulated by unknown **subjectively interested others,** of behavioral modification, given to a political and social purpose. This brings to attention the importance of **Reasoned Motive.** However, all motivations are not certainly honorable. *Subjectively formed motivation directed toward a negative consequence, which it will engender,* is a hallmark of our present complex circumstance. This touches upon the notion of a salesman's mentality, with an emphasis on economics. What's in it for me? This is selfishness!

Selfishness as VANITY is a Sin!

For most, all of their effort is expended toward gaining enough to live on for one's self and one's family, where a legitimate family does exist. There was a certain amount of decency, in reference to responsibility, and respect due a man for providing for his family. At present, in the United States, some other places as well *"persons"* work for the salary, fees, stipends and or benefits that go with the position. There is great interest in *legality* and virtually none in *humility,* prudence, decency and, generally, *morality.* This is a tragedy that is deliberately encouraged by those with the most power, and the most money, determined to enslave the rest in a manner of Sociological Prison. Their object is apparently to destroy Christianity, the creditability of Jesus Christ and, for some, the Caucasian race. Those are virtual enemies of what is held dear to millions perhaps billions of people. Those draw myopic Ideas from an *Ancient and Tribal* past.

Some persons in a commanding or seemingly opportune setting are able to bilk millions some even billions from a malignant form of <u>Democracy become as Socialism in service of **Greed.**</u> **Greed** is the most obviously operative of the **seven deadly sins.** There is little attention given by the really rich and successful to the needs of the little persons, the ones that do all of the service and otherwise necessary jobs, which provide the millions and billions for the fortunate few that, manipulate at the top. And, there are very few indeed. Some of the more fortunate do engage in charity, which many of those (milk) for tax refunds. Nevertheless next to the cost of a ten or fifty million-dollar yacht their efforts are generally marginal at best. Those may receive great acclaim for their efforts, which is certainly somewhat reasonable. The Person is being redefined by sociologists, psychologists and governmental intervention. Notions concerning the Occult figure quite prominently in the Hypocrites plan of divide and conquer the population. Individual liberty is an expression of the self and is all inclusive, beginning with haircuts and dress and working toward a more complex and somewhat misunderstood *"kind'* of being. Today's *"person"* seems very confused concerning what, who and how they are and how they should act. Those are taught to *"Act"* as those engage in one performance after another. A form of Sociological Engineering has deliberately confused today's youth. The engineering works for [the] System, which almost no one understands: many now do what no reasonably sane man would do.

In all instances of subjective as well as objective imposition the past gives impetus to the present as the unknown future is beckoned, becoming (in time) a newly formed reality as part of the construct of an ongoing and complex and continually forming Civilization. In many, perhaps most instances the objectively defined implementations, especially those, which utilize the new electronic forms of technology, are placed in the service of self-interest, which in profoundly significant negative instances will ultimately prove fatal for millions.[54] In fact, this is most likely what will destroy the Civilization introducing a New Dark Age. The New Dark Age is not understood in advance of its becoming and will be a surprise, placing billions in desperation. Those who are the imagined leaders will, very likely in effect, destroy most of what has been more wisely nurtured. *Those are presumptuous fools and shallow minded nitwits.*

The most obvious of these appear in the distribution of pornography and the mass appeal of gambling, both of which, for many, become addictions. Shame and self-restraint have been abandoned by clever use of words in service of self-interest using the technologies of mass communication. Communication should be considered more intelligently and should not be simply babbling on the phone or over the airways.

The computer and the Internet provide the ultimate form of communication and distribution of information, in an implementation, which is marvelously *objective* in complexity and formidable as a means of communication. *Subjectively formed notions,* whether seated in truth or not, are widely available.[55] For the layman, the mechanics of the computer, combined with the intrigue of searching for some personal satisfaction, make the computer a wonderful therapy for the curious, however the ill advised may be *subjectively* assaulted by what is available. The accountant and the money manager find the dependability and *objectivity* of this implementation to be of ultimate perfection, in the accounts receivable departments and in the offices of big government.

Right now well informed stock traders find that the speed of the computer can make trading very profitable.

The courts and the airways are evidence of the theatrical nature, which has been given to *"revised notions"* of historic events, all for interested viewing by a population of poorly informed spectators, with nothing better to do than watch in an attentive however stupefied silence.[56] The extent of any significant consequence, which may be just now becoming apparent, as the result of this unforeseen and complex Problematic, is not generally understood, or is understood only in part. Indeed, truthful dialogue is restrained by the imposed expectations

---

[54]   **The way War becomes** from the encouragement of unknown others is an example. War always has elements of secrecy and intrigue, for incorrectly reasoned objectives. War is always sinful and destroys or partly destroys the lives of all of the victims one way or another.

[55]   **Many notions** are only partly truthful. The minds of those engaged in rather incidental thoughts are inclined to embroider, for effect, what they are saying. The embroidery often has a devastating effect on the listener.

[56]   **The Movies and Television** apparently has done much, to honestly inform and also to distort the factual and effective nature of a perceived or imagined Reality. We can assume that the effect, though not truthfully understood, is having wide-spread influence on the thought content and thinking of those affected, of entire populations, by such imposition. No one can possibly know what the outcome of this will be: all must wait and see.

of *political correctness,* given to the direction of fools and money-grubbers. Ultimately, as in the past, the wisest and truthfully good man amongst us will be crucified by the mass media; silly commentators negatively informed and the (seemingly) liberal. The form of the crucifixion may be different however the effect is the same. This is precisely what happened to Christ as a consequence of circumstance much as is occurring right now, misunderstanding, usurpation and the lie. The men that crucified Christ had absolutely no comprehension of what they were doing and were not able to foresee the consequences that would ensue.

We admonish that Civilization is, in both general and specific terms, an extension of manner, habit and custom, in a substantial and truthfully unfolding reality. Population aggregates stem from the family, the community, the tribe, the nation-state and finally the great nation. For some, in the future the ultimate form will be a One-World Order, under the rule of corrupt law, within which law Christian Morals will be abandoned in favor of Popular Opinion, *driven by unknown masters of finance and the media.* The notion immediately above, as inferred in the title of this critique, suggests we must begin to question just what exactly is being extended, in the domain of a *too subjectively compromised reality,* when such compromise is secretly imposed. May we question this? For what manner and purpose are the present nefarious impositions being pushed and to what will they lead? Who will gain most from this endeavor?

Often we hear spoken of a New World Order. What does this mean? From whence did such concept originate and who will most benefit from this, if and when it might come to be? The Idea is not new. Wealthy and influential men, including some leaders, have always wanted to rule the Civilization, or that part of which those were aware. The Idea of a Master Race is old indeed, dating from about 500 BC.[57] It is the ***will to power*** given to a means of enactment. The means of enactment in the past were dependent upon threat, armies and starvation. The new form is money, finance Capitalism working against the common man. There are elements as in the past; starvation, armies and War. ***Money has moved from being a servant of humanity to being a controlling force,*** which can be used with impunity by who controls the amount and flow of Capital as money. *Those who control the money are very clever in their actions.*

Objectively sustained thinking has afforded us with marvelous technologies, however not many can imagine what might be the ultimate outcome from all this wonderful technical advancement. Certainly there will be much that is good and perhaps much of which will be debilitating: as in War. In many instances, implementation appears to be far beyond what one might reason as necessary and appropriate: much of this is developed in service of foolish and corrupt opportunism. Actually when the entire World has the technologies for rapid and seasonal mass production we will have so much stuff that it should be practically free. This raises two pertinent questions: How much is too much? With this understanding shouldn't the price of everything be declining?

Technologies based upon verifiable and well-understood complexes are very fruitful in achieving the outcome of intention. The modern airplane and the automobile together with the implements for war make this obvious. Engineers know what they are doing and are quite able to proceed with some high degree of certainty, having stood (as it were) on the shoulders of

---

[57] **Mullins Eustice,** *The World Order, Our Secret Rulers.* (Published by the Ezra Pound Institute, Staunton, VA. 24401, Second Edition, 1992).

all the giants who have been before them. However, in the realms of the more philosophical, theological or eschatological formulated thinking, concerning political and moral issues in particular, given to the great variety in the thinking of humans, things are not so good. We are far behind where we must be, if we are to succeed and to sustain as an ultimately complex Civilization, with promise for a better and more enduring future. We have been warned that the present circumstance is not guaranteed of a positive future (Spengler).

Western people, in spite of complex communication networks, are not fully aware of the sentiments *subjectively* held, by most of the peoples of this world and we do not know exactly what their intentions might be. This is certain since all information given is not based on perfect knowledge of the truth. Information, whether truthful or not, is open to interpretation, thus it becomes subjective (given to the interpretation of the subject) in the process. Only the Catholic Church stresses the importance of absolute truth, the continuation of Tradition and perfect knowledge. The Western World, largely become as a result of Catholic thought, which appeals to Mankind, is complex and somewhat evasive to the uninformed, certainly to the heretic.

The Catholic believes all men, are made in the image of the Creator, who shares an infinite personality with His creatures. *This is a most profound **Idea*** whether or not one believes it is true. The Catholic Church is ridiculed for this understanding and conviction as being dogmatic, which it is and must be. In the terms of a Philosopher, *that which is must be as it is or it would be something else.* This applies very much to Philosophy, *as an objective discipline, the dogma is essential.* Keep in mind, Science has many definite tenets (dogmas) upon which our technologies and our Civilization are built. The theologian must appeal to common sense and the Intellect to make universal Christian dogma evident, thus to be more generally accepted as belief. Theologians, prone to a too *subjective interpretation* as they succumb to **Vanity**, are not always convincing, beside which some are inspired to undermine what has been accomplished in this world. Irrespective of subjectivity, **Truth is eternal** and as such [IS] absolute. ***Simply put, what [IS] is ALL, that [IS].*** This is an importantly *crucial* issue, since all mankind does not believe in the same God, nor do those believe in the same way or with commensurate comprehension, ***albeit there can be only one Omnipotence and only one Humanity.*** Humanity presents a very diverse population; it is an ultimately complex, multi-faceted singularity.

Given an understanding of the duality of our present dilemma, it is wise to reconsider our understanding, of what is the consequence of separating Church and State. Given the complexity of the present Idiomatic, this is no easy task, however there must be found (as does exist) common Tenants which might help in the development of a consensus. Religiosity is one thing, Goodness quite something else; history stands in evidence as proof of this. If we expect others to develop a common understanding of what we are doing, it follows we must put in evidence some common held understandings of our own.

In the past some Religious Men, so called, did monstrous things. This was generally the fault of the man or men not of the Institution and is why the Catholic Church, founded by Jesus Christ was and is determined to work from a position of perfect truth. Omnipotent Truth is Perfect Truth, the Truth of the Creator. Nevertheless, the question for some does remain ***who was the Creator?*** It requires mankind, all men, understand this and furthermore that those behave with this understanding as a basis for personal action, controlling all acts of personal volition.

The best Statesmen attempt to do this, to form correct and decent consensus. However they are often missing the main ingredient, which has its origin in morality and the moral order, precisely the birth and life of the Man Christ, who founded the Catholic Church, *for all men, for all time.* Politics must include acquiescence to natural law, which preceded all forms of man-made laws. The rule of law, as presently understood is missing the most important dimensions, defined in the Ten Commandments! *Moral objectivity is based on absolutes,* which are defended in reality as given to past *well-understood incident.* If we do not learn from the past, we will certainly repeat the same errors, which are known as such, however denied. There are moral imperatives and examples of the force of goodness, in opposition to evil. Evil becomes of *misdirected subjectivity* in respect to others, which are exploited, *mostly for profits (a few coins) given to greed.* Most of the World's leaders, are not wise men, many are fools with legal or military protection.

We must modify our instruction and place less emphasis on winning at all costs as, for example, in competitive sports. Win or lose, a sport is supposed to be fun and should be pleasurable for all involved. By placing *so much emphasis on winning a meaningless game* we are training youth to be intolerant and disrespectful in their treatment of each other. This understanding will not go well with those that take pleasure in watching someone be killed in an attempt to kill another.

People who have very little in reference to technology, who suffer because of this, do know that we have much as a consequence of our technology. Perhaps millions imagine all what is ours could be placed in their hands. September 11, 2001 may be just a beginning, albeit a sensational one. And we are not sure of who caused this tragedy and why was it caused? The follow-up may be a surprise, perhaps quite beyond comprehension. How we will solve this existing dilemma could determine the future of mankind, for the next few centuries at least.

It would seem prudent and wise to extend our *objectively defined technological ability*, thus to afford greater access as we set an example for goodness, which others might begin to emulate. This must be accomplished in the name of universal Christianity and acknowledged as such, which co-incidentally is named Catholicism, Universal Christianity. There are religions older than Christianity nevertheless Jesus it is believed came to this earth to save all of mankind. ***Whether or not you believe this you are still subject to the Universal faith.*** To a large extent this is being accomplished at the present time, however self-interest and exigent circumstance, in many instances, may prevent positive consideration for those who are most in need of help. For many of the needy ignorance is the problem thus *"Proper Education"* is the solution, which would include principles ordinate to the Catholic; *that is to a Universal Faith in Jesus Christ.*

There is no other way!

Professor Emeritus; Robert Fiedler
January 17, 2013

CHAPTER IV

SPECULATION THE SHRINKING VALUE OF YOUR MONEY

Speculation, answers the question; What is Greed?

Greed is the Opposite of Humility. Speculation is a functional aspect of *Greed* considered by millions to be a Mortal Sin. *Greed* emanates from the personality of the individual who hopes to make more than might be reasonable, from a monetary or some other form, of transaction.[58] There is, quite often, a degree of dishonesty in such monetary transactions. This is not unusual since greed is, generally speaking, self-serving. At the present time with the fears of inflation and the erosion in the value of the purchasing power of one's own money, this fear combines with the understanding of the existence of stored value earned in the past; right now speculation is rampant. Keep in mind in the United States inflation has been rampant since about 1940, even, to some extent, before that.[59] In 1850 @ $30.00 per month was a decent salary. Right now the wage is many times that amount. Inflation can be found as a cause for much adversity in most places. Inflation is a Politicians way to encourage populations to believe what is not true, imagining they are becoming wealthy. Inflation is a real Problem; it is a form of unseen and silent theft.

The shrinking value of the dollar, for example, is contrived by politicians pretending to be "*the leaders of men:*" inflation robs everyone just a little every day. This is an inherent problem in a Democracy which ultimately will consume itself: or become totalitarian so to control circumstance in favor of the small Anglo-Zionist Elite. This Elite is not well known to, We the

---

[58] **GREED is a mortal sin***:* one of seven deadly sins. Why, is this not better understood? Why, is this not more properly discussed in our *"Great Institutions"* of Public education: First; truthful education is generally private: Second; the removal of Religion from educational institutions has crippled the minds of many: Third; the disagreements concerning what is and is not religious. With many Religions there will always be some disagreement. Additionally, there are those that deliberately defame Christianity, some other religions as well, and especially Catholicism. The Marxists and Socialists of all kinds are somewhat tolerant of various Religions being included in the mix: this creates the confusion that they hope will help destroy the existing Society. Especially the Catholic Faith is a target. *Marxists and Socialists cannot tolerate the truth or anything that is profound or holy.*

[59] **In 1949** one could purchase a cup of coffee for .05 or .10 cents. Now the same coffee is .50 MacDonald's Special (not very good) to $2.50 which is quite an increase. That is a ten-fold to twenty-five fold increase or 1000% to 2500% increase. Divide that by 60 and you have a yearly advance of between 16.66 % or 41.66% per year: frightening! In 1940 a gallon of gas was .11 or .12 cents. Compare that to what you pay today.

People. The Elite are generally comfortably situated and accommodated away from where any trouble is. It is interesting, at least, that many (perhaps most) of the elite are thirty third degree Masons.[60] This should not surprise anyone who understands that we are living in a Masonic Republic. Both Khrushev and David Rockefeller are Masons*: they are Fraternal Brothers:* this is certainly interesting (?). Besides being interesting this makes them brothers bound to a similar form of oath, secrecy; *in fact they are both hypocrites.*

Democracy is self-extinguishing*:* people will vote for more than they can afford, much more than they can pay for. This is a very serious flaw that accompanies Democracy. Democracy sounds good however there are probably (undoubtedly are) better forms of government. Actually a small and honest Monarchy would be much better: one in which the People would know who to blame. ***The money changers-lenders wanted the Kings eliminated*** so they the money changers-lenders could control the money; they did not want a King to have the power of the purse. The money changers-lenders wanted that power for themselves. This is what we now have; the money changers-lenders control most of the wealth. *With our Democracy functionaries are simply moved* from one position to another making it difficult, indeed impossible, to correctly place any significant blame on an individual. Certain individuals are chosen for persecution and damnation by the controlled press. Much publicity is promoted, to confuse the people. Generally such individuals are not the most important they are duped for a misunderstood reason. When a favored Politician commits an indiscretion, even a felony, he is quietly moved to another position of responsibility so to continue the fraud. *This is not as well understood as it should be.* Men, known to be frauds and hypocrites are kept within the System, moving from one *"responsible position"* to another always causing bedlam and unrest; this is subtle however certainly true. The reader can compile his/her own list.

Government is always better when it is smaller rather than larger. Government has a way of growing subtly which is not well understood: not by the politician and most certainly not by the man on the street. The Democracy must control the farce so to sustain it. As governments grow, they become more and more oppressive and will ultimately dominate or they will collapse and be replaced by another. Beside this most modern governments are a mixture, more or less, of one or another form of Political Control. For example our own democracy has much Socialism and some bit of Dictatorship in the mix. The real problems, which are difficult to address emanate from the *character or the quality of the people.*[61] It is unimaginable that a population which is constantly entertained by cheap sex, violence and meaningless athletics will be anything but distracted: generally speaking many in our population are somewhat decadent or illiterate and enamored by nonsense! This is apparent in their manners, habits and customs. One can observe this on the tattooed bodies of a whole class of individuals. This is not all bad individuals must have something to do that is pleasing: especially this is true of the more simple minded individuals. The bright ones are generally creating the trouble: one recalls Winston Churchill

---

[60] **Is it co-incidental** that two, presumably opposing leaders, George Bush (former President of the United States) and Nicolas Khrushev (formerly Leader of Russia) belong to this fraternal Organization?

[61] **The character or quality of the people** is generally speaking a religious question, thus Religion must be included in the policies and workings of any form of meaningful government. Once again the Catholic universal faith seems to be certainly the best choice. It has sustained for over two thousand years and has done and continues to do marvelous things for all people: especially the poor.

and Adolph Hitler for example. It can be imagined (at least) that Churchill and Hitler were similar in their psychological make-up; both could be considered as being quite bright. Neither was a fool but what they did can be considered foolish. Neither was correctly understood for what he really was. Churchill was on the winning side thus he became a hero. Hitler, the loser, had remarkably stereotyped coverage for the World to see; he became a **[the]** villain.

The **"mass thought content"** of the people will direct their endeavors: in America this is not well directed and is not truthfully understood. We suffer from a form of mass-neurosis that is difficult to understand and cannot be corrected. Such condition is being encouraged and promoted by those that are in positions of silent control. The silent control is well financed and carefully directed toward achieving a somewhat sinister purpose. The Sinister Purpose is the New World Order an Anglo-Zionist and Masonic conspiracy to dominate the World; (it is a Conspiracy). One needs to view only the evening television to understand. *How is our tainted reality formed and directed?* Add to this that we are beholden to psychologists and psychiatrists many of who do not even understand the simple problems: certainly they do not understand the complex ones either. No one can possibly have all of the information as required especially when the information changes from one hour to the next. Neurosis is unique and the neurotic elements vary from person to person; they combine in ways that cause both personal and mass behavior that has many negative connotations. All of this finds its way, somehow, to being a part of our misunderstood *Political and Social Thought Forms.* Such forms are composed of what I have mentioned in other places as "pieces of thought." Misunderstanding is further compounded by our contrived two-party System where, in fact, both parties are just about the same. They are kept in close accord, generally speaking, so they can be controlled: the people can be counted on to elect those most beneficial to the System. The people will believe what they are told; that they made a significant choice (?). When a good man appears, like Senator Joseph McCarthy or Ron Paul he is shouted down by fools influenced by the Masters of control. If all else fails the imagined guilty one will be assassinated, pushed from a window or die of a strange illness.

Let us now consider a Specialist in one or another form of what is being inflated: this might be money, real estate art or any other thing. The Specialist is the prominent Dealer and is in the best position to take advantage of circumstances; he will gain most since he will take a fraction of all transactions as a fee: one way or another. The Specialist has a *"Salesman's Mentality"* and he is clever; *he is street smart.* The Specialist may have a significant holding in a given entity, commodity or thing which had been acquired earlier at a lower price. A low price is Time related and relative to when the merchandise was obtained however is generally at a discount from current retail pricing. ***Inflation guarantees that all prices will advance in Time;*** this is a very important understanding. The Specialists positions may have been accumulated slowly over years or they may have happened rather quickly depending on circumstances. If one ignores the Law, important positions can sometimes be accumulated quickly. The Specialist will have built his position quietly and certainly. The Specialist (or Salesman) is an expert at changing notional wealth to real and tangible wealth and must be better understood in this respect. He relies on controlling the emotions of his subjects; for this he is often aided by mass media which informs people. Is mass media dependable? *NO!* Imagine someone paying over one hundred million dollars for a terrible painting by Picasso? This is evidence of the effect of many salesmen working for an assumed profit.

Generally there is a great deal of talking about the inflating value of the merchandise involved thus the *GREEDY* become interested. Consider the Stock Market; as prices advance the greedy will move in: at first the more aggressive ones and later those who are more timid. Each wave of increasing speculation will attract more players who will pay more for what they are getting as the Specialist will continue to take a portion of each trade as a commission. Coincidentally the Specialist's commission will increase as the prices are inflated: he will always get a determined percent of any transaction. In the last phases the general population will join in the fun. Most of this Type will lose their money. They have been given excuses so to believe that this is a legitimate and reasonable position to have occupied. In the meanwhile the Specialists have made a killing. The average investor is who was financially killed: just a little with each play!

At one point the prices will peak and begin to decline. The trick is to be on the short side.[62] People are constantly reminded as prices increase of the inflation in Germany after the First World War. Everyone fears, paying a billion dollars for a loaf of bread. *Keep in mind the Inflation in Germany was a part of the program designed by Bankers and Politicians to destroy the country by this means.*[63] England especially feared the economic status of Germany. Germany did survive and we would too, except at times like this is when assets change hands often becoming controlled by aliens, those least likely to provide support for a people and a Nation.[64] They are very likely hoping for a One-World Government and are determined to rule everyone, every man/woman that may exist:[65] there are also quite likely to be Masons of the

---

[62] **In fact short selling should not be allowed:** never. Short selling removes the responsibility of loss because of declining prices and is part of the SCAM that is called TRADING. It is an important part since millions can be made on the short side thus bringing down price. Prices always drop faster than they advance. It may take years to move a stock to extraordinary levels. Then the average man is encouraged, by the Dealers, to buy so to prepare the specialists to make a fortune on the short side. The Dealers benefit from the commissions. The entire Stock Market is one huge Ponzi-scheme. A few fools entice their acquaintances into a deal and the price begins to fly. When new pilots are no longer entering the System the value falls like a stone. *Some penny Stocks reversed splits of 100 to 500 are enacted which make the investment near worthless.* A few will profit somewhat, this will legitimize the process.

[63] **Keep in mind,** at that time Germany was a very small nation compared to the United States. For details see the Internet under Germany; the First World War.

[64] **If one consider** who has no responsibility to any nation nevertheless some do assume to be a part of one or another nation. The Jew amongst some others is an International individual who makes him comfortable wherever he may be; he is both adaptive and clever. They take all opportunities available; the Talmudic Jew gives nothing in return. The Talmudic Jew believes he is one of God's chosen people and will ultimately be given to rule the World and its People. Such are not the thoughts of all Jewish people only a small percent. However such thought is the cause of many, perhaps most, of the World's problems. Interestingly many of such individuals are not Biblical Jews. They are Asiatic; they are descendants of the Huns and Chasers.

[65] **The Idea of World domination** has been on the mind and in the hearts of many men some are Jews who consider them to be the chosen ones: chosen by God. They are in fact Chasers who have been converted: they are the Asian hoard of which many speak however do not understand. (*See the Internet;* **Koestler, Arthur,** *The Thirteenth Tribe,* 1976). Common sense implies no fair minded God would prefer so small a number of people over the entire human Race. Nevertheless this belief has troubled humanity

thirty-third degree involved in the process of determination. They are planning the worst form of Totalitarianism ever conceived and theirs is the same as any other one-world aspiration. Those are groups, of internationally connected Aliens that protect each other as they inflict damage on everyone else. They are from various countries however they are some of the greediest amongst the greedy. They will rob whomsoever it is possible to rob. They will steal from the dying and the dead as is happening right now. Often the form of theft is not known or may not be truthfully understood. *War provides great opportunity for theft of a profound nature.* Much of the profit from War has fallen into the pockets of those who may be considered as the Elite group and such profit will provide for their control of mankind.

Returning to the subject of inflation; as prices advance some players will take on more than they can afford: they will assume a margin position borrowing what is necessary for their purpose. Many of them are destined to lose for certain when they are faced with a call for more money as prices drop to a certain level. They must pay the price or lose their position. Occasionally one who does this is rewarded, prices advance and he will make a bundle. These are the ones you read about in the financial papers. Financial publications are all over the place *making money for the publishers.* Often their advice is ill-founded and the players who follow their advice will lose much or all of their capital. This is a real cat and mouse situation.

As trading proceeds there becomes more and more anxiety and more and more winning and losing; ultimately panic! This functions as motivation for the Bears and the Bulls. As interest wanes the market for a particular commodity or stock cools off. New players are not likely to appear when prices reach unreasonably high levels. The peaks you see on the charts are formed by the simple-minded buying from the Specialist who is now on the short side of the trade. This is generally the case although there are exceptions: not many we imagine. A Specialist in some instances may also lose a great amount of money however he is generally well covered.

At this time there will be a new bubble forming in a different place which will run through the same cycle trapping a new bunch of **GREEDY** fools. Great sums of money can be gained in this way in very short time spans: by the Specialist and the few lucky ones, more than an honest man can earn in a lifetime doing what is required to keep the System going. Men such as George Soros have no mercy on their fellow man and they will do *"anything"* to make a buck. *Then they use their profits in their vain attempt to tell everyone else how they should live.* This is in fact a form of criminal offense however it is considered good business. This form of understanding must be altered to make it fair.

It must be kept in mind that many so-called *"special situations"* are well understood by one who is close to the action. Those who work in the Financial Industry have information that few can tap for understanding. There is also some deceit and dishonesty involved with some in the business. There is always a manner of legal action or an entitlement for one who has been

---

for centuries and continues to do so. This belief underlies Modern beliefs and confuses the Politics of millions of decent and fair minded individuals. Additionally a Religious concept or Holy Right is rarely discussed without their becoming great antagonism between the parties. This is unfortunate however true since Religion deals with ultimate Issues. One must consider all Issues carefully and not be too quick to judge or to too one sided in their efforts.

scamming the System. The System does have many honest players however Greed is a very compelling emotion for some. Some of who have been imagined to be fair-minded may be in fact amongst the worst of the thieves. Many thieves and liars are caught however the manner of being continues; someone always has a new scheme. The way the market is structured allows for the kinds and degree of dishonesty and deceit as we understand such to be. Time is a very important factor and Time is an absolute determinant in all transactions large and small. Once time has passed it cannot be reconsidered. When a poor man uses his time to accumulate a very small portion against the future it is criminal to rob him of it by means of inflation.

In the last phases of a speculative bubble the general population will join in the fun. Most of this Type will lose most or all of their money. The average investor is killed: just a little.

Too many men do not understand and are not interested in what is truthfully important; What is important are his children, his wife and of course, his Soul.

———⟋⟋⟋∘⦾✦⊙✦⦾∘⟍⟍⟍———

Emeritus Professor, Robert Fiedler
April 11, 2013

CHAPTER V

SPACE, IS PHENOMENAL
AND IS AS NOTHING

To play life's game, is to play by one set of rules, in the space provided;
By the God (force) who (which) created the Universe.

To begin, *space is a profound corollary of Time.* Space is ultimately significant concerning how and why we think and act as we do. *"Without Space there could be no Time."* Space is the most significant absolute and is infinite, nevertheless Space is invisible. **What is infinite must be invisible.** Whatever is visible is defined by the boundaries, such as contains all finite entities. What is *finite* can be *found [In] space.* Coincidentally, Space, as the ultimate infinity is the symbol of itself.[66] It is *ultimate and profound* that what, in fact, [Is], as nothing, contains the **All** that is! The virtual potential of space has no limitation that we know of, excepting those set by the Creator. Whatever else it may be, the universe is a product of a *"Creative Miracle."* Interestingly, we as individuals, are given to comprehend only just a very small Space-time Segment and do not understand the truthful nature of this profound **miracle.**

The Creator must be a masculine entity since the Universe is the result of His being the Progenitor. This is no small matter, *given how many rant and rave upon hearing the mention of God as being a Man.* **God is [Man-like].** Some minds, which have been closed or stunted by too much of the untruth and by adolescent political propaganda, which is rampant and by the 'pedantry,' which, Father Rutler brings to mind:[67] are unable to deal with the truth. There are many today that suffer, as a result of the interpolation of present thought, which is schismatic and is often deceitfully covert; *much thinking and thought is blatantly sinful.* In addition, we are a nation *overwhelmed by childhood fantasies,* which are driven by astounding technical skills, and the investment of billions of dollars (for effect). **Is it any wonder that we have a dearth of serious adult thinkers?** Some other nations are as guilty of this as are we. Personal prerogative and an impossibly naive understanding of Democracy, impose a too politically subjective stance for honest discourse. Objectivity is essential in searching for the truth of any Issue. When one is encouraged by powerful unknown forces, which may have an unknown and obscure messianic goal, in respect to the objectives of those engaged in the dialogue, it is difficult to act in a truthfully and traditionally correct manner. The Creator must have a form of masculine identity since the Universe is the result of His being the **Progenitor.**

---

[66] **Spengler, Oswald,** *The Decline of the West,* Vol. I: Form and Actuality. Alfred A. Knopf, Pub. NY. 1928, 14th Printing, 1976. Pg. 122, (Time, pg. 123). "To name anything by name is to win power over it."

[67] **Rutler** *The Fatherhood of God,* (Homiletic and Pastoral Review, June 1993)

What we perceive is brief compared to all Time and all Space, or so it would seem. In one's perceived Time Segment, we nevertheless become (in a personal biological, neurological and psychological sense) as a center *[our center]* of God's infinite space.[68] We do not suggest that every individual is the exact center of a plotted universe; no one can determine this. The center of infinity could be anywhere. However what one will accomplish is always from, where one is and who that one may be. *We acknowledge and note that what is infinite cannot be exactly plotted.* Only a known segment or portion can be plotted. All human life is centered on an "individually" placed being. Life, in this world of human perceptions, may be considered as a "becoming" toward an infinite existence in an infinite space. This is a Universal Catholic Idea, which is not necessarily accepted by all, nevertheless it cannot be ruled out once it has become within the *mind space* of the individual (Spengler). It is the driving motivation for hundreds of millions of individuals. Furthermore, with a promise of possible salvation, *many imagine* we may [after death] become "one in being with the Father, from whom all good things come."[69] The "All Things" referred to, are located in an infinitely-extensive Time-Space surround.[70] Keep in mind whatever time one is granted is sufficient to gain salvation. The Catholic believes one must be baptized into the Faith.[71] This assertion will create problems for some however the **[All]** exists ipso facto as now and is **then** (as before) and **then** (as hereafter). *See illustration on page 88.*

What is not seen and not perceived may very well be what is most important. For example, ***"the spirit of Christ cannot be seen however is nevertheless very functional in the scheme of (Reality),"*** as we understand reality to be. This is especially true when we consider the

---

[68] **Time** (Fiedler) does not exist without the coincidence of humanness, a human [**being**]. Although the Universe is as it is, cognoscente is dependent upon human neurological function. Coincidentally geological time, as the format for human existence is independent of man's participation. Biological time is continued in the seasons and in the presence of animal life however, such without perception of the relationship between past, present and future. ***Only man has a Soul.*** All other animals have merely a presence.

[69] **Imagination** (Fiedler) is an important part of Humanness. Imagination beacons future time, from a neurological centered humanly perceived Reality. Imagination is a wonderful gift however, should be directed properly so as not to contaminate the effect of such imagination. The source is a particular human presence as exists in the Soul, reaching for an *"infinite beyond,"* which is unknowable. The center of the Self has an unknown and unseen manner of reaching beyond what is apparent. The thought of an infinite beyond has been an important part of Western Thought for centuries, since the advent of Christ.

[70] **Bearden, T. E., Col.,** *Aids Biological Warfare,* Tesla Book Co., P. O. Box 1649, Greenville, TX 75401. ISBN # 0-914119-04-4. Col. Bearden implies then explains that we exist in a time-surround. In such instance all time is cancelled as it occurs, thus each moment is lost in time-space forever, except that it can be documented, in word, sound and symbol, by human intelligence thus sustaining for a limited time. Human intelligence and what is human, being imperfect, cannot possibly convey what is most significant and most necessary.

[71] **Christ** did admonish that we should follow Him. The first step is Catholic Baptism, by which means one is brought into a communion with Saints and other Catholic beings, meaning becoming one in the Spirit of the Lord. The Spirit is found throughout humanity and aids in performing wondrous miracles. The need, for a Catholic baptism brings forth some questions. Millions have been corrupted by an imposition of the pride or vanity of others.

interactive workings of an entire Civilization. *To continue, almost all of what happens between men and nature is unseen by almost everyone on the earth.* **This is the understanding in support of the Catholic assertion that no one can have perfect knowledge.** One would need by definition, to be Omnipotent, to possess an understanding of all of what is known and what has ever been of every single event.

"**Infinite Space** is the Ideal that the Western soul has always striven to find, and to see immediately actualized, in its world around; and hence it is that the countless space-theories of the last centuries possess-over and above all ostensible results—a deep import as symptoms of a world-feeling; *How far does unlimited extension underlie all objective things?* There is hardly a single problem that has been more earnestly pondered than this; it would almost seem that as if every other world question was dependent upon the one problem of the nature of space. And is it not in fact so—*for us?* And how, then has it escaped notice that the whole Classical world never expended one word on it, and indeed did not even possess a word [72] by which the problem could be exactly outlined."[73]

Johannes Kepler recognized that since all astronomical observations result from the intersection of light and the human eye, knowing the principles of light and of vision would provide a link to understanding the connection between, the cognitive and the physical domains.[74] As he wrote in the introduction to his *Optics*: *"What wonder then, if the principle of all adornment in the world, which the divine Moses introduced immediately on the first day into barely created matter, as a sort of instrument of the Creator, for giving form and growth to everything if, I say, this principle, the most excellent thing in the whole corporeal world, the world, has passed over into the same laws by which the world was to be."* We read in this statement that it is conceivable, not necessarily certain, that man might be working with the same manner of intelligence as God however, to a lesser degree. If, indeed, man is made in the image of God who shares, in some small part His divine wisdom with his creatures, then it seems probable that intelligence, thinking and knowing are divine characteristics given each man for a brief period in time in a limited however definite space. *The Time given is always sufficient to gain salvation.*

This divine characteristic set the *"Stage"* for free will, a God given right exemplifying God's respect for His creatures. Millions believe free will has been given by God to every human being, all Mankind, *not some selected group.* If you are human you can think and act on your own volition, as was intended by the Creator. *There are various messianic movements, with mostly political intent, bent on controlling the World: this is a vain and narrow presumption.* Men are of their own volition able to choose one or another without being coerced to do so. Coercion derives from Vanity, which is a mortal Sin. **See our listing of the Seven Deadly Sins.** Coercion derives from the fact that **the will to power** is in force and controls the population. This is obviously wrong since the **will to power** of one then denies the existence of free will for all

---

[72]   **Either in Greek or in Latin.** Locus means spot, locality and also social position.

[73]   **Spengler, Oswald,** *The Decline of the West, Vol. I. Form and Actuality.* Authorized Translation with notes by Charles Francis Atkinson. Alfred A. Knopf, Publisher, NY. pg. 175.

[74]   **Director, Bruce,** *On the 375 Anniversary of Kepler's passing.* Fidelio, Journal of Poetry, Science and Statecraft. Summer/Spring 2006 Pg., 103

others. Christ admonished that to discover truth, as an individual, will set one free, free from slavery, bondage and mortal Sin. This is such a fundamental truth, that it cannot and must not be overlooked or subverted. ***Any Messianic disposition, which denies this, is therefore wrong.*** Christ alone did come to teach *"All Nations"* for which he was crucified by the Pharisees. He was crucified by a mob living at that time.[75]

Mind Space is absolutely unique to every individual in this world. Without elaboration, this understanding is brought to your attention. <u>*The uniqueness of individually formed Mind Space is a threat to those that seek political control,*</u> harbored in the ***Will to Power.*** Such individually and phenomenally formed Mind-Space is a singularity unique to the ***Individual-Time-Space Interlock*** or configuration, thus cannot be controlled. Such space is in fact a psychological extension supported by the neurological, biological functioning of [the] individually formed human body and the control of the human mind.[76] *Mind-space functions as a phenomenal form of "containment" for what we know and what we understand.* The nature of the mind-space is systematic and is determined, to a large extent, by what one has or *"harbors"* as an Idea or Ideas.[77] It is distinct from cyberspace in that the Mind-Space is within the domain of a living being, the individual, whereas cyberspace is a universal given. Cyberspace is a human discovery, which can be entered at will by anyone with the technology necessary to gain entrance. It is true that Mind-Space can interlock with the products of cyberspace depiction however; the product of such interlocking is still a personal possession, which may have positive or negative effects on who enters that domain.[78] *Mind Space is an individually formed human construct requiring*

---

[75] **The Romanoff's** were butchered, burned and mutilated for the same kind of thinking by a mob living (then) and the world has not been as it should be because of it. This mob carried forward in time, in the minds of ignorant dolts, the strange and outdated ***Ideas*** similar to those that crucified Christ. *The murder of the Romanoff's was a Time-Space atrocity based on a carefully planned and executed "take-over" of Russia,* at the time the most powerful and wealthy Christian nation. This take over was orchestrated with precise timing by a group of dissidents combined with bankers and hired assassinates, and was successful because of all the anxious Traitors in the Western world. The motive was GREED ***a mortal sin. The Ideas are made a bit more evasive because there were some Religious implications and many of the Revolutionaries came from New York. This is a difficult subject to approach, more-difficult to understand.***

[76] **It is a tragedy** that the mind content of those such as Karl Marx or Pablo Picasso or any other form of ***prostitute*** did invade and coalesce with the minds of millions of others. In some instances such vainly inspired ***"Intellectual Syphilis"*** overcame the content within the minds of the mostly innocent millions.

[77] **Christianity,** Catholicism in particular, consists of a *"set of Ideas,"* a philosophy that forms, the basis for the theology and the behavioral patterns of a *"kind of person."* In fact it is Holiness! Christ opposed many of the commonly held Ideas of his time for which he was crucified. His Ideas were seen as being a threat to the rulers. He was imagined as an enemy of those in power; this he was. Things are no different today than those were two thousand years ago. Keep in mind *"We the people"* never do anything except live. Those who control the rest are determined in their endeavors and are becoming more certain of such control which is now nearly guaranteed by great wealth and properties. ***Money and the control of Finance provide the necessary means of control.***

[78] **Unfortunately,** for millions, the understanding of cyberspace is correlated with comic book ideas and those that represent violence, killing and mayhem. Youth are distracted by games involving silliness

46

of the discreet biological functioning of the various systems within a particular human body. Bodily systems are synergistic[79] and work together in marvelously complex and very positively comprehensive combinations functioning to promote the life, thought processes and vitality of every human being. At death all such *temporary Human functions* cease to exist. What will/ might replace them is found in the domain of Religious thought and require a form of Faith.

The Catholic Faith, universal and all conclusive, is that Faith which is to a great extent responsible for the development of the Western Civilization and the marvelous thought components, which have provided so much for human progress. Nevertheless since the Crucifixion of Christ there has existed a never ending struggle between Catholicism and those that have a mind, liken to those that performed the Crucifixion. History informs us that there is great disagreement in who is a Jew. Biblical Jews, as such, are very much incorporated into the human race. Much emphasis is placed on the Diaspora, however most peoples have undergone similar fates.[80] Individual members of all tribes have moved from their place of origin to other places. A few may still remain, which is understandable. Only the Zionist Jew uses this as a defense of his being, without including mention of his *sense of exclusiveness.* Some who call themselves Jews have been unwilling to participate in the general workings of the human Race. The most notoriously Jewish persons support the *"Idea"* of racial and religious purity, for Jews. Nevertheless those encourage a mixing and or leveling of all others. By his exclusiveness coupled with his being a moneylender, to the nations of the World, he now finds that he is in a privileged position amongst men. Given the nature of *Usury* and its function in *Time* some Jews have gained an extraordinary advantage in worldly affairs. The history of lending money is a subject all by itself. Briefly, what has happened is that money instead of serving the well being of Humanity has slowly and very deliberately become the Master of Humanity, serving most those that hold the coins? Ashkenazi Jews in large measure, have become Masters, and thereby

---

and gaudily colored forms that represent the vulgarity, cruelty and sensuality representing what is imagined however is unknown and unseen. As such, *the imagination is a dangerous and silently working phenomenon,* to some degree playing into the hands of those who wish to control the world. There is more than one faction with this desire. Only one faction, Catholic Christianity, completely opposes such mind set. Certainly God and His Son Jesus would best understand such maliciously contrived circumstance. *We speak of Catholicism as Christ had intended; men have changed this.*

[79] **Synergism** functions during one's entire lifetime and is manifest as a consequence of trillions of functions, both thoughts and acts. "**In Theology;** the doctrine that the human will co-operates with divine grace in effecting regeneration" (Webster). There is a connection between **Body, Mind and Spirit,** which *must not be excluded* from thinking and/or thought patterns; especially should not be excluded from politics. It is a Primary Motivational force in human behavior and existence. In fact it may very well be the most important consideration. The **Idea** has been eclipsed by Pagan and a Disneyland type imagery that completely obfuscates the real meaning for youth.

[80] **Diaspora**: commonly refers to the dispersion of the Jews after the Babylonian exile. In fact many people moved to different places and today more frequently than in the past. The Jewish Diaspora has greater religious connotation, which relates to their believing that, those are God's chosen people. This ancient belief is responsible for much of the turmoil and bloodshed in our present world. Combined with the use and control of money such feeling of superiority has to a degree *despoiled and somewhat corrupted* the entire Civilization.

control, amongst other holdings, most of the major banks in the West.[81] They may attempt to control the others as well. Time will tell.

When money is loaned at interest over long periods of Time it grows conspicuously. In the course of many lifetimes it become astronomical and becomes a threat to the Civilization. ***This is not well understood and may be fatal to the Human Race.*** The interlocking relatedness is no accident: it is being carefully implemented right now. Corporations must be more truthfully exposed for what those really are. Criminal Syndicalism must be identified and stopped before more enterprise finds its way into criminally inspired possession. The narcotics trade places billions in the hands of criminals that are determined in their sleazy efforts to corrupt the human race. Combined with this notion we have some psychologists pushing drugs, especially on children where such drugs are more harmful than good. This must be reconsidered!

Recent computer imaging, of the interior of the body has been rewarding for the purpose of medical diagnostics. Also, for informing the general population, to a limited degree, of what exactly goes on inside the human body. Nevertheless the understandings that follow are open to the *"thoughtful and personal"* subjective interpretation of those that view, thereafter act upon such information. A Thermograph, senses and confirms the existence of heat within the body, which is a sign of infection or illness, for example breast cancer (Nelson, MD, PhD. and Mark Brown PhD). Vibration Medicine is able to override the waves that function within the body and to make minute adjustments where malfunctions are apparent, for example heart beat and cellular resonance (Richard Gerber, MD)[82]. All such techniques are in consonance with the normally functioning bodily systems and with the *universal order and functioning of the space,* which contains them.[83]

Micro-voltages are found within the functioning cells that can be acted upon by mechanically induced waves so to enhance and correct cell function.[84] Micro-voltages are also found in the aura that surrounds living plants and animals. Subtle forms of energy are emitted from living entities, which can be photographed using Kirin photography. What is within and without from

---

[81] **Mullins, Eustice**, *The World Order, Our Secret Rulers,* Ezra Pound Institute of Civilization.

P. O. Box 1105, Staunton, VA. 24401. pps. 6 to 63.

[82] **Gerber, Richard, MD.**, *Vibrational Medicine, The # 1 Handbook of Subtle-Energy Therapies.* Third Edition. ©2001, Richard Gerber. ISBN 1-879181-58-4, Bear and Company, Rochester, Vermont, 05767.

[83] **"Beginning in 1670** and progressing over three decades, *Isaac Newton* developed and championed his *corpuscular hypothesis,* arguing that the perfectly straight lines of *reflection* demonstrated light's particle nature; only particles could travel in such straight lines. He explained *refraction* by positing that particles of light accelerated laterally upon entering a denser medium. Around the same time, Newton's contemporaries *Robert Hooke* and *Christian Huygens*—and later *Augustin-Jean Fresnel*—mathematically refined the wave viewpoint, showing that if light traveled at different speeds in different media (such as water and air), *refraction* could be easily explained as the medium-dependent propagation of light waves. The resulting *Huygens—Fresnel principle* was extremely successful at reproducing light's behavior and, subsequently supported by *Thomas Young's* discovery of *double-slit* interference, was the beginning of the end for the particle light camp".

[84] **Gerber, Richard, MD**. *Vibrational Medicine.*

the human body (other plants and animals as well), works in concert to accomplish remarkable human endeavor. Acupuncture, the use of light and holistic medical practice is dependent upon such infinitesimal functions. Medical science, when given freedom to inquire, combined with personal discovery, as a consequence of living, combine to provide understanding of what till now has been unknown.[85] Unfortunately there are religious, political and economic considerations that do color what may be done or will be done to benefit from any important discovery.[86]

Micro-voltages combine with chemical substances in *"a spiritually centered force"* that drives human life. The ontological aspects combine with the misunderstanding of what is of a divine nature, and are generally confused, by variously limited notions concerning Religion. All Religions are *"imagined"* to have an equal validity regarding their efficacy. *This is a primarily "Political Notion", driven by the Party, certainly most deficient in the understanding of what is Spiritual.* Our political thought, generally, does not include, the *"Tran mundane"* and that, which is ***Holy.*** As always, complex thought is imposed upon, by political subterfuge and what is only *"imagined"* as necessary. *The separation of Church and State presents an insoluble problem.* Abortion law and the Federal Government's intervention in domestic issues provide glaring example of *destructive and debilitating political interference*. The present debate over the Nation's health programs is a NOW notion of what some imagine or believe will be for the betterment of the people. There is little thought or discussion concerning what is or may be Holy and little cognoscente on the part of those who are doing what *those believe is important*, indeed necessary, as procedure with almost no understanding of the various complex treatments. As such *they are more interested in Politics "Now"* and in being elected for another round of excess.

All forms of life animal and plant also become as evidence of various phenomenal processes. Animals, lack understanding of any spirituality, however benefit from the existence of an ***eternally present power*** over reality that man has determined as his God or as the Creator. All point to one simple question. How can this be?

Thinking is such endeavor and thoughts do have patterns. Thought patterns interlock, within the mind space, ***by means of language, symbol and act.*** When committed to the written word patterns, which engage thought can be observed many times, thus to obviate and reinforce understanding.[87] This in fact is what is prompting and motivating some research in the use of artificial limbs. The advances made recently are phenomenal. The sensory system of the human person is being induced to work in harmony with the prosthesis thereby the individual with a prosthesis is able to perform in a more natural way.[88]

---

[85]

[86] **Privitera, James R.,** MD. & Allan Stang, MA. *Silent Clots, Life's Biggest Killers*, The Catacombs Press, 105 North Grandview, Covina CA.46 W. San Bernardino Rd., Covina, CA 91723, tel. (818) 966 1618.

[87] **The Rorschach test** requires all participants to respond to a form after which response the participant gives a description of what has been seen. This is an interesting test however is influenced by the interpretations of who administers the test. Thus such *"tinkering with the mind"* may not have much, validity. Pp. 8-22.

[88] **The field of neural engineering** draws on the fields of computational neuroscience, experimental neuroscience, clinical neurology, electrical engineering and signal processing of living neural tissue,

Spatial thinking is an important part of everyday living. It is also endemic to all manner of sciences, from astronomy to zoology, and at all scales from the most-minute scale to the largest universal scale. But just what does anyone know about spatial thinking?[89] "Now, how about figuring out who have been some of the world's great spatial thinkers!" Some of my favorites include Eratosthenes (who first calculated the circumference of the earth); Euclid (for his formalization of a geometry); Kandinsky (for his beautiful spatial art); the designer of the Great Wall of China; Copernicus, Tycho Brahe, and Kepler who figured out the movements of the earth and other planets around the sun; Vasco da Gama, Columbus and Captain James Cook for ocean exploration and seeking distant lands; Einstein; the developer of the U.S. Interstate System (I don't know the name); Michael Jordan and Michelle Kwan for spatial thinking in their respective sports; lastly Walter Christaller and August Lösch for their conceptualization of settlement patterns".[90]

Thought patterns are peculiarly formed by means of the senses especially sight and hearing however, other senses play some part as well. Sight is important for the simple reason that man has progressed through time guided by symbols and sounds. Symbols and sounds combine with the effects of incoming experience; the *"ethereally formed"* substance of a peculiar reality. Sight is also important because light is a universal and a constant given. Images travel through space as beams of light. Photons travel within the infinite space of the universe as well as within the interior of the cell. ***There is some reason to believe that living matter is a manifestation of a peculiar form and arrangement of light.*** Interestingly Catholic Christianity, some other faiths as well, maintain ***God is the light of the world.*** Dante in his Divine Comedy imagined Beatrice as being perfect, chaste and as pure light, therefore somewhat likened to God. Angels are believed by some to be a manifestation of pure light, invisible and therefore capable of being anywhere in an instant. Angels generally appear as Man figures, rarely as women and not as

---

and encompasses elements from robotics, cybernetics, computer engineering, neural tissue engineering, materials science, and nanotechnology.

Prominent goals in the field include restoration and augmentation of human function via direct interactions between the nervous system and artificial devices.

Much current research is focused on understanding the coding and processing of information in the sensory and motor systems, quantifying how this processing is altered in the pathological state, and how it can be manipulated through interactions with artificial devices including brain-computer interfaces andneuroprosthetics.

Other research concentrates more on investigation by experimentation, including the use of neural implants connected with external technology.

Neurohydrodynamics is a division of neural engineering that focuses on hydrodynamics of the neurological system.

[89] "**Spatial thinking,** the way we navigate the world and manipulate the space around us, is crucial to problem solving, whether it's routine activities such as parallel parking or more esoteric activities such as designing a building or reading an X-ray. For children and teenagers, developing spatial thinking can determine the course of their career and perhaps their life. And for the elderly, it can mean the difference between mental clarity and cognitive decline".

[90]

babies in swaddling cloth. As mentioned above, three centuries before now, *Kepler in his Optics* made some profound associations in this realm. *(See Internet, Kepler).*

Music also affects thinking because of the intensity and the insistence of the rhythm and beat. The beat, when strong and incessant does affect how one feels and may encourage certain forms of personal or mobs behavior. The vibrations, given off by percussion as well as sound reverberate within the internal workings of the cells in the human body.[91] This is perhaps why music is so compelling, one-way or another. Before coming to any defensive conclusions, consider this philosophically and imagine an extended time period, perhaps two or three hundred years. *To reiterate, even Plato, two thousand years ago, was skeptical of the form and manner of music as being capable of destroying the nation.* One might imagine that music can be an important factor in the destruction of the minds of youth. However the young will grow old. One wonders, how will the adults of tomorrow deal with the problems that those as youth have created today.

Television, especially, has provided a level and degree of intensity and insistence combined with the inclusion of commercial nonsense that is designed to entice even as it distracts from and impairs serious thinking about a subject. It is difficult to imagine what might be the consequence of such desperate programming viewed incessantly. One can imagine that the behavior of our children is directly affected by such inputs. The music, which accompanies drama, is most often more compelling than the drama, much of which has lost its meaning between the commercial messages and the subliminally delivered thought content, both of which may be an underlying factors?[92] As an art form, much of drama has been trivialized and delivered so that the means of delivery, the technologies employed in the sophomoric attempts to create realism, take precedent over the message; they sublimate the Art.

Propaganda is another related issue, which depends upon the reiteration of sound and symbol *in a context contrived to create submission to intent.* Freud knew and had some understanding of this, as do modern advertising executives. What is imagined as truth, when given to the wide audiences found in recent-times functions, as simply stated, to be more or less a form of propaganda. Propaganda has been very destructive on Christianity and especially so on *Catholicism, which harbors the imperative upon which Western Civilization has been founded.* The Church has been the object of calumniation for centuries by all that were Heretics. Millions of individuals left the Catholic Church. They chose to escape the seat of Holiness and Western Culture. (See chart showing the rise and fall of various heresies).[93] Many Priests have been some of the finest and most astute and holy men found in this life?[94] However even some Popes have negated their responsibility and were anti-Popes. The last five Popes come into question for

---

[91] **As a young man** I played a trumpet which I continued until I was seventy. As a quite accomplished player I can confirm, as a musician, what I have written above.

[92] **Jacobson, Steven,** *Mind Control in the United States*. Introduction, by Antony Sutton, Critique Publishing Company. P. O. Box 11451. Santa Rosa, CA.95406. ISBN 0-911485-00-7. LC #85-70431.

[93] **Popes are condemned** because they speak of truth, which is considered infallible. Truth [Is] Reality.

[94] **Ratzinger,** Joseph Cardinal, *Theologische Prinzipienlehre.* 1982 Erich Wewel Verlag, Munich. Translation by: McCarthy, SDN. *Principals of Catholic Theology.* 1987 Ignatius Press, San Francisco, CA.

a strange form of ecumenism, which those have espoused. Politics has corrupted the Intellect and the Papal authority therefore much of serious thinking including theology and the dogma of Catholicism, has been impaired by adolescent misunderstanding, and much has been pushed aside.[95] By serious thinking, we infer thinking that is significantly in reference to the *here and now* and, [the] *there and then,* especially so do we consider eschatology and eternity. Serious thought is certainly more important than the needs of athletic programs and phony classes designed to create a desired form (by some) of social acceptance.

Propaganda, as it relates to health issues is often a form of sophisticated dialectic, conceived to confuse or to sell some drug. One should consider that much of advertising is propaganda, is meaningless, and cleverly written, and simply stated is not true. For example, millions are spent reiterating on television and in print the value of substances known to be harmful to the extent of causing the death of the patient (Contreras, MD). The profit, gained by Pharmaceutical Companies is an absolute disgrace and an insult to the men that know most about the subject however, are not part of the *"Medical Establishment."* There appears to be a form of Conspiracy, or perhaps collusion between Government, the American Medical Association, and the Pharmaceutical Industry to defraud the people and to ban effective and inexpensive products. The government heaps billions, on the Medical and Pharmaceutical Industries, which have been extorted from the people as a form of their payment. "Collaborators in government (and universities) can now get away with open fraud." (Wm. Douglas, MD). As a retired Professor with nearly fifty years experience in higher education I submit that *much of what happens in higher education is a politically motivated farce.*[96] Much is simply a waste of time all such to please a *politically liberal, narrow minded faculty,* too pleased with their own very *"limited expertise".* Many colleges Faculty are suffering from a Socialist bias which is, in truth, warmed over Marxism. Their positions are often dim-witted and shallow; nevertheless those are the

---

[95] **Catholic Dogma** is the consequence of the intentions of Jesus Christ being extended in the work of the Apostles, which were determined by Jesus Christ to go forth as *"the light of the world,* thereby to aid man in his search for salvation, that being for eternal happiness. Even Shakespeare observed *"All that ends well [Is} well,"* and all life ends assumedly well for who are baptized into the Catholic Faith and hold to the doctrines given form as Dogma, persistent, universal, **unassailable and immutable.** This is not something that most *will to understand.* Most find difficulty in following the ways of a perfect being. Some do try.

[96] **We pay too much** for what is often near worthless learning, providing that a few athletes are given unreasonable opportunity to practice in preparation for making it in the big leagues. Institutions of Higher Learning encourage Team Spirit over serious study. Observe the mindless hysteria that accompanies the big games. Note also the arrogance of the stars that, if truth were known, many would not be able to pass an entrance exam to High School. Even after graduation, if it occurs, without help, many could not write an intelligent sentence. We acknowledge some exceptions, of course and extend our sincere respect. However running on the grass is no substitute for serious study. Busywork is not serious study, beside which only perhaps twenty-five percent of high school graduates are mentally equipped for *"higher education."* The rest require job training and the development of the skills, which we seek from other nations. And, women should take motherhood more seriously and prepare for it with the proper kinds of domestic courses. A woman is not a man! And, a woman should act like a woman: for example no women should be in combat, no woman in the Army. Even men should not aspire to kill an unknown enemy presumed as such by a dim-wit Politician.

respected scholars in the Field, self-centered and arrogant in their pretense. We pay our respect to the good, decent and intelligently informed amongst them.

Much in this world is ordered hierarchically, _Thought Space is hierarchical_ as well. We imagine the standard Intelligence tests do obviate this; however political intrusion coupled with the refusal, of some, to consider reality truthfully creates a problem. Some have made a deliberate and effective effort to determine that the _"Level, of Intelligence Quotient,"_ known as the I. Q. is somehow unacceptable. The Thought Space of genius is far beyond that of others, which is obvious, it is more extensive and provides for complexities and more cognoscente associations than that of a normal person. Nevertheless, Public Education thrives on scholarships to those that kick, bounce, hit or run with a ball, not to forget pole vaulting, golf and gymnastics. Also, young ladies are no longer interested in the domestic arts; such programs have been greatly reduced or are eliminated from the curriculum. There are many prepared meals or just open a can! Many are being encouraged, to prefer kicking, bouncing, throwing and hitting a ball, some even train to become boxers, rather than serious study, and most certainly not the domestic arts that support the family.[97] Millions are spent on scholarships for this kind of _"play day"_, which is of little consequence: except for political purpose. Many athletes graduate without having completed any significant coursework during their too much valued participation in one or another game. Those are like grown children. In fairness to Public Education there are some tokens given, for work of the mind as well however, most do not compare with athletics. If one compares the salaries of the better coaches, considered as such, with those who teach English or Math, one gets the picture. Some coaches make two or three million a year ($2,000,000. or $3,000,000.) per year whereas the teachers, generally speaking, make much less than one hundred thousand, many make as little as twenty five thousand for their efforts. Some Religious Schools pay even less. What is this saying? What do we value most?

The jocks rule! Use your imagination. Athletes earn millions whereas scholarship and intellectual brilliance struggles for tenure. Any persons will spend fifty or a hundred dollars, even more, for a ticket to a football game however, _significant writings are ignored_ and Catholic scholarship, covering two thousand years of patiently devout study, is scorned by many, ridiculed and maligned by others. All this is indemnified in higher education, by much of which is dedicated to what is referred to as deconstruction, which is promoting the deformation of Western Civilization. _The destruction of the Western Civilization, the Western Soul, is the work of the anti-Christ._ Keep in mind, there are many anti-Christ not just one!

There exist Education Courses _which become nauseous!_ If the college student is not able to pass mathematics, for example, there is a class in Educational Mathematics whereabouts the college student who is preparing to teach is taught such heavy stuff as counting, addition, subtraction even multiplication aimed at the level of elementary or sometimes secondary education. With such knowledge the "teacher" may know what a ten-year old should know?

Additionally, in reference to thinking, symbols have been associated with sound to the point where words spoken and written [may] have the same characteristic impact on the mind, as do

---

[97]   **The fast food** restaurants have popped up to satisfy the lack of a mother who has no husband and is working to pay the bills. We respect her for this however probably she has not been wise.

direct experience. The thought patterns are incredibly varied depending on the mind content of various individuals. Every element in the mind affects all the others. Thought patterns are imagined to have a binomial formed structure, rather like the wings of a butterfly in parallel position.[98] (See my drawing of a butterfly on page 87). It can be imagined that what becomes as part of a structure within the mind space can be referenced and imposed upon what is incoming as the result of current sensory perception.

To have some idea of what this means, consider that all snowflakes are imagined to be unique. This may or may not be true however there are trillions of variations and they form patterns. The patterns as seen in the snowflakes are similar to the patterns generated by the electrical forces, which accompany life, in that they are categorical and can be analyzed mathematically. _They are not necessarily understood because of mathematical means._ Life and what we do as human beings, is dependent upon the workings of the brain and the thought patterns that develop one way or another. The thought patterns are phenomenally encoded and inextricably interspersed excepting that they do surface so to provide that we are able to distinguish and to recognize one thing or being from another. Without seeing, one can also recognize bacon, frying in a pan or a skunk standing in one's yard, meaning smells as well as images are encoded phenomenally within the _"Mind Space"_ of every living human being. Exceptions are those somehow inflicted with physical impairment.

Cognitive ability is tied to the genetic structures of the cellular matrix, which combines to form the nervous system. Phenomenally, this is a consequence of the fact that sound, symbol and reality as it unfolds is encrypted within the brain. As a corollary the encrypting, as in writing or carving, has a direct relationship to the movement of the hand in space.[99] ***Movement is characteristic of life.*** Writing is in fact movement that has been arrested so to form the marks, which when structured with consistency begin to form the alphabets in various ways. Form, three-dimensional and Texture, random or controlled extension of a flat grouping, as marks comprise two different categories of visual expression. Color is distinct in many ways and enriches form and texture without adding significantly to the meaning of either form or texture. Color may appear as giving form an emotional quality not given by the same form viewed in black and white. Color has an impact of its own. Color may summon forms of emotional involvement that span all the way back to childhood.[100] _Brown, which is non-spectral, is thought (by some) to be the color of the soul._[101] Tradition has made possible the magnificently extended correlation between living and knowing, observing and expressing, formation of various languages and finally mechanical implementation to accomplish a needed and desired

---

[98]   **See Illustration of Butterfly,** (_page 89 below_). The wings of the butterfly are opposites and rest in parallel position. Those can be compared with an image in a mirror as being the exact opposite as the one outside the mirror. What does this mean?

[99]   **This relates** to what is mentioned above regarding the function of prosthesis in reference to the human mind.

[100]   Generally speaking emotions are deep personal feelings about reality.

[101]   **Spengler, Oswald**, _The Decline of the West, Vol. II. Perspectives of World History._ The authorized Translation is with notes by Charles Francis Atkinson. Alfred A. Knopf, Publisher, NY.

consequence.[102] Tradition also forms, as a continuation of what has been the result of millions of individual *"thought-driven"* choices. *In fact every significant human endeavor of the past is woven within the fabric of Tradition*. Every Tradition unfolds as a product of human endeavor and is supported by its own *"Positive efficacy."* This fact alone makes the work of the political process, as we know it, quite redundant except for contrived economic elements.

The results of political-maneuvering have caused untold misery for the human race. Politicians take and are given too much positive credit for the destruction, which they have caused and for the millions that have been killed prematurely because of Wars, Famines and other misadventures caused, by blundering Politicians. What we imagine as elections that will control the future, to the advantage of the people is of little or no significance. *Money determines the law and the workings of government.* Almost every man can be bought. Except Politics form as part of a complex destiny led by the somewhat skewed thinking of individual beings, such is the **Riddle of Destiny**!

Political Space is divided between what we have come to recognize as various Political Parties. The Politicians party, the people pay the bill! A *two party system* is ideal since the *space* is thus divided in about half. Politicians, in our nation, generally choose to be Democrats or Republicans. Others are rarely even mentioned as part of any campaigning, some not at all. In twenty five years, the name Lyndon LaRouche has almost never been mentioned, even though he has run for president several times. Ron Paul is another unmentionable name. Why is this so? Both men are somewhat independent in their thinking and therefore they are not *"qualified" to be considered even nominally*. Interestingly one is a Democrat (so called) he would promote the ways of Roosevelt many of which were not very good. The other a Republican (so called) who is more a libertarian. The choices are probably the result of who will fund them in their expensive endeavor. The two parties are said to be adversarial, which is ipso facto not necessarily true. In fact, although there may be some superficial distinctions, there is much more, which they have in common. The most important commonality is that they all hope to stay in office for a lifetime, which is much too long. *Career Politicians are a curse on the governing process* as determined by the nature of humanness. Career Politicians exude a level of conceit and confidence that is unhealthy and not in the best service of the People. Terms should be limited; perhaps two terms or three at most.

Ideas form as part of the general misunderstanding inherent in human thought processes. Indeed, it is likely that many voters do not understand most issues. It has long been known by a clever few that when millions of people must choose between A and B, or Yes and No, it is likely

---

[102] **A quality of genius** is found in the conception of the idea of interchangeable parts. This is probably the greatest strength found in modern technology. What can be analyzed as to form and structure then produced repeatedly can be utilized discreetly in many places with the same effect. This understanding, it is assumed can be (to some extent is), applied to the human body, which likens the human body to a machine. However, such understanding depends upon the existence of a sophisticated Tradition of Biologically scientific technique with commensurate understanding. The Soul of man is apparently lost in the attempts to redesign humanness. The Soul is an *infinitely distinct* element, which cannot be reproduced.

they will split just about evenly.[103] *Often husband and wife vote differently,* which is dumb, and effectively nullifies both votes.[104] Actually it would be better if husband and wife had only one vote, with double weight. This would encourage them to have a consensus in their own family. This is the first step in making the system work. However the Modernist imagines that husband and wife should be independent in their thinking. Such independence may be a cause for separation and divorce. Husband and wife should work at becoming one in being with the Father. Political posturing provides a basis for such differences, even when neither knows and does not understand the substance of Issues. At present, to win an election one must convince just a few *"on the fence voters"* and the election will be won. Many elections are near even, won by just one or a few percentage points. Thus about one half of the voters decide the election. However only about half of the people vote therefore most elections can be won with a plurality of about 26 to 28 percent of the eligible voters. In matters of fact this suggests that perhaps **two or three percent** of the voters, having been driven by *properly applied motivation (?) can determine the outcome of the national elections.* This is why pressure groups like the ACLU, the Radicals, Ethnic blocks and counterfeit votes have so much influence. Keep in mind many of the dead are still voting; this is because our system does not clear out all who have died.[105] Nevertheless the winners do control [somewhat] the situation for a time after each election. Generally speaking thought-content of the voters can be formed by means of propaganda repeated incessantly for the effect it will have on the thinking process. This is especially true of the simple minded, the nearly illiterate, and they are legion. The reader can investigate some questions on his own.

Uniquely individual inquiry and experience combine in a manner governed by genetics, intelligence, biology, physiology, and time-space location. Therefore, to some extent, one can know and *(possibly)* understand ideas and events derived from the continuum of experience

---

[103] **Col. Mendall House,** who was not a colonel at all, **[was]** a close and very influential advisor of President Wilson. Though he remained almost completely unknown, he was the brains and the Traitor that was largely responsible for much of what President Wilson did do. His legacy from a somewhat remote past, to this day, can be held responsible for much of what happened since. Balzak did comment that only about five thousand persons were responsible for most of the [then] current history. Perhaps today those responsible for what happens are perhaps no more than twenty thousand. Many are blood relatives, much as were the former aristocrats. (See Ferdinand Lundberg. *The Rich and the Super Rich* [also] *Our Crowd*). Those most influential own the large corporations-become-cartel. One-world, the Global Village, International co-operation, Outsourcing are euphemisms for total (as in Totalitarianism) political and economic control. The United Nations Army will be formed for the protection of the One-World government and those owning large pieces of this one-world monstrosity. The individual will be powerless and will have only an imagined participation in the scheme of things. The reason the United States must be destroyed is so that few, eventually no newcomers will be able to assemble great wealth, with which they could upset the scheme of things. What we witness is a sustained effort of one **[Idea]** persisting, over several Millennia.

[104] **Democracy has one of the significant flaws.** *The most ignorant of voters can nullify the voice of genius.* This is precisely why voters must be (1.) well educated, (2.) twenty-five years of age, (3.) gainfully employed, with records of income tax payments for a minimum of five years and (4.) They must own property and have paid their taxes.

[105] **Front page article** The Washington Times; May 2, 2013. "American Civil Rights Union, ACRU's, lawsuit to end voter fraud". The state of Florida alone had 50,000 dead voters on the rolls in 2012.

as encountered. Of primary significance, ***Tradition is the prime containment*** and holds man's understanding, as being a broad containment structured in accord with an evolving language and level of understanding, which is locked in that same language and symbol.[106] Since space is unbounded,[107] and we are perceptive human beings, one's perception is as a peculiarly mortal center for individual humanly contained knowing and understanding. This is true, however perhaps difficult to imagine, as regards pertinent individual becoming. To believe this, with absolute certainty, just look out the window; watch for the Sun, Moon and what is between. ***Space is the absolute accommodation*** and encompasses all the "in between" of everything. Infinite space comes right down to meet every one of us, no matter who you may be, no matter where you may be and no matter when you may choose to observe this.[108] Furthermore, there exist quanta of space within the cellular structure of your body.[109] Do you know how life has come to be as it is?[110] Every individual should consider the All and the Every-where thus to aid in formulating a humanly humble understanding of reality. To lead one to a profound sense of humility in reference to what is *{should and could be}*, is the obligation of truthful education.

Truthful education must include respect for and the extension of the Western Tradition founded in the Crucifixion of Christ and the becoming of ***Christianity.*** Thus the Catholic Church, Bride of Christ must be included in the equation. The word Catholic, taken from the Greek means universal; it means all men. Though of singular significance, we are as individuals, just an infinitesimally small part of an unbounded and unlimited reality. We do not know how or why

---

[106] **Modernism** generally often denies what has occurred as being old fashioned or redundant. This may be true in respect to mechanical invention however is not true in respect to Philosophy or Theology that maintains certain universals as being immutable. Given the present state of language, higher levels of communication are difficult for many of the world's leaders, *recently emerged from a hut*. It is impossible, for most. When such mind space as existed in a hut is privileged to consider what might be done with modern weaponry, one can understand that the death penalty for arms distribution to savages is understandable and easily justifiable. Western Politicians although those may mean well, with their simple-minded, venal and arrogant leadership places all of humanity in a position of peril.

[107] **Director, Bruce:** Article, *Recovering the Generative Principles of Modern Science.* On the 375th Anniversary of Kepler's Passing. Fidelio, Journal of Poetry, Science and Statecraft. Spring Summer '06. Vol. XV. 1&2.

[108] **Bearden, Thomas** *"Aids, Biological Warfare"*). "The Universal space is a *"plenum"* whereabouts all energies from all space are virtually extant in every quantum of space."

[109] **Budwig, Johanna MD.** Quantum space exists within and around biologically formed structures providing space for activities, which occur within the body. Space, within the cells provide accommodation for what is required of life *including formation of electron clouds necessary in the production of life's energy*. Openings scattered over the cell walls provide space for passage of minute factors into and out from the cell interior. Passageways, meridians are *"laced"* within the body providing means for the transport of energy and life-force from place to place within the organism. Finally, *at inception, hollow tubules form to lead the cellular development of the body,* including the differentiation, which produces the organs and other physical requirements for the life of the species. The unseen, existing as space has as much as or perhaps more import than what is seen.

[110] **Oparin, A. I.,** *the Origin of Life.* Second Edition, 1953. Dover Publications, Inc. N. Y. Originally published, by the Mac Millan Co. 180 Varick Street, New York. © 1938. L. C. # 53-10161.

all that is did come about, nevertheless we are gifted to enjoy, with others of our kind *all that has been provided.*

The key word is "provided". *The Question remains. Who was the Provider?* The answer is that it must have been [Is] an omnipotent, Progenitor, eternal, an infinite Being, whom history and the accumulated wisdom of humanity has determined is a God Being *(Fiedler).* The Catholic Church, founded by Jesus the Christ, *crucified on a stick,* teaches that all men must be treated as being equal as they certainly are in the sight of the omnipotent one called God. God is the Father [*progenitor,* of all that is seen and unseen], Son [*Incarnate,* personified as man, *crucified* for our sins] and Holy Ghost [*Spirit* existing and extending in all of an infinite space]. *Mother* is as the earth, *a fertile place* wherein nurturing (gestation) and formation of a new person together with an immortal Soul is the miracle of life. To say *"Mother Earth"* has profound and transfinite meaning *(Fiedler).*

Man can somehow manipulate certain things, within little cubits of space. And, at the present time man is contemplating [conquering] the universe! *For a temporal Creature, this is an absurd notion.* The Idea of capturing Space, though quite stimulating, may be nevertheless preposterous, especially given a very limited individually perceived view of reality. When Politicians entertain an Idea such as this there is no ending to the various programs, which those contrive, secretly and in the open. They that are of the "Star Wars" *mentality* seek control of what is infinite, however, quite beyond human control. *The Star Wars mentality functions best to format entertainment for children and adults arrested in adolescence.* The explosions, noise and creatures which display a vilified humanness function to distract and amuse as *they imprint fantasy,* which in some cases is perhaps so powerful as to blur or override one's understanding of humanness as a reality. *To conquer or command all that is, has been the ultimate wish of the vain hypocrite and presumptuous leadership for centuries.* All those, dictators demagogues and assumed as leaders have harbored this insane notion, which is assumed in Nietzsche's contribution to civilization as the *Will to Power.* Fortunately all former Dictators are now dead!

No human being can or will conquer Space, *which is composed of nothing.* No man can or will sublimate an omnipotent power that cannot be known or seen. *Man is not God!* Eternity, which is what Space is all about (together with all Time), can only be approached from the position of an omnipotent existence, known only to One, Triune God.[111] *There can be only one first cause and one Omnipotence; all else is as being subservient in order.* Reality is, without question, an ordered phenomenon. Although the politically inspired Democrat or Republican does not or cannot understand Reality, there is a *descending order* in the universe. Those that follow a man-made Religion are not sufficiently adept to understand Reality. Whatever is "Ordered" must present a descending or ascending configuration, *such is the nature of being ordered.* What is not ordered is chaotic,[112] which is generally the obvious factor in most human endeavor, and in

---

[111] **Triune God, a** universal God must exist as such, which understanding is the foundation of Western Civilization. And, which understanding sublimates all other understandings of what and who and how is God? Omnipotence as defined, thereby understood requires that this is so.

[112] **Tradition** is what places thinking in an ordered progression, especially so regarding Time, history and human belief and behavior, which can be defined as ordered in an ascending sequence leading to a God-head. The Barbarian or Savage is at the bottom. Jesus the Christ is at the top. Most men have

the Mind Space of billions of individuals, excepting certain scientific endeavor? Science has ordered domains of thought, which in turn represents a form of *Tradition.* One or another form of specialized thinking provides a basis or means for establishing a Tradition.

Physics, a subject dealing with objective reality, as being generally time, electricity, force and light, has perhaps advanced the most. The computer is the best example, a new wonder of the world, the consequence of micro management of electric impulses. Certainly Physics in its many applications is beyond most human understanding, especially when such understanding has been limited within the confines of Public Education. Certainly some of genius ability have, attended public schools however *their genius was not founded by their education.*

Chemistry also has discovered, in part, certain heretofore-unknown truths, and Chemists at the present time begin to understand Reality with more certainty. Notwithstanding, the use of such knowledge is not always for the benefit of all. Much, motivated by the Politics of controversy, is used for the destruction of others; to create War. The present controversy has as its reason an age-old antagonism, stemming from the difference in Religious thinking between the most prominent Religions: Islam, Judaism, Buddhism and Christianity for example separate humanity and the subsequent misunderstanding is problematic. Henceforth China and India will have a more dominant role this because of the *politics of numbers.* Just now everyone is concerned with the availability of resources to provide all with the American dream. Keep in mind it is a dream.

Every person is a creature *within a complex totality, a totality, which is* **unknown and beyond any form of human comprehension.** Attempts at comprehension which, postulates all time and the totality of mankind, is the subject matter of what we define as philosophy or religion, having epistemological as well as eschatological components. Comprehension of *what is unseen and unknown (?) requires Faith* however, man's limited understanding has confused this issue almost beyond imagination. It is very easy to fake certain attitudes as is well known to the hypocrite. However, eventually by our actions, we will as individuals incur whatever settlement is demanded, of the time we have spent in God's good Space. *The Universe is His!* This should

---

imagined God, or what they imagine as a Deity, who will provide a manner of guidance. This has taken and continues in the direction of promoting what is good for the concerned individual(s) and his/their kind and was or could be antagonistic to all others. Presently certain elements within Islam pursues a dogmatic disregard for all others not Islamic. *This is an adolescent notion in the minds of millions;* those (mostly youth) that do not have the intellectual and moral disposition, which would guarantee a higher level of human understanding. Wisdom is a product of old age! Unfortunately, misunderstanding of *"Religion"* creates problems that are, presently, insurmountable. The politician does not and cannot benefit from greater understanding being, as it were, *politics is beholden to economics and the sins of anger, murder, lust, vanity and greed.* To be well meaning is not enough. What is required is a form of consensus, communion within a holy Tradition, convincingly expressed so to be well understood and therefore effective. *All governments must endeavor to eliminate the effects of "Gigantism" and efforts that "conspire" to control humanity.* The Civilization should endeavor toward the reforming of Nation-States wherein a true consensus leading to human happiness and fulfillment is a more attainable possibility. The Nation-State provides the best opportunity for individually inspired self-expression a World-wide conglomeration does not!

be obvious without explanation however seems not to be so. This presents an existentially significant idea for contemplation.

We may begin with a simple question. *Where?* Interestingly it requires only four letters from our alphabet to inquire of a profound notion. The answer is brought forward in history, in that each is born to a location and moves in time and space as part of a minute factor within that extension, that same history, however becomes a particularly pertinent history, involving he/they/who are involved.

For any such question the answer is the same. *There!* Interestingly it requires only four letters from our alphabet to answer a most profound question. A simple answer, concerning one's location in space, qualifies whatever may be a particularly pertinent existence. The understanding of the answer requires that one is cognoscente of objectivity in proximity to the person, event or object in question. The expression can also have an intellectual dimension as well, then requires as it infers a higher level of intelligent understanding, including the awareness of attendant circumstance and a consideration of both past and future time.

Where and how shall one build His house? The Children's story of the three little pigs exemplifies the moral, implicit in this peculiar endeavor. Structures are seated in a place, where they will remain and will become a part of the landscape viewed by all, that venture within sight of any such structure. As such, any architectural form or structure becomes part of an architectural tradition. In the recent past, we have built mobile homes, which require the support of an extensive technology. Still there does remain the Nomad, seated on a horse that roams from place to place, as has been done for centuries across the great, plains, of the several continents. Also, still in evidence are those that build their dwellings from natural materials found in close proximity to where they are. These are used to build the traditional form of their house? However, the most complex *Civilizations have been built in place* as is apparent in the present great cities and those, which remain, from past antiquity.[113] At present the technology is awesome nevertheless there do remain serious problems of crowding and sprawl. In terms of architecture, the architect-artist attempts to leave, his mark, on the building, which he considers as [HIS] work. This, of course is an expression of *VANITY*, a sin. Buildings have taken on the meaning normally attached to painting or sculpture, however are much larger and they are neither. Here scale is an important consideration. A building, which has the intention of functioning for a reason has become as an artifact, *viewed as Art, which it is not.* This is a question that is difficult to answer and goes directly to the meaning of words. Architects and their followers will have great indignation with this assumption.

A building is primarily functional, as having been built for a purpose. Sculpture or painting is primarily esthetic and deals with the *Ideas* that some individual man has. Most sculpture and painting is derivative coming from the work of others. Only a very few artists have been real innovators. Most of what is assumed as modern Art is not Art at all. Buildings may accommodate sculpture or painting however cannot replace them, since those are not the same things. Modern buildings are the work of many people and as such the individual is lost in the

---

[113] **Mumford, Lewis.** *The City in History,* *Oct. 1961. Revised, 1968. ISBN-10; 0156180359 & ISBN-13; 978-0156180351.*

complexity of the construction. _Technology has widened the technical comprehension of any structure however has not changed the meaning._ This is an important point. The scale, of a building, dwarfs anything, which might be placed inside that same building however, should not overcome the essence of the artifacts placed therein. Calatrava amongst many others does not understand this point. And a building should not attempt to appear as a bird or something, which it is not. The Milwaukee Art Center is guilty of this infraction. The architect did not know, truthfully, what he was doing! He worked from a point of vain comprehension which is a bit sinful in some ways and according to some of the best of Western thinking is an oxymoron.

To use a building as a symbol for a place deprives somewhat the place of being what it is. Symbolism cannot be imposed on anything, it requires time to develop. To hire an architect from the other side of the world, from a completely different culture and disposition, to design a hallmark for a strange place, is not worthy of creditability, it is a faux symbol. The symbol, to be meaningful must originate in the place for which it is the symbol. This is a broad subject that will be addressed in a different volume. Because seemingly happy people roam around a building does not justify the philosophy underlying or any reason for the building.

If one wishes to gain most from occupancy, any house, city, nation-state or civilization must be cared for, maintained, though not forever, only as long as it may last. A structure will stand where it is placed however, cities, nations, cultures and civilizations require profound attention as they "evolve" and become different from time to time. They are essentially the products of _"mental restructuring"_ in response to pertinent needs and the availability of Ideas and Materials. Such restructuring is limited by the amount of money one has to spend on the project. Additionally most such structures have developed within a traditional framework. This is obvious in the many subtle similarities of intent and expectation. Referring to the two paragraphs directly above one can see how the elements of architecture and language, combined with other limitations, make this a very broad and complex subject.

Some speak of being in control of their life, which they may be. However, given that which is significantly important, each of us will control very little, for a very short time in a very small space.[114] _Enter what we define as economics!_ One's dwelling must be paid for, as all structures must be paid for, in time or money and it must be maintained in time or in money. Money as currency is related to both time and place in nearly unimaginable ways. Currency has its own, energized domain, which interlocks with the expectations of who has possession of it. This author has considered the subject of Money, in other volumes. Significantly, money travels in space and time, in a lateral or an extended time/space pattern. The velocity of money varies from place to place and is an indication of the nature of commerce. The velocity of money forms as a vortex absorbing what is as it provides for a future store of value. It functions much as a funnel directing liquid through a determinedly advantageous space. Electronic transfers, for the rapid dispersal of _notional values_ and of _real wealth_ have added new possibilities, for good and for evil. International Bankers envision a one-world currency, which they will control. **_Total control, Totalitarianism_**, they envision as being possible, enforced and sustained by the control

---

[114] **Each and every encounter** has an important set of consequences attendant thereto, with absolutely unpredictable effects. The migration of peoples makes this even more interesting as well as problematic than when individuals were more certain to remain close to their place of birth

of money (currency)[115] *and the force of weaponry.* Socialists seek sameness in populations, fearing the significance of the singular mind of Genius. Socialists are small brothers to those that are Dictatorial and Totalitarian.

Any form of Political Control aims at sublimating a uniformly inspired population to the *Will to Power* of an elite ruling group, which controls commerce and the minds of men; we now call them Politicians. Like all men Politicians can be good for Society or they may promote evil. Actually to some considerable degree political control is a fete which is already very much accomplished. **The minds of men** can be controlled by means of brainwashing, which may require threat of intimidation even death or simply a form of encouragement. More recently behavioral modification, *a form of patterning human thought processes,* has been the euphemism for mind control and is practiced, more or less, in the public schools.[116] This is often quite subtle and comes to the classroom as a *"mandate"* from the state or federal government. Disguised in language behavioral modification attempts to condition the child or young adult to accept certain tenants regarding what is and is not acceptable behavior.[117] Changes are brought about gradually so as not to alarm those that would object to the destruction of our Holy Tradition. The very word *"Holy"* or any word connected with what may be holy is removed from public and much private discourse. Especially Catholic Symbolism, pictures of the Holy Family, the meaning of Christmas and Easter, all are deliberately confused in the minds of youth. We have *Christmas trees and the Easter Bunny* as well as many various saccharine symbols that distract from the meaning of such events. Public Institutions of Education work to deny the Catholic Christian God as do the *Commercial Elephants* pandering for profit. Some Federal Judges with contempt for what is holy Tradition are doing whatever they can to destroy all vestiges of Catholic Christianity other Christian forms as well. Coincidentally witches and goblins, warlocks and Harry Potter are best sellers. Those are encouraged for the profits, which those earn for the often anti-Christian producers.

Space, as displaced, is *given to the definition and qualification of all tangible form.* One must be aware that the human body is that substance or that defined physiological space, the place (so to speak), within which we do (in fact) exist. This must be so otherwise we could not be at all. "To be or not to be [is] the question." How then, shall one become? Given an individually functioning mind, all thoughts that we will ever have are ethereal and intangible, which accompany the phenomenology of a particularly human living presence. It is axiomatic and

---

[115] **Currency,** the term, implies the present value of money; of this moment. *Ideally money retains the same value as when it was acquired.* That is to say, it remains constant in regard to the expectations of who did acquire the currency by some lawful means. *This is a question of morality as well as economics.* As a matter of fact, *economics should be the servant of both money and morality as it is rather a matter of accounting for what exists and for what moves from one person to another.* We have given a perverted form of Economics, per se, a too important role in the recent development of Western Civilization, especially where about conflict is concerned. And we have made economic gain the Holy Grail of endeavor. This is a monumental mistake that, ultimately, **will kill the Culture** (it has done much-harm at this writing) **ultimately it will kill the Civilization.**

[116] **Sutton, Antony,** *How the Order Controls Education.* Research Publications, Inc., P. O. Box 39850, Phoenix, Arizona, 1983. ISBN 0-914981-00-5

[117] **This is especially apparent** in the realm of Sex (homosexuality) and perverted type Behaviors (there are many).

logical there can only be one of any individual being. The *"cloning of cells confuses"* this issue considerably, in the minds of those that will profit from or be the objects of such endeavor. This is what is important each person is an individually unique, biological/physiological being, the life of whom is given, as a gift from an omnipotent force, God, the Father [progenitor] Creator of all that is seen and unseen. Believe this and you will be well on your way to happiness. *Thus we might consider that an omnipotent force is as the motivation for the propagation of the human race.* Nevertheless, there are many that do not believe this. Understandably what is corporeal involving the biology and physiology have an understood continuity, whereas what is spiritual and of the Soul does not. One cannot change from one body to another however, one's thinking can be patterned in different ways, and actions can be or will be modified accordingly.

Who but God [?] may have created what is, including each and every human being? Gestation is a biological process, whereas inception is mysterious, phenomenal and existential in implication. Parts and processes may be observed, nevertheless absolute understanding is evasive. The parents are only a means and are entrusted with a great responsibility of nurturing the body and soul of their peculiar **extension into the future.** *Any form of future extension is determined by the past.* Therefore we are well advised who would form and maintain a clear and decently determined Biological and Physiological Tradition. Most will not understand the meaning of this assertion nevertheless it is of ultimate significance, especially now that ignorance is "tinkering" with the reproductive process. Tradition generally, is what feeds the Intellect and makes advances in thought possible. We share with each other, as we occupy a very minute part of God's Universe however each individual person is quite necessary, *one or another way*, to complete a profound, magnificent universally functioning totality. Furthermore, we should never forget, all human events happen in God's good space.

> *Every human being has an inherent or inalienable right and responsibility;*
> *In the peculiar portion of space, which he occupies (displaces);*
> *To become the best he can to benefit the human race.*

One can imagine a forever, based on a mature understanding of the continuity of the species. Biological continuity does provide a concrete and truthful example of extension in time/space. Evolution of the species is an issue, which we do not intend to introduce at this moment. It is possible to imagine space/time as being infinite [∞]. Nevertheless, whatever is the nature of All Space is not open to peculiarly limited Human understanding. We believe, those who are locked within a segment or portion of Space must be content to admit there does exist an unknown absolute beyond the present moment. This understanding drives man to discover many new things however *no single human person can possibly have an absolutely complete grasp of anything.* Nevertheless, as each human person is locked within a *space/time segment or domain*, there can be physical and intellectual reciprocity, between proximate individuals at any moment. The most intimate of such occurrence is mating, thus to create a new human person, having an individual Soul, destined for a possibly eternal existence. It is important that this should be better understood and that all men and women learn to meet their responsibilities and to assist in the nurturing of their children. *Children are begotten because of a man's decently romantic, vain or impetuous nature.* In each instance, the father, as well as the mother must bear the responsibility for their own behavior. Children are the body and soul become because of the most intimate form of cooperation. The children of such union deserve to have a father and a mother and should not be bused between parents or from place to place because of a parent's inability to live as responsibly committed adults. Our celebrities have misunderstood this imagining that money will make a difference, it won't! What money has done is that money has made possible the marriage to several different partners; homosexuality confuses this issue as well.

Where, is an important consideration just as important is when? Where one is conceived has to do with who are the Parents, especially one's mother. Mother is primary, the first place for all of her children to be. Like all living creatures only a few from what is a potentiality will ever be born into space.[118] For humanity, the mother's body is a very special place, wherein the chromosomes combine to determine just how the offspring shall become.[119] Recent understanding has determined that the mother is primarily responsible for the genetic structures of her children, only accepting those chromosomes that are, for whatever reason, superior to her own. Conception and pre-natal development are both mysterious and holy. No one knows why an individual becomes as he/she does; one knows only that others exist. Mother's body has also, in the recent past, become a very dangerous place, especially so for the first born that opens the womb. There are spiritual as well as historic connotations hereabouts, which are beyond our intention. Therefore, it is quite likely that many, having been conceived, will not be born at all. *Presently, it is estimated that, in the three decades prior to now, there have been hundreds of millions of known abortions worldwide,* millions more which have been uncounted as well.[120]

Abortion may seem rather ordinary, acceptable, a matter of [mature] adult choice. Abortion is no incidental matter. Ill-educated individuals speak of a woman's reproductive rights suggesting what is sinful has more *"rights"* than what is natural, spiritual and decent. Remember *everyone has the right and the responsibility to not fornicate indiscriminately* merely for sensual gratification or as a reward for an illicit inclination. This calls to mind the monumental tragedy that is pornography. Where someone is, individual placement in space (on this planet) determines what one can and will do. Mating is part of what humans do. Individually men and women should determine beforehand that they will only participate in what is lawful, decent and fair to all whom they encounter including the *"one whom they choose"* as a mate. Humanity has advanced to the position of understanding the value of perseverance in an adult conjugal relationship. It is unfortunate that some are determined to pull man back to being [again] as a lustful barbarian or a cruel and lustful Savage. As mentioned elsewhere, *the preponderance of*

---

[118] **Nature is prolific** in regard to the extension of a species always providing most generously for the becoming of the young. Many plants have tens of thousands of seeds. Roots and stems can be propagated as well. Fish and various insects propagate in thousands however, most serve as food in a never-ending struggle for existence. What we imagine as this struggle is largely misunderstood however, is a very natural process. Man as well as animals, utilizes the substance of both plant and animal for his own survival.

[119] **It is most unfortunate** that a woman's body has become the object of so much lustful attention. Dress and manners can encourage the wrong type attention. Our television is most aggressive in displaying the wrong manners which exacerbates the problem. Pornographers have caused irreparable harm to millions of youthful woman, which because of their beauty are routinely violated by ignorantly moronic and bestial male attention.

[120] **Human Life International**, Jan. 2000. 4 Family life, Front Royal, VA 22630 USA. hli@hli.org (internet E-mail

personal and social problems are the result of fornication. It is possible, indeed necessary to structure one's thoughts so as to avoid doing what is known to be destructive to the individual and to the community. Education is supposed to inform correctly as well as to point the way to goodness, decency and contentment. Job training has assumed a too important role in the system. At this moment in America, other places as well, individuals of whatever intelligence and ability can find a place to work and to earn a living.[121] What is needed is a generally applied sense of fairness and the will to cooperate with others. Men that do simple tasks should be paid sufficiently to live respectably and less emphasis should be placed upon the attainment of unnecessary economic advantage. If this occurs there would be no need for abortion.

Immigration *is the consequence of people wanting to move to a different, presumably better, place.* When like individuals group and sustain a community as has happened, in the past, such groups maintain familial characteristics and they strive toward the becoming of a Nation. Nations are comprised of groups and individuals having common attributes and shared aspirations. In proximity individuals learn from each other, language is an obvious means together with one's observations of what exists. Societies and Cultures develop as a consequence of their respective and sustained achievements, which are obviated in their *Tradition*, as artifact, habit and custom. Who went where? What did they do? Both are very important questions. As such Tradition is a valuable containment from which the present and the future are the beneficiaries. Public education encourages the young to be independent, creative and to abandon Tradition.

The hypocrite or the ignorant Practitioner-become-educator encourages youth to abandon the source of both knowledge and method of continuing the Tradition which is their birthright. Having abandoned Tradition, youth will drift and can be captured by one or another Philosophical Imperatives. *The one most generally pushed* by the establishment is Socialistic; it is collectivist, Marxist and is anti-Christian, tentative and politically imposing. To argue against this is difficult since often there has been a lack of truthful knowledge conveyed within the educational system (except perhaps in the hard sciences) therefore youth has little or no defense.

Creativity, it must be stressed can be found at all levels of intelligence, from the fool to the genius. Psychologists dance about when a fool does something nominally creative. Our system,

---

[121] **Interestingly** the jobs that are readily available are not the ones that most would wish to consider. Imagining one's self as being educated encourages a form of vanity which causes one to disallow what they are properly suited for. Many of the simple-minded, now have college degrees, which are worthless, in that those that hold them are not maturely informed, not able to think clearly and intelligently in problem solving. They will learn necessary information and how to behave from living their life: the elders are wiser than the young. In time, experience will teach them much that they do not know as youth. Their own lives are corrupted by sin and they are not willing to cooperate with a truthful and loving mate. So how smart are they? Almost fifty-years of teaching in the university allowed me to observe that most of the best students came from other places than the United States. Foreign students are becoming the professionals in this country, which seems dedicated to nonsense. Our government does not send the foreign student home after graduation. If they have a child in this country the child is automatically accepted as belonging; they have instant citizenship. This is the consequence of a Law, which is no longer necessary. We have enough people and should solve existing problems rather than making new ones.

being presumed as Democratic has determined, that the Creativity of a clown or a fool, those being the more mundane forms of creativity are best for mass distribution. Highbrow stuff is more limited in reference to economic gain and must [often] rely on subsidies or donations. The finer forms of pleasure and entertainment are not sufficiently encouraged in the schools; athletics are pushed relentlessly. There is little significant understanding of the meaning of great literature and how this supports a finer existence.[122]

Limitations imposed by placement in space determine that most potential is never realized. It is impossible, that all potentialities could be realized! Because this is so, we understand that all potential is not required, only some. Because of this, various peoples have developed differently. It is incumbent upon the community that the best forms of thought and methods of accomplishment should be encouraged. *No community can afford to pander to ignorance!* A categorical imperative is at work here. Fish survive as fish in the ocean or in water, because they are fish. The fish is of a nature that provides for this. Man will survive, because he is man, Millions believe He is made in the image of God, however, given free will and aptitudes given to no other creature, man is also burdened with responsibilities. Nevertheless, all humanity could be, probably will be consumed in one gigantic earthly-Devastation. Man, if he is to become one in being with the Father, could/does have an opportunity to move toward an open-ended infinity, an endless space.[123] Nevertheless, that some could be given to share in God's infinity does not infer that every man will be as God. *Man is the Creature God is the Creator.*

Regarding political, psychological and social issues, space is a primary determinant. Proximity to a friend or foe has always been an important factor in determining what men do. Immigration involves moving from place to place, thus to better one's existence, as being free from danger. This is simply the reaction to pleasure or pain. When populations move to a new place there is thus a degree of infiltration, with subsequent sociological, psychological and perhaps political consequence. ***Ideas move with people.*** Such movement of ***thought forms*** carries positive as well as negative connotation. *Psychological infiltration involves the movement of an Idea from one mind-space to another.* When ideas enter the human mind they coalesce with existing thought-content and have unpredictable consequence. Individuals, with just and truthful motives do attempt to help in the assimilation of the stranger, unselfishly so. This can serve either Good or Evil purpose. *Nevertheless, there are many that would take advantage of the confusion, which is caused when ideas are in conflict and new ideas are certain to impact an existing understanding.* Much of present politics is centered on this and other related issues.

Tradition defines the determinedly mindful-progress of a people and does provide a particularly formed [time-space] insight into what should and does happen. It is a form of social, psychological and ideational insurance, which guarantees the direction of learning and

---

[122] **Athletics,** while of modest importance is given most attention and the most funding. In a university the football coach may be paid two or three million a year, whereas the other *"scholars"* do not earn enough to pay the rent.

[123] **Cathey, Bruce,** *The Bridge to Infinity.* Quark Enterprises LTD, 1983, 158 Shaw Road, and Brookfield Press, P. O. Box 1201, Auckland, New Zealand. ISBN 0-86467-024-9. This is a highly technical work however the illustrations make it somewhat understandable for the average man. The author is obviously of a genius type for his understanding of the material found in this work.

knowing.[124] A primitive Tradition, may have existed as a singular form however, presently societies are much more complex. The hypocrite and the opportunist are able to profit, one way, or another, from the movement of populations, and will encourage abandonment of Tradition in favor of **evil ways,** *often imagined as progressive or as being modern,* so to accomplish some obscure objective, hidden within the hyperbole. We recognize this as Modernism. To a considerable degree, **Modernism is a disease of the Soul** and of the community. _Modernism compromises proven Traditions_ as it encroaches upon important intellectual, psychological and sociological aspects of one's existence as well as that of a community of men. Religion becomes as a political forum with a veranda about which the minstrels stroll as they mesmerize the devout, with guitar music and dancing girls, rather Pagan, to be sure. We'll have no Gregorian Chanting, thank you. The curiosity of youth draws them toward what is noisy and exciting, whereabouts **they intimidate each other to become part of the festivities.** Chastity and continuance are old-fashioned for those that seek the most excitement from life and who assume that they, **in their ignorance** will improve upon what has taken two thousand years to develop. Youth is restless and seeks to participate in a more Democratic approach to Holiness imagining they will improve upon the wisdom of those that have lived a hundred lifetimes, during the past centuries. _For most youth mind-space is rather small, it is right here, right now._ Right here, right now is advertised as being superior which is certainly not truthful advertising.

State controlled, elementary and secondary compulsory education **works hand and hand with primitive and atavistic religious concepts** and is determined to destroy the foundations of the Western Civilization, especially targeted is any inference to Holy Roman Catholic Tradition, which is the foundation of Western Philosophy, Culture and Civilization.[125] State controlled education is considered necessary where we have the march toward a socialist dictatorship, a Marxist-inspired one-world order. Certainly the defense against such mindlessness has been weakened, with the *"politically contrived"* separation of Church and State. It is imagined, quite incorrectly that, *there is* **some manner of empty space** *between what is secular and what is holy,* beside which we must *"honor all methods of worship"* except the most important one. Only a politician, a weak minded fool one seeking a new term, which will be extended to a lifetime, at the public trough (example, Ted Kennedy) could imagine a void within the mind of men that separates the intellectual framework of Church from that of the State.[126] It is fair to mention that many teachers and instructors do not prefer public education for employment however, the pay is better, and there are many guarantees that private schools cannot offer. Public Education is

---

[124] **The direction of learning and knowing** can be controlled by education, coercion or force. Generally the strongest elements within the society/culture will control both learning and knowing. All the strong forces are not always apparent.

[125] **Blumfield, Samuel,** _Is Public Education Necessary._ Barnes and Noble, 1981 edition.

[126] **The workings of any human mind** *exist as* _an individually determined complex, a singularity._ Because we have chosen to offer education in segments or disciplines as a matter of convenience, it does not follow that the mind is so separated. Certainly bits of mind content can be called upon so to clarify thought however, even then there are time-space influences bearing upon individual thoughts, which have their origin in a peculiarly formed psychological and spiritually determined matrix, which is difficult to understand. Without the guidance of a confirmed Tradition, what is close in time will form as being probably of greater significance.

an insidious monopoly, which few are able or choose or to stand against. All Bureaucracies are self-serving and self-proliferating.

Individuals and groups comprise various nations and, for various reasons, do not necessarily agree with a stranger. When the share the same *"living space"* serious conflicts may be engendered between foreign or alien beings. This issue relates to autonomy and is made complex by political issues involving race, manners, habits and personality traits. Keep in mind *personalities emerge from and within a unique mind-space.* The determinants are very complex, involving the consequence of inter-relationships, which have become, *in unknown ways, integrated in the mind, **inextricably so.***

Social Conflict obviates the need for astute abilities of statesmanship which few men now, or ever, might possess. Even when one antagonist has such abilities, there is no guarantee that he will ever meet another one of his kind at an appropriate moment. *Statesmanship demands the kind of learning and knowing, which few men possess* and as such they are not generally Politicians. Politicians imagine superior force must be applied. Nevertheless War leads to death and enslavement. Millions have suffered, and died unnecessarily because of a sense of greed, driven by misunderstanding, associated with a place to be, a Space on this earth.

Most do not and cannot consider all ramifications in Eventuality, pertinent to each and every circumstance. This is not done, because it is virtually impossible to do so, or some may not choose to do so. Very often, the most important and comprehensively truthful information and understandings, having been colored by means of deception, propaganda and intrigue, are not known by many, the honorable amongst us, who are involved in the most important tasks and the subsequently determined consequence. Too often the information and the level of understanding required, in an acute circumstance is beyond certain limitations and/or comprehension of the parties involved. This is particular to the "emerging African Nations" that have leadership just a short way from the jungle. Additionally, the abilities necessary in the formulation of a truthful response may prove ineffective when an effective process is deliberately subverted, by the introduction of a carefully contrived and seemingly appealing intervention. Complex circumstance almost certainly will create some manner of failure, one time or another, which will be exploited by cleverness (*Our Presidents have been victims of such subterfuge*). Often, reality is beholden to a manner of deceit, because of some secret vested interest hoping to profit from what may happen when circumstance is cleverly controlled. Presently, entire nations have become entrapped and ours will be proven to be no exception.[127] Their collective behavior might be likened to the behavior of a dope addict;[128] the nature of the entrapment revolving around a medium of exchange, the value of which is deemed as money or credit.[129] This is significant,

---

[127] **Wilton, Robert,** *The Last of the Romanovs, How Tsar Nicholas II and Russia's Imperial Family were Murdered.* Copyright © 1993, the Institute for Historical Review. First British Edition, pub. 1920 in London by T. Butterworth. First U. S. Edition published 1920, in New York by George H. Dorn. French Edition, pub. Paris 1921. Russian language edition, pub. Berlin 1923. ISBN # 0-939484-1.

[128] **Inflation,** just now, we recognize as the "Opiate of the masses." The nation was in a state of euphoria, even as our debts total in the trillions of dollars, near worthless dollars to be sure.

[129] **Wickliffe, Vennard B. Sr.** *The Federal Reserve Hoax, The Age of Deception.* Meador Publishing Co., 324 Newbury Street, Boston 15, MA. Seventh Ed. Pp. 14-70.

appropriately so, since in a modern Civilization, money is required to move objects from one place to another. *Space is an important part of any economic transaction,* one way or another.[130]

Because we do not find that we are always in the right place (at the right time) we may lose some advantage; the advantage we would have, if we could alter reality, or if reality was different from what it really is. Then, to proceed with lamentation and self-denial will be of little use however, what are demanded are understanding, penitence and a contrite and willfully good heart. What is demanded, in a word, is *Virtue. Simply stated, one must know his place of being and the potentials offered there from.* Everyone can only begin from where they are; where they may go is a matter of personal volition, combined with will and opportunity; anyone may gain or lose by their own activities. One may gain Human Dignity and aspire to reach the stars, from wherever one may be. This is God's intention; that each should choose right (that is correctly); thereby the best things will happen. Much of what happens in this world, which is unfortunate or disastrous, is not completely understood and is a consequence of the sins of our fathers. *War* provides a category of Sin that very likely has had a negative effect on millions. *Fornication* is another root cause of unfortunate events. Decent and proper behavior, in respect to all others is assumed in the meaning of fairness and provides the most secure basis for self-esteem. Such behavior will propagate as good luck for the future beings affected thereby.

Nothing in this world is guaranteed, however, all Socialists pretend that, which is considered by those same socialists to be important should be as a guarantee. After, which mundane proclamation, all Socialists begin to steal from their brothers *so as to have something to pretend to give away;* then to lie, so as to have something to say. The most sophisticated form of this, *what might be reasonably called a plague*, is found in the incidence of Inflation and various other forms of theft, all for the purported good of the man being robbed. That is how it should be; so we are told! Inflation guarantees that all costs and pricing will increase from year to year including all governmental spending. One wonders why politicians lament the fact of greater debt each and every year; it is guaranteed!

To deny the meaning of Reality is ultimately destructive and should be called by its proper name, Ignorance. The response is often Indignation or Ingratitude; this is compounded by Ignorance.

1. *Indignation causes one to be intransigent, unwilling to change one's mind, to accept that one is wrong. For one to admit to wrongdoing requires humility, a virtue, which may be lacking.*
2. *Ingratitude is that disposition, concerning vanity, a sin, which prevents one from admitting to truthful understanding, even though such is obvious.*
3. *Ignorance is that state of being in the equation of existence which emanates from Slothfulness, a sin, the unwillingness to truthfully seek, and is the cause of many of the maladies, which we can name! The good reader can form his own list.*

The spaces in the cities, for example, are deteriorating because those who live in them are too lazy or too corrupt to make them better, without some manner of bribe. The bribes are often

---

[130] **Spengler, Oswald**, *The Decline of the West, Vol. II. Perspectives of World History.* Authorized Translation with notes by Charles Francis Atkinson. Alfred A. Knopf, Publisher, NY.

provided by the government: the big numbers will go to those involved in fixing what is wrong. *The little man will get just a little and be more crowded than ever.* And such attitudes aid and abet the speculation that follows as urban renewal and restructuring, so as to drive populations away from well-seasoned and compatible neighborhoods.[131]Our government, though well meaning, or seemingly so, offers little help since our government, at various levels, works for the advantage of the moneyed interests and the speculator. Government pays little attention to what evils are really being perpetrated. When it does it is certain to promote the concept of One World Government and the **Socialist Paradise, imagined by every fool in the last three hundred years.** Economic gain is the primary consideration and motivation for those who pretend to make things better. Too often forgotten are the lives, aspirations and needs of those, that will be affected. Present methods are justified almost totally on profit motives, at a time when government is squandering and wasting unimaginable billions on needless and mindless warfare. *A collision of Cultures need not be inevitable* and will only occur as is planned and orchestrated by those that hope, for one reason or another that this will come about. Nevertheless, the United States a nation pretending to help millions of antagonistic aliens, imagined as enemies, should be able to offer substantially better alternatives for our own people. We continue to suffer from more of a bad thing be it noise, pollution crowding or too high taxation. Perhaps it is time to think small, inexpensive and fair.

> ***Return to the Town Square, open space within the city, admit sunshine and clean air***
> ***Curtail mindless movement, work to prevent economic gain from speculation***
> ***Create a more soulful and peaceful existence: as God intended.***

We should punish elected officials who spend our money, millions, billions, now trillions, completely ignoring the needs and wishes of those who elected them and who provide the money? May we punish appointed officials, who we may never know, for working in the best interests of organized crime and the destruction of our nation? Traitors must be called by their proper name. Then, they should be tried and given a proper sentence, in proportion to their indiscretion. To be a Traitor to one's own nation and family should be considered as a capital crime and, as in the past, the penalty should be a death sentence, which should be carried out in ninety days. *Jim McVey was treated this way.* Actually he may have been railroaded so as to cover up for others involved in the Oklahoma City bombing; how many explosions were there?

There is a manner of moral responsibility, each to every other, to provide an atmosphere, within which goodness will flourish, whereabouts petty crime, syndicalism and hopelessness are discouraged, by the positive attitude and behavior of proximate beings. Slovenly behavior and listlessness are learned behaviors (Skinner), as are prudence and thrift, albeit, some people never learn. Many are inclined, because of slovenly and misconceived behavior, to foul their own nest, to be indifferent to the garbage and rubbish that is strewn in the space of their front yard and in their mind's space as well. *Some lounge in the hallways of the tenement, which they have fouled with ugly marks and their slovenly and arrogantly aggressive behavior.* We do not doubt that there are many good people living in what are slums however, wretchedness, crime and the filth that accumulates in the "great" cities of our nation has an overcoming influence. We are all creatures of God, [The] Infinite Being, who has provided each living person with Free Will. Free Will is the

---

[131] **Jones, Michael, Ph. D**. *Fidelity Magazine* (Issue, #?, date)

means to individual salvation. However, each individual must earn, by word and deed, that final resting place, in space, whereat some may ultimately become, One in Being with The Father, and at which place they will spend Eternity; a very long time, indeed! Eternity is all time beyond now! Seek Goodness and you will find that you will have come to the best possible place of all places.

What does it mean to be in a state of Grace, to be free from the stain of Sin. What exactly is meant when one is forgiven of their sins? Life, in this world, requires that each acts with respect for The One Who has shown The Way; that is, The Son of God, Whom we call Jesus. To ignore this, as the most important part of living, is to ignore the best advice which, has been given to mankind. It is very easy to corrupt those with whom one might associate (Syllabus of Errors)[132] therefore we are admonished to love our brother, as we might (indeed) love ourselves. Also, we must avoid all occasion for sin, for ourselves and for others. It is absolutely imperative, that sensual love becomes only as spousal love, one man for one woman, one woman for one man, as husband and wife. *Marriage is of Sacramental significance and must be considered as Eternal, with a complete and lasting commitment.* One who refutes this assertion, rooted in the obviousness of the biological formation of the Human Race, will suffer certain and grave consequence. One cannot defy the propensities of human nature and remain in the most honest and truthfully human state of being. Humanness demands goodness thus to provide for the best possible unfolding of existence for the self and for those with whom one might be placed in proximity, most assuredly family members and close associates. Seemingly intelligent men point to the past and to the habit and custom of a savage or some Asiatic Prince or Mogul and attempt to excuse their own illicit behavior because this was the way of the savage, the barbarian and the Tyrant; this is simply stupid. We do know better. We are informed by a holy Tradition and by the Golden Rule. *Abandonment of one's mate and children is an inexcusable affront, which leads to indignation, self-pity, destruction of the libido, insecurity, and a sensing of an ominous future.* Thus the mind space within the self is scrambled, as what was must convert to what is. That overpaid celebrities set such a poor example in displaying their lustful ignorance is truly a travesty and is destructive on the world's communities. The cute sluts and lustful adolescent-appearing male figures are not experiencing love. What they experience is loss of self-control, loss of dignity and loss of their soul as they corrupt innocence. *A big belly exhibited at her wedding is no sign of a virgin bride.* Having succumbed to a variety of *"[sticks], and various forms of perversion"* the ladies [?] are used up before the Honeymoon. No expectation here, *just brag about how much you spent for the farce that is imagined as a sacred wedding?* And be certain to wear a beautiful white dress; don't forget to tell the world how much the dress cost.

The personality is that human factor, a functioning of the self, which is in evidence moment by moment. Conscious acts are largely a matter of personality meaning they are personal in nature and unlike any other. Often times, personalities are in conflict, which is a matter of compatibility or *"the communion of souls."* Whether or not one is in communion with others has a strong influence on discreet human behavior. Every being functions by means of neurological mechanisms with all that this entails, including the development and functioning of the personality. Personalities become of circumstance playing upon existing propensities and potentialities, which are idiosyncratic. A given experiential manifold can yield an unimaginable

---

[132] **Pius X, Pope** *The Encyclical Quanta Cura and the Syllabus of Errors.* Issued in 1864. Reprinted by the Remnant, 2539 Morrison Avenue, St. Paul, MN 55117.

and/or unforeseen consequence. An ever-widening range of possibilities, exist among what is possible, unfolding with the developing and maturing mind.[133] Mass communication we imagine can play a significant role in determining the nature of such maturity.

Given a huge number of brain cells, which each individual possesses, billions, some are confident that humanity will stay ahead of the game. This is not a certainty, however, or could anyone know much in advance, what might become of the human race. Because this is so, we must pay more careful attention to those elements and manners of input, which are given to masses of individuals, so as not to encourage latent atavistic tendencies. If present world news has any value, it suggests that a return to more primitive habit and manners, in the most civilized populations, so called, seems to be on the increase.[134] Within certain groups, comprised of marginally literate, incorrectly informed individuals, we find questionable precedent. There are millions roaming the streets of the densely populated cities on the verge of submission to an incitement to rage. The mob can be dangerous and provides the *"cannon fodder"* so to accomplish what the political Conspirators have planned for the people. Consider also those who are neurotic, deemed as social outcasts, however are presumably respectable individuals. There are many men and women in important places who, because of greed and vanity, both of which function through the personality are unable and/or unwilling to allow others to benefit from what exists. The men responsible for the French Revolution, later the thinking of Karl Marx, somewhat responsible for the subsequent atrocities of two world wars, have corrupted the physical space of the earth as well as the mind space of humanity. Where business as usual is the method of the day, a serious study of history seems beyond who are paid for leading humanity.

Philanthropy, which sounds like a pretty good word, is largely self-serving, often for tax purposes and to enhance the image of the giver, especially when the giver is a large corporation. Thus, Philanthropy is group-serving, for a variety of reasons. Some wealthy-individuals may be more truthfully involved, in giving for honorable and praiseworthy involvement. Others may be neurotically involved in a personal way. Tax laws are often side stepped to protect large accumulations of wealth, which otherwise might be open to confiscation because of looting by the tax collector. Keep in mind the tax "collector" is a looter. Interestingly corporate theft is also given some protection, when the sums involved are significant (Milikin/Keating). Certainly, there are many generous people, however, even they can and do make mistakes, which effectively may damage or destroy the meaning of what they attempt to do. War is brutal and kills millions, nevertheless those that profit from conflict, are some of the generous givers.[135] Thereafter they may provide assistance to the blind, the somehow physically impaired and

---

[133] **Thinking** has become more problematical and is more complex in nature, _because of the overload of extraneous information provided by mass-media communication,_ often designed to modify meaning and to create illusions. This is a Phenomenon, which has become apparent in the most recent past century. The trend will accelerate dependent upon new forms of mass communication. Often the information is presented simply as noise, with no significant comprehension of the quality or meaning of what is being conveyed.

[134] **Body mutilation,** tattooing, piercing, pornography, addiction to substances and various forms of maiming the self all suggest that your son, your daughter, your wife or husband may be somehow negatively influenced.

[135] **Quigley, Carroll,** Ph.D. _Tragedy and Hope._ Chapter V.

emotionally distressed individuals, home from a needless conflict. The problem with charity for those who are reasonably able to work is that it robs them of the opportunity of doing for themselves that, which will enhance self-esteem as they develop the skills necessary for survival.

Presently the collective conscience, weakened by too much misdirected attention, given to the subject of psychology has, to a considerable extent, been corrupted. The corruption of mass mind presents a very complex and difficult issue. This is an assertion, which can and will draw some indignation from many quarters, since there are so many widely varying opinions, however it must be considered. Psychological tinkering, in various instances has done great harm to a great number of individuals (Carl Rogers, William Coulsen).[136] To repent, after the fact, will not repair the damage done to a fragile mind, or return what, significantly, has been destroyed. Psychology has been at the forefront of a very debilitating Modernist movement having its emphasis on the perverted sexual encounter.[137] Interestingly, philanthropy is often directed toward those that have been victims of war and/or psychological distress. War is certainly avoidable.

Fine Art, beginning with *Picasso,* has been used as an implement to further the aims of perversion and ugliness and to denigrate women, reducing them to become the eager and submissive object of carnal pleasure. The last works done by a *lustful little Twerp* are some of the most disgusting scribbles that have ever found rest on a sheet of paper. The man, Picasso, was a disgusting lunatic that was praised because of the millions made by those that promoted his brand of decadence. The space in the world's Museums are full of stultified nonsense displayed as art, for the benefit of ignorant participation, which views with pleasure the destruction of Christianity and all forms of traditional Beauty. Donors, with more money than they can spend, take part in the philanthropy as they donate or loan to museums works of art, some of which appear to be the work of lunatics, *imagined as men of genius.* Much of which is considered as art, which occupies vast public spaces could be better placed on a few sheets of paper with a short statement. However, those imagining themselves as artists have neither the ability to draw or to write that would be necessary to present ideas as ideas *without the need for tons of silly stuff.* Model making and the tableau, are of some interest but might best be kept at a small scale, It is not necessary to overcome an audience with pretense. Theatrics does not enhance the esthetic quality of any work rather it distracts and often appears simply silly. Shakespeare had it in one short phrase *"Much to do about nothing".*

Considering fine art of the Twentieth century, a group *"imagined as respected, world-renowned"* art Critics (five hundred in all) did come together to choose a urinal, by Du Champs *"imagined"* as the century's most profound artistic expression. One wonders how much artistic talent might have existed, amongst such an erudite group. Ulysses by James Joyce was deemed the best of what was written; Ta, Ta. Certainly, this was the *"presumably astute"* opinion of a group within which, many would heap criticism on the works of past genius as being outdated or decadent. We do not necessarily concede, to the opinions of seemingly educated elites, become foolish, stupid or simply silly in their endeavor. Those that judged the urinal as Art were stupid

---

[136] **Jones, E. Michael Ph. D.,** *Libido Dominandi, Sexual Liberation and Political Control.* St. Augustine's Press, South Bend, Indiana. © 2000 E. Michael Jones. ISBN # 1-890318-37—*Fidelity Magazine* x

[137] **Reisman, Judith, PhD.** *Kinsey, Crimes and Cosequences.* Third Edition. The Institute for Medical Education, P. O. Box 15284, Sacramento, CA 95851-0284. ©1998-2000-2003. ISBN # 0-9666624-1-5

in their decision however; such stupidly conceived corruption of the intellect and of the Arts does receive international attention. Such mind-space is full of bubbles and feathers and of course, some dung. Keep in mind, like every other product, *Fine Art has become a business.* The market has been flooded with a commodity, deemed as being Art, and is driven by pricing, which has little or nothing to do with what Art should be. Much of what is imagined as painting and sculpture is the work of technicians hired to paint or build what is required. *Wrapping a building or installing a fence is not Art and does not emanate from the soul of civilization or of man.* Rather such is the work of a technician, a charlatan or simply a faker. There are many spoofs as well that are viewed as Art. Anything can be called Art (just a word) however this is confusing to youngsters that imagine they are involved in what is an important form of expression. Right now the Arts are important in the destruction of both mind and soul of the Civilization, wherein the work of an individual man is completely eclipsed, by what is made by a machine or a technician with expensive implementation. Great Public Spaces, smaller private spaces as well, are devoted to the efforts of those with little or no talent for the work of the hand and the mind. Only what is advertised sells and only what sells is advertised. *This is a serious turkey in the egg situation*. Apologists for the *New Academy* are legion and a dumb and disinterested population is easy to convince.[138] The work of superior ability, even genius, is not patronized *unless it is profitable for the Businessman.*

Modernist thinking, especially regarding young adults has destroyed their *"Mind-space"* much of their innocence, their honor, their consciousness and *their sense of shame,* by means of publicizing, for profit, that which should remain as intimate, as private, between a Physician and a Patient, or a husband and wife. This is not always the case; however some individuals, including some well-meaning practitioners, attempt to gain wealth and notoriety by accepting, as entertainment, various maladies, deformities and deviate behaviors. This, in turn, inflicts some change in attitude concerning what should be considered Holy. *The imagery conveyed in pornographic Publications attaches to what is in the young mind and provides for content destined to encourage prurient behaviors.* Although there have always been opportunists, it does not help to hide behind this as an excuse. Good men should remain good and coincidentally help others to do the same.

In the recent past, intimacy has become the focus of prurient public attention. Intimacies should not be brought to public attention, in which instance the nature and subtle beauty of intimacy is destroyed. Intimacy requires quiet mind-space, seclusion in a cloistered space, involving the procreative aspects of loving, touching, mating, and *"being together"* as husband and wife, destined to form a new human beings. *Sex is not a joke!* Whilst being pleasurable, *sex should not be viewed as mere entertainment.* Pornographers are most conspicuous in such endeavors even as they are the most despicable of the maggot-men that have gained prominence from Blasphemy, lewdness, sin and the ruination of love and of lives.

---

[138] **Fifty years ago** I gave a lecture at a Public Museum. The lecture was titled *"The New Academy."* I pointed to the coming deterioration of what is called Art. The lecture was well received and my indictment has proven to be correct. Nevertheless the average man still has little interest and almost no understanding of what Art is and must be to be called Art. How many know of brown as being the color of the soul; non spectral and moody, the perfect transparent pigment for creating a soul-inspiring artistic Image?

Regardless of Where, God aspires to love every individual with an infinite love and compassion; nevertheless, God does have some very definite and clearly defined expectations. Some may not understand just exactly what are His expectations, however, all can imagine, at least, that Godly expectations are of the highest and most compellingly profound order that is possible. *We should imagine that God considers each of us, in His good Space as one of His perfect creatures and then, we should act so as not to disappoint Him!* In God's good space it is expected that each person will use individual intelligence, sustained by Free Will to advance the nature and being of humanness. A positively motivated Volition, given to the light of the accumulated Intellect of the past two millennia, should make this possible.

There are reprobates that will not be retrieved by a patient and all loving God. This love is discreetly expressed in the birth, of all that have lived, the living and all that may live in the future. The advent of birth, given the nature of biological reproduction, is an unimaginable blessing, no matter where or when. Tyrants, thriving on sin, especially lust and greed, have destroyed the lives of millions. Nevertheless, all human beings must aspire to meet the highest expectations, in which instance salvation (hopefully) shall be the reward. This has not always been understood. This is precisely why God did send his only Son to teach and to inspire. The Word, with the guidance of the Holy Spirit has permeated the mind space of the entire human race. We are admonished that in the last days, *"Christ will come again."* This chapter has not been an exposition on bible prophecy, or the history of religion, which can best be done by others. However this has been rather a common sense appeal to the reader with some pertinent understanding in respect to the nature & function of space, for example what is sacred and holy?

Space exists as a self-absorbing Infinity [∞]
Space as such is (THE) Symbol of Space
This must be as it is with an Infinity

This is true, only if one believes in the existence of a Supernatural and Eternal Presence;
God the Father; God, the Father is, among other Things, simply an **Idea.**

Nevertheless the Idea is a persistent one.
[∞]

Human mind provides the biological-psychological space.
This is the space, wherein the past and the present intersect.
Then the known past is augmented, and is thus able to collapse.
It collapses upon the presently discreet moment, upon **Now time.**
All this happens in what we can define or understand as mind's space.
Neurological function, which becomes of a synaptic accommodation, is the
Physical-psychic means of configuration, providing the necessary electronic paths.
Such paths attempt to define complex levels of known and reasoned thought.
Within the mind we find *"Nested Concepts"* one found within another.
There are apparently sixteen (16) levels of concepts (Royal Rife)
For each individual, the process of thinking is absolutely unique.
All the discreetly known past, with or without comprehension, is compressed in Time.

The Past as remembered is carried, within a single eminent and functional moment.
Space, which appears as nothing, as the sky, is symbolic of itself, which is nothing.
The present moment is evolving toward an unknown, and is infinitely becoming.
Every human being is aware of Infinity manifest as the sky, symbol of Space.
It is the future, as one may perceive [It] to exist.

$$S = S \ n < > S$$

Manifest awareness is the knowing, as is evident in the individual mind become.
Knowing is a product of the neurological and specifically formed cellular complexity.
Intellect as knowledge, is accessible through language, this is of absolute importance.
Knowing, to any degree, is derived from the advent of individual human experience.
Act is as a response to or consequence of a (our) truthfully perceived reality.
Knowledge becomes and is within individual mind, content, is thereby localized.
Knowledge is a phenomenal product of [a] People, [a] Culture or [a] Civilization.
As having been actualized, history is or may be widely evident: the lie distorts history.

Space is as self as is Space

Reason and pertinent objective, or reasoned understanding of any consequence may be
individually understood, creating, as it qualifies history, for the individual.
Given the nature of humanity and individual humans, truthful History may be obscured;
By forms of deception, in Time, by a Lie or widely known as reasonably understood past truth.
The present moment, in space, provides every single human being a unique opportunity for
individual involvement destined toward the perfection of that particular living person.
Everyone should strive to be perfect as Catholic Christianity defines perfection.

There are many ways to do this.
The future [holds in space] what is possible, from this moment Foreword.
All potential is held in future space-time.

Whatever is possible will happen, as an event in space-time beyond now.
In Space each moment is wrapped in a segment of time. All will be aware who are in the
"Sphere" of influence, which is coincident or is a parallel event, in a particular *place-moment*.
Consequence will be favorably or unfavorably obviated, at a *space-time point* beyond.
Each moment has also been surrounded or wrapped in a *place-certain time segment.*
The truthful meaning of all current conscious acts, intentional or inadvertent will be made
known, to a small part of humanity in future space-time.

Whatever is possible will happen at a certain space-time, in the future?

However the question remains; does mankind learn from the past mistakes?
The answer is that, most men certainly do not learn from the past!
The War on terror or any War makes this blatantly obvious.
War is a complete abrogation of our present reality.

War is cowardly, sinful and must be stopped.
To glorify war is primitive and barbaric.
Technology does not make it better!
It is much worse now than ever.
It is the way of the coward
And the way of a Fool
And will destroy
The future!

Think of it?

Fiedler © 1-11-2000 Revised 2-18-2002 & 11-15-2006 & 12-1-06 & 6-4-2013

On the 50th Anniversary of our Wedding.

For a more complete understanding of Space wrapped in Time,
See Thomas Bearden's work in "Aids, Biological Warfare,"
Tesla Book Co., P. O. Box 1649, Greenville, TX 75401. ISBN # 0-914119-04-4.

Below is drawn a Butterfly Symbol suggesting endless Time.

Below is a graphic attempt to define past, present future in a Time-space format. The heavy line through the center of the form is the present moment; it is Now Time. The Wings of what is apparently butterfly-like are past-future, future-past and represent the before and after; typical of each and every event. P1 and P2 are typical of the pattern formed in Time by singular events. The singular events are persistent and completely unique. Moments are depicted by points on a line suggesting, once again a Time factor; an ordered progression from moment to moment. The BW is as a butterfly wing arrested in time and space; the total drawing is of a single instant. This abstract form has been repeated backward in time and will be repeated again in future Time; Top Image and Bottom Image. It is cyclical and continuous in Time. The Large Infinity Symbol at the bottom of the form suggests unending Time. The small images are the before and after. The parallel lines suggest simultaneity of events.

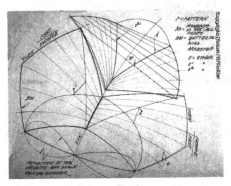
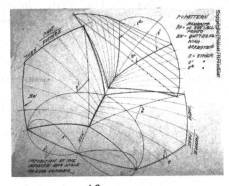

Before　　　　　　　　*After*
Two small illustrations, an abstract Butterfly; Artistic interpretation.

The images are alike because before and after an event can be deemed equal. Before and after can be imagined as being mirror images one of the other. The misunderstanding or incomplete understanding of time is a mysterious quality in human thought. Specialists have a superor understanding of reality and even they can be wrong.

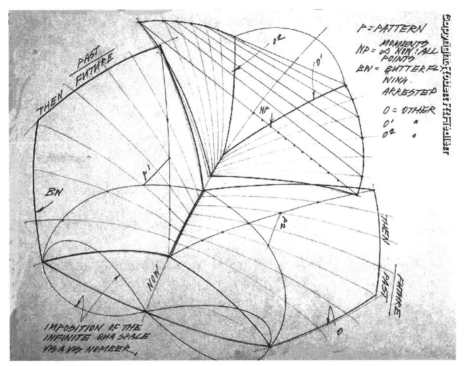

One large illustration, the Butterfly; Artistic interpretation.

The Butterfly

This is a drawing that symbolizes Time.

The central vertical line represents now, the existential moment.
The figure eight at the bottom represents infinity; all time in all places.
The left wing form represents past, future; is as then.
The right wing form represents future, past; is as then.

The right upper-hand corner has a brief description of the piece.
One will have to think independently from there about Time and what it means.

Time is related absolutely to Space.
In phenomenal ways each requires the other to be what it is.

———

CHAPTER VI

PSYCHIC SPACE IS PERSONAL AND EXISTS WITHIN A SINGLE MIND.

The Apocalypse is Unseen, Silent and Certain

Psychic Space can be understood or imagined as existing within the inner-cranial voids wherein thinking occurs. Every individual has synaptic space between the proximate neurons found in the brain tissue. It is a small space however it is Space. It is believed by some that thinking occurs in this *inner-cranial space*. This is consistent with the Scriptures that proclaim all was created by a God who thought of one thing or another and the object appeared as if by magic.[139] It is imagined that a word was necessary so to call prominence to a thing or sequence. This of course is somewhat religious and we cannot deal with all of that just now. However the mention of it is important and it does fit with what is explained below. In fact there is so much knowledge and so many trillions of Ideas that one must take a broad view when dealing with any issue.[140] This author's education was greatly varied and quite extensive in both academic and economic or social issues. However, that said everyone must apply their own intelligence to the materials postulated below. *What is written, in this volume claims, demands and requires that one read with an open mind,* this will help one to learn to think in a more profound manner. Some Issues are unclear and will remain so nevertheless one's thinking is important and determines what one will do. ***Much of what is written is as an assumption***: the proof or disproof is up to the reader however the reader must apply an open and non-prejudicial mind.

---

[139] **That God does exist** is not believed by everyone, and there are different imaginings concerning who is this God.

Think of God as an Idea. Time, Movement and Light combine in Space and give opportunity for a Means, (he who we call God) which are required for creation. Think of this and avoid searching for a man-like form for God. *No one knows exactly what a trip-ret creature looks like.*

[140] **Every human being** has thoughts and thought patterns, there are very few exceptions. The mind as well as the body, is what distinguishes one being from another. In the common scheme of things we are told there are no absolutes, however this is incorrect. *Every single person is an absolute being* some are more prominent than others.

One's time-space format will distinguish the inputs and guarantee that each person is unique. Some will state this is a part of God's plan. This is also obviated by the fact that the DNA for every individual is absolutely unique. Who may have thought of this? This is certainly a supernatural God-like understanding.

To follow thoughts and thought patterns is interesting and can be amusing or it may produce difficulties in the mind of the thinker.

Psychic Space is ephemeral and difficult to understand. _Moments lived are recorded in the brain, one at a time,_ in order and ideas accrue to the individual being. Such moments are a cause in one's becoming. Such moments impose upon _"present-time moments"_, and work toward the development of the personality. _**All such moments remain embedded, known and unknown, within the Psychic Disposition and become a part of the personality of the observer, for a lifetime.**_ One's ideas and personality can be considered as the result of this particular _"understanding"_. Good experiences, in a general sense, given in childhood will have a positive consequence in future Time whereas, in a general sense, poor experience will have an opposite effect. This is rather difficult to understand because all individuals do not respond in the same and known manner. We do not know how and why ideas form as they do. Certain _"positive experiential clusters"_ may function positively and will/may negate some of the negative ones, thus counteracting or altering somewhat their effect on the individual. The study of Psychology attempts to deal with this phenomenon.[141] Some practitioners are more successful than others whereas some may actually be adding emotional stress to a patient. One will have to search on his own to find the answers.

In children today we find many abnormalities of one sort or another. Such abnormalities take up a great portion of their psychic space. For example *Autism* is a disorder of neural development _characterized by impaired social interaction and communication,_ and by restricted and repetitive behavior. What is happening in the mind of someone so inflicted? Apparently if we accept some studies we imagine the child's brain contains much more than is obvious. Autism is a developmental disorder that appears in the first 3 years of life. Autism spectrum disorder (ASD) is a range of complex neurodevelopment disorders, characterized by social impairments; communication is strained accompanied by various disorders that make it difficult or impossible for the child to function in a normal manner. Studies are being conducted to better understand and learn to help children so impaired; therapies are being developed. Such impairments probably have cause which may go back for generations and would therefore be very difficult to determine. Some forms of illness are known to have this feature, emanating from a distant past.

In adults with greater apriority experience we see addictions of various sorts, some are very extreme. Narcotics, alcohol and strange behavioral patters are seemingly more prevalent than in the past: this may or may not be true, we don't really know. The shooting and murder of innocent victims is abhorrent. Rape, child molestation, shacking-up, perverted sex, gang-banging and many other problems appear to be growing in spite of efforts to curtail them. The young women that accommodate the gang-bangers are most unfortunate in their personalities and desires. Some corrective programs actually reinforce what was heretofore considered an abnormality.

Additionally many individuals respond in unison to conformities dictated by the creators of _"now time"_. Those most obvious are generally made apparent by jewelry and the personal taste

---

[141] **Psychology,** in a general sense, is too concerned with method and not concerned enough with a deep and holy understanding of reality.

in dress and right now by the emergence of numerous tattoo parlors. There appears to be a strange relationship between what and who one is to the various forms that are chosen. Both criminal types and athletes seem to be leading the way for the tattoo parlor; and then, to where we can only imagine. This appears to be a form of self gratification where other *more refined* forms, carefully learned and patiently practiced are missing. Many males use the tattoo to prove how tough they are. They imagine enduring some form of pain will make them appear, at least, to be brave and strong. It would be better if they would use their time and intelligence to care for and nurture their families; their wife and the children which they have fathered. Such as this combined with the autism found in children is providing a tremendous challenge for the thinkers and the scientists in the community. The problems are increasing with the increasing population.

Most individuals are mostly good however they may occasionally slip into behavioral patterns that are similar to those suggested above. *This writing* in some respects may seem a bit pessimistic however life is only unusually positive for a few individuals amongst us. <u>*The World is a wonderful place, the beauty; the grandeur and the extensiveness are all outstanding.*</u> Children are a wonderful gift to the parents and to the community and should be recognized as such. We must teach them properly urging against sinful behavior and with the understandings necessary to form a better place emotionally and intellectually for them to become as adults. We will best inform the child by our own actions; if we are good and decent and have no abnormal or weird characteristics the child will benefit from this. We must not attempt to encourage a child to mature too quickly; some adults are inclined to do this. We must discourage all forms of improper behavior and concentrate on goodness and on the Truth.

Much Psychic Space is consumed by Politics within the nation and the World. Politics are driven largely by Economics. The fact is that all individuals do not agree on substance and procedural methods. Who could have imagined someone like **Stalin** or **Churchill** would be able to lead their people into and through one of the bloodiest conflicts in history. For a time it was imagined they were Hero's and friends. Actually, they were to a degree a part of the cause of the conflict. Both imagined they were right, in fact both were wrong. In many ways they were just as Hitler in their understanding and vindictiveness nevertheless Hitler, the looser, has to bear the stigma. The image of Hitler was created by others who have divided and personally contrived interests. The U.S. as characterized by Christopher Story analyzing the *Domestic Security Enactment Act* of 2003 as being what he calls **"The Coming U.S. Nazi regime".**[142] Keep in mind the Nazi Regime was promoted by Hitler and his colleagues. With Barack Obama we are pursuing a path similar to that of the (infant) Nazi Regime; control, deny and punish dissention; some punishments are fatal.

Psychic Space provides for Thought Clusters to combine creating Ideas both good and bad. Apparently Stalin, Churchill, Hitler and Obama and many like them have some of the same thought clusters from which they draw their understandings and commit subsequent acts; we will have to wait to find out the results for Obama. It must be noted that the general-understanding of right and wrong are relative and are determined by those dealing with the

---

[142] **Kramer, Father Paul, B. Ph., S. T. B., M. Div., S. T. L. (Cand.)** <u>*The Mystery of Iniquity*</u>, Unmasking Iniquity.

questions; who is doing the thinking.[143] Also **Greed** and **Vanity** play a large part in determining actions, often the actions are a disaster, one may hope to have what another has and will kill to have it; Greed and Vanity are mortal Sins. Who knows how to fix this? Two thousand years ago *Christ had all the right Ideas however he was crucified because of his Ideas.* There are others who espoused the same type of teaching and were also killed and in the future others will be killed because of this. In some writings it is said that life is as War, antagonistic and brutal. Why must this be? Stalin is said to have killed sixty million people and is considered a Brute. Churchill watched over the death of millions as well although he is considered a Hero, this is because he was on our side. Stalin was considered a brute; it was not always clear whose side he favored? Churchill was properly educated: this is what millions have been taught by a mass media. The content of his education was highbrow and very proper no doubt. Nevertheless his deliberate actions left much to be desired.

At present the West appears to be in a state of gradual decline. About one hundred years ago Oswald Spengler pointed this out in his writing *"The Decline of the West", two volumes, published in April 1926 November 1928.* The first sign is the number of people who are reproducing wantonly with many of the men having little regard for the nature of or caring for their own children. The men wish to be soldiers and hope to become a Hero. Why is this so? This would be an interesting subject. Many of the today's children were conceived because of the sinful behavior of these same soldiers. Mothers, are more caring however, are being taught by Television and other forms of encouragement to behave as men. Men are more generally interested in the sex portion and many give less regard to their children. Young men forget their more significant responsibilities; reproduction guarantees the future of the species. The government provides some help except this is not what is truthfully needed. What is needed is for a man to behave in a more Universally Christian decently formed moral manner until a suitable opportunity presents itself; matrimony provides this as it has in the past. This requires self discipline and denial of some sexual urges. Illegitimate children, by Christian standards, are often *"pawned off"* on grandparents and often supported by monies from the state. To solve this, the government refers to the illegitimates as *"love children"* which completely negates the meaning of love. At times this works well with little or no stress: this becomes as an accepted Ideal. At present entire communities wait for the dole. With the money provided many will by narcotics and liquor: they become *"spaced out"* and are irresponsible. Such as this is the cause of turmoil and agitation often leading to beatings and murder. The consequence is most often meted on the children who inexperienced and fragile suffer from the effects: the suffering is not always knowable and may not even be apparent to others. The number of child beatings, kidnapping, torture, rape and murder is telling us something. Hello! Are we listening? Do we understand?

---

[143] **What is relative is not absolute,** it varies in meaning and tenor, is open to adjustment one way or another.

This is a principal that is a part of the inflation that everyone fears so much. Some leader's favor a bit of inflation others do not; some ideas are absolute in their intention others are not. This is an understanding that lies beneath all of the financial transactions performed at present. Inflation is not a good idea where money and trade are being determined. *Inflation will always go beyond control.*

The Psychic Space of our children is too often consumed by the Television and the Computer to the point where they are often unable or unwilling to communicate with those around them. Imagine a child being placed in front of a television from perhaps six months to view all the mayhem and the silly and some stupid commercials which make their environment almost intolerable. The commercials are thought to be good for the economy. Millions are paid to some celebrities for appearing on a commercial. There is much talk of education however many students receive very little serious learning in our often beautiful schools. Serious learning is in the fields of philosophy, history as fact, the meaning and influence of religion, mathematics, the sciences, ethics, human behavior and seeking the Truth; to mention some important ones. There are certainly very bright students however the System does not encourage them as it should. There are some very good programs however in many too much emphasis is placed on method rather than *content and meaning*. Much of the information may be slanted for a political or social purpose. Academics are often lacking whereas special programs and sports are pushed beyond reason. And who then is considering the *Soul* of the child? Religion is undergoing an assault from the Left and has been and is being reduced or will be in the future. A university program in the past was largely concerned with Theology and Philosophy. Who at present follows such a program? When they do they are exposed to the wrong forms of content which, in fact, should be exposed honestly for what they really are.

Much of our Psychic Space is consumed by what is called music much of which is as frightful noise with little or no reason to be listened to. Here we witness a takeover by ignorance and bad manners; all for fun of course. This is a political as well as a cultural and social aberration in a once proud and dependable people. There is also fine music however how many are tuned into such stations? Early Philosophers (Plato and Socrates) called attention to our being mindful of music as a stimulus for the destruction of the people. *Music apparently influences the deeper aspects of our consciousness.* The dancing is as that of a savage with no respect for the body or other individuals. Dancers are *"letting it all hang out"* so to speak. Children as young as three or four are dressed as adults and compete for prizes which very likely will teach them to be selfish and vain: *Vanity* and *Selfishness* are both sinful. Their parents encourage this and participate in the destruction of the *"Psychic Disposition"* of their own children.[144] Who now considers and contemplates on what is Sin? Who is the Devil and how does he operate? *The Devil is an Idea and the Idea operates through any and all who would entertain it.* This is a relative understanding open to different points of view, some are wise some are stupid.

The Psychic Space of millions of "grown-ups" has been and is being overcome by the present *"beat of the times"*. Much of their behavior is revolting and the treatment of their own appearance is often disgusting. They imagine themselves as being different in a special way, cool, with-it, a mover and shaker. But in reality they are disgusting and vulgar; disgusting and vulgar have become normalized in the eyes of foolish people. Coincidentally there are millions of examples of primitive and simply barbaric behavior. The recent outbreak of tattooing is an obvious symptom of a form of social decadence however is considered as an art form. The art,

---

[144] **The Psychic Disposition** of the individual when combined with the Psychic Disposition of millions of others, make up the Collective Disposition, confusion and the general ignorance of the population; this is also known as the Collective Psyche. Our problem is that Ignorance and ineptitude have been given too much attention and authority. This is a real flaw in a Democracy.

for the most part, has deteriorated to that of a child. Young men and women are allowing their bodies to be brutalized by some pervert with a needle that enjoys scribbling on the flesh of another human being. There are many silly images, silly cartoons, ugly scrawls and moronic, interpretations of other things.[145] There may be a few good ones amongst the drivel.

In many places the men are dressed as soldiers; killing who they do not and cannot know. They gain a certain sense of importance driving around in a truck with a gun in hand; never will they do any meaningful work. They follow a vain and often perverted leader and imagine they are doing good for some ancient, medieval or present Idea which most do not comprehend. Men, so called depend on their women to do most of the menial and manual work. There are some good amongst them however with the present political situation they have little influence. The young soldiers are prone to rape and brutalize the women who they come into contact with. They hide behind a total misunderstanding of Religion what it is and what it is supposed to accomplish. They consider violating a woman to be a symbol of their manhood. They are most certainly wrong; they are not men they are rather as an animal or beast, perhaps an insect; a disturbed and perverted human being.

The Psychic Space of some is confused by an Addiction to narcotics which has been and is a growing problem; the laws do little to curtail this. Narcotics, provides an income for crime and the violence associated with the gang-bangers. The narcotics trade is in the billions of dollars and seems to be unstoppable. Those that deal in the sale of narcotics are probably the worst form of human being. They commit atrocities against often innocent beings just to create an atmosphere of fear and a perverted form of respect for who they are. The Devil is in charge of every one of them, many are hooked unknowingly.

The Psychic Space of a prostitute as it combines with outrageous sexual behaviors even amongst the so called civilized patrons shows the nature and extent of degradation. Even the more civilized are drawn into one trap or another. In a mindless search for identity individuals are often led astray. The process is generally slow, it may take years however for millions it is a certainty. In the past Religion did in fact curtail some offensive behavior however that too is being removed from the mainstream as individuals attempt to create a Religion that fits their strange and unusual requirements. There are many presentations that are designed to show Religion as being evil. Perverted and strange creatures act out the various roles to disprove Religion as being good. Celebrities play conspicuously in the formation of new and deviate Religions and generally have the backing of the establishment. The Celebrity has a false sense of self worth because he/she has been given so much money for almost nothing. They may be generally involved with Religion for some misunderstood reason.

---

[145] **In the New Federalist Magazine,** January 16, 1995 there appeared a very interesting Article by Thomas Wolfe. The title of the Article is *"Don't Entrust Your Kids to Walt Disney!"* The Author states that *"Disney has helped entrap several generations, in a regressive enforced infantilism, as they take their children to see the films that they saw with their Parents years before."* Disneyland is an important factor in keeping our population in a state of perpetual childhood; not exactly healthy for adults. Disney has become a real stain on Culture and Civilization of the Western World and is spreading to other venues as well. It is suggested that you obtain and read this article. Having done this you will be in a better position to understand some important elements in the dissolution of our Culture.

All of what is listed above is silently working as much of the Western Civilization is crumbling enamored by technologies and entertainment that seems to be, generally speaking, unnecessary. Our somewhat silly and very expensive Wars are a distraction for millions and hundreds of young men are killed and wounded. Our Wars are contrived and advertised for the benefit of the American people to weaken their resolve and their military strength. When a young man is killed it affects the entire family parents, brothers, sisters, wives and children if there are any. Right now women are being destined for combat; *this is a serious and unreasonable tragedy.* If one man or woman is killed we play a bugle over the grave, hand the family a flag and believe this is enough payment for the death of who served his/her country; this too by itself is a great tragedy.

What are the deadly Sins?
There appears to be seven deadly sins.[146]

- **Lust**—to have an intense desire or need: "But I tell you that anyone who looks at a woman lustfully has already committed adultery with her in his heart" (Matthew 5:28).
- **Gluttony**—excess in eating and drinking: "for drunkards and gluttons become poor, and drowsiness clothes them in rags" (Proverbs 23:21).
- **Greed**—excessive or reprehensible acquisitiveness: "Having lost all sensitivity, they have given themselves over to sensuality so as to indulge in every kind of impurity, with a continual lust for more" (Ephesians 4:19).
- **Laziness**—disinclined to activity or exertion: not energetic or vigorous: "The way of the sluggard is blocked with thorns, but the path of the upright is a highway" (Proverbs 15:19).
- **Wrath**—strong vengeful anger or indignation: "A gentle answer turns away wrath, but a harsh word stirs up anger" (Proverbs 15:1)
- **Envy**—painful or resentful awareness of an advantage enjoyed by another joined with a desire to possess the same advantage: "Therefore, rid yourselves of all malice and all deceit, hypocrisy, envy, and slander of every kind. Like newborn babies, crave pure spiritual milk, so that by it you may grow up in your salvation" (1 Peter 2:1-2).
- **Pride**—quality or state of being proud—inordinate self esteem: "Pride goes before destruction, a haughty spirit before a fall" (Proverbs 16:18) Lust—to have an intense desire or need: "But I tell x

The seven deadly sins are presumably damning or may be so. There are others which are apparently less serious. They are named Venal Sin. What one should be concerned with is to know and understand the difference. Even the lesser sins should be avoided as a matter of habit. If ones sinning affect another negatively that too must be considered. The most obvious in such instance would be in rape or some other form of distressed sexual occurrence.

When a child is born to a woman who does not have a husband she will face a more difficult time with raising the child. Without the love and companionship of a faithful mate life can be bleak and will be difficult for the woman. She may turn to Prostitution simply to make enough money to support herself and her child. This is tragic! Generally speaking mothers love their

---

[146] **The seven deadly sins** are taken from the internet with a brief explanation of each sin.

own children and will do anything for them. Men often don't give a damn and they desert the mother and the child, they look for another woman, perhaps younger or prettier or even another man, for sexual pleasure which may be despicable, *"Lust plays a dominant roll"*.

Murder or killing another is always sinful; *"Wrath"* comes into such decisions. War is imagined as being necessary and comes about because of differences in Ideas or because of wanting what belongs to another; this is *"Envy"*. War then becomes largely because of *Wrath* and *Envy"* certainly *Greed* is an important part as well. _Munitions makers and their distributors_ _pile up millions and billions making the junk that is used in killing another of God's children._ The stuff appears awesome; the planes and tanks, submarines and aircraft carriers, rifles, bazookas and now the drone type weaponry. Our politics confirms the use of warfare and therefore *encourages killing.* Youth learn this from the adults in the community. The men who start the Wars are generally not known by the soldiers. The Officers are generally intelligent however they are not wise. A soldier is respected for killing others however he/she may also be killed. This is considered as bravery which it might be; *or is it foolishness?* When a man or now even a woman faces what is imagined as an enemy in combat they will have no choice. The *"Vanity and Pride"* of Womanhood causes them to want to be soldiers and kill like the men. I some situations one must then kill or be killed. This is a difficult choice for some and may be a cause for conscientious objection. Others accept being a soldier as a duty, which it can be; they imagine this is how life is; which is true for now. America provides many benefits to their soldiers the ones not killed or somehow wounded in action. They are offered a university education and some helpful financial benefits without having to pay for much of what is given.

Economics is a cause for much sinning *"Greed is the motivation"* for much of this. This may be called good business, shrewdness or, luck and is a _time-space phenomenon_. Some are given opportunities while others may take opportunity believing they are smarter than the rest. *Some may be smarter however some are simply thieves.* The thieves will do almost anything for money used to support their often outrageous life style. In many countries the money is often used to support a drug habit. Such life-style may be considered a form of reward for whatever they might have done, right or wrong. Morals fall by the wayside as opportunism become more effective.

Gluttony and Laziness are rather more personal and have to do with habit and what one sees in the immediate surroundings. They are somewhat familial or tribal involving people in families and tribes. They have to do with the kind of foods and the amounts consumed. They also involve learning from parents and friends. Many people are obese weighing much more than they should. Some obese persons weigh twice what would be normal. In some places nearly half the population is considered obese. This is difficult for the organs in one's body and causes many forms of disease. Some Doctors have warned of this however who listens and acts on the knowledge gained? Health clubs and gymnasiums are filled with people trying to lose weight when a simple diet would be more effective.

As the above notions and eventualities occur they become a part of the *"Psychic Disposition"* which I have referred to in this writing. The notions and eventualities pile-up, and become *absolutely unique* in how they are related and in what they mean to the individual and to the community. In the very complex process of thinking, individuals become confused and cannot even understand themselves. *Combine inadvertencies with the lies and distortions* *and the communication slips into **a difficult to understand abstraction.*** This abstraction is nearly impossible to explain or to imagine and cannot be fully understood. One can discuss imaginings and understandings without comprehension of their meaning. In our modern world comprehension for millions perhaps billions is nearly impossible. A lack of comprehension helps all that desire to have a one-world order which relies on a manner of confusion to be established. The manner of confusion involves individual lack of comprehension.

What is called the Establishment, attempts to keep "We the People" in a state of confusion and anxiety.[147] The establishment inveighs upon the Psychic Space of every individual and produces the various effects that we see in a population. Many diversions are imposed and advertised relentlessly to keep the ball rolling. In many respects the Establishment is succeeding.

—⁓◦◦⌀◦◦⌀◦◦⁓—

Professor Emeritus; Robert Fiedler
April 12, 2013

---

[147]   *I have written briefly about the Establishment in Chapter I of this work.*

CHAPTER VII

THE PHENOMENOLOGY OF
EXISTENCE; PART I

It is a time-space occurrence, a discreet presence of a physiological-biological entity.
Among other things "Human Existence" is a Complex Consequence.
No two Humans are the same: each is profoundly unique.

Space and matter have distinguishing characteristics which are found at all levels of existence from the very smallest to the very great.[148] ***This must be true or the Universe would not and could not function.*** The Universe is a beautifully designed and executed Space believed by millions to be the result of the presence of a Divine Being whom they call God. This Divine Being may exist for millions as only an *Idea.* Others by Faith believe in His truthful and real existence. This Divine Being has been given to numerous evaluations from the simplest to the most complex of human thought patterns. Many believe what is as Reality is a product of God's word. Besides being a person, for a Catholic Christian, some other Christians as well the person of the Christ Jesus is a_*profound Idea.* At present some physicists are seeing relationships between what is spiritual and what, is temporal. *Some imagine they have found a God particle.* Spirit and form are now *seemingly* somewhat better understood than they were formerly. Nevertheless we cannot be certain if the newer or present understanding is correct. The understanding comes from the realization that an atom is imagined as only about one two-billionth part matter: the rest is space. How can the average man understand this? The Spirit is a non-material form: it cannot be seen with the human eye nor can it be touched. It is a phenomenal enigma. The Spirit often manifests as a ***Thought***, or is imagined as an ***Idea***, that not many truthfully understand nor can they explain just, what it is. The understanding as present in Catholicism seems to be the best form: Catholicism is God's Religion and is Universal (from the Greek). Catholicism covers all men whatever Religion they may have been born to and whatever they profess. Eventually humanity must acknowledge there can be only one God, one Omnipotent and one true Faith. Jesus said, "I am the way, and the truth, and the life" (John 14:6). The Ideas in which many perhaps most men believe, is of little or no consequence to

---

[148] **If one views an atom** and a constellation there are similarities found in each: first there is more space than matter; second there is infinitely rapid movement; third the components verge upon being composed of Light and finally the entire-form is moving through space, which is as containment: Space is [The] containment. This is theoretical however is believed (by many) to be how matter resides, sustains in space.

88

existence. Against an Omnipotent Force each man, is as a fleeting moment.[149] We are not certain what will happen after death; this introduces the Trinity and the appearance of what is deemed as the Soul of a particular being. This Idea is corrupted by Sin especially *Vanity.*

Humility is a necessary Virtue; *Primitive men* and some not so primitive have given the Spirit all manner of strange and some comical forms, without the least understanding of what this in fact means and will mean in the future. Their misunderstanding, supported by centuries of incorrect thinking, has given us our mythologies and our false understandings comprising important parts of the present collective and general understanding: this can be imagined as a *manner of collective or mass confusion or a manner of mass neurosis.*[150] Presently there exist preposterous components *(thought clusters)*, in the thinking of whole populations, groups of people that encourage a strange and generally *misunderstood trip* concerning: **What is Reality.** For many the present is perhaps, more confused than the past because of the rapidness of communication and the imagined freedom of speech which makes the headlines. All of this competes with the incessant and banal advertising to sell a nearly worthless product. Furthermore this combines, intellectually, emotionally and spiritually with an over-emphasis on athletics and games. No one understands truthfully exactly what is happening to the thought process that leads one to act; however it is profound. Various forms of odd human behavior such as murder, rape, theft and cheating, for example give somewhat qualified evidence into our strange existence and behavior.

A form of general misunderstanding too can be understood as a form of mass neurosis in the imagination and is creating what I have referred to in other writings as a form of Mutual Insanity which involves the entire population of the more advanced nations: (seemingly so). The neurosis is carefully nurtured by those that hope to utilize the mental unrest of the general population. This is what happened as the French Revolution was formed, some other Revolutions as well. *Individuals and groups are brought to a high level of pandemonium and can be incited to do un-Godly things.* The slaves of the Devil are foremost in this cadre of malcontents. Mass neurosis is an evolving condition that seeks for a form of expression which is not knowable in advance: only those who are involved in the expected take over, if indeed this is what is occurring, understand partially what is happening.[151] Such a mental condition, can and will cause various forms of unrest, riot and revolution: millions will die as have died in the past, this will continue others will suffer. This state of affairs is well known to selective elites and is exploited by those who are attempting to rule the World. ***They have named it the One World Order.***

---

[149] **Ultimately,** what anyone thinks or knows imagines or experiences is of absolutely no consequence in the *Universal Order* of things to other than who are living at that time and who are nearby.

[150] **This is exacerbated by Lucifer**—former Angel of light, by his rebellion against God, he became Satan— the devil. This enemy of mankind bases his reign of darkness over the world on the lie. To him the lie is "sacred", because it is by lying to the men and women who believe him that they thus enslave themselves to his will.

Men such as Joseph Stalin, Karl Marx, Pot Pohl, Fidel Castro and many others were enacting out the Devil's wishes.

[151] **The take-over** will have been accomplished if and when we have a one-World Government.

The selective Elite might be named as the Anglo-Zionist, Masonic, Communist, and Marxist Conspiracy.[152] Their will to dominate all others goes back for over two thousand years and longer: *it is carried in the hearts and minds of vain and preposterous individuals*. This same type individual may also be Banker to much of the World and has been for centuries; he holds the coins. This Banker is a man without a country who plans on dissolving all nations into a World Federation. He assumes "It" will be controlled by him. This is why some things that occur are inexplicable: they corrupt present thinking in a very real way with nearly unimaginable Lies. Ever present is the Liar confusing those who are not well informed, confusing those that are not at all interested. I must apologize because all Bankers are not this way only those well connected who belong to the Anglo-Zionist Conspiracy. Unfortunately they control the great Banks of the world: the ones with tens or hundreds of billions which very often have been extorted from various governments. And there were and are the Bolsheviks who plan to destroy *"this Civilization"* and replace it with a form of *"Collective Madness"*. One can imagine there are a number of conspiracies working to establish the control of the World: religion plays a significant role in some of these imaginings.

In Genesis it is acknowledged that *"In the Beginning was the word."* Accordingly the word apparently preceded the becoming of the Reality that we know and enjoy: one way or another.[153] The word *"calls to meaning"* some form or manner, a person, place or object, of what we perceive as Reality. Furthermore it is believed by millions that God created the various elements and various Heavenly structures that we all recognize and appreciate: it is believed by some that he did this in six days: furthermore it is believed that on the seventh day He rested. *No one knows how long His days were.* Beliefs are sometimes difficult to understand therefore Mythologies grew from some beliefs as explanations for what had been and was occurring at one time or another. In fact this is what propels much, or most of man's thinking and thought processes. _The Mythologies contain various understandings of Reality,_ some are perhaps correct others are not, and the Metaphors which have captivated the thinking, the soul and the being of Humanity may be true in part or simply false. *This is dependent upon one's learning and education and what one presumes to know.* The structure and use of language as generally understood bears importantly on this point. *This is why a nation, as such, must have a single language in which all of the citizens are fluent.* If you do not have this you cannot have social and intellectual compatibility which is essential for a nation to survive.

Neuron Biology and Neuron Science is (seemingly) made to appear as two difficult subjects: they deal with the functioning of the mind and the brain. Brain function, and the consequences derived there from are elusive. Recently it has been determined and is now believed and somewhat understood that thought originates in space, between the proximate neurons located in the brain. *This is consistent with the understandings advanced in Genesis:* the thought originates

---

[152] **The complexities** in combining the various Political means, causes great confusion. To define what is the truthful Political Reality becomes nearly impossible.

[153] **The Word** precedes the Act much as the transparent tubules precede the development of the various organs and parts of the body. This assertion has both spiritual and scientific meaning. The meaning is defined by the intellectual capability of the thinker who knows of this as being extant.

in (God's) space.[154] The various problems we face grow from *a misunderstanding of past reality and from confusion regarding just how was the Universe formed.* What power was great enough to propel the becoming of the Universe?[155] Millions have and do consider that this was an Omnipotent force, a God-force. This brings us back to the same question: Who was or is God? This question propels and asserts influence on all that is, was or ever will be nevertheless it is not answerable. ***No one really knows who is and what is this God being.***

Presently some Physicists are considering what is known as the String Theory which suggests that, matter is composed of quantum-size bundles of energy. We can observe with an electron microscope that what we consider as atoms are mostly space. It is imagined that "the particles take up only one two-billionth or less of the space that the atom actually occupies."[156] Some of the drawings which I have presented in my *"Fantastic Sketch Book"* a complimentary volume are to a great extent, an interpretation of "String Theory" and are symbolic and suggestive rather than literal, real or depictive. The lines in that work must be considered as being lines of force which manifest in different ways and in various degrees. This is a concept perhaps quite difficult for many to understand however the lines give the *"abstract evidence"* of something being present. Consider what is present is as a force moving along the lines and is very small: one two-billionth 1/2,000,000,000 of a space-defined magnitude.

Additionally it has been recently advanced as an Idea that the genetic components found within the individual are mostly those of the mother. It is now considered factual (by some) that the mother will allow only the better genes of the father to become involved in the combined genetic-structure, of a new human being. This is quite logical and is probably correct, due to the fact that the mother is an incubator (care giver) reaching to the future whereas the father is the progenitor (the cause) bringing forth substance from the past. Therefore, it is assumed that the most important genetic components are from the mother.[157] *Although woman is not God she has the upper hand in producing the next generations.* These are difficult issues for ordinary,

---

[154] **The word** must seemingly precede the act or understanding since it **is the vehicle** for both act and understanding. A word has mystical properties which few understand nevertheless all benefit from them.

[155] **There are two aspects** which 'might" be considered. The first is the geologic or foundational element: the second has to do with living forms. The geological elements were necessary so as to support the various Life Forms. Evolutionists insist that the life forms evolved from lower to higher levels of being. This is an Idea about Life that has no support given the nature and complexity of the Life Forms. There have never been found any transitional fossils in all of the fossil records. Beside the Life Organisms are generally speaking so complex that they must have always been as they are at present or they could not have existed. A Species or life form is consistent from generation to generation and its complexities guarantee it will remain as it is never changing. If one views a variety of animals this should be obvious, however there are skeptics. The evolutionists may have Time on their side since no one can perceive what may have happened billions of years ago.

[156] **One two billionth** is a small fraction of anything tangible: It is a minuscule portion. One-trillionth is infinitely smaller: what is infinitely small is very near nothing!

[157] **It is imperative** that the woman should be protected so to advance and promote the development of the species. When women behave as men the species will have unimaginable problems: this is the Reality that makes the acceptance of sex as a game a most insidious notion. Love is not a game: love is

quite disinterested, individuals who are concerned with the trivia of the day rather than great scientific, philosophical or religious thinking: thus, such issues are avoided or may not be within the view of most persons. The concepts are left waiting for the attention of just a few.

When we observe the declination of the various components that comprise the civilization this is not difficult to imagine. The brilliant are certainly apparent however the averages are brought down by those genetically inferior in their make-up. A bringing down does not imply any racial or sexual connotation however has to do primarily with how one lives and how one's ancestors lived in the past: one's actions determine health and all related human issues. Often, when considered such Ideas lead to antagonism and bad feelings. In some quarters such understanding, if expressed, would lead to conflict. One can imagine, at least, that the mother is most important since the child resides within the mother for nine months. This period includes the time necessary to develop all of the necessary human features, physical organs and the traits preparing the child for birth. Nevertheless millions of men see a woman as being inferior; they are fools! *Birth is the advent of a new Soul,* contained within the individual as a Spirit. To be born is one of God's blessings. At death, it is believed by many that the Soul will leave and be free from the body and function on a new and different plane of existence. The "Idea" of a soul is already in the infinite space. This is a part of mythology that is held to be true by millions disparaged by others. There are different imaginings of what is the Soul; no one really knows rather they imagine what a Soul might be. Whether or not and how this might be or is true is a profound enigma. The only way to know is to die: after which no one is certain of what will happen to a Human Being? We understand that the body will decompose however we do not know what will happen to the soul; this derives from the complexity and intricacies of living.

The composition of the brain, mostly existing as a form of *uniquely energized water,* is what functions to connect the individual being to a time-centered reality: to the existing and phenomenal environment.[158] *To have Time* there must be Movement. Within the environment exists all of that which is possible in any environment. No one knows how this came to be however, this is the reality within which we find ourselves and other Creatures. The other Creatures have their own distinctive features that provide for and establish what and how they are. We as Humans presume, probably correctly, to be at the top of the vertebrate class of life forms. Nevertheless an insect, a primitive creature, probably has the best chance of survival.[159]

Distinctions as exist are encoded in the DNA which, by itself is enigmatic; phenomenally so. This is difficult to contemplate: more difficult to understand. How might one know exactly how a gene will influence the health and/or behavior of those who possesses it? Present researchers, are addressing some of the questions, at this moment and are discovering amazing qualities given to existence. The extant qualities are profound, beyond the realm of human thought: *for now.*

---

a necessary and stimulating function necessary for human survival. *Humanity cannot survive without truthful and eternal love; that is forever.*

[158] **It is alleged** that the brain is about seventy percent water. The quality of this water is very distinct and provides a place for thought to occur and for the various neuron-biological functions to develop and to be remembered. It is a/the receptacle for humanness however, as such, is not well understood.

[159] **There are trillions more** insects than human persons and they are a more functionally primitive Creature, therefore they are very likely able to survive where humans will not or cannot survive.

They encompass a variety of what are termed as disciplines: including theology, biology and neurology: others as well, which encourage and enhance the functioning of the brain in various common endeavors.

The similarities are provided in the most ingenious and profound ways. Water, air, light (as both illumination and heat), movement and minute waves which cannot be seen or perceived by untrained senses make up a *"Divine Array"* from which all happenings can occur. *Whatever can happen has already happened or will happen in the future:* unknown beyond this moment in what we perceive as Time. What will happen to man in the future is largely in the behavior and doings of newly born individuals.[160] Great geological deformations will obliterate the existence of man; will such be the workings of a God Being adjusting His universe? Time is a consequence of our perception and understanding of the fact that the earth is rotating, defining each day: and of the earth's movement around the sun, which defines each year. Therefore, Time is a corollary of Movement. *Apparently there must be movement so to define Time, one way or another:* Past or future. Beyond this there are presumed, and there do exist, longer cycles, which are more difficult to understand given the finite duration of individual existence. The longest cycle (for now) is presumed at about twenty-five thousand years and is a corollary of the "Precession of the Equinox."[161] The cycles involved in the workings of the Universe are long of duration and complex in their constituencies and in there meaning; they may involve millions of years. They can be only partially observed in a short period of Time: that is for a brief time. However, given the present understanding of Time astronomers and mathematicians can postulate from Time segments that are observable. Such postulations may or may not be correct (?). Given Time as being forever, will any of this make any significant difference?

The Idea of God we might imagine or believe has apparently been present for all of known human existence. Who and how God is provides a very special and fundamental place in the life of nearly all beings. Man stands in awe at the marvelous, beautiful and profound elements that make up the World and the space around it. We attempt to "conquer Space," (whatever that means) and work acidulously toward this effort. Is such work futile? What are we searching for? If we find something what might we do with such information? *Will we have greater and more destructive warfare than we have now?* More than likely the answer is Yes. Comic books are full of things from outer space, dragons and strange appearing creatures. Such imagery corrupts the understanding of the young; some of the older folks as well. Are Comic books prophesying what will or may happen? One mythology suggests that the US is working for peace in the World however the US is in part a military dictatorship, billions of dollars are made by certain groups within the establishment in the production of armaments. The establishment wants to continue on this path. The people have very little to say in this matter; however they provide the funding

---

[160] **It is certain** that if we continue on the present path some youngsters will grow to be barely an adult, they will join the army or be conscripted to work for the Bankers. While in the Army they will be given the proper tools for killing another man's children: they will not know them. Or, they may be killed in their efforts. Which is better?

[161] **Crittenden, Walter:** *Lost Star of Myth and Time.* St. Lynn's Press, POB 18680, Pittsburg, PA 15236. "As we will soon see, there may be a simpler model to predict precession, one that is based on the laws of elliptical orbits. Such law isn't weighted down with the problems of the modern theorem—and it comes from the ancients." ISBN-0-9767631-1-7: LC #2005927480. (page 86).

and some of our young even die for the cause. Most do not understand the reasoning of the Complex.

The smallest spaces have the same potential as the greatest expanse however the expressions are distinct, given the determined scale. A manner of Determination is what drives man to do what he does. Most of what influences the comings and goings of the age is contained in unknown and unseen forces. They are *ethereal, esoteric, unknown* and some other forms which comprise a somewhat ordered "Pallet" for the Phenomenology of existence: they are transfinite and generally not perceived correctly with the senses. *I have done drawings which attempt to clarify and promote the understanding of what is happening without the use of number or known symbols (See my "Fantastic Sketch Book")*. When one considers how we act and how we live one can know that our understanding is somewhat flawed. The way we live and the obsessive need for conflict in how we behave, provides tangible evidence that this is true.

War is the most obvious of this evidence. When one considers War, madness is the only correct explanation: *it is a form of malicious Greed tending to Vanity.* People are not all the same and it should not be expected that this be so; nor should one kill those that may be different from their own person.[162] There were, Cannibals and head hunters in the past however men have developed since then into more sophisticated beings: so we imagine. What might happen to encourage men back to such form of behavior? Head-hunters and cannibals were a strange group attempting to display their courage by such activities. Their reward was to cook and eat their enemy. The appeal was to a vain understanding of manhood, warped by ignorance; fear a very strange understanding of reality. Cannibals were primitive creatures; given our understanding.

If they had a form of religious expression it may have played a part in their being as those were. Selfishness over the necessities of life played a dominant role as well in the development of such malicious and anti-social behavior. Certainly sex was also an issue, to "show off" for the hand of a maiden, this is understandable, but was given to an incorrect and unholy form of expression.[163] When we consider the innumerable intricacies of any living Creature, especially the vertebrates, that top the list one is amazed at the complexities and intricacies of the various Creatures: especially so concerning their *"thought content"* if such there be. In support of such complexity Carl Sagan postulated that the DNA found in a single cell, if given to written expression, would fill a library as great as the Grand Canyon.[164] This may or may not be true

---

[162] **Some Moslems** believe if one does not believe in Allah or insults the Islamic faith that they should be "smitten"; meaning they should be killed for such thinking. This is barbaric and is conceit in its worst form. It is difficult to imagine how such mind set can be replaced by a more fairly adaptive understanding. Killing *with very few exceptions* is sinful. One is allowed to kill in self defense. Also men have determined that killing is acceptable to remove a mortal threat from the community: we call this Capital Punishment. This seems like a good idea however it does have some serious flaws.

[163] **In the past** women have been abused as part of the showing of male superiority. Recently in India there was a brutal gang rape of a young woman. The act received world-wide attention. However to change the attitudes of a nation with millions of people is a difficult task; it might require drugs or a secret endeavor.

[164] **Dr. Sagan** stated that several Grand Canyons would be required to define the nature of the content within a single cell. Keep in mind you have several trillion cells in your body each one of which can communicate with the others. The means of communication are not completely understood however

however it is worth some of your time to consider it: even if is merely half true. Keep in mind, Carl Sagan was no fool. He had the computer generated means and the intellectual ability to consider the question. We are sorry for his passing from this world to what may be the next. Who knows what will be the next World?

Interestingly, *to repeat,* there are no species known, from amongst the hundreds of thousands existing that provide any definite form of evidence of evolution. Evolution is an **Idea** that some hold in opposition to the **Idea** of Creation. Many men are not able or ready to admit that there may be a superior force, a God force and they seek reasons for believing in evolution. Nevertheless all species seem to have appeared initially just as they are at present: as if by magic! If it is not magic it is *"something"* like magic. Most individuals do not think seriously about such subject matter; however they should spend some time contemplating it.

Men are very distinct in the formation and function of their personalities which, in fact, govern much of their behavior: probably most or all of it.[165] Tyrants come and go with the wind however they affect the behavior of millions, perhaps billions, of individuals concerning their personal activities: some are fatally affected. This is a question involving the presence of Good and Evil, is very complex and is worth a volume of its own. I have written on the subject before however not everyone wants to consider such topic on their somewhat limited reading list. Individually men and some women are distracted by athletic events the news and their own personal misfortunes. They are not necessarily interested in great or deep thinking. Athletics require muscular control and physical strength whereas great ideas demand the higher forms of an interested and determined mind which is able and willing to deal with difficult Issues.

Tyrants are generally vain and by various forms of aggression they attempt to cover their own lack of self esteem and worth as a human person.[166] Their aggressive conceit is a mask for their feeling of inadequacy, which blossoms into abstruse behavioral patterns. Their behavioral patterns are mostly incorrect and are the cause for the suffering of nearly all who are victimized by contact with them. They do have a strong influence on a small part of an extensive reality however, like all others they will die relieving the populations of their mischief. "In the end we are all dead." (Shakespeare) Tyrants are often given credit for being brave or courageous and are *given to honors for killing another man's son, or daughter or wife.* In fact they were and

---

there is sound, movement, hormonal factors and other perhaps generally unknown (for now) methods subtle and evasive. The cell is as complex as a great city, all compressed in a very small site. The cell is responsive to various stimuli, known and unknown. One could go on however this is fundamental to what Dr. Sagan said and postulated.

[165] **Personalities can be trained** and/or they may develop in strange ways. Personalities, together with some other features, provide a way of distinguishing between individuals. The personality sets the situation for belief: Belief is adjunctive of personality function. One's personality, how one is, is what causes behavioral traits, which can be assessed as positive or negative. Whether positive or negative may be a supposition of another known and unknown individual. Negative personalities are often given to fame, which causes them to act as is imagined by the Master that controls them. This is a very complex issue and is a force in all social and political maneuvering.

[166] **Vanity is a Cardinal Sin**, one of the seven deadly Sins and is the cause of much of the World's anguish. It is often associated with young love however this is quite incidental in the greater scheme of things.

are **FOOLS:** unable to understand and sustain a decent thought; this is a Tragedy, of the most profound kind![167]

Many perhaps millions of modern men and women do not consider sin as Sin: they call it by a different name. Especially the sins of the flesh are encouraged by our modern advertising and sales routines. How many near-nude women have you witnessed on Television pushing a product? Often the nude image with breasts and groin are covered up somewhat with a ghost-like diffusion. What is considered as sinful is often treated as humor and as such is tolerated by even the seemingly good people. Sin is also equated with fun and the pleasures and is made thereby acceptable. Satan, the Devil, has many ways of disguising what he is doing and he is certainly very clever. Exactly who is Satan?

Satan as an Idea affects reality in strange and unpredictable ways. Those possessed by Satan obfuscate Reality for the millions whom they affect. This is one of the unseen and only partially understood commonalities of their presence on the scene. They are a strong and personal influence where such influence is not generally wanted or needed. They "bend the Reality" for millions of innocent beings whom they infect, it is an infection, with the wrong and incorrect notions of what life should be.[168] The misconstrued idea of Patriotism is used to encourage the

---

[167] **Napoleon was considered a Hero** by millions of Frenchmen until he invaded Russia. He entered Russia with about four hundred thousand men and left with a mere ten thousand: the rest lay dead amongst the rubble which he created: a few may have deserted for the love of a Russian peasant girl, who knows? **How much good did he do for France? None!** (We have Heroes just like Napoleon!) One can cite other notable examples: all vain Fools! When vanity assumes a decidedly political role we find men like Karl Marx expressing a malicious and ignorant form of the misunderstandings of the human race. Nevertheless our great Institutions of learning (?) pay homage to his malignant form of intransigence in their hiring and educational practices. For one hundred years and longer our Universities have been stacked with Marxist Professors playing the wrong tune on the same string. They have been thought to be progressive and aided in the development of Modernism: *an eccentric and incorrect form of thinking*. As this was occurring Catholicism and Christianity have given way to this unsocial and negative form of thinking, which has led to monstrous consequence; the butchering of the Romanov's for example. *This is because it is not well understood how the human personality functions or is it imagined beforehand what a vain form of ignorant maliciousness can do.* Hiring objectives are generally tied in with the personalities of who are hired and how they relate to the Administers of the educational process. This is not good however seems to be unavoidable, it is what we have had. It is an important part of Reality.

[168] **Many men** and a few women are in this class however are considered Heroes. They are considered heroes by those whom they have helped to mold into a likeness and acceptance for a curious form of thinking. This is a very complex issue however is understandable. The Hero was often a warrior type or now is also as a Politician. The warrior types were considered brave and were generally well protected; *were they brave or just stupid?* The warriors killed their enemies and ran away with the lady. If a lady was involved she may have been a prize or she may have been abused and killed. They regarded sex as something that was owed them by the ladies whom they encountered; sex was often as a reward for their bravery, probably there was not much feeling of love, compassion or respect for the opposite female sex: she was merely a comfortable pit. The movies are full of this type of nonsense. Their passion was most likely driven by lust or a strange form of loneliness. The present Politician uses words and the deeds of men, actually boys, conscripted into service by a corrupt and retrograde form of compulsion: or they may

youthful warriors in a form of *"murder for pay:"* they are servants of the people, so they are told. This makes the role seem honorable which in some few instances may be the truth.

There are different forms of tyranny: political tyranny has the most profound and widespread influence. All Dictators are Tyrants: Stalin, Hitler, Castro and Mao for example were all tyrants one way or another. One might also consider some of the good guys: Wilson, Roosevelt, and Churchill even George Bush. All of these leaders have skeletons in their closets. Even such as these, considered somewhat more gentle have had strange and illusive ways of addressing an issue. This is true because they are victims; they are trapped in a present which they do not completely control and do not fully understand. They do not understand [all] of Reality: and all are somewhat dishonest. There thinking was not all wrong however the effects are generally quite negative on the populations.

Dishonesty has different ways and means of expression and ties in with many other forms of sinful behavior. Dishonesty is sinful and requires that it be supported and kept alive by more and more dishonesty. In a manner, it is the building of an edifice requiring of ever more deceit. *Keep in mind the liar is perhaps the greatest threat to any Nation.* Our World is built on a combination of both truthful understanding and much misunderstanding however is often punctuated by the Lie. *Some lies are deliberate whereas others form from misinformation and misunderstanding of what may, in fact, be truthful.*[169]

All Conspiracies have and promote a manner of false understanding, which expresses the needs of the Conspirators in their unnecessary and unwelcome being. Conspiracies often develop around issues involving economic gain or political control. *Conspirators often work and are developed in collusion with the governments of this world,* which provide the substance and protection for their being and growing. On the face this may appear reasonable and a good idea however, when extended in time it develops into a sinful form of bureaucracy and finally into a form of Totalitarianism: *for a period of time.*

---

be talked into submission. At present in our country, if they return alive rather than in a body bag they are promised a form of education, *compatible with the present understanding of Reality.* Every effort is used to keep them alive so they can continue the mayhem and the killing. One can understand where this is going and no further explanation should be necessary. However we should better know and understand the meaning of the words of George Washington: *"Stay home"!*

[169] **Lies** are an important part of contemporary Mythology, which by itself is or may be a product of wishful thinking or romanticizing over an issue. Mythologies are interesting as stories: they make a good subject for a Novel or some form of fictitious writing. They can be very appealing to ignorance and are an important ingredient in the formation of some personalities: whereabouts can be found various and distinct forms of understanding. Individuals who read the same book several times because of the effect it has on their understanding and emotions are often not well equipped to deal with the reality that they must face: they withdraw. In my judgment, *Novelists and mediocre writers have done near irreparable damage to the Culture and to the Civilization.* Presently the mind space of the collectivity of human beings is being flooded with more bad than good Ideas. This is an important element in directing the Politics of humanity, there will be consequences the kind of which we now can only imagine: clever men understand this. The cartoon and the character have a prominent place in advertising which should be replaced by a more sensitive and mature understanding of graphic imagery.

Conspiracies now encompass a variety of what are termed as disciplines: including history, the social sciences, philosophy and politics to name a few; some others as well. Governments have grown so large and represent so many individuals that it is impossible to contain them within a single imperative. Philosophically they are not consistent nor can they be in a multi-cultural settlement with many thought forms and ideas. The Democratic *"notion"* is that all forms of humanness may be compatible: this is a false and destructive *"notion."* This notion is a basic part of the Bolshevik philosophy, if one can call it that. Thought forms and ideas become competitive and some undermine and confuse the meaning if others. This is impossible to avoid and cannot be corrected without Divine Intervention.

Given thinking as a process it is important to understand that one thought does or may influence another. It is also important to consider the timeliness of a thought. Individuals cannot remember their thoughts beyond a short time frame, they wander and change emphasis. Where and when did the thought originate and for what purpose was it intended? *Conscious thinking is directed toward an objective: the objective may or may not be understood by everyone entertaining the thought.* Also, for billions thinking is transient: thoughts change from moment to moment and are thus quite evasive to contemplate. Add to this that the cells in your body communicate with each other; the communication is hormonal and electronic, and is not definable. This is truly a very real chicken-egg situation. Thinking is an ephemeral endeavor.

Imagine a thought has originated one, two or more thousand years ago. If it is carried forward in time: by now, we are told and understand and believe that everyone knows of it. ***Thoughts*** concerning important matters do sustain. From such thinking we have metaphor and story-telling: which is persistent however may change from one teller to another. Ultimately the origin and reasons are lost to common understanding: nevertheless the thoughts, as such, do persist. This is a factor in all religious thinking. The question arises: is this a truthful thought? *In most instances it is not and never was a certainly truthful thought* however is *"imagined"* to have been so. This functions as a basis for one form of the LIE, ignorance or an unawareness of the truth. In each case the consequence is the same, which is unfortunate however true. For most individuals the daily routine will help to clarify thinking however some confusion is also added: a little bit at a time each and every day.

The United States Constitution is perhaps the best writing on what Government should be however at present our president Barak Obama does not agree. He does not agree because he does not understand the Constitution truthfully; he imagines an understanding. *He wishes to change things to suit his form of misunderstanding.* The Constitution is brief and was written by men who had, in their time, an insightful and decent understanding of humanity. There may have been others with decent inclinations: this we cannot know. It should be continued in its intended form and not changed or altered by various amendments that will destroy its meaning and effectiveness. Our Presidents and the other men, some Senators and Congressmen whom we have elected have not done well in their understanding of the significance of this document. Additionally many individuals in government are hypocrites having hidden motives and desires which they are promoting as part of their job. We cannot be sure of their motives or their goals. Many have allowed pressure groups and their own belief of self-worth, ***"their"*** understanding of what is right, to prevent an honest and truthful understanding. One can imagine their feeling of self-worth is significant in their decision making and does affect their thinking.

Men in the present who think deeply are few in number and their thinking may be overcome by the past contradictory thoughts of many others, many now dead: perhaps they may have been dead for centuries. Critical thinking of the present must also deal with the many forms of thinking that are incorrect or only partially true. It has always been this way however with mass communication it is worse now than ever and will become even worse in the future. We are building a new and more confusing Tower of Babble than we had in the past. The past was filled with demons and dragons: the present has metaphoric creatures, of a different species, formless and faceless entities created in the Hollywood Studios: they are protected by a corrupt Law and by the misunderstanding of the people. In addition we have great concentrations of wealth in just a few places which will, most likely, determine what will happen to the people now living and those living in the future.

Inordinate political and social pressures that, in the past, did not exist confuse issues and create a false understanding with a false sense of what is reality. All of this is part of the contemporary scene. The Idea of a One World Government is a consequence of such blatantly false and irresponsibly incorrect thinking, and must be avoided. The general Tenor of the contemporary scene, in the minds of millions, is seemingly tending toward a Marxist or Socialist form of government: both will benefit the rich more than the poor. In addition, there are the great Corporations (?); they are mostly owned by the already rich who own most of the important stock, they control the Corporations.[170]

The Floating Dollar as a Threat to Property Rights

What follows are to some extent excerpts from an article by Seth Lipsky, Founding Editor of the New York Star. They are adapted from a speech delivered on February 16, 2011 at Hillsdale College National Leadership Seminar in Phoenix, Arizona.

A changing value of the dollar, or any currency, will destroy this or any society.

Generally that change is called inflation. At first in the beginning it feels good for those that benefit from a small increase in the value of their possessions and perhaps in their income. However in time it becomes a fatal flaw in any system so plagued. At first people feel more prosperous because of a small increase in their salary. Such increase will probably be spent on something not truthfully necessary. And because of the nature of the game they will spend a bit more than they can afford in hopes of getting a bit more for a salary in a year or two. *One must understand most people cannot add or subtract, mathematically they are virtually illiterate;*

---

[170] **Some Corporations** may fail however the truthfully inside ones will sustain or morph into something different: the money will be closely guarded and is the best guarantee for success. A particular kind of Stock not common Stock will guard the money; there also exists the somewhat protected international bank accounts. Some corporations are controlled, by what are known as criminal elements; no one knows how many. Criminal elements have gained billions which they invest in various enterprises to increase profits.

given time as an added element those are totally confused by what is happening. They feel rich: of course *this is only a feeling* and has little to do with their reality generally speaking. [171]

The significant wealth is held in just a few places by those with the forty or fifty million dollar yachts. Also consider that the Queen of England has about 60,000 near priceless works of ancient, med-evil and Renaissance art: the forms are as drawings, paintings, suits of armor and books for example. The Rothschild's are said to be, collectively worth about nine trillion dollars: that's a lot of wealth even for a rich man. The Rockefellers collectively own much of the pie as well. Then there are the speculators that turn ideational wealth into real wealth using the stock and futures markets as a means: George Soros for example. Stock markets have become too complex so as to be beyond the understanding of most individuals. Many of the trades of the experts are computer driven based on algorithms and they work well for their beneficiaries. We imagine some of the profits generated this way will find the common man. The millions or billions in commissions will go to those who run the show. Most individuals will require some form of *"expert advice"* for which they will pay a price: generally the average man will pay more for the advice than the advice is worth. The expert makes a tidy profit on every transaction: guaranteed by the Law. *The laws are questionable and are often lost in Time.* Only the Specialists are able to find and make the best deals: they control the prices. Many experts have been found to be thieves as for example George Soros, who, it is alleged made a billion

---

[171] **The basic problem** is that the currency (money) at present is treated as a commodity. Currency should never be treated as a commodity which will change in value from day to day. The value of a currency *must remain stable,* inviolable, never changing up or down. The objects which the currency will purchase will vary in price relative to supply and demand; they will go up and down somewhat however such variations should not be allowed with the specie; in kind or in coin. Silver and gold are not the same as paper money which can be printed in any amount. Printing, in fact, guarantees that eventually the paper will be worth just about nothing. At present, the already wealthy use the fluctuation of money value as a way to generate hundreds of millions of dollars in profit, however their paper money will be worth less every day; this is the same for the poor man.

"Kurt Branham Barton NFL Ponzi-Scheme: Kurt Branham Barton NFL **Ponzi-Scheme**: Triton Financial Founder Faces Sentencing For Fraud. AUSTIN, Texas—The former CEO of a Texas-based investment firm was sentenced to 17 years in prison Friday for a **scheme** that used former NFL players to bilk hundreds of investors out of more than $50 million. Several of his victims watched as . . . Huffingtonpost. com · 11/4/11. He was convicted in August on 39 counts, including more than a dozen each of wire fraud and money laundering. The charges could have carried up to life in prison. Investors including Barton's family and church members thought their money was for real estate deals and business loans. Prosecutors say Barton spent much of the money on himself, using it to pay for such things as a luxury box at University of Texas football games and a $150,000 car. Former NFL quarterback Ty Detmer testified during the trial that he considered Barton a close friend and lost most of his life savings, about $2 million. Other athletes who prosecutors said promoted or invested with Triton were Heisman Trophy winner Earl Campbell, former NFL, quarterback Jeff Blake and NFL kicker David Akers. Akers said he lost more than $3 million. None of the athletes were accused of wrongdoing. The Ponzi scheme bilked more than 300 investors over four years before ending in December 2009, prosecutors said. He was able to raise about $75 million from investors, only about $20 million of The Ponzi scheme bilked more than 300 investors over four years before ending in December 2009, prosecutors said. He was able to raise about $75 million from investors, only about $20 million of it ending in legitimate investments."

from the Bank of England, or Bernard Madoff the great swindler of billions.[172] There are many that are less-notorious as well.

The Idea that one should receive more pay for being employed for a longer period of time is a part of what pushes inflation. The simple minded agree with this notion. This is a cause in part for so much cheap and shoddy junk which we see in the market place. There are virtually no skilled craftsmen except in mechanical industries or from just a few places: they produce the best of the best. We must develop a better understanding of how inflation is driven and what are the ultimate consequences. *If one expects more for the time spent on any job then all will naturally have to pay more for what that job produces,* whatever it might be. In fact this simple understanding should be taught throughout one's formal education.

To demand more for simply being employed for a longer period is what has motivated Labor Unions. The leaders of some unions are often somewhat criminal in their activities. No one will be any better off except those who work for the Union. ***The laborer will be in the same relative position.*** However this is, in part, what makes inflation possible: indeed it then becomes a part of the cause. There should be a top salary for any form of employment and it should not be raised as an incentive merely for time spent; *the top wage should never be raised.* All this talk about merit increases and cost of living increases is simply part of a misunderstood totality; such thinking will destroy nearly all working men and women. *Simply stated the Union hype is* **Bull Shit!** It rewards organizers and their hangers on for all the wrong reasons. Given this consideration employment should be hierarchical and remain as such indefinitely. If one wishes to have more money they should learn a skill, find a different job, or develop their mind to a more competent level, thus to provide for their intention. This, of course, would require effort and time and with so many meaningless things to do most do not even consider this as a possibility. The really wealthy hire help and need not consider this. They might be sold a watered down program from one of our institutions of learning, six to ten weeks, however such programs are often somewhat inferior. Real learning and significant understanding takes a great deal of time. To study any subject completely is a serious and arduous task; learning is no job for someone who is too busy with what he/she imagines they must do.

Some individuals are not worth as much as others and we must be willing to understand this and truthfully what does this mean. *There are various levels of ability and not all are the same.* This is to some extent a negation of the Democratic Principle and must be understood for what it is: keep in mind *Democracy is an idea and like any System has many flaws* and the belief in the equality of all men is one of them; in fact this is a somewhat Bolshevik's notion. This is only true in respect to a Divinity which many have largely abandoned in favor of silly sex and Rock Music; now we have Rap. You can't have it both ways! And: we must live with this: forever. Some individuals might be considered as being "Gold Bricker's" they seek rewards for doing almost nothing. They will work next to a productive person and do less making it necessary for the good and decent man to do more. Right now with modern methods of manufacture most must do very little of anything. Nevertheless they complain endlessly for ***higher and higher wages***. Much of what they have is wasted on what is, in fact, unnecessary. *"A fool and his gold are soon pared".*

172

Democracy asserts all men are created equal however they forget to include "In the eyes of the Lord." This is a more significant omission than one might imagine: There are others as well. Many youngsters spend their youth playing games which one can imagine has become as a social disease: certainly a form of mass-neurosis. Those spend their time kicking, throwing and bouncing a ball and expect to know something from such endeavor. We imagine they learn something about the game from their efforts however it is merely a game. This is a commercially sponsored issue since there is so much money to be made for some individuals so involved. Youngsters know they can make millions as the population watches those kicking, bouncing and throwing a ball. They are physically fit however not always socially or intellectually well adjusted: they are not properly centered given Reality as it is. To pay a man millions-per season for standing in left field or at first or second base is outrageous when others with functional abilities cannot even find employment. The residuals are outrageous and the system has a foulness that is imposed by *"the inept and curious having fun".* Individuals will spend fifty or a hundred bucks, some will spend thousands for a box seat, to watch a meaningless game: the excitement is profound and the noise is deafening. The movement, noise and cost make the event seem important and everyone has got to participate so to be with it and to be modern! All of this should find a more legitimate place in the scheme of things allowing for the development of the mind and a better understanding of the truthful nature of Reality.

Many adults, seemingly educated, are suffering from delusions laid upon them by a System which is out of control. There are too many worthless degrees where about the individuals spend a lifetime wondering what happened to those so programmed. The nature and reasons for thinking have been and are being confused for the millions of pretenders. The pretense is all about us; however no one seems to notice and only a few are wise enough to see the effect of acts on subsequent consequence.

And the athletes all muscle and not too many with brains must see what they are doing to the System: if they could see. This would not change anything with each man for him-self. Whoever could have imagined a golfer with a few clubs and a bit of skill could amass a hundred million plus fortune for hitting a golf ball? The Corporations that pay outrageous sums, a million dollars a minute for advertising on Television, would be better advised to make a better product *(in the United States)* and lower the price for the average consumer. Make the boxes smaller so to reduce shipping costs. Stop the bold promises that every year brings a remarkably new product. The best products remain nearly the same from decade to decade. All of this could not happen if the consumer were just a bit more alert.

The floating dollar suffers under this pretense making some believe that they are superior whilst *others maintain life from stealing or finding edible garbage.* When one gains millions because he is a thief that is no sign of prosperity rather it is a sign of decadence and a degenerate existence. All this occurs as millions are spent on ways of killing one another including women and children, the old, the sick and the lame.[173] After the episode of Sin and Shame, *they call it war,* everyone complains of the butchered participants. And everyone seems so interested in

---

[173] *Children are often chosen* for what adults know will kill them in their efforts. They are baited with promises of Heaven which they cannot and do not understand. The real cowards choose the children because they have not the understanding or the guts to do what the adult imagines might or will be fatal.

the children. The men so called who are killed are generally not much beyond childhood. A few older men are slaughtered as well: why must this be? Then follow the rebuilders who make fortunes _rebuilding and cheating_ who they are working for. This is what the pretenders, the miscreants, who sit at the top imagine is good for humanity. _The System is deformed by a cadre of cheaters and liars_ who are sucking blood from their brother.

A changing value of the dollar, or any currency, will destroy this or any society.
Our dollar is now worth about $.02 to $.05 from what it was worth in 1940.
A $15,000.00 house is now $200,000.00 (same house 75 years old).
There has been improvement in the quality of some things.
A $2,000.00 to $3,000.00 car is now $30,000 and more.
A $.05 cup of coffee is now $1.75 to $.3.00.

This happened while our Politicians insist there is no inflation.

And the Chairmen of the Federal Reserve have all insisted there is no inflation.
Make your own list!
You can prove you are smarter than the Chairmen of the Federal Reserve!

———∾∾∘⌇∘⌇∘∾∾———

Professor Emeritus: Robert Fiedler
January 18, 2013
February 28, 2013

CHAPTER VIII

THE PHENOMENOLOGY OF EXISTENCE; PART II

Those that imagine they are saving the World for the good people, at present they are called Politicians, appear to be the cause of most of the problems. They have been and are somewhat the Warrior Types: aggressive and insensitive to the fact that *"All men are created equal: in the eyes of an omnipotent God."*[174] The warrior types are` often vain and malicious and do not see the various connections between all of Humanity.[175] They may wear a pin striped suit or decorate their bodies as a Savage; however their effect on humanity is probably more often bad than good. They often seek personal wealth and riches for them *(they are selfish: a Sin)* and hope to be remembered for their seemingly heroic activities *(they are vain: a Sin).*[176] One can imagine, in fact that they are, although perhaps unknowingly, simple mined men of the most mundane and common type. Many are, one could say, profoundly stupid however they often, not always, gain much for themselves for a brief time: in this life. They fail to understand the meaning of *"In the end we are all dead."* They do not contemplate that they too will soon be dead: *forever.* With a complex of religious and irreligious thinking combined together with the snide activities of those who hope to rule mankind, working to destroy what is good and what is Christian, we encounter very difficult circumstances. There exist in contrast ideas that are known to be destructive partially or completely nevertheless they are encouraged by the Ideas of the money grubbers and others, many deceased: Marxist, Stalinist, Socialists and all forms of the reactionary ignorant attempting to destroy the Civilization created by Christianity. They imagine that they can create a better World however they do not even understand this one.

---

[174] **No one is certain** of what this means, nevertheless it is an important point to contemplate while one is living.

[175] **If one would trace** back for thirty generation they would find almost all people related genetically.

[176] **Selfishness and Vanity** are, in the Catholic and some other faiths, both considered *mortal Sins.* Mortal Sin is not considered as it should be which has become a significant problem in the Public Schools. Mortal Sin is damning and can be very destructive including rape, beating and ultimately murder. An over-emphasis on a concept of the value of the self adds to the problem whereabouts an over emphasis on self-worth most generally leads to aggressive behavior. The prisons and the ghettos are full of this type of aggressive individual. In the past people did believe that Mortal Sin would prevent one from being admitted to Heaven and people were taught not to commit such Sin. Heaven, as an Idea is overlooked in favor of what is more mundane and perhaps trendy. Presently thinking of Heaven is considered by many to be prudish and not honest and open. That there is a Heaven may or not be the truth however the effects were generally positive. No one knows for certain what will happen after death however the Idea of Heaven is compelling. *Heaven is a reward and must be earned heaven is not a Democratic right.*

Forever is a long time: forever is all Time beyond now.
Forever also includes all past-Time.

Man's inventions, although some are very good, will ultimately lead to his destruction. <u>*Men generally do not understand what they have done*</u> and they are uncertain or ambiguous in how to use their implementations: meaning their inventions do not always serve them as well, as they should. There is no question that man, collectively speaking, is intelligent and capable of many wonderful, achievements however generally speaking *"he is not wise"* in the use and application of what he has.[177] Additionally men are not able to communicate well with others because of language, habit and custom. There are head-hunters that see the head of another as a prize for their own bravery. This is a somewhat metaphorical understanding which is based on a complete misconception and misunderstanding of the *"other form,"* (other than the self might be) of human being which in such instance one, holding a contrary point of view will become defensive and unyielding. This is understandable however difficult to correct. In the past cannibals would enjoy, if one can imagine, eating an enemy at a feast to celebrate an *"imagined"* victory. Today we have different rewards however the Ideas that promote the "feelings" and understandings are similar. Most all "Ideas" are related to what has happened in the past: true invention is very rare.

The word "imagined" is used frequently in this writing because much of what is done is done because of one's imagination and has nothing to do with the truth as Reality provides. Reality exists as exemplifying the truth: whatever exists, what has happened is as a form of Truth, one way or the other. Every single act adds to the totality as part of what is Truth. When individuals correspond, using one form or another of communication, they do not always get all the important details, innuendo or context correct and they are not aware of what is the proper order. Sometimes to forget the details is an important element in the governing process.[178] In addition an individual will sometimes use deliberate distortion of fact; *they "Lie"* to achieve a personal goal. Many individuals are opportunists: they seek personal advantage from any and every effort expended. They do not mind cheating another and will try to do so if they *"imagine"* they will not be caught. They will do or say what they believe is in their best interest to do or say. In contrast some individuals are absolutely truthful or this is what they attempt to be; this is to be respected. <u>*This is not so complex, as one can pretend it to be.*</u> Much of present dialogue is overly wordy with much of what is true being missed in spite of this: additionally those who pretend

---

[177] **He** (as mankind) has allowed a certain number of somewhat alien individuals to control his Politicians which [He], in fact, imagines are governing the country. Beside this, the Politicians generally speaking have all of the faults and only some of the good qualities of anyone. Add to this that many of our Politicians it would seem appear to be, simply stated, TRAITORS: they are working for other Ideals which are contrary to those upon which the US was built. Add to this the personal sins of the men in politics and you begin to understand the problems. This is to be expected since the scope and rapidity of unfolding events cannot be known *"exactly"* to any one man. Various *"specialists"* are appointed to oversee what is actually happening. *Space being what it* is one cannot be in more than one place at any given time. If the specialist is somewhat of a hypocrite, knowingly or unknowingly, the matter is confused between the parties.

[178] **We have Laws** that defend a fifty year moratorium on some of the happenings in politics, thus this can be considered as quite important.

to lead do not always use words well. There are many clichés and certain *"space determined"*[179] uses of language that add to confusion. Youth are not being taught the correct and proper use of words which is fundamental to communication and subsequent understanding. Also there is too much meaningless group activity in the schools with *much too little of significant learning:* significant learning is somehow made to seem boring by our present poorly understood methods of teaching and the distractions exerted by what is unnecessary and probably unwise. Learning is a difficult consideration when so much falsehood is perpetrated by others whom we do not know.

Consider what is written in this presentation. The French Revolution is still largely misunderstood by most individuals. Even though we have had over two hundred years to figure out the details of what happened they, meaning the common men, do not understand what really occurred or why it did occur. They do not understand because they were given mostly false information. Also, this is largely true because most are not interested in the French Revolution! However our present time is largely a product of what happened at that time. Each period in History is a *"product of the past"* more or less and projects into the future. Recent history has been dominated by War, Finance and Politics of a perverted nature. War and Finance are in close association and Politics, of a perverted nature is imagined to be in control. In fact money is the ruler with the Politician beholden to that same money: *even without truthful understanding of what the money is and what the money must do to sustain the Civilization.* Beside this many are convinced there is no relationship between Politics and Religion when in fact as a matter of truth **Politics** and **Religion** are as one. Whatever is Political has Religious elements especially concerning **Greed** and **Lying** both of which are Sins: Sin is a religious issue politics is concerned only with some of the subject matter.[180] The religious issues are too difficult to consider so they have been eliminated; this is a fatal flaw in our system.

---

[179] **By space determined** we mean different linguistic forms, colloquialisms and Idea specific uses, to name a few.

In the book *The Empire of the City* there are considered *"five Ideologies of Space and power."* The five considered are 1. "One-World." 2. "Pan-Slavic." 3. "Asia, for the Asians." 4. "Pan-Germanism" and finally; 5, "Pan-American Isolationist." At the time the book *The Empire of the City* was written these five seemed prominent. At present there are others known and unknown. The essence of the five Ideologies of Space and Power are where one is, in a geographic sense, what is the Time or period and how does one or many think.

As the technologies involved in communication are perfected the number of space determined elements is increased. With Television and other forms in a few seconds one can observe what is happening anywhere in the World where the technologies are in place. If one is not made immediately aware there are ways of storing and transporting information for viewing at a later time. The information can also be altered so to change the meaning depending on the intent of who is in charge of such information. This fact is cause for many world problems.

[180] **The Seven Deadly Sins; Anger** (Enraged; Wrathful, Irate, Indignant, Feeling or Showing Anger). **Envy** (Grudging Desire for Another's Advantage or Excellence). **Gluttony** (One who Eats, Drinks, or Indulges to Outrageous Excess). **Greed** (Selfish or Acquisitive Desir, beyond Reason). **Pride** (Haughty Behavior, Ostentatious Display, Excessive Elation, in Your Success. **Sloth** (Laziness or Indolence [Insensitive to Pain or Slow to Heal]). **Lust** (Sexual Desire of an Intense Longing, to an Unrestrained, Sharp Degree).

Money as currency must have an ***unchanging value*** against which all else is and has been honestly determined. This fact which is implicit in the creation and use of money will control any situation: to ignore this will be fatal to the segment of humanity that does not understand this. Inflation can be promoted for long periods of time. Honest determination is a matter of truthful history and comes from the past. At present money is as a commodity which fluctuates in value and provides for speculation and usurpation: the thieves take full advantage of this believing they are smart. *In fact they are fools: money as currency is devalued by inflation ultimately it will become worthless.* Inflation is the most significant element in our present milieu. Many of today's prominent billionaires exist because of two flaws in the System. The *first* is the fluctuation in the value of our Currencies; the *second* is the ability to convert imagined wealth into real and tangible wealth:[181] the means for this is at present one functional use of the currency.[182] This should be easy to understand however those with the power to make this known, work and promote their actions in favor of the present unworkable misunderstood and decadent System. There are some inventors that have developed an idea which turns out to be very profitable, they make millions even billions: they are not the problem if they are honest. We *"imagine or believe"* many or perhaps most are honest. Keep in mind *"excessive wealth"* has been named by former Pope Benedict XVI to be the eighth deadly sin.

Internationalism as a political understanding is imagined, by those with the great wealth, to provide the means to sustain what is often *absolutely criminal and most certainly sinful.*[183] It will be as the Devil's assistant, Satan's handmaiden and will impoverish the world: this is presently

---

Excessive Wealth [in March, 2008, Pope Benedict XVI added the 8th Deadly Sin of 'Excessive Wealth' to the list of Deadly Sins.]

[181] **This conversion** is one of the main functions of the present stock markets. To prevent this, short-selling should be abandoned: it should be made illegal to short-sell. This manner of subterfuge is somewhat irrational and must not continue. It must be better understood for the damage that it does to the system and to the millions that are robbed because of short selling. The Specialists who set the price periodically will issue a reverse-split of any number that they assume will make money for the Specialist. If you own one million shares of a penny stock for example such split at 300 to 1 will leave you with only 33333.3 far fewer than the one million which you had purchased (1,000,000). This is a clever "trick" that every small investor faces. *(See writings of Richard Nay).*

[182] **This works especially well** for the Specialist, an individual that spends his time watching the fluctuation in prices. The slang term *"buy low and sell high"* here comes into play. This is even better when you are in a position to set the price. One can easily understand where this is going: right into the bank account of who are the most-wealthy already.

[183] **A One-World Order** was Cecil Rhodes dream for a World of peace and tranquility, "ruled by a benevolent despotic intelligentsia and so to create peace for all eternity." (*Knuth, The Empire of the City*). *Cecil* Rhodes had a fertile *"imagination"* and had stolen so much he imagined his was a form of serious and profound being: he was neither. Cecil Rhodes is dead however his Ideas are, in one or another living being, alive and well in one form or another. Different groups of people have forged such Ideas into different political forms which must be better understood and intelligently considered. History has been and is still advancing one moment at a time. It is becoming more difficult to control the outcome of a moment. The truthfully wealthy imagine they can control Destiny with money; the present advance in the price of gold is an ominous sign that this not happen.

being accomplished at this written. At least one third of the World's Population is already impoverished, millions are starving. The most significant wealth from their Nations is under the ownership of giant multinational Corporations: Rio Tinto and British Petroleum for example or Exxon. A few Natives will work for the Corporation however the wealth goes to the United States or Europe. There are a few other players: China, Japan, the Middle Eastern countries and Russia. The truly elite from such places have the thirty, forty or fifty million dollar yachts. Interestingly many of the men, who own the yachts, are _despicable bastards_ that will pay some whore a fortune for fornication and for other sexual favors. Lust is a deadly sin. The women who oblige them are no better than they are: such women are the worst of womanhood, they are _unmitigated prostitutes_. Our Television interviews some prostitute types who are given to appear as Celebrities by the sophisticated presentation. At the present time great emphasis is placed on the size of one's breasts. Some women have opted to have operations and injections so to make the breasts absolutely grotesque; they do this so to be able to perform in adult presentations of sex and obscenity. No thinking adult would want to see any of their presentations.

This is a serious dilemma. How might one address such problem? It is nearly impossible. Never the less such as this will be settled by death: death takes every Human Being: sooner or later. It matters not at all how much you may have paid for your yacht or how many whores you have pricked: it matters not at all that your breasts may have been large or small; Death is a certainty.

The Civil War and the Rothschild fortune was and continues to be two situations of sinful, over exuberant and unnecessary behavior: with the slaughter of tens of thousands of innocent youth: all this so some could amass a fortune. The War was fought because of misunderstood reasoning. **Why?** The Rothschild fortune at the time of the Civil War is _"imagined"_ to have been at about one billion dollars, $1,000,000,000.00: and growing. That was the beginning of their well established fortune now estimated by some to be about $9,000,000,000,000.00 that is nine trillion dollars. This is an increase of 9,000 times. In 1850 $30.00 a month was a good salary; never the less we are told over and over that there has been no inflation. If one calculates that number in terms of percent the Rothschild fortune has increased 900,000%. Divide that by years and you will have an increase of 5062.5% per year. This number will grow as time passes and time will certainly pass. Put another way the increase in their wealth is about $44,000,000,000.00 44 billion per year: 44 times the original $1,000,000,000.00. This illustrates the effects of inflation and compounding interest on a very large, sum. How much is a billion? Very few individuals can even begin to consider that as a number.[184] This money is not all in one

---

[184] **A.** "A billion seconds ago it was 1959. **B.** A billion minutes ago Jesus was alive. **C.** A billion hours ago our ancestors were living in the Stone Age. **D.** A billion days ago no one walked on the earth on two feet. **E.** A billion dollars ago (by present Time) was only eight hours and twenty minutes, at the rate our government is spending it". With these numbers in mind: let's take a look at New Orleans . . . it' amazing what you can learn from a bit of simple division. Louisiana Senator, Mary Landrieu, a Democrat, is asking Congress for 250 billion Dollars, to rebuild New Orleans: an interesting number what does it mean? *A.* If you are a resident one of 484,674 of New Orleans, every man, woman and child will each get $516,528.00 dollars. Not too bad! *B.* If you have one of the 188,251 Homes in New Orleans, you will get $1,329,787.00 dollars *C.* Or if you are a family of four your family will get $2,066,012.00 dollars. This is why the country is broke! Simply stated our Politicians are just plain **_STUPID! The Rothschild Dynasty,_**

place: there are many affiliates and others involved in this takeover of the Civilization. This is a somewhat difficult number to contemplate but we must learn to understand what this means.

Such wealth is not concentrated in a single person however, is a basis for a consortium, which ultimately will have and control everything. Inflation provides a temporary cover while the figures are advancing. *In the West we are witnessing this advance right now.* Information such as is above suggested should be given to every human being as a part of their education. However it is not provided because such information is *"imagined"* by the controllers to be beyond the minds of the plebeians. The problem is most youth as well as their teachers are not able to comprehend such numbers and *to figure out what such numbers mean.* This affords protection for the usurpers. We have many teachers that cannot do simple math: they would find the issue being discussed as being for others to consider. *What others?* Those that designed the system: no doubt! The System was not designed by knowing individuals rather it happened one small imperceptible issue at a time: it is an important part of human *"Destiny"*. Those working the System made slight adjustments to better their own circumstances and "Presto" we now have what we have; a monstrosity.

Who has captured ownership of the great cities since the Civil War? How have they done this? Can we allow this to continue? Unfortunately I don't believe there is anything that anyone can do to prevent it. What has been done and how it has been done places impediments that economic considerations will prevent from being corrected. We must allow History to unfold one event at a time: we call upon Destiny to help us in our endeavor of correcting what is in fact *"Absolute Evil"*. *Ultimately there will be an Apocalypse as suggested in the prophetic writings of wise men.* In the end we are all dead so it will not matter: Right now planners are again considering a collective or socialist approach. Such approach will not and has never worked. In spite of our intelligence and inventive nature every single man and woman is limited by time and will soon be gone. This is the reality of every Epoch! We will not live as corporeal humans forever.

Consider Slavery: Slavery was wrong and was Sinful, like most things that are wrong and sinful the reasons were economic. At the time Slavery produced profits for the slave owners and land owners and growers of cotton. Slavery would have succumbed to invention of the various mechanical implements that followed in due time: all this could/would have happened without a War. However no one should be kept as a slave. There were other important political and monetary Issues that were involved as well.[185] It matters not at all what the Issues might have been they are in the past: they are History. Nevertheless they were *"imagined"* as being important at the time. There was certainly some lying and distortion of fact in favor of the liars and profiteers: History is filled with such nonsense however it has been effective and is responsible for the killings, in the last two hundred fifty years of tens of millions, one can

---

it is a Dynasty, is said to be worth $9,000,000,000,000.00 dollars. That's trillion: and that number would take you back millions of years: figure it out, use what is given here to do that!

[185] **England** was attempting to recapture the United States. The Bank of England once dominated the Western World and what ever happened there: at the time of the Civil War their influences was no longer as prominent. However, even today our Federal Reserve System is owned in large measure by affiliates of the Bank of England.

"imagine" at least two hundred million, most of them were innocent including women and children. One wonders what the World would be like if there had been no Wars.

The general population was given *"Gone with the Wind"* an epic and timely story formed by the *"imagination"* of a clever writer. It is judged as a good movie which perhaps it is. There was much technical advancement in the form of the Art (so called). The Art was diversionary and in some ways interesting. *Who can ever forget Scarlet O'Hara or Rhett Butler?* "Frankly I don't give a damn," Was Rhett Butlers comment to Scarlet. Hollywood imagery and the thinking that is attendant thereto are dominant forces in our present time frame. Much of our *"present Psychic Space"* is consumed by Hollywood home to the wealthy and famous. Stars are born there. I would certainly question the reasons, acts and future consequences of such as Hollywood.

Hollywood is a good example of a form of contrived and sophisticated commercial decadence: Hollywood presents thought content and thinking that is dangerous to our Culture and to Civilization in general and it is becoming worse. Hollywood is showing more crotches and nipples than ever before: there is just about no restraint. Those who produce many of the shows seem to be perverted in their understanding of sex. *"Imagine"* the misinformation given to youth by the great films. The young men are handsome and the ladies are beautiful however as people they are exploited and used by others for profit: again we see **Economics** as primary. Interestingly many of the Stars (so called) are from broken homes.[186] The money wealth of some is imagined to make things better than they are. Many Hollywood Icons never had a real soul-mate and companion. Some depend on alcohol, or narcotics to make it through the day. Judy Garland was victimized some time before Whitney Houston.[187] Right now Whitney Houston is praised as presumably being a Saint which shows the degree of misunderstanding present right now. Whitney Houston (died 2012 of an overdose) is one of the latest victims of over indulgence and a strange understanding of God's immutable principles.

Presently men are re-enacting battles fought during our great Civil War. One wonders why? It is a rather overly involved way to learn History. There are certainly friendships that may develop however it is a distraction from life at this time. Those so involved, I am guessing, get

---

[186] **Apparently acting** as being someone else provides a major good that they derive from their effort. Perhaps this has a deep seated root in their lives which influenced their choice. To consider the question further we find many have had numerous husbands and wives, four or five or six and more, a mixed bag of children and innumerable lovers (so called) in between. Albeit, we understand many of such type spend the last years of their lives without a mate a lover or even a decent and caring friend. Certainly there are some exceptions which we respect for their integrity.

[187] **Judy Garland** was a victim of *"Now-time"* that being her time of life; there are many others like her. "Despite professional triumphs, Garland struggled immensely in her personal life. Her self-image was strongly influenced by film executives, who constantly manipulated her on screen physical appearance. She was plagued by financial instability, often owing hundreds of thousands of dollars in back-taxes; she married five times, her first four marriages ended in divorce. She had a long battle with drugs and alcohol, which ultimately led to her death at the age of 47. In 1997, Garland was posthumously awarded a Grammy Lifetime Achievement Award. Several, of her recordings have been inducted into the Grammy Hall of Fame."

all the details right; however they seem to miss the point given by the reality of War as an event. Many have probably been in some service already and they will be proud if their son, even their daughter, goes off to fight and kill another man's children. *Keep in mind it is the future that is being killed. Who understands this?* One wonders how the imagination of someone else articulates with the reality of the present in regard to such unnecessary and destructive conflict. Consider the photograph depicting the artillery piece and four men which is provided in this work. I believe the facial attitude of the man on the left (fig. 1) and the man second from the right tells a great deal about this conflict which was archaic, belligerent and senseless. If you are interested, you can learn some of the details from the many books written on the subject of the Civil War. However, you must be truthfully interested.[188]

Following is a brief history of some of the wars. **The Spanish American War;** Theodore Roosevelt advocated intervention in Cuba: this was typical: imagined as being good for the Cuban people and to promote the Monroe Doctrine. While assistant Secretary of the Navy, he placed the Navy on a wartime footing and prepared Dewey's Asiatic Squadron for battle. *"Imagine"* how proud he must have been preparing a squadron for battle; this even sounds somewhat dramatic, before the killing starts. He worked with Leonard Wood in convincing the Army to raise an all-volunteer regiment, the 1st U.S. Voluntary Cavalry. Wood was given command of the regiment that quickly became known as the "Rough Riders". This is a romantic sounding name probably coined to gain support for the senseless War.

The Americans planned to capture the city of Santiago de Cuba to destroy Linares' army and Cervera's fleet. To reach Santiago they had to pass through concentrated Spanish defenses in the San Juan Hills and a small town in El Caney. The American forces were aided in Cuba by there-independence rebels led by General Calixto Garcia.

From 22-24 June, the U.Ss V Corps under General William R. Shafter landed at Daiquiri and Siboney, east of Santiago, and established an American base of operations. A contingent of Spanish Troops, having fought a skirmish with the Americans near Siboney on 23 June, had retired to their lightly entrenched positions at Las Guasimas. An advance guard of U.S. forces under former Confederate General Joseph Wheeler ignored Cuban scouting parties and orders to proceed with caution. They caught up with and engaged the Spanish rearguard commanded of about 2000 soldiers led by General Antonio Rubin who effectively ambushed them, in the battle of Las Guasimas on 24 June. The battle ended indecisively in favor of Spain and the Spanish left as Guasimas on their planned retreat to Santiago.

The photo in this work (page, 152) is of a Battle Cruiser, typical of the time. Like the men with the cannon during the Civil War the sailors on board that ship: *"imagined"* they were near invincible. They were not. The ship was destroyed on July 3, 1898; *So much for being invincible.* Most all military hardware is useless for anything but killing and it soon becomes obsolete when new inventions are brought forward. All of this nonsense is extremely expensive it accomplishes very little. At the present time there are acres of abandoned airplanes and tanks and trucks all paid for with the sweat of some good man's brow? All wasted for the purpose of killing the, generally speaking, decent people, with whom some might disagree. Certainly there is some

---

[188] **See Photograph 2** "The American Civil War".

value in the materials that can be salvaged however this is nothing compared to the cost in life and treasure. The costs are figured as a percentage of a contrived national accounting statement.

The murder of the Romanoff's and the Czars family was an incomprehensible blunder. The men who planned and did this are the worst form that humanness might ever take. One of such men was a German born American Jacob Schiff who it is believed may have provided $20,000,000.00 toward the accomplishment of that effort.[189] Furthermore he was *"imagined"* to be civilized and decent: both wrong, he was only partly civilized and certainly indecent. Schiff was the golden boy of New York and Wall Street; a real insider. After the War he made profitable investments in the Soviet Union *which was against the law of the United States:* so much for the law. The other executioners were despicable cowards and maliciously ignorant flunkies. *Lenin was an unmitigated Bastard:* he was cruel and ruthless and aided in the destruction of all that had been and was good in Russia. The murder of the Czar and his family was followed by the theft of the hundreds of millions of rubles and gold and the various bank deposits of the Russian Monarchy. How could all of this wealth disappear? Who claimed it?" Also stolen was the one hundred forty thousand acres of land owned by the Czar. ***Did this land simply disappear?***

Russia, one hundred years later, has still not recovered from the tragedy. For cleverness and as part of a plan for world domination, that act of barbarism is unequalled in World History. We read today in our controlled press that at present much of Russian commerce is controlled by organized criminals. This may or may not be true however it is *"imagined"* as being true. Interestingly many of who participated in the revolution, a number in the mid four hundreds, came from New York: to which some had immigrated so to become American citizens.

In opposition to the organized crime which we *"imagine"* does exist there is much talk of consecrating Russia to the Virgin Mary thus to bring Russia back to the Christian fold. This may or may not happen very soon; we must wait and see. We won't hear much about this in our

---

[189] **Jacob Schiff was born in 1847** in Frankfurt am Main, Germany, to Moses and Clara (née Niederhofheim) Schiff, members of a distinguished Ashkenazi Jewish rabbinical family that traced its lineage in Frankfurt back to 1370. Schiff was educated in the schools of Frankfurt and was first employed in the banking and brokerage business as an apprentice in 1861. After the U.S. Civil War had ended in April, 1865, Schiff came to the United States, arriving in New York City on August 6, 1865. He was licensed as a broker on Nov. 21, 1866, and joined the firm of Budge, Schiff & Co. in 1867. He became a naturalized citizen of the United States in Sept. 1870

It must be understood that there was a struggle between the Ashkenazi Jewish and the Russian Christian peoples over religious issues: some other issues as well. The antagonisms go back for Centuries and are not well known by many people in the United States. *(See Internet, Arthur Koestler, the Thirteenth Tribe).* There were many strange happenings. The reader will have to inform himself from what is available on the subject. One can *"imagine"* that killing the Czar and his family had some symbolic effect thus to even an *"imagined"* score. This is a very complex issue which deals with an ancient epoch in time and many forms of behavior. The Jews were seen by many as enemies and thus were treated as such which may be understandable for various reasons. Some forms of hatred have their origins in the distant past however are kept alive for various reasons: political and religious. However with the control and reporting of news primarily in Jewish hands it is understandable that there would be some preference to the Jewish side of any argument. How might one obtain a real understanding of the truth?

carefully controlled press. What would this mean in reference to the mundane political, social and economic factors involved? The Russian people have for long had a religion however the rulers, generally speaking, control the wealth and the rulers plan and promote conflict for one or another reason: if they have no reason they will invent one. *Youth, barely adults are drafted into service to fight each other so to support the Establishment's programs.* This is clever however not wise. Many of today's youth, theirs and ours are trained to kill an imagined enemy.

One wonders how so great a crime, to overcome Russia for a time, was pulled off and who, in fact, benefited most from it. We know however it is difficult to prove. There are many speculations however the whole truth will never be known. All of the players are now dead. However their progeny and followers have the advantage of tremendous wealth: beyond the imagination of the most astute observers. This is true because of the scale of the World and the millions of people that inhabit it. Why should not such criminal activity be punished? Such activity will continue corrupting the present and is a threat to the future of all good men.

War is the reason, so many are distracted from the Reality that surrounds them. There are other distractions as well the most obvious being entertainment, athletics and more recently Sex. Youth aspire to have the outrageous income of an entertainer or an athlete that makes millions on **pretense** and simple **body movements.**[190] There is too much emphasis placed on making it financially. Too little emphasis is placed on decency and simply being good. A Great War requires the participation of millions of individuals, thousands of tons of supplies and many forms of outrageous preparations. The inventions are astounding and mostly unnecessary except to fight the War. When the War is on the other side of the Planet it requires extraordinary group-effort just to get to where the fighting is. After the War one is expected to rebuild and reconstruct what has been destroyed the day or year or century before. This is good for business: or is it? What shall we do with all the bodies that are piled around the places of the engagement?

For the Romanoff's special considerations were observed: this was necessary to escape detection. The bodies were not treated well: *certainly not like nobility.* They were dismembered, cut up, one might say butchered, thereafter burned with acid and fire and finally buried in a mine shaft under the floor-boards. It was *"imagined"* that they would not be discovered too soon.[191] The evil men that did this did not live very long after the fact however they had done their dirty work and they were expendable. They were dupes, morons and certainly they were very cruel.

---

[190] **Millions of viewers** flock to the various events, contrived to make money for the promoters. Certainly some events do fail however most are successful some monumentally so. The ability that some have to make or to steal money has created a new class of aristocracy; such has replaced the persons of more legitimate nobility. Presently the wealth of the Super-rich is astounding: hundreds of millions can be made by a lucky few. There is really no solution for this except humility, temperance and prudence on the part of the players. One cannot force another to be good however each should retain a fair amount of dignity in respect to the accumulation of wealth.

[191] **Wilton, Robert,** *Last of the Romanovs, How Tsar Nicholas II and Russia's Imperial Family were Murdered.* Copyright © 1993, the Institute for Historical Review **(See photos in the book between pages 95 and 96)**. First British Edition; pub. 1920 in London by T. Butterworth. First U. S. Edition published 1920, in New York by George H. Dorn. French Edition, pub. Paris 1921. Russian language edition; pub. Berlin 1923. ISBN # 0-939484-1.

During the First World War millions of Russian Christians were killed most of whom were innocent of any maliciousness, indecency or transgression. Currently they might be considered, by such as our leaders to be collateral damage; (remember the comment by Madeleine Albright). As devout Christians they were hated by some others. Notable amongst the others there were the converted Jews, Ashkenazi Jews Asians that were descendents of the tribe of Bulan who had his people convert to Judaism in the 7th Century. *This has created some hatred for Jews in general which is certainly wrong.* However some individuals search for ways to justify their hatred for another: **this is the working of the Devil.** The Devil was also motivational in the murder and butchering of the Romanoff's. The killing of an innocent family is difficult to understand. However one cannot discount the *"Idea"* of a Devil. Keep in mind the idea cannot be dismissed: even though we are not certain, of whom the Devil influences and of how such influence will manifest. **The Devil; exists in Cyberspace as an Idea.**

Nevertheless there are Opportunists that enable some to benefit from every form of evil endeavor and they do. In the instance of the Romanoff's history was on the side of the Opportunists who were able to move in and take over the wealth and workings of the greatest Christian nation on earth. The fact that the Opportunists were not Christian is something to consider. One might consider discrimination as we pretend to do in America: to do so is good for Politics. We have, in this instance, contrary religious beliefs which intervene and make understanding for the average man nearly impossible.[192] The average man has no comprehension of the nature and scope of this dilemma however, it has to do with one's belief in God and what is immortality: and what is the meaning of death. The Catholic (Universal) Christian notion is that one should love his brother; to make this more effective one should love most he who hates him. The conflict has been ongoing and will not cease to be. It is the basis for *"Philosophy, Eschatology and Religious Thought"* (other thought forms as well) which emanates from the deep recesses of the inner-self and is an often unknown however certain form in the way of human being. At the present time there is some effort to better understand what is happening however even in such instances there may be unknown motivations and misunderstood reasoning *"all imagined"* which encourage specious acts.

In Time, clever men have been able to manipulate this understanding to their own advantage. For example given the compounding function of currency wealth, with interest applied to the principle, a long period of time will produce what are *"imagined"* as profits. At the present time what is imagined is no longer a metaphor: It is a primary influence within our Civilization and is an *Economic Reality.* Lyndon La Rouche talks about bankrupting Wall Street; this might be

---

[192]   **This is one examples** of a prime reason why some insist that Religion is the cause of so much trouble. In some few instances this may be true. In addition there have been strong antagonisms within the various Christian Religions. A most extraordinary example is the action of King Henry VIII in his absolutely defiant refusal to accept the Doctrines of the Church. Such defections including Martin Luther and others are advanced by the unknowing as they attempt to discredit Christianity: especially so with Catholicism which has been the basis for the Western Christian Civilization. Catholicism, which is the Universal Faith, is believed to be Godly inspired (?): **Do you believe this?** There are indeed strange forms of Occultism in some Religions. However Catholic Christianity (meaning universal, from the Greek) is not such Religion: Christianity augers for goodness and the virtues, for the abolishment of sin and for a life of Holiness, all of which, are good and can have only positive consequence.

a good idea. Given the present System in time all the wealth of the world will be in the hands of only a few. The transposition is occurring as this is written. This is what modern warfare is about and the plan, if there is a plan, seems to be working. Who were the planners? *The Bank of England* is a most powerful source behind this venture and is a complex entity residing within the City of London.[193] And *Wall Street* with the imaginary and questionable transactions is an important part. Lastly there is the greed of the general population which is very much misunderstood.

The Romanoff's are gone, although they did rule Russia for nearly 300 years (1650-1917) such Monarchy has come to an end: *for now.* Before the Romanoff's for nearly 500 years were the Rurik's (1157-1598). *These two families formed the legitimate Monarchy.* They were real Nobility! Whether this was good or bad we cannot know for certain. However it certainly never erupted into the kind of slaughter that has been apparent in the two World Wars. The art and Architecture in pre-war Russia is nothing less than astounding. Russia, at that time was one of the most exceptional Countries ever to exist. For this reason it may be considered as having been good. Coincidentally however of great importance in 1915 their currency was backed by 125% gold and was thus very valuable: consider this was after 800 years of the Monarchy. With gold at about twenty dollars an ounce that was very good.[194] The poor man's currency was worth a great deal. Compare that to our currency which has declined by about 98% from its original value since 1935: it now requires nearly one thousand dollars ($1,000.00) to acquire what could have been had for twenty dollars ($20.00) until our great Mr. Roosevelt took over.[195] One thousand is one hundred times twenty

---

[193] **"The City,** in what is perhaps the most arbitrary and absolute form of government in the world is an international financial oligarchy. It uses the allegoric "Crown" as its symbol of power and has its headquarters in the ancient City of London, an area of 677 acres; it is not under the jurisdiction of the Metropolitan Police and has its own force of about 2000 men. It has a night population of less than 9000:" *(Interpolation by this author).*

[194] **This alone** says a great deal for having a Monarchy in which the Monarchs are, generally speaking, honest and where Honesty is better understood. Democracy is destined to fail. When an ignorant Dolt has as much influence as a wise man, ignorance will prevail. At present many of our leaders are Dreamers and self serving fools. The only determined leadership is of a Socialist Type which harbors an idea of superiority. Any *"Idea"* is only temporary and must be given up to a known and *functional understanding*: for example such understanding is in the absolute value of a currency as a means of exchange. If this idea were promoted then the rampant speculation would cease the World would function much more to the advantage of the common man.

[195] **Mr. Roosevelt,** it has been alleged, was a Dutch Jew. He must have had some reasons, known or unknown, for doing what he did. He was perhaps one of the most destructive individuals that ever ruled our nation. His basic philosophy was most likely anti-Christian. This is somewhat proven by his various mistresses. He never admitted this which makes him an imposter. He lied so to place us into a War against Germany which had devastating consequence. It is understood he was worth over fifty million dollars: in the early thirties and forties those are really big bucks. Churchill also hated the Germans which was probably more a matter of personal conceit: he saw the English as a superior group within the race. In fact in many ways the Germans were and are beyond the English. Hitler was a monumental tragedy, for Germany and for the World as well. Nevertheless Hitler was against the Bolsheviks and would have rid Europe of the Communist consequences and *perhaps the Bank of England.* In the end we are all dead: Hitler was no exception and the German people would have formed a different future for Europe and for

(50 x 20 = 1000). The American people are constantly reminded that there is no inflation: ***this is a monumental Lie*** and Deception that must be better understood. <u>*Economically the Monarchy was much better than what we now have.*</u> Much more could be said however the reader must avail himself/herself of some of the pertinent information from our bibliography.

The First World War: was a European war, between 1914 and 1918, the war to end all Wars: we are laughing over this one! The War began shortly after the assassination of Archduke Franz Ferdinand, shot to death by a Bosnian Serb Gavrilo Princip in Sarajevo, Bosnia. Blame was spread around and the great Powers *"imagined"* there interests were somehow involved. They took sides, War was declared and millions were killed who had nothing to do with the incident. Twenty million, perhaps more or less, were traded for *"The One* "Archduke Franz Ferdinand. How could any sane man have *"imagined"* such an outcome? There were great feelings of indignation including settling the problem of Slavic nationalism. What exactly is Slavic Nationalism but two words which, since that time, have not often been uttered: interestingly many Slaves have come to the United States they have blended with other people as was more natural. On July 28, Austria-Hungary declared war on Serbia. Soon after, France allied with Russia. On Aug 3 France and Germany declared war against each other. On the night of August 3-4 Germany invaded Belgium shortly thereafter Great Britain declared war against Germany. ***When will this madness be better understood?*** When will such madness be stopped? ***Never!*** There is so much money in fighting it will never be stopped: not in this lifetime, probably not ever. You can inform yourself about this Great War by reading some of what has been written on the subject. <u>*Certainly whatever you read will have been slanted or editorialized*</u> to make the author's point more believable. You will get different ideas about the War depending on whether you read works written by the victor or by the loser. In any event it is past History and you can access only a small part of the truth.

The Second World War: was a global conflict between 1939 and 1945 involving most of the nations of this World. All of the *"Great Powers"* were involved. The *"Lesser Powers"* did not have the means: they stood by and watched having only a small piece of the action. They did not have the money machines as the Great Powers had and not the number of people either. The World quickly divided into two Camps the Allies who were the good guys and the Axis who were the bad guys. This assertion as to good and bad will depend on what material is available for your review. The United States has been papered with reports favoring the good guys: we saw ourselves as the protectors of the World. We did much for many nevertheless we did kill many as well. Who can imagine however how much of what we do is secretly directed from the City of London. Who can imagine how much money and how many political favors change hands. And, who profits from all the machinations of the truthful insiders? The number of deaths

---

the World. Their intelligence and their technical ability they have been very willing to share: history has proven this. What are most important in all occurrences is the will and the reasoning.

*   **The Bank of England** is the driving force within much of the manipulation in the money and financial markets. They work in concert with our Federal Reserve and ***are intent on controlling the World using money as a means.*** They set the value of the currencies and are important in determining where the World is going. Right now China Russia and India pose a threat to this old established system of wealth: ***it is the wrong system, too much for just a few, too little for the rest!*** However there are solutions which are not collectivist.

during World War II as reported is between 50,000,000 and 70,000,000 no one is certain.[196] Many deaths would have been from natural causes however most were needlessly slaughtered.

Initially before World War II Germany was a magnificent deposit of art and architecture. The bombings destroyed much of what was there however it has been somewhat rebuilt.[197] Of course at that time Germany hoped to conquer Europe which was nearly accomplished when the United States entered the War on the side of England and became one with the Allies. _We should not have entered this War._ If we had not entered this War an ongoing History would have accomplished much to correct what was wrong and, of course, Hitler would now be dead: so would everyone else who were then in power. The problem was that Germany though a very small country had a most prominent intellectual and inventive ability.[198] This bothered some of less capability: notably the English who had some difficulty with this. George Washington advised us to **"Stay Home"** we would be safe here. I think he was right however the money powers in Europe, especially The Bank of England, had and still have other things in mind for the United States. This relates to the existence of our fraudulent Federal Reserve System, which is owned mostly by European Banks and U. S. Banks with close European ties.[199] The English, in particular have their eye on our wealth and prosperity. No common man knows how the Banks are related however we can _"imagine"_ that many are related. The same, Group of individuals are involved in their ownership as they have been for a long time. The English _"imagine"_ they are still fighting the Revolutionary War. Right now President Obama is one of our crippling forces: we will have to wait and see: be that as it may.[200]

---

[196] **Such butchery** is difficult to assess however it did occur as a **consequence of Sin**. Only a few individuals will talk seriously about what is sin. Sin is dismissed, most often as a sign of having fun. Those who attend a church may be inclined to think of sin only on Sunday: by Monday they have forgotten.

[197] **Drawings** for the demolished buildings were still available and they were used for this purpose, which was to rebuild their Culture. This was interesting, that a barbaric Culture would have had the sense to maintain the technically significant drawings for their magnificent buildings.

[198] **These are current figures 2010.** Germany: Area: 357,114 sq. km. (137,846 sq. mi.); about the size of Montana. Cities (2007): _Capital_—Berlin (population about 3.41 million). _Other cities_—Hamburg (1.77 million), Munich (1.31 million), Cologne (1 million), Frankfurt (671,000), Essen (567,000), Dortmund (581,000), Stuttgart (602,000), Dusseldorf (586,000), Bremen (548,000), Hanover (521,000). Terrain: Low plain in the north; high plains, hills, and basins in the center and east; mountainous in the south. Climate: Temperate; cooler and rainier than much of the United States. Many Americans thought of Germany as a large country which was not true.

[199] **The capital stock** is controlled by ten Banks, six of which are foreign. Mac Masters, _the Reaper. "The controlling stock in the Federal reserve is held by:_ (1) Rothschild Bank of **London,** (2) Rothschid Bank of **Berlin,** (3) Lazard Brothers of **Paris,** (4) Israel Moses Seif Banks of **Italy,** (5) Warburg Bank of **Amsterdam,** (6) Warburg Bank of **Hamburg,** (7) Lehman Brothers of New York, (8) Kuhn Loeb Bank of New York, (9) Goldman Sachs of New York, (10) Chase Manhattan of New York". Notice _"our Banks"_ are all in New York and have close connections with European interests. Much of the staggering wealth of this international banking cartel is illegally and unconstitutionally extracted from the American people.

[200] **Some suggest that George Soros** has backed Obama which may be true. George Soros is wealthy and has ideas which are not in our best interest. He is _"imagined"_ by some as an opportunist and a fraudulent speculator.

In 1941 the Axis launched an invasion of Russia: this was a fatal mistake that caused the Axis to be defeated. You can view on your computer hundreds of frozen and dead at Stalingrad at the point where the Axis began to decline. You can still watch movies and Television programs about the Great World War II, even as we prepare for World War III which may or may not occur.[201] This author's assumption is that there will be a World War III worse than the other two. The news media, largely controlled by interested aliens is not totally truthful. For our somewhat free people the news will make certain that you and your children and your grandchildren will not forget how we defended the World against the **"Hun."** _What we did was preserve the World for the wealthy Aliens and their progeny._ We see all the latest military hardware that is being produced for the billions we are forced to spend and we, some of us, are impressed. We are rather like the artillery man in our illustration, we feel invincible: _we are not invincible time will tell and Destiny will prove this_.[202] The details of the Second World War some true and some false and some a bit of each can be assessed by anyone interested: there are hundreds of books written on the subject. You are warned to be selective and not too gullible as you attempt to learn about the Great World War II. Keep in mind we are always on the brink of some catastrophe which we are told is about to happen: this is necessary so to make everyone feel insecure and of course many individuals are insecure for other reasons as well.

On December 7 of 1941 Japan which aimed at being the main power in Asia attacked the United States and bombed Pearl Harbor. It is _"imagined"_ that Roosevelt knew about the attack three days before it happened however he did nothing, rather he allowed for the destruction of much of our Pacific fleet and the killing of scores of our young men. During this attack our Navy was somewhat destroyed and _"had to be rebuilt."_ The rebuilding was good for industry and placed millions of ladies in the work force. This has not changed: most ladies are still working to pay the taxes and the costs of a monstrous and very unconstitutional Government. Now the ladies are deserted by their men and must raise the children with little or no help from the _"man that took advantage of them"_. The break-up of the family is a dire warning. Circumstance has been altered somewhat since we blundered into the Second World War.[203]

The Korean War: June 25, 1950 till July 27, 1953: another opportunity for profit to the Bankers and many insiders. This conflict was of a smaller scale, a model for future small scale conflicts.

Fortunately for the World Soros will soon be dead. Unfortunately his son will survive him, and carry on his efforts.

[201] **Grab a beer** and sit down at the Television to be entertained by moving pictures of the murder of millions of the innocent including women and children.

[202] **How does this relate to now?** Right now many of those that control the money and the Law are working to bankrupt this nation. The people who purchase all the junk from China help them; as the people sink further into debt. Check what you can find on the Internet; **the Cloward-Piven strategy.** This strategy seems to be working right now as millions have been added to the lists of who are being subsidized; they are the takers. Soon we will have too few of the givers.

[203] **Presently mothers** must place their children with care-takers while they are working to pay the bills for what has been imported from China. Mother's love is no longer dependable. This will have grave consequence for the people and the nation. Pick up the paper and read about the signs of the times: this is scary. Just recently someone found a new-born infant in a sewer pipe. Where was mom? Where was dad?

There have been other Wars since then; they are continuous. We *"imagine"* we are doing the World a favor in clearing out all the World's enemies. This may or may not be true. Keep in mind one man's enemy is another man's friend. What we are doing is preparing the World for a one-world government which will most likely be governed by Socialist types of one form or another. At present the United Nations is the front for such activity. Matthias Chang, a Chinese Catholic has much to say about this in his book *(Future Fast Forward)*.[204]

Since the end of the Korean War China has gained a position of prominence with cheap labor and exports to other nations, principally to the United States. China has exported tens of millions of things to the United States many of which are questionable.[205] The smart Chinese buy thus retrieve our junk metal, make something from it and sell what they make back to us at a profit. China also has purchased and owns much of our debt something in the range of a trillion dollars and more. China quite recently supported the North Koreans in a War against us. Presently we *"imagine"* **China is our friend.**

For now this may be true: in the future that may change.

We have assumed as we presume that we are making the World better, this may be a false presumption based on our *"imagination"* and our peculiar and particularly flawed idea about Reality. There are certainly millions that would not agree with such assumptions or our methods. Politically and intellectually things are not consistent: they are certainly all mixed up. One can understand the complexities leading up to the present moment in time however *what they mean in the aggregate is not so clear*. Meaning is always evasive since reasons and planning varies from one person or group to another: and much reasoning is contracted in secrecy.

We do know that there have always been the same types of individuals existing that exist at this moment. There have been a few wise men and many who are foolish some of which have been malicious: scoundrels, liars, thieves, hypocrites and fornicators. This will remain much as it is however one must remove the means of assistance that are built into our way of living that aid and abet the wrong type of being. Our understanding is labeled as being anti-social which is not exactly correct: rather we must face the fact that many men and women are sinful beings. One cannot discount and should not underestimate the effects of sin, they are tremendous. There are also millions that are decent and do fear their death and the Lord. Religion has attempted to do

---

[204] **Chang, Matthias,** *Future Fast Forward, the Zionist, Anglo-American Meltdown.* First American Editions, 2006, American Free Press, Washington D. C. 20063. Mr. Chang makes some insightful points in his writing which cannot be denied and should be carefully considered.

[205] **Americans like cheap junk**. Americans have not reserved taste for things that are sensitive and beautiful, they want many and much. The Idea of present style has overcome our people especially it has overcome the idea of value in time. Many Americans are vulgar: dress and entertainment prove this every day. The Celebrities dominate the scene with their vulgarity and silly sexual encounters, expensive, vulgar homes and shiny big and fancy cars. Many men like their women to appear like a whore with the smallest and tightest bikini so to expose *"nearly all"* of their womanhood, right down to the bone. Other men are no better with their yachts and simple minded women on board. Nevertheless such fools imagine they can lead the World to better things: we suggest this will not happen. As a nation we are just about finished leading a band of somewhat subservient nations.

away with this disparity of being and attendant behavior however we are not all of the same faith and many antagonisms arise because of Religion. Some individuals are ready to kill another that does not believe as they *"imagine"* is correct. This is tragic however true.

Some politicians are overly exuberant and their type has placed the World and its people in an untenable position. Economics is the driving force however has become a manner of stealing within sight of a contrived form of law. Economics is necessary so as to be able to carry on a form of legitimate trade amongst individuals. The best situation would be a reversal of rising prices as is presently occurring. Can one imagine that this will happen? Falling prices would help the poor to gain an advantage in their being. Rising prices are always co-incident with inflation. Inflation is necessary so to sustain our present System. *Our present system must be restructured so to promote stability in pricing, better yet a lowering of all prices.* This would be a slow process however we should aim at pricing similar or equal to what was the pricing in perhaps 1935. I have written of this in other places: I believe this is possible. There is little advantage in having a bushel of money when it will only buy one carrot or a cup of coffee.

As prices fall some billionaires will generally be eliminated since they depend on our corrupt System. No individual requires a billion dollars. As mentioned in a past footnote the Pope Benedict XVI has declared excessive wealth to be the eighth deadly sin. What they do with their money is their business however they further corrupt an already unworkable System: they make it worse. We must do two things: **First** we must find a legitimate way to prevent all forms of short selling in the stock market. **Second** we must prevent specialists, others as well, from turning vast amounts of notional wealth into real and tangible value. *These two things combined are two of our greatest economic problems.* And we must stop Inflation and reverse the trend; it must be done slowly so not to further destroy the poor.

We must not engage in senseless and costly Warfare. We are killing millions of the innocent as we attempt to protect a largely untenable System. Apart from what is here mentioned; we are killing many of our children by abortion. This is truly sinful. A woman's rights do not include allowing for the murder of her own children. Much of such *"murder"* is a consequence of consenting adult laws which in fact encourage fornication with multiple sex partners. *This is bestial as some beasts do kill their own offspring.* How many young women are becoming beast-like? The writings on such subject are almost totally without any understanding of a truthful spiritual Reality. The experts who write on the subject have eliminated the understandings of Catholic Christianity. This is a subject for another volume.

Spending must be cut to more reasonable levels. Imports should be somewhat restricted and where possible items should be made closer to home. We should employ our own people. We had this before the drive toward Internationalism began. *Internationalism is like a disease that will infect the world's population negatively.* A few food items might be imported however we do not need crackers made in England or China. Even to move potato chips from San Francisco to Florida is simply stupid. No one gains anything from this in any way except those that set up the too-large Corporations; they create the deals for speculation, the money goes to just a few. What happens is the small producers, if they are successful, are bought out by the giant Corporations. This is ruining the culture: where are the mom and pop industries? They simply cannot survive the competition. For example, potato chips can be made anywhere: even in your own kitchen.

What is this mentality, the Internationalist Position? *It provides a means for one entity to become a monopoly as in the Corporation.* We over-value such entity and eventually we will have only the choices that one such as those will provide. With flavor and freshness being issues our foods will be laced with preservatives and shelf-life ingredients most of which should not be eaten. Look at your foods and see what is in them: it's scary! Perhaps one might limit the size of a Corporation to engage only within a limited geographic domain. This seems like it would be a workable solution to this problem. To open another MacDonald's in China does no good for the United States or for its people. Such act simply places junk food in another location!

All of what is written above is dependent upon one's health and how one feels. It is my contention that generally speaking even where food is plentiful our health is failing. I speak hear of physical and *Mental Health as such health is supportive of Ideas,* thought content and the individual's understanding of the world and its people.[206] We are in a period where individually we are overburdened with thought content that we do not and cannot possibly understand. This is a cause for much of the anxiety which we see. Much of our life is overburdened with meaningless Ideas and activities that have been implanted into the Civilization by greedy and self-serving lunatics. **This assertion** is made with the recognition that most of what we have comes as an imposition of the will of another on the collective consciousness. The totality of Human Being is slowly being challenged and will eventually be overcome by this fact. It is a fact that is difficult to understand and more difficult to deal with. There is little promise of a better tomorrow where the population is so beholden to the thoughts and ideas of just a few: and they are self interested, greedy in the extreme. I use the word *"lunatic"* as the only way capable of suggesting how they are: those presuming to know so much. *The Culture and Civilization is working toward a somewhat self imposed destruction.* Although politics does play a role politics are not the cause of our dilemma. What is the cause is deeper and more complex. Who in fact believes because we have an *imagined Democracy* that those whom we elect are doing so much for so Many?

We as a Nation are being strangled by too much of what is useless for both mind and body and especially the soul. This is tragic however true.[207] In the beginning things for amusement and pleasure were smaller and more suited to Humanness. At present all of our Ideas for amusement and pleasure are grotesque, they are too large and they overshadow the participants who are seeking even more grotesque forms of distraction: they call this amusement. Amusement and everything will be better in the future. They are wrong.

If one studies health one will understand that it is best to eat food that was grown *within one hundred miles of where one was born.* Actually this observation may or may not be true, however is consistent with the fact that we are *"from the earth"* in a very real sense. Who will

---

[206] **Cancer** in 1900 took the lives of about one person in fifty which was 2%. Right now that number seems reasonable. At present Cancer is taking about one life of every two people that die which is 50% of all deaths.

Right now that number seems much too high! How did we arrive at this point? We suspect that part of this is due to the fact that more disease is attributed to cancer however we submit that there are other reasons as well.

[207]

believe this? Many of today's health and social problems are due to the nature and kind of diet that we have. There may be a profound connection here that we do not, perhaps cannot or will not, understand. Food can be grown most places where people live. In the past certain foods were staples for one group of people or another: beans, rice, grains, fruits, fish and some other assorted items. The diets were restricted and the cooking was generally not too varied. This was probably good. In the West it was discovered that some imported foods were *"imagined"* to be better: they were exotic. This is not an expose on diet however diet is an interesting factor and mention of it should be included with this presentation.

So now: What shall we do about the money?

As a nation we are strangling ourselves with the effects of Debt. We have allowed, indeed encouraged, Specialists to plunder our wealth as part of one System or another which those same Specialists have devised. The Specialists include salesmen and various entrepreneurs that seek to make a profit on our involvement with them. The premier group consists of specialists in the stock market. Whenever an Idea arises that appears to be one from which they can profit they put *t*hat Idea, into the System. In simple terms *they are expert at converting imagined wealth into real wealth, properties and gold.* The billionaires that one hears about are amongst those that are doing this to the Nation. There are certainly very profitable inventions however those few inventors that do exist are not the problem.

The problems are the Sinful ways which have been perfected and made to appear legitimate one way or another. Men generally speaking have discounted the effects of Sin on personal and commercial activities. One reads of some movie stars as having had five, six, seven or even more soul mates; they imagine this as marriage, as an auxiliary part of an overpaid and corrupt existence. They also have various encounters during their hunting. Logically how can one person have so many *"Soul Mates"?* Marriage by the best and most profound thinking is supposed to be permanent and a means to extend the Species with the becoming of children. Christian Marriage has been considered a Holy Institution, Christian Marriage is a Sacrament, permanent and inviolate; to love, honor and obey till death do us part. There are a few exceptions that must be considered however they are few. The present dialogue on same sex marriage is simply nonsense. If two individuals want to live together that is their business. *The talk about equality misses the most important elements concerning sex or in fact any truthfully important issue.* It provides an outlet for various personal characteristics. The subject is too broad to be included here. However the dialogue emanates from Public Education's failure to teach Philosophy and Religion truthfully: the curriculum is contrived mostly for Social and Political effect.

Do Politicians not understand what it means to be a child and to be dependent upon both parents? Most Actors appear to be perhaps good people in many ways however they are not in command of their own Reality and have very little understanding of the important and most critical issues concerning life.[208] When one understands the workings of Commerce the set ups, the squeezes, the lies and the misrepresentation, all legal of course, one realizes that the laws favor the most unscrupulous of the players. *Giant Corporations grow because of the Sin*

---

[208] **Many Stars** are themselves from broken homes. They don't know or understand what is Holy, requiring of Virtue. No one has ever taught them about such things.

of **Greed.** It is a common belief that any Corporation must get larger and larger or they are not successful; this is a vain aspiration. ***Vanity is a Sin!*** They do this by consuming small competition which they buy out. This is often done with the assets of the smaller corporation or with a form of corporate credit. These are absurd conditions they are sinful and should be stopped. They must be stopped, sooner rather than later. Truthful Ownership must be, in truth, more widely diverse. The stock market affords diversity in a limited way. Nevertheless there are still some individuals with millions of shares in a Corporation; this is greed. ***Greed is a Sin!***

All the talk about the National and World Economies is mostly *"Bullshit"* talk for the sake of having something to say. *It is part of the subterfuge that is built into the System.* No one can be called responsible for this. Listen to the reporting on such events, it is mostly nonsense as those doing the talking are uncertain of what they say. In addition every single one is made confusing by the imposition of commercial messages for selling a product that, generally speaking, may not be needed by anyone. *And we do not need all the compassion as pretense* that leads to ever greater warfare: we need simply **to stop producing the armaments that are developed to kill another man's children.** Balance of payments, who owes who how much has become as a disease of the present. Since the French Revolution, and the becoming of Modern Financial and Commercial transactions, the most important things have been getting worse. We are told who our enemies are, by those that are planning the next takeover of another man's country. All this, as stated immediately above, are the ways, cause and effect of a badly tainted Political System.

What we suggest above cannot be corrected with political means. The Issues must be addressed with more sensitivity by who so ever can be counted among the concerned. What we now have are understood as political accommodations which, to repeat are Sinful and they do not work. Sin never works. *What will work is Virtue: honesty, fair play and truthfulness.* This will come as a consequence of having properly educated youth. We are too late to make all adults over so to become more virtuous, this will only work with a few who are concerned, interested and willing. Youth must be trained with a more Catholic sensibility meaning a sensibility **universally fair and applicable**. They must become their brother's keeper not just in Church on Sunday however on the Street every single day. We must begin this education when they are very little, in the home. The Child's parents must co-operate in the effort: the parent must contain his/her own lust, and the use of liquor and narcotics to solve a problem and should restrain from obvious vulgarity so as to not influence the children badly. The adult must attempt to be virtuous, cut the foul use of language, learn the proper words for decently inspired communication and should not resolve to name calling and hateful utterance toward others. Parents must be tolerant of others, even when they don't agree. One can teach much by example as is well known. Our television programs should be less spiteful and all the obscenities and screaming should be curtailed.

Adults must act like adults. Adults should turn off their Televisions except for only the very best programs. There are some good programs. Adults should do more for themselves the hand crafts, for example carving, crocheting: learn to play a musical instrument. There are thousands of things that one can do for such forms of amusement. Do the kind of things that builds rather than destroys both you and your country. You will be proud of your achievements even though they are perhaps small and not advertised. Give up the need to win at some meaningless sport, sport is a game, temporary and fleeting; treat it as such. Spend some time alone, learn to love and appreciate yourself as a good and decent person without help from some opportunist. Curtail your lust, or it will destroy your Soul. You do have a *Soul;* this is an Idea about life and living. Everyone's Soul is a profound summation of all that they have been and of all that they are.

Money must be understood as a means and should not ever be considered as a commodity that fluctuates in price from day to day. When this occurs speculation in currency is the result with just a bit of clipping every day on every fluctuation. Such fluctuation is, most generally, toward larger numbers. ***This is the Mortal Sin of the age!*** Money is what may remain or does remain of your past life. The value of the money is the value of your past life. Ask yourself: Was my past life of any value? If your past life had any value then the money that you have saved from that past life should still be worth what it was when you earned it. *This is easy to understand however the System works to deny you this understanding.* **The System is wrong in this respect.**

No political System is for the people. All Systems are divisive they are designed, knowingly and unknowingly by men. The men that design the system are all Politicians of one form or another and they do not have perfect understanding of anything: Perfect understanding is God's understanding. Think of God as an ***Idea.*** Although God may or does exist do not try to give God a personality or an appearance. You will always be wrong. God exists as a driving force for Humanity and is not a person as you know a person to be. God is perfect meaning he favors all equally: this too is what a God is or may be. And you must understand God is everywhere as is the Space of the Universe.

At this point a belief in God is essential to the functioning of the Human Race. The Idea of there being a God is essential for every single man, women and child without which they are lost. *We are not speaking of any Idea of God as being correct rather we speak of the Singularity of omnipotence.* The Catholic Church as founded by Christ, who is believed to be the son of God and *(from the Greek)* is the universal Church for all mankind. Christ came to save all men; this idea must be better understood and taught to our children. God is an omnipotent singularity, infinite, timeless and perfect. This understanding is made functional in the language which everyone should understand. This understanding will save Mankind, one soul at a time. It will make Life perfect for everyone! Without this understanding all other understanding becomes corrupt and will be ineffective. *A correct understanding of God* will help to do away with all forms of thievery and mayhem. All War will cease. Who wants to kill his brother: only a fool would do this.

An understanding of the presence of God should be the most important goal in all forms of education from the beginning of life until the end of life: for every single individual.

Only with a truthful and consistent belief in God will all men prosper and survive peacefully.

Peace Be with You.

———

Professor Emeritus, Robert Fiedler
February 1, 2013.

CHAPTER IX

WHY ARE WE AS WE ARE? HOW DID WE GET THIS WAY? PART I

Here is an attempt to understand the present mind-set with various intentions.

Keep in mind the level of understanding, the meaning and intent of any dialogue and what one receives from such dialogue are all temporal they are ephemeral: they are ever changing. Ideas exist as sounds in space or as marks on a surface and are abstractions open to Various Forms of Philosophical, Moral, Social and Political interpretation. There are many forms.

We are confused, our understanding is generally incorrect: Or, only partially correct.

***Especially is the understanding of most of the Politicians incorrect:
Or are our Politicians working against the common interests?
Are our Politicians truthfully and virtuously informed?
No doubt, some appear on the side of an Enemy!***

There are always times of uncertainty and wonderment. Some events are neutral or natural whereas others are contrived or invented for the effect they may or will have on the population. The population is *"We the People"* and this includes everyone in this nation. At present it includes people from all Nations. All Propaganda includes some or very much of what is untrue and the world functions in response to the propaganda. The world functions in respect to what is in part untruthful or simply a Lie. ***Many occurrences are, in some part, a result of somewhat contrived and politicized information.*** Modern Communication has made it more likely that the messages received by that same population will be for the effect they will have on steering *"We the People"* in the proper direction.[209] *We the people must be steered* so as

---

[209] **The recent past Republican Presidential Primaries** are an excellent example. Ron Paul was ignored whenever possible whereas Mitt Romney and Santorum were featured initially for no special reason. This is an attempt to condition the public to reject Ron Paul and choose one of the other two. Interestingly Santorum dropped out of the race for seemingly personal reasons. Ron Paul, generally speaking was perhaps the best Conservative Candidate: he is for the people and did see things as they should be seen by a Presidential Candidate. Apparently he did not and does not belong to the Secret or somewhat Secret Societies to which many other Politicians do belong. Many influential ones are 33rd degree Masons: they appear to be in control of much of circumstance. Interestingly Khrushchev was a Mason as is the present leader of the Soviet Union. This is an aspect of One World Government that few understand. The real

to allow the "assumed as being elite" to gain control of everything in this world. The people must be steered so as to move in what is imagined, by those that control circumstance, as the right and proper direction.[210] The *Politicians* and those who control them will determine what is that direction? In a Democracy, it is imagined that everyone will have a say in the Governing process. *This is an ideal which is in fact not possible to attain* except with very small populations however nearly everyone existing, believes it is, and works under a pretense caused by such gross-misunderstanding.[211] Those with the real power that control, the money and the Commerce are well covered in their endeavor as those proceed along a nefarious path, toward a One World Socialist and Totalitarian government which they and those like them will, in fact, attempt to control.[212] Socialist and Totalitarian governments benefit, from the sins and various imaginings of the populations. *Socialism becomes as an aid to the meanness of whom we imagine as being Satan or the Devil.*[213] Most Politicians are admired for doing what no one can understand. A small group has control: however such control is for very short periods of time. Before there were Politicians, so called, some Royal Families held their peoples together: the Rurik's and Romanov's in Russia are good examples. However they were despised by some and in the end the Romanovs were butchered by an alien group with atavistic and primitive urgings.[214]

---

controllers appear to have a plan which they hope will be implemented by the people: this is a Democracy we are told. President Obama is **"apparently"** a fraud. There appears to be written evidence that he was schooled in Indonesia. At the time no one could attend their schools unless they were Indonesian. His father was Indonesian. His mother was an American who had deserted, by that is meant betrayed, this [her nation] nation.

[210] **Webster, Nesta** *"the French Revolution, a Study in Democracy".*

A study of the French Revolution will give evidence of how this occurs guided by unseen and somewhat misunderstood forces. The people will follow the leader as is intended by those who may profit from the endeavor.

[211] **In a Presidential election**, other elections as well, when the two sides have a nearly equal amount of votes nearly one half the population will always be disappointed: having lost by perhaps just one or two percent. The System guarantees this type of outcome. Only about half of the voters vote; elections can be won by 26% or 28% of voters.

[212] **This is a process** which is slow however is apparently working quite well. There will be set backs however they will be temporary. In political writings it is assumed that one will have to step back occasionally before continuing forward to new and better forms of control. As it unfolds this is a process difficult to define and to understand.

[213] **Think of the Devil as an idea** or a form of *Thought Cluster* that is negative in implication and seeks to destroy rather than create a decent reality. Why one becomes possessed with the Devil's evil is not well known and is not well understood nevertheless all will suffer from the consequences. The Devil is certainly an unholy creature.

[214] **Many individuals in the Alien group** were from New York: the number is given as approximately 450 they were mostly Jews and originally many of them had come from Russia. Once in America they became citizens and returned to Russia as American citizens. Once in Russia they were able to take part in the Revolution with the protection of American citizenship. This was a form of International hypocrisy aided by some hypocrites in our own nation. Some of the hypocrites are known others remain unknown. We believe Jacob Schiff was prominent in the butchering of a decent family.

The present has many variations which are all mixed up, devised and improvised in curiously formed ways. Intelligent men know this and are able to exploit one element or another so to serve, their immediate purpose and to some extent their long range plan and ultimate objective: which is **World Domination.** The Stock Markets are prime examples of this phenomenon: some small players do make a bit however it is meaningless in terms of the total value and nature of the market. Since NOW, as in the past is in a state of flux, the leaders must remain cognoscente, and act according to their long term goals.[215] Long term goals may go back for centuries: even millennia.[216] As in the past all present leaders will be replaced by new talking heads: those new heads, in fact, share the same *thought content, ideas and understandings* of a pervasive and perverse Reality.[217] Our leaders, generally, have been educated to do what they learn to do in the state supported educational system: the Corporate School.

Keep in mind *the man, whoever he is, is not as important as the Idea.* Great men and scoundrels from the past are now dead however their Ideas may linger for centuries. ***Ideas give form and direction to action***: it has always been this way and will continue into the future. Both good and evil ***Ideas*** move forward in time influencing the next generation. *Keep in mind also* the real Power in Politics and finance is in the hands of those few who, in fact, controls the big money.[218] Historically money and value have moved within small groups, the more fortunate participants. Money is the means. Generally speaking, there are always places for the perpetrators to hide from detection. This will be even more certain in an International setting as is being planned right now. Because of the scale of the endeavor, the larger domain of Internationalism will protect the vested or *"entrenched"* interest better than Regionalism. ***Money is considered as a commodity which is a fatal mistake: money must have an unchanging value, an intrinsic***

---

[215] **One cannot be certai***n* of exactly what is happening in any given circumstance: as they say, *"That's Life."* Thought and thinking are transient, moving with the time of the day and/or with whom one might be interacting. There are various levels of Communication some are understandable some are not: this further expands the difficulties which might be encountered, in a personal dialogue. Use of language may obfuscate meaning for many when the levels of intellect are distinct, different: one can understand this is a difficult issue to contemplate. In some other places I have written on the meaning and use of language including what I term as "Psychic Space".

[216] **If one will take time** to read the text contained in *"The Rise of the House of Rothschild"*, *page v to page xiii,* in the very beginning of the book one will have a good idea to help understand what is written thereafter. The book generally deals with the various exploits of a nefarious cadre of people; some were liars and thieves.

[217] **The mind-content** of the talking heads and of the truly wealthy is as the mind content of others *"of their kind"* who lived before them and this is not easily changed. Each learns from the others with who they are in contact. This is a basic concept in education and is related to *"The presence and nature of Reality"* in kind. It is familial, social and tribal and more recently has broadened into being National, and also International. Thus the leaders do have some adversaries and their general sense of being is often incorrect: their adversaries very likely are from different forms of World Groupings often defined in religious terms. No one can change this at this moment.

[218] **Money is a means** without which nothing or at best very little can be accomplished. As civilization becomes more complex the need for money increases. When the need for money increases also ways of cheating others are increased.

value, without this all the paper money will become worthless as time passes. As long as there is Inflation there will be raising prices; wages of the common man will go up as the inflation continues however the common man cannot beat the system; the common man cannot keep up! This is why he is referred to as the common man.

Ideas give form and direction to action!

The Jewish question is so confused and so confusing that it is difficult to consider. Much is as metaphor and confusion is given by some so to promote more confusion. *Confusion creates a cover for what one is doing.* One must study the old Jewish writing to best understand where the ideas of some came from.[219] Generally speaking most all Biblical Jews have been assimilated and are a part of the Human Family. They live peaceably amongst other human beings. However the Ideas that some who call themselves Jews (however are not really biblical Jews), still cling to are cause for much of what is wrong in the present world. They are, in a sense, imposters: they are converts from the Khazar Empire.[220] They are Zionists. Importantly they control much of the wealth accumulated in the Western nations. *"In its own circles, world Jewry works constantly for Jewish Nationalism and to (some degree there are those who) work for domination of the Gentile world. Socialism, communism and the revolutionary labor movement, are primarily led by Jews or dominated for the greater part by Jews; they are also basically international. Some do demand an international world order for the Gentiles and a separate, distinct and exclusive nationalism for themselves. The reasons are obvious, Jewish nationalism—as the sons of Abraham—is the basic principle of Judaism. (The truth of this statement is one of the outstanding and uncontroversial facts of history). World domination by Israel is decreed by Jehovah."*[221] *(Parenthesis is by this author)* At present they are employing clever means using the financial markets and the help of some Big Banks and Governments (largely under their control) to attempt keeping what they have amassed and gaining more of the worldly goods: money, property land and various commodities. We cannot imagine that all Jews agree however many can be controlled by those that do. From what is written above one can see that there is a definite and absolute relationship between Religion and Politics. The converts to Judaism favor and encourage a separation of church and state however only for the Goyim: those whom some such as the convert perceives being as beasts, animals and deserving of death.[222]

---

[219] ***Rev. I. B. Pranaitis, The Talmud Unmasked.*** *Secret Rabbinical Teachings concerning Christians. Imprimatur, St. Petersburg, IMPRIMATUR, St. Petersburg, April 13, 1892. Kozlowsky, Archbishop Metropolitan of Moghileff.* The writing in this brief text gives one a notion of where some Ideas have come from. Keep in mind they are Ideas about the form of Reality. In some instances these Ideas influence behavioral patterns.

[220] **Chang, Matthias,** *Future Fast Forward, the Zionist, Anglo-American Meltdown.* First American Editions, 2006, American Free Press, Washington D. C. 20063. page 167. *"**The Khazars** were a Turkic people from Central Asia. **They were a warring people** . . .* At the height of their influence they were in the Northern Caucasus, Eastern Ukraine, Crimea, western Kazakhstan and north-western Uzbekistan. They had influence in Hungary and Romania." *The interpolation is from this author for brevity.*

[221] **The Beasts of the Apocalypse,** *Olivia Maria O'Grady, @ 1959 & First Amendment Press 2001.*

[222] **This form of thinking** represents a rather ancient idea carried forward by a small number to the present day. Some others will refute such an assertion. No one knows exactly how all such ideas fit together however there is conjecture and imagination which figures prominently into such circumstance.

Some of them, an imposing few, are determined to use their wealth to conquer the world.[223] Some of their Ideas are symptomatic of **Bigotry** and **Vanity** yet some still hold to them. As such they, a small group, are determined to destroy Christianity and especially the Catholic Faith whereas some others are receptive and supportive of the *"Idea"* of Christ as the Messiah.[224] There has always been some antagonism between Catholicism and Judaism because of the theology being somewhat different. This is understandable and need not be an impediment in World peace. In fact for many, Religion is much better understood than in the past. The study of Religion is acceptable to dignified scholarship and much popular opinion.[225] *Keep in mind Christ came to save all peoples not just certain ones.* All are welcome into Heaven if they have lived a decent Catholic-type existence; by that is meant ***universally acceptable***.[226]

No one group will destroy the Catholic Christian Faith however some of their mischief is a bit threatening. Some Jews believe they are superior to all others and because of this they remain somewhat isolated from the Human race. In the past some have been deliberately prevented from being a part of Humanity: nevertheless some were at times very exclusive and preferred their own Kind. The Rothschild's made a habit of marrying their own cousins thus to keep their wealth in the family. This is also understandable and reasonable when the genetics are considered; uncles are not necessarily genetically related to nieces. The Jews even had their own laws and punishments allowed by those among whom they lived. This was certainly unusual: contrarily they were excluded from many occupations. However this is not now the case in most Western places that we know of. Especially they are prominent in politics and banking and law: They control most of the major Institutions considered to big to fail: especially big Banks. We are certain that this protection is to a great advantage for them. *There are other forms of the Zealot in other religions as well.*

The Rothschild's were in the right place at the right time to do what was done thereafter. If the Rothschild's had not existed there would have been another family, probably a Jewish family

---

223 **It is the belief of some** that the Fortune of the Romanoff's provided a significant portion of the economic basis for much of what has been done in the past nearly one hundred years. Most of the important antagonists of the Russians during the disastrous Revolution were, in fact, Jewish Khazars. Many of the Functionaries had come from New York. This is an interesting fact that few are aware of. (See footnote 212 immediately above). Many of the revolutionaries came from New York. They had become US citizens so to be able to return to Russia in time for the revolution: a well planned and brilliant although most unfortunate political and social maneuver: *unfortunate for humanity.*

224 **This idea** must be reconsidered and a new dialogue should be formed. Compatibility is possible only when thought forms include tolerance. What is exact in truth is not always correctly understood and known and one must allow for this in a dialogue which is certain to encourage various acts. This author opts for a dialogue of fairness and consolation as the world moves forward.

225 **Matters are made more complex** therefore difficult by Islam. Islam is distinct from most all other religions and the radicals of Islam would destroy all who do not believe in Allah.

226 **This is a difficult Issue** for most thinkers however it must be considered. Keep in mind, there can be only one Omnipotence, God; we will all succumb to His will; one way or another!

that would have filled the role.[227] This considers the time from about 1750 to the present day. We consider this Time-frame as the "Modern Period" in European and American History.[228] During this period the American Republic was formulated and began to function. We _"understand"_ there was much hardship during this period and certainly a great misunderstanding among the people. You can obtain various History books to inform yourself of the details which are less important than the overall concept that is being delivered here. We caution that you are certain of the truthfulness of the writers: this must be carefully checked so as to not fall victim to the propaganda that is written as History. Such propaganda is both debilitating and confusing for the reader. In fairness, some Propaganda is simply because the author did not have all of the correct and truthful information. Keep in mind if one has no information that is probably better than having a _package of lies_. Keep in mind _the greatest enemy of humanity is the Liar._ Lies are the Devil's tool and are involved in all deceitful and harmful motivations. Lies can be very motivational when accompanied by martial music and a sense of patriotism. Million have died because of this as the munitions makers become wealthy.[229]

Think of money as an idea. What is it and what should it do? _Presently the perversion of money is creating great havoc on the poor people of this world:_ many other people as well including large numbers of whom we define as being the middle class, which is indebted beyond reason.[230]This has been true in the past as well: not much has changed. In fact, given a more equitable long terms understanding the World could be quite different as it should be. **GREED** must be curtailed in favor of a more decently minded understanding of circumstances. People, as children, should be taught to appreciate and respect the person of all others: they should be taught to be Christian in the truthful sense of the word. Christianity augers for loving all others and for truthful brotherhood: The world may not yet be ready for this. **Christianity, as Catholicism, is God's Faith.** To explain who is God is a difficult assignment. This I attempt to do; I have attempted to do this in a different writing as well: _The Eve of Annihilation_, which includes some imaginings. For a while there will be a sustaining of other Religions however the Religion of God, the Father, as progenitor of the Universe, is Catholicism which I believe will eventually be triumphant: many certainly hope this will happen. Children should be taught to love their brother and when they reach maturity they should refrain from hating

---

[227] **At the time** the Jews were not allowed in many occupations and industries however they were allowed to be money changers: This may have had something to do with an infinite cause or an imagined punishment: this is difficult to know, more difficult to understand.

[228] **The United States** is a descendent of the European Culture and Civilization. There were also native cultures that did in fact exist in America however they were not as powerful as those in Europe and they succumbed to what may be considered, not necessarily correctly, as superior technical and ideological or spiritual forces. The technologies are more obvious than are the more ideological or spiritual elements.

[229] **Grand Prix, Don, Col. USA Ret.** _Barbarians Inside the Gates, The Black Book of Bolshevism_. GSG & Assoc. Publishers; P. O. Box 590, San Pedro, California. ISBN # 0-945001-79-7. First Printing 2000.

[230] **Recently** the president has ordered a change in the debt structure of home ownership. Reduced interest loans are being financed to help the overburdened. This is not a good idea. Those helped will probably incur more debt with what they imagine they are saving. Again this is a part of the Cloward-Piven Stratgedy to bankrupt the government.

and killing whom they do not agree with.[231] Nothing is more important than this! There is the Commandment: ***Thou shall not kill!*** No one has the right to take the life of another except in self-defense: even then it might be questionable. The present state of affairs with War and killing must be brought somehow to a close. Men must lay down their weapons and do things that are more important: love their wife truthfully and care for their own children. Young men should quite their carousing, find a decent woman to love: love unto death do you part. This is how it should be. The rather unusual tattooed men that one observes at this point in time are somewhat of a negative mark on Civilization. This is telling us something; do you know what it is that is being told, what is expressed in this form of imagery? Is this the Devil speaking to us?

Presently Some of Physicists are becoming more to appreciate the value of a Divinity. How else might what is have come to be?[232] There seems to have been a Supernatural Power which created all that is. "Infinite Space is the ideal that the Western Soul has always striven to find, and to see immediately actualized, in its world around; and hence it is that the countless space-theories of the last century possess-over and above all ostensible results—a deep import of symptoms of a world feeling. In how far does the unlimited extension *underlie* all objective Things?"[233] Nevertheless what about the Space? We understand that at present the World and the Space is almost totally empty: according to some physicists even an atom is mostly space. It is alleged, from some research, that the atom is only *one two billionth part of matter* and the rest is space. *The movement, the form, the nature and structure of the atom have properties in common with the solar system.* The difference is in the scale and the velocities. The small particles contained in the atom, because they move so quickly in the space make the atom appear to be solid.[234] Can one imagine there is a correlation between the speed of the evolving forms in an atom and the speed at which the planets move about? Is the velocity an effect of the scale? What would this mean? This is phenomenal and has a spiritual tenor which we do not understand. This is a combination of form and movement that few can appreciate. *The solids found in reality seem to be products of the infinitely fast movement of the smallest elements in existence which appear to occupy all of a limited space simultaneously.* ***This is as light.*** *The smallest elements, are very likely quarks of light? They may be referred to as* **God Particles.** We do not know and cannot understand what this means however many believe God, an Omnipotent One, is the Light of the World. This would mean that God resides in all matter as he resides in all space. ***God's presence is infinite.***

---

231   **In the Unites States Constitution** it is stated that everyone has the right to pursue Life, Liberty and a state of Happiness. Happiness is a matter of personal volition and cannot be legislated except to protect such right.

232   **Divinity is only a word**, nevertheless the meaning is what is important. To be divine is to be unworldly, ephemeral and transfinite. It is imagined by millions that the Universe was made from a word. A word precedes all that is: a word is definitive in the most profound sense of being. Before one can understand anything there must be a word to define it. "In the beginning was the Word;" Genesis.

233   **Spengler, Oswald**, *The Decline of the West, Vol. I. Form and Actuality.* Authorized Translation with notes by Charles Francis Atkinson. New York. Alfred A. Knopf, Publisher, NY. 1926.

234   **Matter** *is the form of a vector sum created by motion: (Fiedler)* the track of a particle, given to infinitely fast movement, and appears as a form of matter in Space: the Space provides the accommodation for the placement of such event.

Thus light is eminently important. In Genesis it is said that God is the Light of the world! What does this mean? If God is the Light of the world and if all matter and form are made of light then *God is as all matter and form.* This is difficult to comprehend: except by faith. The Catholic Faith seemingly acknowledges some of this understanding. Other faiths do not quite come up to so doing. The Jewish faith, what is generally considered Jewish is too political and is overly concerned with the things of the earth. Additionally some Jews set themselves apart from the rest of humanity as being somehow superior: a chosen one, chosen by God to dominate others. This is a *VAIN* notion and is *childish* however has been very effective in forming the Soul of many Jews. Many Rabbis assume to be holy men nevertheless this feeling about others is a part of their make-up. The Jew is a human being just like all other human beings and has not a special roll of leadership except some are trying to assume what is not there's to assume: to rule over and dominate all others. Moslems are too concerned with Mohammad and with Ala: they apparently miss the point of existence. Ala is not an Infinite Being: omnipotent and timeless. Culturally they have been prominent and have created some beautiful works of Art however their understanding and comprehension of Reality is not as comprehensive as in (Universal) Catholic Christianity. Moslems are somewhat exclusive and unlike God and his Son Jesus they are not infinite in their becoming and in their being. Their Prophet was a man not a divinity and their prophet did not raise from the dead.[235] These are profound and serious issues and must be considered. In addition many of them see a woman as somewhat inferior to a man and the woman has little rights except as determined by a man. Nevertheless it has been discovered recently that the woman, generally speaking, controls the genetics therefore the nature of the newborn. *Women given a deep understanding of their bodily functions control the future of mankind.* Such position makes the woman superior in a real worldly sense. To repeat after the event of conception the man is finished. The man represents the past in the element of his seaman. After conception the man is finished whereas within the woman's body a new life is formed; given a small segment of Time and an Eternal Soul or Spirit. Other Religions have their own shortcomings which are not apparent in Christianity.

Religious Belief
Parte II

At this moment we encounter religious beliefs some of which beliefs can be very antagonistic to the beliefs of others. This is true because Religion deals with the most important aspects of human existence, of living and dying. Much of Religion has been given to sophomoric interpretations by mediocre preachers with minds not able to deal with the ultimate complexity of existence. Because of this there thinking is irrelevant concerning the vital elements given to existence.[236] Like all thought content, Religion is victimized by the *LIE* and ineptitude in

---

[235] **For forty days** after death Christ walked on the earth. No one else had ever done this nor has anyone done this since that time. This is apparently presented as history: we have no way to prove this except by what records there are concerning the incident. The records apparently are truthful and well acknowledged.

[236] **The chatter** over whether or not women should be priests has brought forth the most absurd criticisms and arguments imaginable. Christ Was a Man: **God as progenitor** is a man, he is masculine by definition: woman is an incubator: the roles are distinct, and *they are not interchangeable*. Certainly there are some women that are very holy, nuns for example. They do have a place in the order of what is however

respect to the populations. Also the levels of understanding vary from one to another person which confuses understanding. Religion is compromised by various *"Thought Clusters"* many of which have originated and expanded in the minds of fools.[237] The fact is modern history, since the time of Christ, has had a new and different tenor: Catholicism. Catholicism is the basis, the philosophy for all modern Christianity.[238] Catholicism also influences the thinking and *"Thought Clusters"* of millions of non-Catholics. At this time, many in the World cannot or will not attempt to understand the nature and elemental goodness embodied in this Catholic Philosophy. Catholicism has formed into a driving force and its effects are seen in much of the World. *It is also the only formidable antagonist to those that seek to rule by means of a One World Order.* Those who wish to dominate are what I have called the **Money Grubbers.** Money grubbing is a mortal sin emanating from **Vanity** and **Greed**. The present *"contrived"* debt crisis is one of the simple-minded *"Socialist Means"* to weaken the constructive force of Christianity, which is the driving force of Western Civilization: however what is contrived will never work because it is basically dishonest and is fraudulent. The ignorant hypocrites that promote this form of intransigence should be removed, if possible, from positions of power: replaced by honest, decent men who believe in and understand: ***who or what is God?***

Catholicism is attacked by many other religions: unnecessarily so. One in particular, has its origin in Asia. The King, Bulan in the seventh century, invited representatives from the various prominent religions to meet with him, so to benefit his people whom he believed would benefit from having a religion.[239] They chose the Hebrew faith. *The meaning is that currently there are two types of the Jewish faith:* the traditional Biblical Faith (with a long history) and the new form which can be defined as a *"New Form Zionism"* (essentially a worldly and intransigent form

---

they are not men and they are not progenitors and they cannot be Priests; Priest is a matter of holy Catholic Dogma and cannot be changed. There is biblical, historical and biological evidence supporting this assertion. However one must understand what this is and what it means: **very few do**. The present lack of serious learning when such learning is a requirement of existence is a flaw and will burden our continuation as a Culture and as a Civilization. *Politics will employ every means to negate the truth of Reality.*

[237] **I define a thought-cluster** as being composed of interrelated Ideas with common or purposeful intent. The nature and scope of the *"Cluster"* is changing and is merely tentative. All thought is tentative changing from moment to moment, inexorably so.

[238] **Catholicism,** as this is written has about 1,250,000,000 members: that is almost one quarter of the World population. And the numbers are growing. *(See, Catholicism versus Christianity on the Internet.)* Right now in some places, Catholics are very much persecuted because of their beliefs.

[239] **Chang, Matthias,** *Future Fast Forward, The Zionist, Anglo-American Meltdown.* First American Editions, 2006, American Free Press, Washington D. C. 20063. Pg. 167. "Sometime, during the 7th century, King Bulan adopted Judaism to replace Pagan worship and the people in Khazaria converted en masse and invited Rabbis to establish synagogues and Jewish schools. When the kingdom collapsed after the invasion of the Russians, the Khazars scattered throughout Eastern Europe and Russia. These Jews are therefore not the progeny of Judah, or of any of the twelve tribes of Israel. They were converts. Today they are referred to as "Ashkenazim Jews", and Chaim Weizmann, the President of Israel, and many Zionist leaders today come from this Khazar lineage. That the Khazars are the lineal ancestors of Eastern European Jewry is an historical fact acknowledged by Jewish historians and religious textbooks as well."

intended for the purpose of *political domination and control of a people*). Not many people are aware or understand this; one can check on this in the more complete and objective history texts.

Political domination apparently requires control of the money, *the means for carrying out the necessary commerce of any community.* This is an ultimately important point to consider since all humanity deals in a form of trading one thing for another. It was imagined that money would be that element which would serve as a common denominator. This is one of the prime motivations for modern commerce: indeed money is a miraculous invention. And, to repeat, money must maintain a constant value and **must not be considered as a commodity like all other commodities.** Wages should be decently structured and maintain a constant value as well; for future Time. This would help the poor and the less fortunate in planning for their future.

Some Zionists are closely aligned with the thinking, meaning and intent of Adam Weishaupt the founder of the Illuminati.[240] The very title, Illuminati, is somewhat suspicious since it is a Secret Society: more or less. The term Illuminati sounds respectable, even scholarly and infers a special form of wisdom. Ideas founded in the Illumines run through the thinking of many men. Most are tired, worn of wear and have solved nothing. What we need is not Illumines of some strange and occult form rather we need intelligent men with self control *who are decent and who are honest and not greedy.* Furthermore they must be willing to nurture and raise their own children without the distraction of covertly formed and poorly run programs of government intervention. There must be less emphasis on silly sex and sex as entertainment. Armies should be disbanded so men can consider the important issues of existence: a wife and their children the next citizens of the World. Killing someone from the other side of the World, for reasons that they do not understand, cannot be justified in any way: except *as a perverted political maneuver.* Keep in mind the Killers are young men barely more than children. They are encouraged in this madness by middle-aged morons and old fools who have made a life of killing others. *WHY?*

Men must control their lust and their illicit passions: many of course do this. This is a simple issue that has been made complex by the bad habits of the people. *The bad habits of the people are motivated more and more by television, pornography and raunchy books and movies:* such are the Fool's undoing. In a word we require that men and women remain decent and committed to caring for each other and for their own children. Without this, no system can or will function properly. *No imposed Social Program can replace genuine love and sincere caring of a parent for a child.* To imagine otherwise is to be blind to Reality. Such as this, must be supported by the Virtues: Humility, Patience, Temperance, and a genuine Love for others. Nothing else will ever work. A good family can endure many forms of hardship and still remain happy, even content.

The French Revolution (Illustration I) was a disaster for Catholic France and generally speaking for Western Civilization. There are books on the subject describing the nature and

---

[240] **Adam Weishaupt** was a renegade Catholic Priest who attempted to convey Ideas of his own. He is long dead however some of his ideas are still functional, in the flux of thought forms: one way or another. His thought form, which is in fact a perversion of a form of thinking, articulates well with that of the Zionists determined to control the World and its riches. One will sense vanity combined with a general conceit and a pathological personality. None of this is good, certainly not for the millions of innocent victims.

effects of a bloody revolution.[241] The French Revolution was an example of man's disregard for his fellow man and was as bad as any form of behavior might provide. It was arcane and included the behavior of men and women as cannibals. Ms. Webster, the author, has also written a book on World Revolution which is a compliment to the work on the French Revolution.[242] Both books provide the necessary insights to understanding the nature, scope and objectives of Revolutionary Thought. A bloody Revolution is no joke: indeed it can be and generally provides a display of the worst form of human manners, motivated by the Devil; by hatred, lust and greed.

From Adam Weishaupt and the French Revolution we move to the middle of the nineteenth Century and the Wars that were being fought at that time. The money lenders saw and took advantage of what was happening and they provided the funding for the endeavor: this was considered good business *"for the money Lenders"* that profited greatly from the conflicts. Many were to a considerable degree responsible for the conflicts: at least in part. Like most Wars those Wars abandoned goodness and focused on gaining the field and ultimately on gaining victory. The Victory was no longer noble rather it was savage, deceitful and most unfortunate. By 1850 it is believed that the Rothschild fortune was at about one billion dollars. That was a great sum in 1850: enough to provide well for the family. The mid-century Wars in Europe had a parallel conflict, in the United States:

The Civil War; The Civil War (Illustration II) (began in 1861 with the battle of Bull Run and continued until April 9, 1865 when Lee surrendered at Appomattox) is very well documented however much misunderstood for various reasons that were given to the people: freeing the Slaves for example. This would have happened without the War however the outcomes would have been somewhat different. Keep in mind all Slaves were not treated inhumanly: many were treated quite well. However many families were separated. Unfortunately we here only of those that were brutalized: we cannot know for certain how it might have been different?[243] In fact the Confederacy should have known that bravery could not provide for the fact that they were only one-half the number of their much more industrialized and better equipped opponent: from the beginning they were in a much disadvantaged position. And: very few understood the monetary

---

[241] **Webster, Nesta,** *The French Revolution, a Study in Democracy.* First Published 1919, Republished 1969. Second Edition, The Christian Book Club of America, Hawthorne, CA 90250.

[242] **Webster, Nesta.** *World Revolution, The Plot Against Civilization,* Veritas Publishing Company, 7th. Ed., 1994, Cranbrook. Western Australia 6321,

[243] **American Civil War Facts and Timeline;** Approximately 2,100,000 soldiers participated in the war on the behalf of the Union, while 1,064,000 participated on behalf of Confederates. The death toll in the Union camp was 360,000 of which 110,000 were killed on the battlefield. While 260,000 died in the Confederate camps, 93,000 lost their lives on the battlefield. More than 10,000 soldiers representing the Union were under 18 years of age. *More than half of all deaths during the American Civil War were the result of disease (not bullets).* The primary culprits included typhoid fever, dysentery, tuberculosis and pneumonia. The physical destruction was severe and fatal for many. These are some of the few details, actually quite unimportant in the overall scheme of things which was more focused on controlling the World and it riches. Who understands this? There are still groups that re-enact the Civil War for amusement and for something to do. They appear to be mostly or somewhat blind to Reality. Nevertheless they do enjoy doing this and this forms as a basis for friendship.

and political strivings of their adversaries. If they had better understanding they might/could have found another way.

As a parallel venture in time the Nobility and the Kings of Europe were being eliminated, one by one; this was a profound mistake. This continued until July 16, 1918 when Czar Nickolas was murdered together with his wife and five children, his servants and those who were in his favor.[244] (Illustration III) A complete synopsis can be had in the book *The Last of the Romanovs, How Tsar Nicholas II and Russia's Imperial Family were murdered.*[245] The type of thinking that motivated this atrocity had been seething for two thousand years and was related to the need to dominate: to the **"Will to Power."** The will to power is difficult to understand and more difficult to control. *The killing and murder of the truthful nobility was necessary so that what was Nobility might be transferred to the money-lenders and their kind.* This has been established and we have a new form of elite. This is made more complex by the becoming of very wealthy movie stars, athletes and promoters and by specialists in the stock and real estate markets. We have a vulgar and profane new group of multi-millionaires and billionaires. They have replaced truthful nobility.

The Spanish-American War; April 25, 1898 till Dec. 10, 1898 is pictured (Illustration IV). Movies have been made and stories exploited about Teddy Roosevelt and his rough riders bring fiction to correspond with an important historic event. One is led to fantasize on imagery and the existence of noble warriors riding horse-back against an evil foe. At this point in time there was becoming an understanding of the power of imagery to support a Political Notion and programs for correction.[246] Such movies as were made were followed by those depicting the First World War: *"All Quiet, on the Western Front"* comes to mind. At present this is advertised as a classic

---

[244] **The Russian General Prosecutor's** (7-17-2008) office says remains found last year near the city of Yekaterinburg have been identified through DNA testing as those of Grand Duchess Maria and Prince Alexei—two of Czar Nicholas II's five children. A written account left by one of the killers, Yakov Yurovsky, indicated the royal bodies had been soaked in acid and thrown down a mineshaft. He said two of the victims were burned and buried nearby. Those are the ones identified Tuesday. The remains of Czar Nicholas, his wife and three daughters were buried in 1998 in Saint Petersburg. At a minimum, says Lukyanov, monuments to communists who toppled the czar should be removed and street names should be changed. He says there are streets in Yekaterinburg within blocks of the place where the czarist family was killed that still bear the names of their executioners. Lukyanov notes, however, that Russian communists continue to oppose the removal of monuments to their former leaders. Nicholas II is leading an Internet poll conducted by the Rossiya television network and the Russian Academy of Sciences to name the greatest Russian. Some see that as an indication of renewed interest in the country's royal past. The Orthodox Church, which canonized the czar, is holding memorial services Wednesday and Thursday to commemorate him and his family.

[245] **Wilton, Robert,** *The Last of the Romanovs, How Tsar Nicholas II and Russia's Imperial Family were Murdered.* Copyright © 1993, the Institute for Historical Review. First British Edition, pub. 1920 in London by T. Butterworth. First U. S. Edition published 1920, in New York by George H. Dorn. French Edition, pub. Paris 1921. Russian language edition, pub. Berlin 1923. ISBN # 0-939484-1.

[246] **Jacobson, Steven,** *Mind Control in the United States.* Critique Pub., P. O. Box 11451, Santa Rosa CA 95406. ISBN o-911485-00-7. LC # 85-70431. Mfg. Apollo Books, 107 Lafayette St., Winona, MN. Pg. 22&23.

movie: perhaps it is. At this moment in time it was discovered/imagined that there was really great power in the movie as a tool for propaganda. Since then every form and manner of thought control has been considered and is being applied to some fictitious presentation. [247]

The First World War 1914-1918 (Illustration V) [248] was fought concurrent with the elimination of the Russian Monarch and his family: this was the first of the Great Wars, worldwide conflicts encouraged by the money-lenders.[249] The money-lender always appears as being somewhat altruistic in his pretense to help one side or the other: both sides in fact as circumstance would provide such necessity. The money-lenders always had the collateral of the winning-side they would finance and the loser as well. *President Wilson lied to the American people about an incident that, in fact, never occurred.* This provoked our brave and courageous leaders to prompt action against Germany. It is an interesting fact that a great number of Americans were of German decent and they carried the potentiality of the Germanic peoples in their gene Pool. Nevertheless they did respond, as planned, and entered the War against the Germans. *The results, genetically speaking, were a catastrophe for Germany and for the human Race*

---

[247] **Jacobson, Steven,** *Mind Control in the United States.* Critique Pub., P. O. Box 11451, Santa Rosa CA 95406. ISBN o-911485-00-7. LC # 85-70431. Mfg. Apollo Books, 107 Lafayette St., Winona, MN. Pg. 3&4. "The most effective way to conquer a man is to capture his mind. Control a man's mind and you control his body. Most people don't pay conscious attention, to the things that affect them subconsciously. They don't usually know what to look for . . . . *Stop conscious thought and the mind is in its most suggestible state and is more susceptible to programming than at any other time."* This book should be read by everyone.

[248] "**The assassination on 28 June 1914** of Archduke Franz Ferdinand of Austria, the heir to the throne of Austria-Hungary, was the proximate trigger of the war. Long-term causes, such as imperialistic foreign policies of the great powers of Europe, such as the German Empire, the Austro-Hungarian Empire, the Ottoman Empire, the Russian Empire, the British Empire, France, and Italy, played a major role. Ferdinand's assassination by a Yugoslav nationalist resulted in a Habsburg ultimatum against the Kingdom of Serbia.[10][11] Several alliances formed over the past decades were invoked, so within weeks the major powers were at war; via their colonies, the conflict soon spread around the world."

[249] **The Money-lenders** were apparently aware of the value of the Russian currency when equated with gold. The Russian currency, at that time, had a gold backing of about 125%. The Russian monarchy, as servants of the Russian people, had hundreds of millions in various Western banks as well as a fortune in jewels, Art, Architecture and many other precious objects. This was known by the thieves that stole the Russian Nation from its people. The invaders created reasons why the Czar should be retired. When they reached a point of current understanding coincident with the Reality they murdered the entire Royal Family. *This was probably the greatest crime of the twentieth century.* The vast wealth of Russia combined with the money swindled from the various contrived stock markets has given a small minority tremendous economic power. They have become the *"New Nobility.* Keep in mind at the time of the murders the value of gold was at $20.00 an ounce. With inflation, the one we are not supposed to notice, the value of gold is presently at about $1,500.00 per ounce. The money changers have made a fortune on this maneuver. This is preposterous and should never have happened. Roosevelt raised the price of gold in 1932 to $35.00 an ounce giving Bernard Baruch a tremendous advantage along with some others of their kind.

as well: millions were killed unnecessarily.[250] However the bankers profited greatly from this fiasco: we are still treated to the movies and stories about the quietude on the Western Front. The dissemination of the gene-pool perhaps the most lasting aspect of any warfare is rarely mentioned in political writing.[251] This is unfortunate and is probably due to the greed or hatred of the combatants.[252]

The Second World War 1941-1945 (Illustration VI) under the *imagined* mindful-direction of a somewhat failing President Roosevelt was as bad or worse. ***We were given lies by our esteemed President*** so as to encourage us into this conflict: as we were deceived by lies into the First World War. *Simply put both Presidents were liars:* womanizers as well. *"They told more lies, than the cross-ties on a railroad or stars in the skis."* The drums began to beat and the Nazis became the enemy of the World: even as the bankers pocketed the spoils from the conflict. Our national debt, *which is a phony number,* expanded considerably because of the nature of the Federal Reserve System. The nation was mobilized and the stories that came from the conflict were grotesque and fantasy like. We still see movies about the Great War as we enjoy a beer in the comforts of our inflated meaning over-priced accommodations.[253] Such pricing has placed millions in a state of virtual debt from which some will never recover; time will tell.

Since World War II the US has had continuous involvement in various forms of conflict: Korea, (Illustration VII) Viet Nam, Cambodia, Laos, Iraq and now Afghanistan and Pakistan to mention those most important. This is being portrayed as being good for the people of other Nations. Some good may have come from this but at what cost. The fluctuation in the price of gold is just part of the cover-up of Reality. Not to worry: we have a money machine in the Federal Reserve. The Federal Reserve is papering the world with our once valued dollar, ***now worth about two***

---

[250] World War I Statistics: Number of German soldiers killed in battle during World War I: 2,000,000.[1] Number of Russian soldiers killed in battle during World War I: 1,700,000.[2] Number of French soldiers killed in battle during World War I: 1,400,000 [3] Number of British soldiers killed in battle during World War I: 900,000.[4] Number of American soldiers killed in battle during World War I: 50,000.[5] Percentage of total French population killed or wounded in World War I: 11%.[6] Percentage of total German population killed or wounded in World War I: 9%.[7] Percentage of total British population killed or wounded in World War I: 8% [8] Percentage of total American population killed or wounded in World War I: 0.37%.[9] Percentage of American soldiers serving in Europe who contracted sexually transmitted diseases during World War I: 10%.[10]

[251] **Pendell, Elmer PH. D**. *Sex versus Civilization;* Noontide Press P. O. Box 76062, Los Angeles, CA, 90005. © 1967 Dr. Elmer Pendell. This work discusses the declination in the intelligence of the general population and the imagined lack of the intelligence which would be necessary to solve existing and future problems. The work might be considered, in some respects, as prophecy. Such information should be given with the attendant facts and projections, as part of any Education: Public and Private.

[252] **Sat. July 25, 2009:** Harry Patch the last veteran to serve in the trenches in World War I, died today at the age of 111. He served in the battle of Passchendale where three of his friends died and he was wounded. The First World War is finally over!

[253] **World War II Statistics:** Military Deaths Civilian deaths Total deaths; **Deaths as % of 1939 population**

		Military Deaths	Civilian deaths	Total deaths	Deaths as % of 1939 population
Totals	Population 1-1-1939 1,978,167,400	22,572,400	To 37,585,300	To 62,171,400 To	3.17%
		25,487,500	55,207,000	78,511,500	

cents ($ 00.02 C). That money machine is determined to destroy what was the greatest Nation in recent History. This is being accomplished as the main focus of a Conspiracy. *The Conspiracy has determined to take over the entire World for the good of a few.* Who are the few that will benefit from this take-over? Very few know who they might be. The cost of the accommodations and luxuries featured in our slick magazines should begin to inform even the most intellectually dull: if they could simply count, add and subtract those could have an idea about Reality. The disparity in the wealth is some indication however even this is not conclusive and is mostly misunderstood. Invention has provided some inventors with astounding profits: we need not know who they are however we do know that some do exist. There is nothing wrong with this as a part of human progress. We do not require a form of totalitarian dictatorship to deal with good luck and good fortune: all benefit from legitimate invention. All benefit from honest endeavor no matter how profitable it might be. Conversely all suffer from the Lies and the cheating of many amongst the *"Well Connected"* who are generally the most wealthy.

The Corporation and the legalities that protect it form as an interesting element in the totality. The Corporations are held as stock and various forms of legitimate paper which can be purchased by anyone with the funds to do so. This provides a cover for the real owners: the individuals with millions of shares. There are many investors involved in various ways however in fact the present Idea of a Corporation is not a good one. *The Idea forms as a perfect foil for the great wealth of the thieves that are stealing the World and its riches from the millions who suffer from famine, pestilence and persecution.* Add to this that the petty warfare and the disease and abortions that claims the lives of millions every year. There must be found other ways than the Corporation to deal with the problems and a burgeoning population. A selection of soap scents or the lace on one's panties is not sufficient: such is superficial; is actually a form of *Vanity*; a *Sin*.

Is there a Conspiracy? Yes!

Is there a Conspiracy?[254] We are told there is no Conspiracy. In fact there are many and they do compete each with the others. To begin, a Conspiracy is secret or somewhat secret, and requires financing, money and ways to make profits. This does exist in many forms, most of which are tightly held by the conspirators as stock, mining interests, precious metals, diamonds, newly found elements and various forms of property; especially in the great cities, for example New York, Chicago, Los Angeles, London, Paris, Berlin and Tokyo; there are others as well. There are also criminal syndicates that have their own forms and means of theft. They are considered illegitimate. And new methods and procedures, largely focused on elements used in warfare are being found, developed and utilized. *The most significant of the Conspiracies* is in the business of finance and banking: which provides for the source and distribution of money wealth and paper profits. *For the opportunists paper profits are very important: they can be transferred into real wealth as is being done on a continuing basis.* All efforts depend on a form of financing which provides entrance into the arena of wealth building. Wealth building is as an Art form: one transaction depends on others and they multiply; in some instances they have grown into

---

[254] **Conspire,** *Conspired, Conspiring: to plan secretly an unlawful act: plot. Webster.* It is well known that much of what is done is secretly planned in advance and executed privately with little or no meaningful detection. This is the reason for the Lie mentioned in other places in this manuscript. Interestingly: to lie has a certain tainted glamour.

a Colossus. People who manage large sums of money understand some of this, perhaps not all; however the wealth which they control will provide ample cover for the owners in most any circumstance.

What is a Conspiracy? Any act done in secret is to a degree a Conspiracy. Some are more effective and have wider influence and some are of little concern. *The Conspiracies that exist in financial dealing will probably have the greatest influence on the greatest number of people.* This is understandable and is the cause for a form of *"Collective Anxiety"* where about large numbers of individuals are **held captive by their own mind.** People control or lack of it, are important elements in directing the path and direction of society. When individuals are distracted they are likely to do dumb things which could prove their undoing. The dumb things often involve spending more than they can afford or spending on things which they do not need. Both can be considered as foolishness.

This understanding works well in a consumer oriented Society within which there is so much to buy and not enough money immediately available to pay for what one wants. Our credit system seems to encourage overspending and falling into debt. This often has little or nothing to do with what one in fact needs. *Wants and needs are of different species and must be understood as such.* The understanding should be discussed in any competent educational system so to provide protection against making the same mistake over and over. Given the educational System this is not generally happening and is not universally encouraged. We, individually and collectively are more deeply in debt to the Controlling money interests than ever however there are so many distractions that few in our Democratic Republic even notice what has and is happening. There is an entire cadre of attorneys that make a living solving such dilemma. During the Holidays, especially Christmas the most holy day of the year, the shopping and buying are incredible; in fact they are outrageous for the most holy of all days. Our public Education system will train technicians however there are very few real thinkers. Many cannot figure the simple interest on the debts that they have accumulated. Programs abound that ensure you can be debt free in just a moment or two; such as this further encourages the problems to continue. Presently the debts are in the trillions and climbing rapidly. The interest alone is mind boggling: millions by the minute!

This climbing of the Debt is the final reward for two thousand years of patient and secret money-grubbing! *The clever seem to have outwitted the self-praising wise.* This has been known and is understood by the manipulators and most of their henchmen. In 1959 Congressman Usher L. Burdick was interviewed on a radio by T. D. Horton Chairman of the Executive Council of the Defenders of the American Constitution. At the end of the interview Congressman Burdick had this to say: *"Ever since we have had any recorded history of the use of money and the control of money, every czar that has controlled money has said, every one of them let me control the money and I don't care who makes the laws. What surprises me, by following that process, we haven't lost the government completely."* **Not yet!**

Money, *what it is and what it should do* should be **THE** primary subject in any well formed educational system of a free people. Money must have and must maintain a constant level of value. *As such it is a store for human effort: indeed for human life.* If it does not do this it will allow for speculation in currency and eventually the Nation will be destroyed: our Nation is being destroyed as this is written because of a lack of understanding regarding this rather easy to understand factor regarding money: ***what it is and what it should do.*** The problem is, no one really wants to understand this very simple and elemental fact. Greed for some implies possession; when greed enters the mind the people will follow the call of Greed.

About the time of the murder of the Russian Royal Family was the establishment of the Federal Reserve System in the United States. To begin, let the reader understand that *it is not* *Federal* (it provides that a group of private entities can print and distribute the money) *and there* *are no* *reserves* (but there are tricks to fool the Public). The System was designed to be the model for a World-wide currency and in fact, at present, the dollar is the World's reserve currency. Even if a different currency were to come to be it will be modeled on the same suppositions and with the same intentions.

As an aside the compounding of interest on great sums of wealth did increase the basic stipend and there was and is more on the way, with Wars and International Finance. To repeat, it is imagined by some that the present Rothschild fortune with their various associations and connections is in the realm of nine trillion dollars ($9,000,000,000,000.00).[255] At a mere 2 1/2 % interest this provides an income of $225,000,000,000.00 per year; ***two hundred twenty five billion.*** This is truly an economic disease! Additionally, it is the opinion of many that about one half of the World's wealth and properties belong to about 350 individuals. How did this happen? This writing has been my attempt to explain briefly just how it did happen. To better understand the reader must avail themselves of the works listed in the bibliography. Given the various ingredients it did happen and had little to do with the known political movements except it did very cleverly exploit them. Rather it was centered on the financial structure and operation of the perverted Banking System and on a very poorly understood and cleverly contrived Legal System. All the reasoning and evidence for an indictment for fraud are there to see: however to understand more completely you must be interested enough to read some of the works cited in the accompanying bibliography: as many as is possible.

The Leading Families
Part III

The Few believe "The Few must have everything"
Greed is insatiable. Who has most seeks more and more: And more.
He who has little will get less and less: admittedly there is some lack of responsibility.

The victims of organized pillage will always be the Poor, the ignorant and the poorly or inadequately informed. Those with a weak will are especially vulnerable; there are many. Generally the Poor have not means, financially speaking, to cover any rise in social or physically imposed tragedy: they suffer with only the hope of a better tomorrow. They are in the wrong place. In the past, due to invention or the discovery of some needed or wanted commodity some of the Poor did gain power over others which began what is now being considered. Such good fortune, small at first propelled some into a regal existence of plenty. Also the power of

---

[255] **This may or may not** be exactly the number however even if merely close it represents a great fortune, actually a financial colossus. Certainly it is divided amongst the various participating entities.

some was extraordinary and they controlled, by physical means the lives of others. The concept here is more important than the name of the man: the Reality is the exploitation of *the Will to Power!* All of past Humanity is dead. However the **Ideas do remain** and are still functional and have become so complex almost no man can understand what they are and what they mean. The money made by the Elders is given to those that survive; this is somewhat complex but is understandable.[256] Big money will move in time from one generation to the next. In all events *the Will to Power* sustains. *This is a perfect compliment for the imposition of a politically contrived and economically inspired control of the masses.* There are others as well: some still unknown? If this is not better contained there could be mass drugging or simply the annihilation of millions by war or starving.

We cannot define all of the past in this brief publication for the intelligent and well informed reader much can be understood by inference, innuendo and the gaining of truthful knowledge: from past history as it did in fact occur. Once again it is suggested that the reader pursue some of the thoughts by obtaining and reading the works cited in our references: you will be amazed at what is the truth. The Internet can provide the reader with the required details. Because of the presence of *LIARS* and the *THIEVES* even a study of past history may not be adequate, when the History has been edited somewhat, by that is meant distorted. *Serious study is lacking having been overcome by sporting events* which dominate the time that is absolutely necessary to learn and to know. The salaries paid to some outstanding athletes says it all: millions are paid to some men for bouncing, throwing or kicking a ball: Recently a Football Star was given a contract from the Green Bay Packers for over one hundred million dollars for five years; forty million the first year. One wonders how much does the promoter get? The community is more interested in being distracted from their menial existence than in truthful learning and knowing. This combined with a phony Democratic prerogative, controlled by the persons at the top, make what is happening possible. Other Nations and peoples have their own sets of imposed or imagined problems many volumes have been written on the subject by various individuals: who reads what has been written, who understands the meaning of what they read? Some other peoples are simply too primitive and cannot be included in the present dialogue, except by interpretation. Such, class of people are human beings like anyone else however they can be a real threat to the more decently determined individual.

The division of subject matter areas into fields of specialty prevents the necessarily broad framework of knowing and understanding that is a requirement for truthful participation in serious Philosophical thought. University study, at one time, placed high regard on Philosophy, Religious study and Eschatology, what might be considered as supernatural knowledge. With the secularization of Universities and the prevailing Democratic prerogative, *"where it is imagined"* that all can learn at the highest levels, this has changed.[257] Universities, at present, are more concerned with technologies and what are called the Professions. *Such as this is fine for*

---

[256] **Lundberg, Ferdinand,** *The Rich and the Super Rich.* A Study in the Power of Money Today.

[257] **Everyone can learn something** however learning is categorical in a descending order from Genius to Fools. Every individual is not equipped to be a brain surgeon or an inventor. This is a matter of aptitude, propensity and will. Individuals must be willing to study and to go forth from their existing position: most dullards would rather have fun. Many simple minded individuals are more interested in entertainment and in sex; they seek pleasure.

everyday expression however for learning, knowing and understanding this is not sufficient and is a mistake. It is known that most everyone can learn something however those with the proper level of intellect should be considering the higher forms of learning: Philosophy, Religion and Eschatology, which deals with the supernatural. All youth are not equipped or are they interested in so doing.

Additionally problems with personalities may and do function often with negative consequence on the totality.[258] We have marvelous technologies, often aimed at killing a man's son or daughter and almost no understanding of what this means. Every person has and should have an opportunity to live life without being threatened by some moron with a gun. That this is not happening is absolutely pitiful! What we require are well educated leaders and a population of decently inspired individuals who will endeavor to understand the truthful meaning of reality and of History.

At pres*ent* there is some debate of the debt issue. Once democratized, the people demand more than is reasonable: and more than they can afford to pay for. How might this be solved? Will placing another contrived program in position to afford temporary relief be a good idea? All will be better for a short while. There are too many of such programs and no one wants to give up on what they imagine is their Right in an imagined Democracy. Rights must be intelligently determined or we would have chaos and murder. In the meantime good men have created much for all to enjoy and there is even some prosperity.[259] Nevertheless the real thinking concerning this issue has already been done by the wise and shrewd money-lenders. They will simply bankrupt a nation and then help themselves to the wealth that remains: this is done rather secretly and slowly so not many will realize what is happening. This is clever however not wise and is certainly very deceitful. ***This is exactly what Inflation is accomplishing!***

The Federal Reserve System is one of the real problems, the existence of a fraudulently conceived and managed Federal Reserve System, is never mentioned with any form of constructive intent.[260] It was designed one hundred years ago by a foreign-born alien Paul Moritz Warberg, to do exactly what it is doing: to destroy the economy and prosperity of this

---

[258] **Reisman, Judith, PhD.** *Kinsey, Crimes and Cosequences.* The Institute for Medical Education; P. O. Box 15284, Sacramento, CA 95851-0284. This work obviates the destructive force of the works of a somewhat perverted mind given to wide spread attention. Kinsey was and remains as a *"Nothing"* (of course he is now dead) however the Ideas that found a place in his mind were and are very dangerous to humanity. One must read of his work to understand the nature and consequence of his type of meddling.

[259] **There is a waiting list** for fifty million dollar yachts, that no one really needs except as a means to display a form of Worldly success. It is *VANITY* of the worst kind. Christ warned of this however most do not understand what this means. A fifty million dollar yacht is viewed as a manner of good fortune; how such money was acquired is not generally well known.

[260] **Wickliffe, Vennard B., Sr.,** *The Federal Reserve Hoax, The Age of Deception;* Meador Publishing Co; 324 Newbury Street, Boston 15, MA. Seventh Ed., Pp. 14-70. This is a brief book however is very concise as to meaning, The Federal Reserve System is a complete Hoax, *it is a fraud!* It should be abolished and restructured to fit the Constitutional Dictates of the Republic. If this does not happen, America will cease to exist as the Land of the Free and Home of the brave. The entire book should be read: in fact it should be required reading in our Public and Private Schools.

presumably free Nation. The Lords and Ladies in the past saw Freedom as a threat to their monopoly on an opulent existence therefore some of them were encouraged and in fact did support the programs involved. At the time, they could not have imagined the productivity of the human Race which, if the Political nonsense were removed would provide amply for every man, woman and child. It is true that at various times much of the Nobility was destroyed, as a part of the greater Plan: they were beheaded or worse.[261] Some participants in the plan met with an untimely death. However the money influences, having originated in the distant past still controlled the situation. The book on the French Revolution by Nesta Webster outlines and leads *"We the People"* to be aware and to understand the possibilities for the most brutal form of human behavior imaginable: executed by the drunken *"Slobs"* of that era. Their behavior was unconscionable, crude and did display the worst form of human involvement against another of God's creatures: there will be more drunken *"Slobs"* in the future. The book on the French Revolution is compelling and makes for better use of time than any of the Futuristic forms of nonsense by Spielberg: *"Writing as Entertainment, to sell tickets to enable the author to buy a too-large house."*[262]

When an Idea has been adopted it may take centuries to eliminate the actions and consequences caused by that same Idea. This too is a part of History. Additionally Ideas *"morph"* and become different from the original in various ways; they may improve circumstance or be a disaster. This is very difficult to understand and even more difficult to correct *in fact it is not possible to correct this.* Ideas motivate men they move from now to then, they change one way to another and are always effective: on everyone involved. And, everyone is generally involved!

Professor Emeritus, Robert Fiedler
May, 2013.

[261] **Webster, Nesta,** _The French Revolution, a Study in Democracy._ First Published 1919, Republished 1969. Second Edition. The Christian Book Club of America, Hawthorne, CA 90250. This book should be required reading of all students attempting to be well informed. We cannot deal with the details at this junction except to suggest one read the entire book. It will keep you on the edge of your chair: for very good reason.

[262] *All of such as this,* forms as a manner of success: in this world. Nevertheless it avoids any understanding of what is an Infinite and enduring Entity: it completely ignores the presence of a Divine Being.

Painting of the Bastilles. There were seven men held in the Bastilles when captured.

I.   **Artist's interpretation *"Storming of the Bastille"* Suggests what may or may not have happened.**

In 1789 when the angry mob broke through the walls and stormed the Bastille they found only seven prisoners inside: four forgers, two lunatics, and a young noble. However, it was not to free the prisoners inside that the battle was fought. Instead, it was to bring down the single most important symbol of the King's power. The Governor of the Bastille, De Launay, had his head cut off and paraded around the streets of Paris on a pike. In the end eighty-three attackers were dead, and seventy-three injured. The guards only suffered one death and three wounded.

When prisoners were released from the walls of the Bastille, they were allowed to go only if they agreed never to tell what they had seen or what had happened inside the feared prison. This lack of knowledge about the Bastille helped to create a mystique of horror and terror that the King could use to coerce certain things out of people. However, the reality of the Bastille was much different than the mystique created by the King. All of the rooms until the year 1701 were left unfurnished. Wealthy political prisoners were allowed to bring in their own furniture many even brought their own servants with them. Meals were of generous proportions, and more luxurious meals could be bought if the prisoner was wealthy enough. Most prisoners were docile. They had their own personal hobbies and a few were even allowed to visit the city of Paris on parole. The Bastille was much more comfortable, even homelike, than the horrific rumors that circled around France proclaimed. The prisoners were allowed to walk freely around the fortress, talk with officers and other prisoners and play games.

Men with cannon, Civil war. In the end we are all dead.

II.   The American Civil War Photography (1861-1865)

The men shown in this picture are certainly all dead: we are not sure of how they might have died however "In the end we are all dead" (Shakespeare). Shakespeare put it simply however everyone can understand what he said. Some others talk incessantly about death however no one understands what they are saying.

Undoubtedly these four men felt superior standing with the cannon, an advanced weapon for the time: they may even have thought they were somehow invincible. Certainly no one is invincible.

The personality takes control of the man and allows for the Devil, that being Evil, to invade his being. When this occurs the man works for the Devil, metaphorically speaking. However no one knows where the metaphor stops and where the truthful reality controls one's being. This is a factor in all warfare: in fact it is a factor in just about everything that man does.

Each one of these men displays a form of guarded arrogance in their countenance. Do you see what it is?

The man on the left although he is the shortest of the group exudes a certain self confidence that is telling. The man second from the right has an attitude very similar to the shorter man. The remaining two appear to be somewhat docile. One wonders if any of the four was killed in the senseless struggle.

Battle cruiser, Spanish American War. The ship was sunk.

III. Spanish cruiser *Cristóbal Colón*. Destroyed during the Battle of Santiago on 3 July 1898.

This is a typical naval vessel of the time.

Theodore Roosevelt advocated intervention in Cuba, for the Cuban people and to promote the Monroe Doctrine. While Assistant Secretary of the Navy, placed the Navy on a war-time footing and prepared Dewey's Asiatic Squadron for battle. He worked with Leonard Wood in convincing the Army to raise an all-volunteer regiment, the 1st U.S. Volunteer Cavalry. Wood was given command of the regiment that quickly became known as the "Rough Riders.

The Americans planned to capture the city of Santiago de Cuba to destroy Linares' army and Cervera's fleet. To reach Santiago they had to pass through concentrated Spanish defenses in the San Juan Hills and a small town in ElCaney. The American forces were aided in Cuba by the pro-independence rebels led by General Calixto García.

From 22-24 June, the U.S. V Corps under General William R. Shafter landed at Daiquirí and Siboney, east of Santiago, and established an American base of operations. A contingent of Spanish troops, having fought a skirmish with the Americans near Siboney on 23 June, had retired to their lightly entrenched positions at Las Guasimas. An advance guard of U.S. forces under former Confederate General Joseph Wheeler ignored Cuban scouting parties and orders to proceed with caution. They caught up with and engaged the Spanish rearguard commanded of about 2000 soldiers led by General Antonio Rubin who effectively ambushed them, in the Battle of Las Guasimas on 24 June. The battle ended indecisively in favor of Spain and the Spanish left Las Guasimas on their planned retreat to Santiago.

The murdered Romanoff family. Real aristocracy ruled Russia for 900 years.

IV. Last of the Romanovs:

Olga, Nicholas II, Anastasia, Alexei, Tatiana
720 x 599 · 73 kB · jpeghistoryinspiredmusings.blogspot.com

The Romanoff Dynasty (1650-1917) followed that of the Rurik Dynasty (1157-1598) which represented Russian Royalty of that period. The Rurik's were nobility for almost 500 years, the Romanoff's for about 450 years.

The Romanoff's were murdered ruthlessly by a new form of aristocracy: communism, Marxist socialism. In fact with the help of various traitors and hypocrites the Marxist stole the nation from its people. The Rurik's and the Romanoff's were legitimate keepers of the Throne where as the ones that committed murder and thereby took over for the hypocrites were not.

This is a complex issue dealing with economics, banking and the suppression of the Worlds people for the demanded and stolen rights of a few: those few have managed to acquire vast wealth and live beyond the means of any previous King. Our present system must be reconsidered so to make it more responsible to all people not just the Money-grubbing thieves that presently control nearly all financial transaction and most important circumstance. Their wealth has grown in time because of the compounding of values upon present holdings. This is mentioned above in this article immediately above.

The Romanoff's were decently inspired leaders of their people: perhaps they did make some mistakes however in time they would have been corrected. Importantly, the Nobility, generally speaking represented the most intelligent, gifted and enlightened amongst our kind. There were some fools and scoundrels in the mix however they were not the majority as may be the case right now.

Men in a trench, the First World War. They are all now dead.

V.   The First World War

On June 28, 1914, in an event that is widely regarded as sparking the outbreak of World War I, Archduke Franz Ferdinand, heir to the Austro-Hungarian Empire, was shot to death with his wife by Bosnian Serb Gavrilo Princip in Sarajevo, Bosnia. Ferdinand had been inspecting his uncle's imperial armed forces in Bosnia and Herzegovina, despite the threat of Serbian nationalists who wanted these Austro-Hungarian possessions to join newly independent Serbia. Austria-Hungary blamed the Serbian government for the attack and hoped to use the incident as justification for settling the problem of Slavic nationalism once and for all. However, as Russia supported Serbia, an Austria-Hungary declaration of war was delayed until its leaders received assurances from German leader Kaiser Wilhelm II that Germany would support them in the event of a Russian intervention.

On July 28, Austria-Hungary declared war on Serbia, and the tenuous peace between Europe's great powers collapsed. On July 29, Austro-Hungarian forces began to shell the Serbian capital of Belgrade, and Russia, Serbia's ally, ordered a troop mobilization against Austria-Hungary. France, allied with Russia, began to mobilize on August 1. France and Germany declared war against each other on August 3. After crossing through neutral Luxembourg, the German army invaded Belgium on the night of August 3-4, prompting Great Britain, Belgium's ally, to declare War against Germany.

Men with tank, the Second World War. Those were not invincible.

VI. German Tiger Tanks, World War II

World War II, or the **Second World War** [2] (often abbreviated as **WWII** or **WW2**), was a global military conflict lasting from 1939 to 1945, which involved most of the world's nations, including all of the great powers: eventually forming two opposing military alliances, the Allies and the Axis. It was the most widespread war in history, with more than 100 million military personnel mobilized. In a state of "total war," the major participants placed their entire economic, industrial, and scientific capabilities at the service of the war effort, erasing the distinction between civilian and military resources. Marked by significant events involving the mass death of civilians, including the Holocaust and the only use of nuclear weapons in warfare, it was the deadliest conflict in human history,[3] resulting in 50 million to over 70 million fatalities.

The war is generally accepted to have begun on 1 September 1939, with the invasion of Poland by Germany and Slovakia, and subsequent declarations of war on Germany by France and most of the countries of the British Empire and Commonwealth. Germany set out to establish a large empire in Europe. From late 1939 to early 1941, in a series of campaigns and treaties, Germany conquered or subdued much of continental Europe; amid Nazi-Soviet agreements, the nominally neutral Soviet Union fully or partially occupied and annexed territories of its six European neighbors. Britain and the Commonwealth remained the only major force continuing the fight against the Axis in North Africa and in extensive naval warfare. In June 1941, the European Axis launched an invasion of the Soviet Union. The USSR joined the Allies and the largest land theatre of war in history began, which, from this moment on would tie down the major part of the Axis military power. In December 1941, Japan, the major Asian Axis nation, which had been at war with China since 1937,[4] and aimed to dominate Asia, attacked the United States and European possessions in the Pacific Ocean, quickly conquering much of the region. In response, the United States entered into military operations on the Allied side.

Men with tank, the Second World War. Those were not invincible.

VII. Korean War

The **Korean War** (25 June 1950—armistice signed 27 July 1953[28]) (was a conventional war between South Korea, supported by the United Nations, and North Korea, supported by the People's Republic of China (PRC), with military material aid from the Soviet Union. The war was a result of the physical division of Korea by an agreement of the victorious Allies at the conclusion of the Pacific War at the end of World War II.

The Korean peninsula was ruled by Japan from 1910 until the end of World War II. Following the surrender of Japan in 1945, American administrators divided the peninsula along the 38th Parallel, with United States troops occupying the southern part and Soviet troops occupying the Northern part.

The failure to hold free elections throughout the Korean Peninsula in 1948 deepened the division between the two Sides; and the North established a Communist government. The 38th Parallel increasingly became a political border between the two Koreas. Although reunification negotiations continued in the months preceding the war, tension intensified. Cross-border skirmishes and raids at the 38th Parallel persisted. The situation escalated into open warfare when North Korean forces invaded South Korea on 25 June 1950.[30] It was the first significant armed conflict of the Cold War.

CHAPTER X

THE NATION STATE

A Nation State is that State which is closest to the individual.

Every man should be as close as is possible to the law and to the governing process. He should, in fact, be the law and should be responsible for the administration and governing of that same law. In a Democracy many imagine this is how it is; however this is a general misunderstanding. If such were true there would be little problem with the man or the law. I understand the above sentence is a generality however it is supported by a large measure of common sense. If men were allowed truthful participation in manners of Law, there would be little reason to disobey that same law. Youth, if taught properly would understand this and be, generally speaking, more co-operative. We are training our youth, inculcating them, by means of a perverted form of Television to be selfish and barbaric. Youngsters learn rapidly until they have reached puberty therefore it is wise to teach them properly sooner rather than later. If they do not learn correctly they will learn incorrectly nevertheless they will learn; one way or the other. All individuals learn much from their own experience and by witnessing the behavior of others.

How close can one be to the Law? Every man should and could be a part of the Law. The Law provides a framework for moral certitude which must be considered from a universal perspective; a Catholic perspective where all men are equal under the eyes of an omnipotent God. Those who do not believe this should imagine they do believe as they may imagine many incorrect and contrary ideas. *Such as this is important thought however, is not and will not be considered by public education as it presently exists.* This is a most unfortunate situation whereabouts the philosophy that, in fact, has determined what we understand as Western Culture and Civilization is prevented from being included as an important element in educating the youth that have grown up in this existing world. The word Catholic implies a universal understanding (from the Greek), followed by proper and correct behavior.[263] This is nothing new and should be understood as exemplifying the truth as it is. A little well understood Law is much better than too much legality. *The Law,* in truth should be limited for use in some rare cases where common sense has been forgotten. At present some lawyers are paid in the millions for settling cases that are simply foolish. They become celebrities!

Legality should protect the innocent citizen without contrivance or moral corruption. Presently the laws have been perverted so that the innocent become the victim of the law. In the United

---

[263] **It is true** that some Priests have behaved badly however that is a personal issue and does not discredit the Church as such. Other Faiths have the same problems.

States Police Officers are jailed for enforcing the laws intended for the protection of the honest citizen. This does not speak well of law or the method of enforcement. This generally results from a form of politically motivated pressure to protect who is imagined to be innocent. This is outrageous and is an understanding that few might imagine. It is understood that all men are not wise however Police Officers who have made a mistake should be better trained and accept the teachings of the Catholic Church and generally speaking the teachings of Christianity. Some have in fact done this. Such understanding is not within the framework of presently administered political and social thought, which is confused by intransigence and moral corruption. Who would understand the dimensions and consequence so caused? This appears to be caused by serious philosophic and moral issues overcome by "Dancing with the Stars", "Super Bowl" and simply stated "moral corruption" of various sorts.

One cannot accuse everyone of being immoral nevertheless many are (somewhat) morally corrupt and they add to the problem without realizing what they are adding. Many gamble just a bit, have had only one or two affairs, lie only occasionally however are otherwise redeemable. *Most people are good most of the time since this is, generally speaking, the best way to be.* However our entertainment often glorifies Sin, perverted Sex and Unholy ways. The reader can pick his own examples from the many offered.

Christmas, one of the holiest days of the year, has become overcome with commercialism and buying stuff to present as a gift, which has become a requirement. Easter is also plagued with the same nonsense however focuses somewhat more on adults. In the last few years Halloween has been given much more attention as the Holiday center for the spread of Paganism and unchristian ways. One could go on however the picture should be clear enough at this point.

Whether one, as an individual, believes in God or not is not relevant in the totality of the ongoing of Humanity; nevertheless such belief is fundamental to our way of life, to our *"thought clusters"* and to our actions. Importantly such belief is a philosophic and cultural given; we have no choice however must accept what is reality. Life, one way or another presents opportunities of various kinds which must be accepted and understood; if this is possible. In the past this was not always possible however presently this is very possible. One can know and understand much of what is. If and when this knowledge is put into honest and fair action the world will be a better place because of our efforts. Christ admonished men to seek truth believing that the truth will set men free. How many men understand truthfully the meaning of this and what is implied?

Politics is not the same as Theology nevertheless some men treat it as such. This is flawed thinking and will lead to incorrect actions; this is obvious considering the many recent Wars, and more are planned for the future. This is a form of insanity justified with music and parades, with medals and a promise of an education. The reverence held for Politicians is certainly misplaced especially considering how many of the Politicians are lecherous fools, many have sworn to other oaths than to those appropriate to their charges, some have been and are felons and others are simply stupid. There are some good ones in the mix as well which provide a degree of cover and respectability for others, to such as those goes our apology. Nevertheless many spend a lifetime in the office; this is incredible!

Political nonsense is protected by Law and often financed by the Corporations that build the armaments. Is victory in War an ideal that men hope to achieve? Who might have imagined what did happen to the _"slings and arrows of outrageous fortune"_ which have become the weapons of our present epoch? The World will be certainly destroyed unless some change their ways; time is running out against the fact that this will happen! The present economic crisis should be enough to alert intelligent men to cease Warfare and concentrate on feeding and providing for their children and for a growing population.[264] With effort directed toward gainful and significant tasks the earth can sustain a larger population than now exists. This must include the cessation of all forms of politically and socially brewed conflict. Insurrectionists should be jailed, re-educated in the ways of a civilized and cultured population. _Race is not an over-riding issue._ Religions too should be tolerant each toward the others. One can have various faiths included however it is our belief that Catholicism is the one true Faith. _Christ came to serve and save all men!_

One's Faith is a personal characteristic; Faith comes from the family and the environment which one is born to however may be difficult to understand. Where one is born provides one with a manner of Faith. Those that have not well understood Faith should and sometimes do attempt to find one faith that is pleasing. This is not always a good way and may prove to be incorrect, illogical and unreasonable; however this is reality. At this moment tempered tolerance is certainly the best choice. One need not push their Faith in the face of a different set of beliefs however one can remain dedicated and open minded simultaneously. This is one of the functions of brain power: _co-operation with others without dissention_. One can be trained to develop such a technique; in fact one can do this without any help from another: what is required is the _will to understand and appreciate_ the feelings and beliefs of another without animosity. In a Nation State, whereabouts the Law is curtailed and individuals are given the responsibility of governing themselves the _Will of the People_ is an important factor. A common and unified understanding of the meaning and substance of _Will Power_ is necessary then a Democracy can and will work[265]

Individually and collectively men must demand a cessation from warfare. There is no need to fight someone on the other side of the planet; this is a consequence of the political and economic bungling that has been going on for centuries, promoted by a wealthy however uncaring elite.[266]

---

[264] **There are, always Economic Crisis,** developed carefully for political gains by men that control circumstance.

[265] **The will to power** is the power of personal volition and is a driving force in the make-up of most individuals. The power of the will can, and at times does, have a tangible force when enacted with-in the framework of an acute situation. An omnipotent being has the strongest will imaginable which created the reality that exists; this is as a God form. Most individuals it is imagined would believe this.

[266] **"The British system** with its perennially imperial influence on the leading combination among the money-systems of the planet, has been, since the accession of William of Orange and, then, since the death of Queen Anne, the consistent, either direct, or contingent cause of all of the major economic crises of the planet since the onset of the 1492-1648 launching of a virtually permanent state of successive waves of mass—murderous warfare within, and reaching beyond the European system. The most notable of the launching-pads for the reign of warfare centered upon the British East India Company and its outgrowths, has been what is called the Liberal system, the system which bans actual truth in favor of the degraded

Those who have most wanted even more, whereas those with the least will get an even smaller portion in the future. We are reminded that this way of bungling has made it better for millions however more millions are starving than before. The numbers on both sides of the equation are increasing, consistent with the increasing populations of the earth. This should not surprise anyone who can think; divided a larger number into equally imagined proportions and you will have greater numbers on both sides of the equation. Presto! What is so unique about this? Proportionality should be understood by any educated individuals nevertheless we doubt that this is true given present circumstance.

The conflicts that we experience have their origins in a distant not always well understood past. What remain of the conflict are the **Ideas that motivated the conflict,** which Ideas can sustain for centuries; they will exist in the minds of some future born individuals. The children and men of the future will receive their ideas from the past; this is a truism that cannot be denied. In the minds of new adepts the **Ideas** will acquire (perhaps) a new or broader meaning. *In such instance the meaning is the most significant ingredient.* Those that preach insurrection and revolution are, in truth, not well informed; they are ignorant or are simply attempting to destroy what better men have created; in a word, they are *Jealous.* Jealousy is a Cardinal Sin, a mortal Sin and a mind-numbing attitude that cannot allow another to enjoy what the other did create.[267] One can imagine that such types do not understand their own beliefs or limitations.

Many young men have sat around in coffee shops and restaurants hoping to change the world; to their imagined image of what reality should be. They are waiting for their next attempt at illicit or perverted sex with some young lady with "hot pants" or "requiring a place to sleep." They are scoundrels that have done the work of their masters. Often they have been perverts or simply mean. They work for the Bankers without any knowledge of how this could be. [268]

Many of them have a very slight education and have probably read the wrong books; revolutionary authors that had not a clue of Reality. Given the youthful age of many they did not nor could they understand the consequences which would befall millions of people because of

---

system based on "pleasure and pain," the Liberal system rooted in the designs of Venice's Paolo Sarpi." (Lyndon La Rouche)

[267] **Young Men fight the battles conceived in the minds of old fools** attempting to bring myths buried in ancient history to the fore. The young bleed and die whereas the elders occupy lavish quarters acquired from the wages of sin. All the while an exclusive cadre of Miscreants with vain expectation, till the day they die, dream of conquering humanity. In the past many have held the idea of a master Race nevertheless they now rest silently, stiff and cold, buried in the ground, or burned: *we will see only the ashes.* This is the story of life, which is perpetrated by an inferior and incomplete education. See **Quigley, Carroll,** Ph. D. Tragedy and Hope. A History of the World in our Time. Chapter V.

[268] **When money is master** and economics the most significant endeavor there will become all manner and variety of sinful ways. Money can be and often is a corrupting influence when it has become the master. At present it is the master whereas it should be returned to being a servant of all men as was intended. Money transactions should be scrupulously honest, *like keeping the scores in a football game* and other sporting events. The essence is simply not understood for what it really is. Athletics is a distraction appealing somewhat to ill-educated and brutish character; *however the scores and results are catalogued and placed into archives.*

their incorrect forms of thought. They were too young, spaced out on drugs or too drunk to think great thoughts; nevertheless the Culture and Civilization (generally speaking) has been reeling from their silly kinds of notions and the nightmares taken from their perverted dreams. Many were involved in extra-curricular sex or perverted sex; the wrong kind. As they became older they (probably) lusted after the _younger more-attractive ladies_. Novelists have built fortunes pandering to Ideas such as these; for money that could be earned thereby. The novelists are often held in high esteem. One wonders why,? Better writers often receive very little or no attention?

When the news is controlled and in the hands of an alien, as is presently the case in many instances, the world will suffer. The enemy is the perverted financial establishment which has grown over the centuries; the establishment is Anglo-Zionist and has determined that it will rule the World, one way or another. Such men with their great wealth insist on a one-world government. The self-acclaimed leaders of the World have gained control of many of the channels of communication; movies, theatre, television, newspapers, magazines, publishing houses and some others. They have used their position to brainwash millions of the immature young into imagining that the self-acclaimed leaders are doing the right thing. The youth carry their Master's banners in the streets and shout the slogans that were given them by the perpetrators. Youth carry the banners of Marxist, Socialist and Communist organizations without any significant understanding what they are doing. Look around and you will see.

A One-World Government is often mentioned being pushed by the establishment elite together with the (seemingly intellectual) pimps that make a few nickels for their agreement with the silly notions being pushed. Certainly; we are reminded incessantly as though we already have a One World Government. We have a Constitution which is perhaps the best document, of this world, for the limitation of governments from becoming what a One World Government would be. This Constitution, at this time, with its legal and genuinely lawful checks and balances is the best offering to the millions of common men in this world. _**World control of Government is the worst possible type of Government.**_ The individual will be made totally ineffective with this form; except those "chosen for their functional ability" will be rewarded for their questionable efforts. A World Government places all the power in the hands of the "chosen few" that will enjoy unimaginable luxury. The chosen few are those that have designed and want this System. We are very close to that right now, and we have been moving closer each day. Read the portion of this book describing real wealth the kind that has grown over centuries. The average man will have no inputs and no recourse; all men will be ruled by a stranger that will not be known. The stranger will be very well paid!

We will have meaningless elections, as in some instances we have at present. The greatest influence will be that of money held by one or another of the ruling elite. In such instance men like Barak Hussein Obama will be given command of the highest office in the Nation; he will do as the _"money"_ commands. Simply stated this is political and social madness. Why should a Bedouin, an Alien (imagined by many as a Traitor) have been elected to the office of the Presidency of the United States; is this for real or is it someone's _sinister imagination working behind the scenes?_ Consider how much opportunity you or your representatives have had to help your own influence in Obama's spending spree. Not much; nevertheless everyone will be encouraged to pay for all of Obama's "somewhat stupid excesses and profligate spending;"

certainly you will understand how all of this is for your benefit and for the benefit of the People, of course! [269]

Following is a quote from the Czech Republic; it speaks quite correctly with the assumptions made in this volume. Some people have the vocabulary to sum up things in a way that you can quickly understand them. Someone over there (in Europe) has it figured out. It was translated into English from an article in the Prague newspaper, Prager Zeitungon. *Quote* "Far more dangerous than our President and those around him are the _legions of the ignorant who still do not understand what his administration is doing to their country._ This is not entirely his fault. It is also the American media who refuses to tell people the truth. The danger to America is not Barack Obama, but a citizenry capable of entrusting a man like him with the Presidency. It will be far easier to limit and undo the follies of an Obama presidency than to restore the necessary common sense and good judgment to *a depraved electorate* willing to have such a man for their president. The problem is much deeper and far more serious than Mr. Obama, _who is a mere symptom_ of what ails America. Blaming the prince of fools should not blind anyone to the vast confederacy of fools that made him their prince. The Republic can survive a Barack Obama, who is, after all, merely a fool. It is less likely to survive a multitude of fools, such as those who made him their President."

At present the dialogue focuses on charity and Christian compassion for the little people of the World many of whom, in fact, have been kept from accumulating any significant or truthful knowledge. Except for the earnings from unusual or significant invention most are kept from accumulating any form of significant wealth as well. Millions are near destitution most of the time. *Young women turn to prostitution and young men turn to crime.* The good people in the community tolerate and to some extent encourage both of the sinner types. Gambling, drinking and various forms of entertainment push the whole parade. Christ determined the Theology, which has given literary form to some of the best examples in present Western Thought and Philosophy. This Philosophy should function to provide for all of the people; given there will always be exceptional circumstances. This clarification makes it possible for the average man to participate in the coming together of past, present and future as is expressed existentially in the Catholic Faith. Man is, thereby, afforded an opportunity to understand, to a degree, the meaning of what is infinite. All of the teachings of Christ oppose any form of negatively collective Philosophy, as such, and emphasize the meaning of true brotherhood. True brotherhood is not collectivist; true brotherhood is honor in action. Some other Faiths may do this also; nevertheless _the Catholic Faith as illuminated by Christ, in its original form, is a complete and perfect Theology._ It is believed by millions that Christ was a perfect man; one must understand this. If Christ was simply a metaphor men must also understand the significance of the basis for this metaphor. *Understanding the Reason for the being of Christ is absolutely imperative.* It is believed, and is historically proven that Christ, in fact, was raised from the dead and ascended into Heaven; however not everyone believes this. No one else has ever done this, which is a

---

[269] **If one divides one trillion** $1,000,000,000,000. By 300,000,000 the number (approximately) of citizens in this nation one will have $3,333.00 for every man woman and child now in the country. Obama talks about many-trillion dollars and more. The man is a FOOL! Do the mathematics, if you can, and you will understand better. Barak Obama is not only a FOOL he is, considered by many, a TRAITOR as well. For millions he may be a nice guy; Time will tell.

truthfully phenomenal occurrence. There are billions of individuals that do not believe this however, they should consider the *meaning of this understanding; if indeed they can.* The Establishment will do everything possible to confuse the people and is most definitely in a general sense anti-Catholic!

The ascension of Jesus Christ could be considered allegorically, metaphorically, symbolically or as a reality. Christians consider this an important part of reality actually the most important part. If one considers this event in any way other than a part of reality it is still (probably) the *most important event "imagined" and has been most effective. Nevertheless, the whole "Idea" has been considered by all forms of human being not all of which are necessarily generous.* There is much antagonism, even hatred in considering the presence of Christ. From this event forward in Time there has become a whole set of positive miraculous and holy doings which have very much influenced the existing world. Christianity has separated past and present in such manner so as to favor goodness over evil in unnumbered and uncounted ways. The real Catholic Faith places great emphasis on *the Soul of man and the existence of Heaven.* The nature of the Soul is difficult to understand, for billions of men it would be impossible; it is an ephemeral and somewhat ghostly entity.[270]

The technique of repetition, repeating the same message over and over, does work to establish an objective. Propaganda thrives on this notion which has become very effective. Ever since the Russian *"take-over"* in the twenties the technique is being perfected. *In fact there was no Russian revolution* it was a very well planned and orchestrated take-over of the wealth and power of Russia by an Anglo-Zionist conspiracy. The threads of continuity continue to this day and are ultimately complex. *Simply stated it was Grand Larceny, a monumental theft and it was a Conspiracy.* The same approach has been planned for the United States, however Time has changed and the new technologies will help to prevent this from occurring like it did in the past. Therefore, the weapons of the "intruder gangsters" have been refined. At present the financial markets do present opportunity for a complete take-over of the monetary aggregates of the Civilization. We cannot exist as a people without a form of money to facilitate exchange. However the compounding of interest and the costs of executing such a plan are staggering. They are beyond what could have been imagined when the scam began. **It is a scam.**

Inflation which provided a cover for the main event continues at an accelerating pace reducing the purchasing power of all the little money; inflation *would not exist* in a Nation State truthfully controlled by the people. Inflation reduces the middle class to a financial non-existence. What is your bank account compared to the billions and trillions now considered as being controlled by the really rich? And, *it was a conspiracy.* All of this was happening under the watchful eye of Alan Greenspan, Jewish Chairman of the Federal Reserve, who has reminded the People "over and over," that there was no inflation. And all of the people believed him because they have been prepared to believe him in our Public Schools. He has admitted somewhat humbly that his

---

[270] **Nevertheless the Soul** is a form of accumulation built up during the lifetime of every single being. One cannot be too definite about the nature of the Soul nevertheless Souls do exist. A soul, to be brief, is one's existential being, which transcends the present in phenomenal ways and beacons toward an eternal existence. *The Soul connects man with what is infinite and perpetual; it is continuous.* **Perpetual Infinity is all that is; in a rarified and extended form.**

judgment was at times incorrect. Why was this? Nevertheless he was continuously applauded whilst basking in the glory of his accomplishments. One wonders; who was he working for? Then there was Ben Bernanke, a Jew, as new Chairman of the Federal Reserve. No sane and knowledgeable man would follow such program for bankrupting his country. Now President Obama has appointed a woman another Jew we will have to wait on this one. People must understand that we are being overcome as Russia was overcome; in our instance the enemy, those that promote a One-World Government, is using very finely crafted techniques of money manipulation.

It is alleged that a great amount of the funding for the promotion of the Russian Revolution (so called) $20,000,000.00 came from Jacob Schiff a Jewish banker. Many of the participants (about 450) came to Russia from New York City; USA; quite interestingly, perhaps coincidentally, they were almost all Jewish. Many had come from Russia to the United States so to gain American citizenship. Thereafter in Russia American citizenship would help them to move about freely; this was the assumption. This is not a condemnation of all Jewish people however is *a condemnation of some Ideas* held by various individuals including Jews. The Czar, his wife and five children were murdered as well as a number of his loyal and faithful servants. Why are such tragedies allowed to develop? Such tragedies are the work of lunatics, *men with no conscience and no truthfully developed sense of Christian or Jewish compassion or honor.* They even imagine as they pretend that they are working for some place in a strange form of Heaven; how can this be? What manner of God would encourage this? Much of Islam has the same *Tenor of destruction*. In respect to belief and Philosophy we are at a very critical place in history for the people of this world.[271] All people in the past have had problems generally contained in a geographic location. The present problem is International in scale which makes it more difficult to understand.

It seems fair to mention that even the supposed leaders like Greenspan and Bernanke are simply functionaries. They certainly must imagine, at least, that they are doing the right things; in some instances this may be true. However, *the System is so complex it is as a perfectly designed trap:* no matter what any man may think he may be compelled by the exigencies of the moment to act incorrectly. In any event the names of the individuals are not important; various others can be placed in the same position to do what the manipulators want them to do. The manipulators are a very select group of seemingly distinguished leaders; many are investment bankers. Even they can be replaced as often does happen. Money manipulation is a never ending problem for free men to deal with.

---

[271] **We live in an era of theatrics**, make-believe, with fraud, in business and accounting. *The Lie becomes as Metaphor:* deceit in marriage and government, cheating in disclosures involving money transactions and a weird form of fantasy peopled by talking animals, logo warriors and barbaric comics displaying plastic forms that appeal to prurient interest and erotic sensation. Combined with this is an incessant prattle selling everything from thumbtacks to swimming pools, confusion is rampant. Within such confusion it is easy for those that control the "Information Highway" to selectively inform a docile and distracted population. Myths, once established are likely to persist for a very long time, possibly hundreds of years. See **Orwell, George,** Animal Farm.

The Nation State is the best form for a government to take being somewhat Familial. Having its origin in the family and the tribe; a Nation State affords opportunity for wide-spread participation in political and related functions. *A small Nation State is the Ideal.* Consider Switzerland and Lichtenstein. A small self governing Nation provides a means for a wide variety of opinions, which can be considered and is a fair way to arrive at truthfully representative government. Small States could compare performances and the better performances could be emulated where possible. This is superior to any form of warfare. Importantly, unlike our present government no decision should be rushed however, a reasonable amount of time should be given to contemplate and determine necessary action, if any, in all instances. [272]

The problem is that the wealthy establishment creatures do not want all points of view to be considered; they want their own selfish and egotistical ways to dominate. This is especially true of those inclined toward warfare. A One World Government will encourage a warfare mentality, at least for the present moment. Ultimately such form will give way to another political format.

In fact a titular King might be a reasonable Ideal to consider; one who presides however does not rule the Nation. Some direction is required and this can be worked out in practice. *Such form of leadership need not influence the quality of the Ideas presented nor would it determine which ones are best.* Unfortunately almost any form of government is as an accommodation with strange innuendo. Nevertheless any determination should be a consequence of the genuine, truthful and reasonable will of the governed. It is important that the governed be educated and fair minded each to all others. The concept of *Christian Catholic moral certitude is most significant* in what is mentioned hereabouts. Moral certitude is an ethical issue and it is important to have such framework; *we have this in the Ten Commandments.* The Commandments are (presumably) given by God. Even if they are not given by God they are very reasonable and life would work very well if all obeyed them. If youth were educated into the truthful meaning of this assertion they would become the type of citizen that is required by a truthfully inspired Nation State. A population must be properly educated to function efficiently and fairly regarding what is being proposed. The youth should not be indoctrinated, as many are at present, into a malignant form of Socialist thinking. Youth should be encouraged in what is truthful, wise and decent. Youth should also be taught what is proven to be negative and evil. Less emphasis should be placed on hearing the child's opinion and misunderstanding. Education is a time for listening and learning the difference between right and wrong.

To educate the youth is not the same as inculcating them in some form of political and social madness. We can now see and understand what is political and social madness; by the presence of our own political and social situation. Children should be taught how to think. We have come to elect a President that millions consider is an enemy of the people that he is supposed to rule. This is an absurdity beyond comprehension. This is the same *"Type"* of situation that was found in Germany in the election of Adolph Hitler. The people were discontented with their leadership and wanted an improvement in such leadership, which was promised by the election of the Dictator, Adolph Hitler. Everything he did was not wrong however *he was a victim of his own strangely formed personality.* This should not be difficult to understand. He

---

[272] All political activity in America must consider our debt position, which is extraordinary. Timing in respect to payment of principal and interest has a too important influence on what occurs.

was unanimously elected by a confused people that had little political understanding of what might and did happen.

Obama in some ways is much like Hitler was; Obama, it would seem, is generally a Socialist. He is a Collectivist *who does not comprehend the forthcoming consequences of his actions in reference to the moral behavior of a leader.* He is not wise but he is clever.[273] He is somewhat

---

[273] **Democrats** Should Be Very Proud Of him, this is exactly what THEY wanted and voted for, the Dem's won . . . and Rep's lost. They must be proud of their vote. Following footnote by by Wayne Allyn Root

"Barack Hussein Obama is no fool. He is not incompetent. On the contrary, he is somewhat brilliant. He knows exactly what he's doing. He is purposely overwhelming the U.S. economy to create systemic failure, economic crisis and social chaos thereby destroying capitalism and our country from within. Barack Hussein Obama was my college classmate." (Columbia University, class of '83) *This is an excellent quotation.*

He is a devout Muslim; do not be fooled. Look at his czars, they are anti-business and anti-American. As Glenn Beck correctly predicted from day one, Barack Hussein Obama is following the plan of Cloward & Piven, two professors at Columbia University . . . they outlined a plan to socialize America by overwhelming the system with government spending and entitlement demands.

Add up the clues below. Taken individually they're alarming. Taken as a whole, it is a brilliant, Machiavellian game plan to turn the United States into a Socialist/Marxist state with a permanent majority that desperately needs government for survival . . . And can be counted on to always vote for even bigger government. Why not? They have no responsibility to pay for it.

Universal Health Care: The Health Care bill has very little to do with healthcare. It has everything to do with unionizing millions of hospital and healthcare workers, as well as adding 15,000 to 20,000 new IRS agents (who will join government employee unions). Obama doesn't care that giving free healthcare to 30 million Americans will add trillions to the national debt. What he does care about is that it cements the dependence of those 30 million voters to Democrats and big government. Who but a socialist revolutionary would pass this reckless spending bill in the middle of a depression?

Cap and Trade: Like healthcare legislation having nothing to do with healthcare, Cap and Trade has nothing to do with global warming. It has everything to do with redistribution of income, government control of the economy and a criminal payoff to Obama's biggest contributors. Those powerful and wealthy unions and contributors (like GE, which owns NBC, MSNBC and CNBC) can then be counted on to support everything Obama wants. They will kick-back hundreds of millions of dollars in contributions to Obama and the Democratic Party to keep them in power. All the new taxes on Americans with bigger cars, bigger homes and businesses helps Obama spread the wealth around.

Making Puerto Rico a state: Who's asking for a 51st state? Who's asking for millions of new welfare recipients and government entitlement addicts in the middle of a depression? Certainly not American taxpayers! But this has been Barack Hussein Obama's plan all along. His goal is to add two new Democrat senators, five Democrat congressmen and a million loyal Democratic voters who are dependent on big government.(This will tip the balance of those living off the government to more than those who must pay for it; and we're done for.)

Legalize 12 million illegal Mexican immigrants: Just giving these 12 million potential new citizens free healthcare alone could overwhelm the system and bankrupt America. But it adds 12 million reliable new Democrat voters who can be counted on to support big government. Add another few trillion dollars

narrow-minded and selfish in his vain apprehension of Reality. He has been groomed by others, of his kind, into believing much of what is not and cannot be true. His understanding of the World lacks a genuine understanding of what is Holy and why it should be considered as such. He is inclined toward being a Muslim which is _antagonistic to Catholicism the root of our philosophy._ He is a functionary in a long line of strangely minded men; he will do what is expected of him when encouraged by praise and compensation to do so. His being the President is irrelevant except for the damage he is doing to what is, in fact, mostly good. His language and appearance are in his favor, he seems to be sincere in his efforts; this may or may not be the true.

One can imagine, perhaps presume, that at some point in time we had a government with some of the qualities being considered. If this were not true things might be much worse than they are at present. To begin we must simplify the process, which has become too complex and which complexity provides justification and cover for many of the wrong notions. The wrong actions are the result of the actions of dissident individuals and the imaginations of fools and Traitors.

Revolutionaries and insurrectionists should be jailed and educated regarding what it means to be decent, fair-minded and good. Most individuals would find value in such programs when the end result was one of positive and worthwhile achievement with a decent salary and the prestige that comes from self-achievement; no one need be tortured. Real psychopaths should remain in prison for life. One must consider execution as a possible punishment for wrong doing. One cannot allow an individual to preach and teach subversive techniques and promote various means of torturing other human beings. Government has been deliberately determined to confuse the people, thus the perpetrators of collectivist and socialist thinking have found populations numbed by the excesses of a too big government. Wars should cease so that the monies and efforts could be directed toward long range infrastructure and reasonable occupational programs.[274]

---

in welfare, aid to dependent children, food stamps, free medical, education, tax credits for the poor, and eventually Social Security.

Stimulus and bailouts: Where did all that money go? It went to Democrat contributors, organizations (ACORN), and unions—including billions of dollars to save or create jobs of government employees across the country. It went to save GM and Chrysler so that their employees could keep paying union dues. It went to AIG so that Goldman Sachs could be bailed out (after giving Obama almost $1 million in contributions). A staggering $125 billion went to teachers (thereby protecting their union dues)."

[274] **_Lyndon La Rouche_** and his associates have brought forth some interesting projects that would make the world a better and more productive place for the teeming millions. However, he has been cast out from the dialogue of the war-mongers and thieves. At present he is an old man and has little time left to promote his Concepts however we hope others may see and understand his monumentally positive methods and procedures that are possible and give true freedom to create a better world for all people. The present retrogressive Anglo-Zionist leadership is imagining and planning ways to reduce the population. How might one accomplish this? We do not necessarily require more people however the World could certainly handle more. What is required is a more intelligent being and participation in what is; RIGHT NOW! The truthfully wealthy must acquiesce to the existing Reality and help those, who are less fortunate, by creating reasonable opportunity for the Poor. To some extent this is happening. Nevertheless the cessation of Warfare would be the best and most productive way. This must be understood and implemented; SOON!

The entertainment industry has made hundreds of millions from romanticized nonsense involving all manner of ridiculous forms of special effects involving the child-warriors of the present epoch. Some productions are blasphemy others specifically sexual in nature and many are simply foolish. This quality of the production infuses the mind with evil, perverse and silly forms of thought content and, generally, what is not needed. Such content replaces or confuses decent and correctly pertinent thought content in the minds of millions; this is not good. Many individuals sit stupefied by the special effects that are orchestrated in a carefully built stage set for the imaginary occasion. Computer technology is widely used for the purpose of the pretense, which becomes as an obsession, with many of today's youth and simple-minded adults. Who hasn't heard of Schwarzenegger and Stallone as being the bestial and excessive defenders of all that is good and worthy? Both men, some others as well, have made millions with their overly romanticized and silly depictions of an impossible kind of man. One wonders; how can they sleep at night on their bed of roses and hundred dollar bills. Neither was man enough to respect his wife who did bore and mother their children. Apparently they were more interested in their own demented happiness. Nevertheless the masses have made them millionaire celebrities. Why?

Professor Emeritus, Robert Fiedler
August 2013

CHAPTER XI

WORDS: MEANING AND EFFECT

As in seeing truthfully and understanding what really is there.

Words form as patterns. The patterns are specific and carry a form and manner of meaning; not always properly understood as to context and how the words relate to what is in the speakers or writers mind.[275] The form that is carried in one mind may be outside a common and generally accepted understanding of another. *The form of meaning may, or may not be, clear:* the form usually is not resolved accurately or correctly in the mind of the reader or the listener: *many only imagine they understand.* Most understand just a portion of any symbolic. The Modern Context for communication is crowded for the attention of those that might see or listen. Language is generally possible of conveying meaning however is unlikely to do so when superseded by extraneous elements: there are many extraneous elements. And, there are also extraneous elements contracted by the liar, the thief and the malcontent: all three Types trade/auger against one's position, in general a nominal position; the interlopers are winning on many fronts. There is some luck as well. Some untruths go back for a millennium even longer and are not traceable

Most Lies convey a false understanding and are simply untrue nevertheless they are effective in a short time span. New Lies are conveyed to cover the damage done by those in effect at any given time. Satan the Devil is the father of the lie.[276] Many of those that presumably lead the people, they are called Politicians, tell Lies that may have the most serious consequences. I will state also that many Politicians are honest; however *their honesty is compromised by the Politicians that lie.* Many Politicians are thirty third degree masons, which, by itself makes

---

[275]   **Specific patterns** are obvious however are not necessarily commonly understood. The patterns form in unusual ways and combine with what exists in a particular mind's being. See my "Fantastic Sketch Book" so to understand somewhat the nature of various abstract patterns. They are beautiful as well as compelling driving the mind to think deeply.

[276]   **Keep in mind** Satan and the Devil are Ideas about Evil and can become a part of any thought pattern. Man has tried to give them a corporal form understandable as a means of knowing them. In fact they may be formless or perhaps they can assume the form of any single being. When Satan or the Devil, as an Idea enters a human person that individual will possibly be driven to commit nefarious acts of one kind or another. For example, a young man in his teens shot a baby in the head, killing the baby. The baby was in a stroller being taken for a walk by the baby's mother. Imagine what such an experience would have on the mother? An entire life the happiness and sorrow were extinguished with a single violent move. New sorrow was added to the mother's psychological disposition. There are many examples of similar behavior.

them in the eyes of many somewhat suspect.[277] In addition many Politicians are not certain of the truth of many issues. Significant truth may remain obscure for long periods, for years: this is because of the former compounded and altered lies. Given such lies Mythologies are created and promoted which all may know of however few understand their origin and purpose. Indeed even the purpose may change or mutate without any deliberate effort on the part of the originators who may be long dead. *Such lies may not even be known as lies by who is telling them:* they *form from exigent circumstance and are woven in with the truth.* There are many: they are part of the Mythologies that millions believe and are ready to defend. *This may become as a basis for warfare: often religion is involved.*[278] As such they are probably the most sustaining and destructive, in the longer term, of all Lies. Some men will kill others as a consequence of a strange form of religious thought.[279]

Honest men and women have always had to sustain in spite of the impositions brought about by the Lie. *The Lie, generally speaking, is the most avaricious enemy of the human Race.* This point seems co-incidental to what happens however is perhaps the most compelling of all intercessions in the progress of Humanity. Humanity will progress in spite of the Lie however the progression will be corrupted for a time by each and every Lie.[280] No one is exactly sure of to where is man progressing? Especially War is a consequence of the compounding of Lies. Imagine what all of the lies contracted during World Wars I and II have done to the human race.[281] There are groups of individuals that have structured the greatest forms of the Lie ever developed by human consciousness and some have been perpetrated for years or centuries and longer World-wide. World-wide perpetration is something rather new and is dependent upon modern communication.

Most Religious thinking is only partially true much of it is metaphorical, or symbolic. Words are not always capable of conveying the exact meaning of every instance and one's ability to

---

[277] **Wardner, James, Dr. Ph.D.** *Communist Infiltration of the Catholic Church.* Video produced by, Most Holy Family Monastery, 4425 Schneider Road, Fillmore, NY 14735.

[278] **Religions** are involved with metaphor or mysticism however they are often not Theology and certainly not well understood Philosophy. In fact who knows the Truth of the many issues in one's life? Many will remain unknown.

[279] **See the Internet.** The perversion of religious practices. Sexual Perversion (Forerunner Commentary)— Bible Tools. "God, without mixing words, judges, "You shall not lie with a male as with a woman. It is an abomination" (Leviticus 18:22; 20:13). Paul includes lesbianism in the condemnation: "For even their women exchanged the natural use for what is against nature" (Romans 1:26). Later in I Corinthians 6:9, to make our understanding absolutely clear, he writes that neither "homosexuals, nor sodomites" will inherit the Kingdom of God (*cf.* Jude 7)".

[280] **The Lie**: the effect and duration of the lie will be sustained by additional lying and misunderstanding brought about by the first instance. It will sustain for as long as it is encouraged by the *tenor and implications* of time.

[281] **Such Lie** is often a part of a Propaganda Effort to encourage a population to do what is considered by intelligent men and women as being inhuman: they have been and are very effective. During the French Revolution and some conflicts since then some people have responded to propaganda acting in the most inhuman ways.

understanding may be flawed, inadequate or may be missing. This is especially problematic in the various schismatic religions that have been invented or imagined by men. In the ancient past this was probably more the case than at present. Ancient Mysticism and the various cult forms of Religion were perhaps, mostly invented by an opportunist seeking a form of gratification.[282] Many included strange practices, even including torture and death, some included perversions and strange sexual practices. Nevertheless some people have believed and followed such mental wanderings for centuries. There are still remnants of such thinking in the *"thought clusters"* of various individuals and groups. Eternity is forever and there will undoubtedly be remnants from the past brought to the next centuries and beyond as man bungles on his way. The assumption is that there is a future for mankind: *Time is not completely understood and is a quasi-holy element: we cannot perceive exactly what will happen and when it will happen.* The Catholic Faith, some other Faiths as well, have Ideas and teachings about this however no one can be absolutely certain of the future. An Economic Future can be predicted somewhat, better than others because of the nature of numbers and even then there is much misunderstanding: however all such False Systems will be eclipsed in Time. All such forms of thinking and the consequences there from will mutate or disappear in time. Ultimately mankind will cease to exist as part of a greater and more universal stellar existence. Here the Soul and eternity become very important to individuals as human beings; destined to become one in being with the Father.

Truthful utterance and script is necessary so to maintain a *"trusting relationship"* between the involved parties; this is understood as Tradition. Without this there can be no real compatibility between individuals. Various sins provide us with a personal example of the consequence of untruthfulness and improper behavior, in respect to sexual and ethical mores.[283] *What individuals do not understand is that honesty is an **absolute necessity** in any personal or social transaction. There is no substitute for the truth.* If one is not truthful there is no point in any form of communication. This fact must be taught and reinforced with the youngest children in the home and in the educational System.

Our entertainment seems to be responsible for promoting the continuation of lies which must be reconsidered and corrected. This is a very subtle occurrence. *It is a monumental tragedy that so many of our teachers, so called, do not understand this.* Our system at present only does this coincidentally. To tell Johnnie to be a good boy is not enough. There must be given many examples of what goodness is; they must be extended from the lowest to the highest forms of learning and knowing. In many instances the anti-social and anti-goodness that is projected on the television is winning the battle. This is obviated by the gang-mentality of many of our youth. Our youth are taught many bad lessons by the television programs and commercials and also by

---

[282] **Pranaitis. Rev. Iustinus Bonaventura.** *The Talmud Unmasked,* Translation of the author's Latin Text. Imprimatur St. Petersburg, April 13, 1892. Archiepiscopus Metropolita Mohilovicnsis Kozlowski. Imperial Academy of Science, (Vas. Ostr., 9 Line, No. 12).

[283] **See Interet**; Bible verses about Sexual Perversion. "Within the Western industrialized world, the United States not only is the undisputed leader in murder, but in rape as well. According to the International Criminal Police Organization's 1990 statistics, England reported 6.7 rapes per 100,000, population; France, 8.1; the Netherlands, 8.9; Switzerland, 6.2; Germany, 8.2; Poland, 5.9.The United States reported 41.2". Note Poland is the lowest; Poland is principally a Catholic country; interestingly the Polish young ladies are very attractive.

what they observe on the street. They learn quickly and some are bound to try the various forms of perversion as their selected form of behavior. *As they do this, their own behavior becomes perverted by degree and can become a threat to others.* The recent trial of Jodi Arias should demonstrate one form of evil consequence, leading to killing.

Hollywood is apparent in the most unfortunate proceedings in the trial of **Jodi Arias** who was victimized by a man that exploited her and then decided to abandon her to a lonesome future *with the memories of his and her adulterous behavior*. Some will imagine she exploited the man. Undoubtedly there was an ingredient of *unlawful sex as is advertised and promoted by the System:* ***by television, movies, stinky literature and pornography.*** This is done for a few nickels profit. The intimacy of their sex was unwise, uncommon and premature; for her to be exploited and abandoned was too debilitating. *This suggests that she might have been a better person than she was portrayed to be.*

The eager news-vendors had little respect or feeling for the person of Jodi Arias. One does not, certainly should not, have outrageous sexual encounters with a casual friend. Sexual behavior is the most intimate behavior. Pornography is an abomination appealing to a few degenerate individuals. To be legitimate sex must occur within the bounds of a permanent and sustaining matrimony; at the very least it should be sustaining till death. Everyone understands some things are sinful; sin has a way of altering the personality of the sinner. In Jodi's instance her sinful behavior overcame her common sense and her sense of self. *Self esteem is very important to all human beings* who, in fact, need this to support their humanness. This is why many prostitutes are doped and held in bondage; you can put the pieces together for yourself.

The trial of Jodi Arias was a travesty it was commercialized by vain practitioners who imagined that they were informing the public. In fact they all missed the most important elements including the Judge. Fairness and goodness demand that the private sexual activities of anyone, no matter what they have done, should be kept as personal. Sex is an important part of who one is, beginning with conception. *Sexual behaviors should not be paraded before the world* by the simple minded and enthusiastic conveyers of the news. In fact in many perhaps most instances the commentators are assuaging their own egos by decimating another human being: a real tragedy. This is a real psychological problem. Imagine the damage done to the psyche and to the soul of the helpless victim of such unfortunate and lustful behavior; and then the trial. This is an example of too much legalese with ***no common sense or Christian compassion.***

Jodi Arias is a victim of her time. ***Her behavior and that of her boy friend were learned:*** they were ungodly and perverted however all of this should not have been offered to the general public as a form of entertainment. Her trial for murder became a spectacle for voyeurs and many with little or no comprehension of the situation. Her spirit had to endure the various claims which were made public by an inept legal system. The circumstances which led to her situation were very understandable however Jodi should not have been subject to the treatment which was given. *The trial was one form of modern tragedy.*

Marriage it is understood is a Sacrament and the Idea of marriage should not be violated with various forms of premature sexual encounters; with sex considered merely as fun. Men and women should learn to control their passion and wait patiently for an appropriate encounter leading to marriage. *The consummation of marriage is a binding act and should be honored as such.* Old fools and young lechers refuse to believe this. Bestial sex is never good for the body or the soul. Bestial sex is promoted by pornographers that exploit a woman, her beauty, her youth and her soul for a moment of ignorant bliss. *Pornography is an expression of ignorance without redemption.* Past actions do affect future occurrences; one can and must understand this and must always be aware. Decent behavior is a learned characteristic and should be promoted from the earliest days of life. Without this the political system, any system, will fail. **War** is an example of the most indecent behavior involving whole societies and civilization, nevertheless we hear about it every single day; who or what is promoting this? Rape is an important part of any conflict with the winners stealing the ladies of another man. The ladies are abused raped and often killed as a punishment. ***Why do so few understand what is really happening?***

The mayhem and killings that we here of, for example gang violence is a consequence of what we are teaching our children. Our understanding of sex encourages unholy perversion and deviations; it is abysmal. Same sex marriage is also a consequence of a generally misguided and misdirected way of being.[284] Television must be reconsidered in reference to the harm that is being done to many individuals, especially youth and to the collective Id; *a compound psychic phenomenon.*[285] Some producers of television spectacles do not want to do this: rather they attempt to expand the envelope (as they say) so to include all forms of human behavior debilitating as well as decent.[286] Simple minded fools respond most to what is decadent, tacky or vulgar: there are many simple minded fools no doubt, however they are unaware of their condition. They should be educated in a more sensitive and positive manner. Outrageous behaviors are a consequence of simple minded folks acquiring the Ideas of fools and perverts imagining they are being *"entertained"* with displays of blatant vulgarity and sinful decadence.

Some Television shows repeat sinful activities, the worst forms of behavior over and over: to some considerable extent it is educating the population to be simple-minded, insensitive and brutal.[287] In fairness we affirm that Television also adds greatly to good things however the evil is what is most often called to the attention of youth and the simple minded viewers. And remember *"The evil that men do lives after them whereas the good is interred with their bones"* (Shakespeare). Democracy forbids censorship however must be better understood and reevaluated as to methods and procedures so to benefit positively the most individuals. Sex is viewed largely as a joke when in fact the human race depends upon a more decently formulated

---

[284]   **See Interet**; Bible verses about Sexual Perversion.

[285]   **A compound psychic phenomenon** is a complex with much of the content and form being of unknown origin. It is an important outcome of the Lie. It is difficult to define and nearly impossible to correct. Much damage is done from this form of imposition. In fairness, it must be stated that some good things come from circumstances with a similar pedigree.

[286]   **What exactly** is meant by the phrase *"to expand the envelope"?* This is certainly a cliché however who thinks of it in this way. *This is the kind of misuse of language that is both confusing and debilitating.* To suggest that it is modern is not sufficient to repair the damage that is done to the general idea of thought.

[287]   **Every intelligent** man knows that repetition reinforces learning which is approved by the best understanding in psychology; to repeat over and over will reinforce an Idea and will make the Idea believable.

understanding of the procreative function. *Sex is pleasurable however is also intimate and personal and should not be advertised to sell tickets to cheap theatrical productions.* How far one can go in the promotion of decadence should be more carefully considered.

Television provides a platform from which anti-social and destructive behavior is promoted as entertainment. If one questions this aspect they are confronted with the idea that some do enjoy the mayhem and therefore it must be included as part of an inclusive mix for public viewing.[288] It is asserted that individuals will choose wisely concerning viewing and how the views are interpreted. *We suggest this is not an accurate understanding of what is really happening.* One cannot choose wisely from the dump of evil and decadence. It is also true that individuals can learn and grow to a more mature adulthood where they do not depend on or need what is, in truth, decadent and infantile. The monsters and falsehoods which are envisioned by clever and greedy producers to become part of the shock of *"make believe"* should be more carefully evaluated. *Most likely they do more harm than good.* Morality and critical discernment are abandoned because it is the right of those with an immature and vulgar nature, seemingly somewhat confused, to produce what is decadent and anti-social. This is a serious problem which is encountered in our Democracy: so called. [289]In fact we live in a complex of Democracy and other Political forms: there is much confusion. Socialism and subtle forms of Marxism are creeping into our once wholesome and decent form of life.

The collective Id is a product of Now-time or Now-being and, it is generally believed, must include everything from the Devine to the guttural and that is precisely why our Democracy cannot and will not work over a long period of time.[290] One can see the signs however one *must be willing to understand and to admit* what they are and what they mean. Our people

---

[288]   **I have written** to a variety of stations and always get the same response. The answers infer that the bad and ugly are the preferences of millions and therefore must be considered in the offerings. Many stupid and indecent forms of entertainment make millions for the producers: certainly the producers are not in favor of changing what is happening. Much of what is at present considered normal was, in the past, considered as a form of perversion: this goes directly to the meaning of words.

[289]   **See footnote 285**; Bible verses about Sexual Perversion.

[290]   **Democracy** appears to be an Ideal Political means that has complex roots in each and every Nation where it has been encouraged to function. This goes back hundreds of years and has taken on peculiar forms. "In Russia for example Tradition says the *Viking Rurik* came to Russia in C.E. 862 and founded the first Russian dynasty in Novgorod. There was undoubtedly certain Democratic-like nuance in their thinking. The fact is that in the course of the 9th century, Viking tribes from Scandinavia moved southward into European Russia, tracing a path along the main waterway connecting the Baltic and Black Seas. *The various tribes were united by the spread of Christianity* in the 10th and 11th centuries; Christianity does relate to Democracy in various ways especially dealing with the behavior of one individual toward another. Vladimir the Saint was converted in 988. During the 11th century, the grand dukes of Kiev held such centralizing power as existed. In 1240, Kiev was destroyed by the **Mongols,** and the Russian territory was split into numerous smaller dukedoms. Some of the Mongols became the forerunners of Zionism and were very anti-Christian. The Mongol Empire stretched across the Asian continent and Russia was put under the suzerainty of the Khanate of the Golden Horde. The next two centuries saw the **rise of Moscow** as a provincial capital and centre of the Christian Orthodox Church." (For a better grasp of the situation as it was see the Internet on Russia: Rurik and Romanoff rulers).

seem not to understand the meaning of the signs which spell an end to freedom and the decent becoming of humanness. This is true because many of our citizens are virtually ignorant of truthful circumstance. The recent Democratic Party presidential promotion showed the people in a state of untamed exuberance, just like in Disneyland, without much understanding of what Barak Obama was saying or what he has in mind for them and for their children and for their country. He seems to be making great progress on what is called his charisma. This is as an appeal to those that support him and he probably understands this. The pressure for a one-world government without the existence of distinct nations or a definite manner of personal being is the ideal that many of the vain Western, Socialist and Communist leaders are pushing. They are imagining that all people are the same so to be better able to control them for the would-be leader's purpose. This has been the goal of the Money lenders and the Masonic and Zionist visionaries for centuries. Our Democracy does not guarantee all that is positive.[291] *Our freedom*

In the late 15th century, "Duke Ivan III acquired Novgorod and Tver and threw off the Mongol yoke. Ivan IV, the Terrible (1533-84), first Muscovite tsar, is considered to have founded the Russian state. He crushed the power of rival princes and boyars (landowners), but Russia remained largely medieval until the reign of Peter the Great (1689-1725), grandson of the first **Romanov tsar,** Michael (1613-45). Peter made extensive reforms aimed at westernization and, through his defeat of Charles XII of Sweden at the Battle of Poltava in 1709; he extended Russia's boundaries to the west. Catherine the Great (1762-96) continued Peter's westernization program and also expanded Russian territory, acquiring the Crimea, Ukraine, and a part of Poland."

During the reign of Alexander I (1801-25), **Napoleon's attempt** to invade Russia was unsuccessful and his troops defeated in 1812, and new territory was gained, including Finland (1809) and Bessarabia (1812). Alexander originated the Holy Alliance, which for a time crushed Europe's *rising liberal movement*, which eventually led to the Russian revolution. In the Decembrist revolt in 1825, a group of young, reformist military officers attempted to force the adoption of a constitutional monarchy in Russia by preventing the accession of Nicholas I. They failed utterly: Nicholas became the most reactionary leader in Europe.

Alexander II (1855-81) "pushed Russia's borders to the Pacific and into central Asia. Serfdom was abolished in 1861, but heavy restrictions were imposed on the emancipated class. Revolutionary strikes, following Russia's defeat in the war with Japan, forced Nicholas II (1894-1917) to grant a representative national body (Duma), elected by limited suffrage. It met for the first time in 1906, little influencing Nicholas in his reactionary course."

[291] **Our Democracy** has a quasi-socialistic manner of confusing the people and is controlled by those with the "Big Money" for the effects it may have on the response of the people. The actuality is that the very wealthy are taking over the riches of the earth and using the profits to control the people: *there is something called a Conspiracy, in fact there are many conspiracies not just one.* Many dismiss the idea of a Conspiracy which is in general a driving force controlled by an elite few; the elite few will vary with the cause. The people are given slogans, *simple phrases that they can remember* and flag. The phrases are repeated over and over until all believe them; they are speech clichés. The people will condemn what they are told to condemn; often humor is involved. Interestingly humor is used to promote killing and warfare; it is also given as an excuse against wrong-doing. This is in large measure an exercise, in remolding a group's behavioral patterns; it is dependable and it works.

In a nutshell, the underlying principle of the Cloward-Piven Strategy is to so *overload the entitlement system* to add so many to the entitlement rolls, that the country's economic system collapses, *unleashing*

is being overcome by excess and by the imposition of subtle however effective political and social means.

All of this is conveyed and may be corrupted by the clever use of a Word. Most of what "in truth" happens is not properly understood for the exact meaning. The Politics are much discussed however not well understood.[292] This is also apparent in the trial of Jodi Arias discussed briefly above. What is heard and conveyed too often shows great lack of truthful understanding: the slogan and the cliché are what, in fact, dominate the various discussions. *The Social means of destroying a Culture and Nation are not well comprehended by the common man and are even less well understood than the Politics.* There are groups notably some Masons of the thirty third-degree, Occultist and the Anti-Christ (there are many anti-Christ), as well as large segments in other than Christian Religions that are harboring the domination of the World as their objective: *this is Messianic.* There methods and means are well understood by the adepts and they are consistent and clever in their use of them. To a limited degree they have been and are being successful.[293] They cannot succeed at controlling humanity however their efforts have caused and will cause significant damage to the Soul of the Civilization. Wars are fought over some of the issues and millions are killed. *The Soul of a Civilization is difficult to understand and discussions of this are generally non-existent or are quite limited; they are mostly flawed because of imperfect knowledge.* Not many individuals understand the Soul truthfully and most are not well equipped linguistically to discuss it. In addition to this they lack a dedicated will: they are not interested. It is a difficult task to tell someone that they are foolish nevertheless someone must do this. A good man or woman cannot influence everyone however should attempt to influence those closest to them in positive ways. Generally this is the responsibility of the parent for the child.

---

chaos and violence in the streets, thus affecting radical Leftist political change in government. What truly intelligent person would encourage this? Until recently this theory has been just that, a theory, and a theory that anarchists and Progressives have salivated over for their want of execution. *But today, we are seeing the fruits of the Cloward-Piven Strategy played out to success in Greece and several other financial destitute countries in Europe* . . . . To summarize briefly the Cloward-Piven Strategy, I turn to Richard Poe who wrote an article of the same name, which is featured at DiscoverTheNetworks.org. Mr. Poe observes that "Mr. Cloward and Ms. Piven sought (and "seeks," in the case of Ms. Piven) to *facilitate the fall of Capitalism* by "overloading the government bureaucracy with a flood of impossible demands, thus *pushing society into crisis and economic collapse."* . . . In a 1970 New York Times interview, Cloward is quoted as saying that "poor people can only advance when the rest of society is afraid of them." He then theorized that activists should refrain from demanding that government provide more for the poverty stricken and, instead, "should strive to pack as many people on the welfare (read: entitlement) rolls as possible, creating a demand that could not be met, facilitating the destruction of the welfare system and *massive financial crisis".* As a byproduct, *"rebellion would be ignited amongst the people; chaos would rule the streets and governments would be damaged beyond repair, many falling to history making it possible for new radicals to assume the roles of oligarchs, ushering in new systems of government and the dismantling of the Capitalist system in particular".*—See more at: http://theatheistconservative.com/tag/the-cloward-piven-strategy/#sthash.CDo4LNfg.dpuf

292

293

Until a child is seven or eight the parent is the most important influence: the understandings of the best of Western thought must be promoted with conviction before a child reaches age eight, if they are not the child may be lost to a new age of Occultism and Socialist nonsense, ultimately lost to an understanding of decency and self-respect and of what life should be.[294] Here once again I refer to the Jodi Arias Trial and to her perverted boyfriend Travis Alexander. This is, in fact, apparent in many of today's youth: their dress, manners and choice of noise as music are indications of the depth and breadth of this phenomenon; *in fact it is a Social Disease.* And all of the youth appear to be jumping up and down as they appear to enjoy the raunchy entertainment and vulgar music.

The Idea of self respect suffers from the bad habits of the individuals. *Prostitution, Drunkenness and various addictions have been carefully encouraged by some criminal-type groups and become the Sins of their victims; this is done for money and for a feeling of superiority over another human being.* There may be psychopathic problems under the surface as well. Most often the other human being is a woman which introduces a dimension of man-woman misunderstanding. The traffic in narcotics is motivated by the sin of **Greed.** If one has a weak self-image this motivates the slipping into negative behavioral patterns which might include the use of Liquor or Narcotics: each provides a manner of escape from what is imagined as a feared or tainted Reality. Many young people want marijuana to be legalized and sold openly to whoever may wish to buy it; they are encouraged by the ignorance and ineptitude of the adults. For the teen-agers smoking, drinking, condoms and illicit sex are not enough. *Many adults encourage such foolish and immoral behavior believing it is natural and healthy.* Millions of people believe this and they follow such thinking with strange attendant beliefs. Some very successful people fall victim to dope, narcotics and prostitution because they have not been "taught to understand" that they will not always be in a youthful position. They will not always be young and healthy; they will lose their vitality and become old with the attendant diseases. At this juncture the Virtue of **"Humility"** is very significant. The virtues must be taught and proclaimed as positive personal attributes and their consequences must be explained to children: over and over by example with reasonable counsel. Children should be modestly praised for being good people. Less emphasis should be placed on athletic achievement and more emphasis should be placed on goodness and on truthful learning.

With a loss of self respect one will have a loss of the respect for others.[295] We are living in an Age when the respect that we have for each other appears to be in a state of decline. Some will

---

[294]   **Catholicism** is the Faith which supports the Philosophy of the West. More of Catholic Philosophy must be given as part of a well rounded and formal education. Certainly the Ten Commandments should be taught: repeated over and over for emphasis. Unfortunately this seems not possible in our Public School system where Religion is disavowed and is **seemingly** excluded. Additionally there are antagonisms between various Christian Religions and some that are not Christian. The word seemingly refers to the fact that there is Socialism and collectivist thought forms replacing decently formulated Religious thinking which is being discouraged.

[295]   **Body piercing,** deforming the body, tattoos and various forms of personal defacement are ominous signs. They appear mostly in the lower-classes and least intelligent of the population however they are making inroads into the higher-income classes as a status symbol; this is especially noticeable amongst young women. Wrestlers, fighters and prison inmates have a variety of conspicuous tattoos. This must give them

pretend otherwise. To repeat; the Television and the various theatrical productions are trying to *"expand a make believe envelope"*,[296] which they are doing. However in so doing they are providing grotesqueries beyond any decently imagined intelligence: we are as a people submitted to the near-worst examples available in the nonsense of the movies and now the rap music.[297]

All of this nonsense is exported to other seemingly decent communities on other continents. Such as this, represents Ignorance overcoming the value of Virtue and Decency. One can easily understand why a Muslim would want to discourage and prevent rap music and some films to be banned. We watch in stupefied silence every form of perversion known to man: this is our entertainment. *We are told we are emotionally healthy we believe this: in fact we are becoming as a pack of untamed children, children of evil and some are becoming as pagans and savages.* The body tattooing and ultimate fighting are the most obvious forms of symbolism however who may understand and admit what this means? People spend money for tickets to games and to watch stupid pornography such as which a truthfully intelligent person would not care to see: this is promoted for millions that can be had this way. Once again this is promoted because of **Greed.**

Body mutilation as *"an imagined Art form"* is no solution; it is a symptom and an indication of the problem that is faced by immaturity seeking attention and a degree of menial self-gratification. *The role played by those seeking immature gratification and attention is an important and significant part of Now-time.* Tattoo Parlors are blossoming like weeds in the desert whereabouts youth and some old folks as well submit their bodies to the scrawling of ignorance, the immature cartoons and decadent forms of blasphemy. This is justified as being good for the economy. The assertion is that if someone wants to do this they certainly can. This is true: tattoo parlors are protected by the Law. Prisons are full of tattooed men and now women who imagine they are expressing themselves so to make them exceptional among their peers. In fact each one is just like all of the others when considering the whole being. There are many more useful ways of accomplishing self respect, including learning a trade or vocation and stopping the lying and cheating, killing and fighting that put them where they are; *in prison.* Many are in need of psychological help which they cannot afford or it is sponsored by the State. Rather they must meet decent and friendly people who will not exploit them. Young women especially are victimized by the carnal and illicit demands made of them by their man. Rape is an unholy form of male expression that cannot be tolerated. In some gangs rape is as an entrance fee and is encouraged by other members who share the broad. The gang bangers are an especially dumb, brutal and indecent type of youth. Nevertheless they imagine themselves as heroes.

---

some form of comfort: they have little else to comfort them. This is a definite form of atavism; it is not a Fine Art, it is retrograde and repulsive.

[296] **Many mention** that they are "expanding the envelope". This has no truthful meaning and is merely one cliché amongst many.

[297] **Plato** suggested that Music could or perhaps would ruin the social structure. Rap music is certainly capable of this and some other newer forms, atonal and dissonant, are capable of such an accomplishment. Nevertheless the New Art forms have been given praise and opportunity whereas better forms are abandoned and neglected.

Some individuals who may read what is written have a very limited and slanted point of view. Many may have insufficient understanding therefore they will have a smile and shift to something more "pertinent" like the scores from a meaningless game.
Others may dismiss much of what is expressed in this work.
And finally some may be insulted by the inference.
To you I say; open your eyes.

We are confused Victims of a great form of the LIE.[298]
Keep in mind the Lie is the most destructive form of Political rhetoric and action.

—————

Robert Fiedler
Emeritus Professor, January 11, 2013. June 18, 2013.

---

[298]   **The World Order, Our Secret Rulers.**

Some of this information is taken from the book by Eustice Mullins: (Ezra Pound Inst, Staunton, VA. 24401, 2nd. Ed. 1992).

CHAPTER XII

WHAT HAPPENED TO THE WORLD
IN THE PAST HUNDRED YEARS?

It should be understood that I am not a researcher. What appears in this writing is a distillation of a lifetime of reading and observation. All of what appears here has a factual basis as history; it can be checked on the Internet and the book sources provided in the bibliography. This writing I define as being deductive logic, intuitively applied. The deductive logic is based on the facts that are somehow known to me and the intuitive element is rather a metaphysical or spiritual Tenor to what is written. **I am not certain that all of the facts are precisely true however I did use what I believe to be the most reliable sources.** *Since there are so many lies and so many verbal constructs, many of which have become a part of common thought patterns and which may have been designed to deceive, when reading this one must move to a higher power for truthful understanding.* [299] *This I attempt to do in encouraging the Idea and belief in a singular omnipotent God, whoever He may be.*

What was the roll of Destiny in forming the past hundred years, more or less, of History? Is this knowable or do "things just happen?" One can trace the occurrence of events and come to a Manner of conclusion however this will be "colored" by one or another point of view. Who is doing, the thinking, will effect what is the outcome of the thought-process. *Our thinking is somewhat of a transient endeavor,* and we are not always certain of how it will be received by other human beings. Thoughts travel in an infinite space and may be misinterpreted by who hears what is said or sees what is written. Recently it has been discovered that once within the

---

[299]   **I have written** about common thought patterns or *"thought clusters"* and the thought constructs devised by men in some other Writings: Such *"Thought Clusters"* combine and are what motivates much of what is done. And, there specific origin and meaning, is difficult to trace and to access honestly. For 2500 years some Ideas have persisted: none more so than the Jewish **_"Idea" that they, the Jews, are people chosen by God to rule over humanity._** This is a destructive and very negative form of **VANITY** and is a Cardinal Sin. This Idea continues and is promoted by many who are not truthfully Jewish; they are Asiatic converts; from the tribe of Bulan and some other places. This is what motivates much of what is called Jewish Politics and because of greed is destroying much of the good that is in the hearts of the truthfully good Jews of this World. Some such converts are clever and dishonest in many of their dealings as is obviated by their past personal known behavior. Read some of the current literature on the various Ponzi Schemes promoted by some Jews. You will quickly arrive at your own understanding of some Jews. Their maneuvering combines with the maneuverings of some others and is a part of what is bringing the World very close to what might become as a massively destructive annihilation War.

realm of the computer the thoughts will remain as they are expressed for an indefinite time period; possibly forever; *they become as a small part of the Universal Order of creation.* They enter the Space and because of new technologies can be accessed by anyone with the proper equipment. This is a strange and completely new phenomenon. This has great political, economic, social and practical applications. The written word has the same problems as those words spoken. One can imagine that this is a problem in all communication; perhaps generally communications should be as brief as possible. In fact at this time the opposite is true the communications grow in length as the discussions continue. This has become a serious problem when one is trying to understand the meaning of our Constitution. In fact it has become absurd in the variety of interpretations that some give to what is precise and generally definite. The computer can handle the information however the computer cannot understand the meaning or purpose: *not yet!* And the computer cannot think: *not yet!* The computer does not have the physic-spiritual components as does the human mind. Certain occurrences are destined to happen, no matter what: we have no way to know what they will be. This is the part of Destiny that is unknown and unseen nevertheless it will have strange and various effects on different people.

To set the tenor for what is happening let us begin with the Spanish American War: a small War by the standards of warfare today. On April 25, 1898 the United States declared war on *Spain* following the sinking of the Battleship Maine in Havana harbor on February 15, 1898. The war ended with the signing of the Treaty of Paris on December 10, 1898. As a result Spain lost its control over what it had once controlled. This War **cost** the United States $250 million and 3,000 lives."[300] This was a relatively cheap War by today's standards and cost only a few thousand lives. This was before the about one hundred years of *"inflation"* and the taking over of nearly every industry in the World by the giant Corporations. W are not certain how the Orient will come into play however it will be very important.[301] The numbers are small, almost unbelievably so compared to what is expressed as the cost of the more recent conflicts. Keep in mind this is the *Devil working through man to accomplish what is evil.* Also keep in mind that the Devil, Satan and Lucifer are metaphorical creatures that exist as IDEAS. The Idea always precedes the Act. We cannot relieve the World of all evil ideas however we can guide the people to making the right and correct decisions, every day. This guidance has become almost as an Art Form.[302]

---

[300] **This is about as many deaths** as were incurred in the 2001 bombing of the World Trade Center in New York. It is interesting to note: that which allows for the advancement of Civilization is that *"In the end we are all dead"*: think of that: *we will all be dead, forever.* Forever is a long Time!

[301] **Both China and India** are difficult to understand because of the number of people and they're having been somewhat isolationist in the past. South America does not weigh in heavily for political and social reasons. When we speak of the West we mean Europe, The United States, Russia, to a degree Australia and small parts of other nations. All of this is difficult to assess because of the evolving and changing nature of the populations and the political pressures being applied.

[302] For centuries men have tried to give the Devil a correct and real form. The form must relate somehow to what is evil. How might such evil form appear when given to graphic depiction? Cartoonists and other artists, often silly beyond belief, have attempted to create such an image. Comic book nonsense is rampant without significant understanding. Unfortunately such nonsense has been incorporated into movies and vainly inspired literature. And such nonsense is also part of the imagery of a collective neurosis which is mentioned in this writing.

"*After the fall of Napoleon,* the Rothschild's turned all of their hatred against the Romanovs.[303] In 1825 it is asserted that they poisoned Alexander I; in 1855 they poisoned Nicholas I. Other assassinations followed, culminating on the night of Nov. 6, 1917, when a dozen Red Guards drove a truck up to the Imperial Bank Building in Moscow. They loaded the Imperial jewel collection and $700,000,000.00 in gold totaling more than a billion dollars.[304] The new regime also confiscated the 150,000,000 acres in Russia personally belonging to the Czar.[305] The $700,000,000.00 in gold was with gold at twenty dollars an ounce: at today's price that would be about 75 times that number or 75 x $700,000,000 = $52,500,000,000,000.00 (52 trillion 500 billion dollars). *Given such numbers one can postulate that they are sufficient to "take over" the world).* Right now the price of gold is fluctuating, quite a bit as speculators attempt to make a killing. This is what is imagined by some as being accomplished at this time: the Romanoff fortune is believed by some to be the basis for this World take-over. This "take-over" is clothed in mystery, murder, lying, deceitful methods and a misunderstanding of the meaning and effects of Religion: it is Messianic to be sure. *Such money by now would have found its way into many pockets, not all of them would be Rothschild's.* The Understanding is that this was a tremendous amount of money to be had and such money would have grown exponentially in time. In collusion with Governments this money was sufficient to create what we have: a very near "One-World Dictatorship". Whom do you imagine holds and controls the remains of this great fortune? Of equal importance were the enormous cash reserves, which the Czar had invested abroad. The New York Times stated the Czar had $5,000,000.00 in guarantee Trust, and $1,000,000.00 in the National City Bank; other authorities stated it was $5,000,000.00 million in each bank (in 1925 that was the equivalent of **at least** $50,000,000.00 of today's deflated currency). At that time the average cost for a new car was $445.00 to $500.00. Mr. Mullins mentions other sums as well.

---

[303] **There seems to have been** an extreme hatred of the Romanoff's (Christians) by the Rothschild's (Jews) probably dating from an early misunderstanding of the meaning and nature of religious beliefs. Many Jews have been separated from other people so they might be better contained in their own beliefs and more easily controlled as a group by their Rabbis.

[304] **That price** was when gold was worth $20.00 per ounce. Today's price of $1200.00 to $1500.00 per ounce would make the value *seem much greater*. If one divides $1200.00 by twenty one will have 60 *times the imagined value*. If one multiplies $700,000,000.00 by 60 one will have today's inflated value. $700,000,000.00 multiplied by 60 equals an astounding $42,000,000,000,000.00; that is forty two trillion dollars. This is the reason Imperial Russia was destroyed. We are told the value of gold will go much higher; who promotes this Idea? It is promoted by speculators that hope to profit from the people's ignorance. Such destruction had little reason for the people and little reason for the nation: *it was the functioning of Greed,* a **Mortal Sin.** Such monies at least a part of such money, is probably being used in an attempt at conquering the World. Such may succeed. If we add to this any legitimate interest that may have been earned on such money the amount is even greater; we cannot know how much greater. In the recent past six months the value of gold has declined to about 1200 to 1400 dollars divide this by twenty and you will have between 60 and 70 times the value adjusting for inflation. $700,000,000.00 multiplied by 75 = $49,000,000,000,000.00 and by 75 = $52,500,000,000,000.00. This is still a great sum of money. We must admit that we have no way of knowing just how much would be the number; but it would be much!

[305] **Mullins, Eustace:** *The World Order, Our Secret Rulers.* Thus we ask the questions: What happened to all that wealth? And: Who now has title to the land?

$115,000,000.00 in four English banks.
    $ 35,000,000.00 in the bank of England
    $ 25,000,000.00 in Barings bank
    $ 25,000,000.00 in Barclays bank
    $ 30,000,000.00 in Lloyd's bank
$100,000,000.00 in the Banque de France
$ 80,000,000.00 in the Rothschild bank of Paris
$132,000,000.00 in the Mendelssohn bank in Berlin.

$542,000,000 Total; a pretty nice nest egg!

Given inflation these numbers can be multiplied by at least ten to arrive at the present approximate value of such holdings. One can easily understand why at present we in The United States appear to be in a state of gradual decline. Happily some believe we are entering a new era of prosperity.

We return to our subject; practically all of these Banks were generally controlled by Jews: actually not Biblical Jews however, many may be considered as counterfeit Jews or Khazars having originated from Central Asia.[306] It appears they have replaced what were commonly referred to as the Huns. At compound interest, since 1916 this would amount to a tremendous sum, no one knows how much interest they may have gotten from this investment.[307] This is quite a bit of money: even for a Rothschild. If you consider the price of gold then and now the number is much greater (see above). Gold speculation has made millions for many generally the already rich.

Apparently Sverdlov and Lenin had early in 1918 decided to execute the Czar and his family. *"There is no need to exaggerate the part played in the creation of Bolshevism and in the actual bringing about of the Russian Revolution by these International and for the most part atheistic Jews. It is certainly a very great one; it probably outweighs all others. With the notable exception of Lenin, the majority of the leading figures are Jews."* [308] (Lenin may have been a Jew). The Czar his wife, children and faithful servants were murdered on ***July 16, 1918***. The Czar and his family were murdered, in cold blood; they had no form of Trial and no opportunity to express their position. Those that planned this atrocity didn't care what was their opinion or their defense; they wanted them dead leaving no rightful claimants to their fortune.

---

[306] **The Khazars** were descendants of the families ruled under King Bulan, the Seventh century ruler of his people. His people were Khazars; they were an Asiatic and a warring people. These people were not Biblical Jews: they were converts to Judaism because it was believed by Bulan that his people needed a Religion.

[307] **It is understood** by many that none of this money and none of the land have ever been *rightfully reclaimed by a rightful owner*. One wonders who now owns Title to this land and how did they obtain Title? The answer is no doubt quite interesting and is a well kept secret. Do some research and find the answer.

[308] **Jews,** as can be imagined, are prominent in most Western revolutions. Many are heirs of Judaism from the past acceptance of the Faith by a somewhat primitive Asian people; King Bulan, 7th. century.

Russia was socialized: this was and is the methods of Socialism: cut expenses except for your own, lock up your imagined enemies; those who you fear, hang-um before the trial. Many of us have read of the various five year programs and how they all were, in fact, failures.[309] This, ties in with many aspects of human behavior and commerce. [310] In addition the leaders, as they were, generally speaking were ignorant, profane and disgusting forms of human kind; nevertheless they may have possessed a manner of perverted intelligence. Thereafter Stalin was absolutely a brute and had an ignorant and disruptive personality: he was also somewhat clever and shrewd. Such as this is the kind of person required of this Type of leadership: no conscience and no compassion only a *narrow-minded and venal insolence*. This insolence is meted on all who might be able to disobey the corrupt leadership under that of *"We"* the people will find themselves captives. The Form and Manner of this atrocity is apparent behind the perverted thinking in the Cloward-Piven Strategy. They encourage riot in the streets to scare and sublimate the decent people in the community. Nevertheless they were given positions in Education to promote and encourage such behavior.[311]Such Idea as held by Cloward and Piven is certainly not decently formulated. What appears in the paragraph immediately below is one consequence of such thinking; there are others as well.

The First World War was fought at the time *the Romanov's were murdered*. Their murder was a senseless killing, including the *killing of five innocent children,* based somewhat on hatred that had been nursed for centuries by vain fools and simple-minded morons; *they were working for Satan, for the Devil.* Many believe when the Devil takes possession of your Soul you will do his bidding.[312] The details are less important than the concept: *a real fool will hate forever* and

---

[309] **If our good President Obama** knew something of History he would certainly know that what he is proposing will lead ultimately to failure. One cannot presume to know how everyone should live. Life is sacred and man has free will to choose as he is able: the consequences of such choice are not known in advance.

[310] **"Because of his need for capital,** the farmer is especially vulnerable to the World Order's manipulation of interest rates, which is bankrupting many. Just as in the Soviet Union, in the early 1930s, when Stalin ordered the kulaks to give up their small plots of land to live and work on the collective farms, the American small farmer faces the same type of extermination, being forced to give up his small plot of land to become a hired hand for the big agricultural soviets or trusts." *Page 254, Internet document, Mullins, the world Order, our Secret Rulers*. The takeover will require some time. The expansion of private farming is occurring, under corporate leadership with the idea or expectation that eventually such farms will become Communes controlled by the State: Obama Types will be given opportunity to lead such Communes.

[311] **In a 1970** New York Times interview; Cloward is quoted as saying that poor people can only advance when "the rest of society is afraid of them." He then theorized that activists should refrain from demanding that government provide more for the poverty stricken and, instead, should strive to pack as many people on the welfare (read: entitlement) rolls as possible, creating a demand that could not be met, facilitating the destruction of the welfare system and massive financial crisis.—See more at: http://theatheistconservative.com/tag/the-cloward-piven-strategy/#sthash.CDo4LNfg.dp

[312] **Keep in mind** whatever "It" may be the Devil is a persistent "Idea" which will not go away. The Disneyland ways of showing evidence of his being are somewhat shallow nevertheless they will keep him alive for the kiddies and the older immature types.

pass the hatred to his children, this is sad however true. The First World War, like all War was a consequence of the people being motivated to levels of hatred sufficient to allow this to happen. We are mostly interested in the cost of this War in money and human life: the human life is irreplaceable whereas the cost when borrowed money is involved earns interest for years given to the lender. ***Everyone knows of this however few understand the meaning of such knowledge.***[313]

Some imagine *that the money stolen from the Romanov's could have been used as the seed money in the attempt to destroy the Western Civilization and especially Catholic Christianity. The plan appears to be working quite well: up until this time.* Keep in mind at the present time all involved are not enemies of the Romanov's, there are others as well: the Dynastic families which have intermarried and begotten families of their own. They are all, knowingly or unknowingly, tacitly involved. This is an Issue that requires a more mature understanding.

To repeat for emphasis*: We suggest that the money stolen from the Romanov's could have been used as the seed money in attempting to destroy the Western Civilization and especially Catholic Christianity: the plan is working quite well up until this time.*

"Financial Cost **of the** First World War—**Spartacus Educational** . . ."

This includes the five countries that were defending something which someone may have valued. When other excuses are not to be found they refer to National or Racial pride. Who remembers what that was? All of the important players are now dead: the last one died this past year, 2012; He was 111 years old.

Allied Powers: Cost in Dollars in 1914-18: United States: $22,625,250,000.00 Great Britain: $35,334,012,000.00: France: $24,265,580,000.00: Russia: $22,293,950,000.00: Italy: $12,413,998,000.00."

The total for the five countries was $116,932,796,000.00. That is one-hundred sixteen billion, nine hundred thirty-two million, seven hundred ninety six thousand dollars. Quite a large sum to waste killing your brother: whom you could never have known. Where will this lead us?[314] We are being bankrupted, destroyed for a generally unknown and misunderstood purpose.[315] The people are sleeping, or attending a noisy sporting event or they are simply lazy.

---

[313] This is what has enabled a few eager individuals and their progeny to capture so much of the wealth of this world: some of the good people have captured a bit as well.

[314] **Russian currency** at that time had a gold backing of about 125 % this is certainly interesting. This is not bad for what Americans were told was a vulgar and primitive people. At that time their Palaces and Artwork was the Standard for the World. At that time gold was selling at $ 20.00 an ounce compared to what it is today, $1500.00 more or less.

[315] **The purpose** was to further the One World Anglo-Zionist need to dominate all other human beings. This is a Socio-Political and Religious Idea that must be better understood and should be curtailed. This is a battle between the Beasts of the Apocalypse and God: the Creator of all that is seen and unseen and his son Jesus. This is true no matter how you may envision or refute God's being.

After the War, there were a few years of prosperity in the United States, followed by the Great Depression, so called. In 1932 our good President Franklin Delano (van) Roosevelt did some spectacular things. He was not necessarily the good and decent person which he was formed to have been by the mass media. Many considered him a hypocrite and a liar, which may be exactly what he was. Only God knows for sure.[316] Roosevelt had four terms which was outrageous for a free people: for a while he was like a King. When *"they"* were finished using him he died just like everyone else however the thieves kept the spoils for their progeny. The progeny are very well off; some may own the $50,000,000.00 Yachts that are mentioned in this writing. This Type of human behavior has been going on for centuries. Roosevelt deceived us into the Second World War and many other times beside this. We still are treated, as entertainment, to all the movies and the mayhem which was a part of that conflict. Here again one finds himself in a Disneyland of sorts, a fantasy of excess. The mind set developed from this Type of participation is nothing less than savage. *Such imagery and the understanding encouraged thereby also become part of the collective consciousness of "We" the people.* This Type of behavior being promoted as entertainment has been and is affecting the entire World. Such as this is difficult to correct since others are just as sick and demented as many of us are. This is a question of ***mass-neurosis*** which, to begin, is difficult to trace and perhaps more difficult to assess.[317]

At present our women are being taught to be warriors. This is part of the silly demand for equality; equal, so to feel justified in killing another man's son or daughter or anyone unfortunate enough to be in the wrong place. *Some others are dressed appearing nearly naked with bulging body parts that appear to be made of wax: in fact much of the bulging is absolutely grotesque, and is surgically applied to satisfy both the vanity of the women and the lust of the men.* Some of the bulges are merely padding in the right places. All young women know of this. Keep in mind both ***Vanity*** and ***Lust*** are Cardinal sins. Sitting in front of the televisions sets

---

[316] **What follows is taken from an article** *about the 1930s economic programs of the United States.*

"The **New Deal** was a series of economic programs implemented in the United States between 1933 and 1936. They were passed by the U.S. Congress during the first term of President Franklin D. Roosevelt. The programs were presumed as responses to the Great Depression, and focused on what historians call the "3 Rs": Relief, Recovery, and Reform. That is, Relief for the unemployed and the poor; Recovery of the economy to normal levels; and Reform of the financial system to prevent a repeat depression (this proclamation is rather humorous, considering what has happened in the past seventy five years). The New Deal produced a political realignment, making the Democratic Party the majority (as well as the party which held the White House for seven out of nine Presidential terms from 1933 to 1969), with its base in liberal ideas, big city machines, and newly empowered labor unions, ethnic minorities, and the white South. The Republicans were split, either opposing the entire New Deal as an enemy of business and growth, or accepting some of it and promising to make it more efficient. The realignment crystallized into the New Deal Coalition that dominated most American elections into the 1960s, while the opposition Conservative Coalition largely controlled Congress from 1938 to 1964."

[317] **A Neurosis** may be considered as a mental disease, certainly a mental impairment. Today some psychologists, too influenced by contemporary political pressure are changing the meaning of words that would apply, to such forms of behavior. Many are more interested in having a government grant than in seeking real solutions for the problems they are supposed to address. They fall into the comfortable trap of complacent behavior: for a price of course. I am not, nor would I want to be, a psychologist so I leave this to your own inquiry.

many are being programmed to accept non-sense as enjoyment and Sin as being quite common, which it certainly is. Such as this is our entertainment together with the football; there exist the great teams of tattooed athletes. Given Sin you can choose which Sin is your preference, there are no limitations; remember you are considered to be an adult expressing yourself. Any form is acceptable; where, will this lead?

The Second World War was a really big disaster for millions. Millions were killed; uselessly. The cost was approximately $288 Billion (1940 dollars): Be aware the First World War cost the United States only $22,625,253,000.00 which was less than one tenth of the cost of the Second World War. This cost factor is what is most interesting to the Bankers and Money-lenders. This is a function of inflation. The common man is told that things are relative and inflation doesn't matter. He is told he is better off now than before; this is true however such thinking evades the Issue. Those with the intent of controlling everyone else are considering centuries. This has been going on since the time of Christ and the take-over is becoming nearly a reality. They know their assets will sustain and they will have a greater percentage of the total. *Such spending will bankrupt any nation given the time required: we are no exception.*

End of the War; In terms of losses in human lives which maintain the *"genetic pool"* and material resources, World War II was undeniably the most destructive military conflict to date. It was a global-military conflict that saw 61 countries taking part in a war that lasted from 1939 to 1945. The major participants were the Allied powers, specifically the United States, Great Britain, France, and the Soviet Union, who were at war with the Axis Coalition of Germany and Italy in the European Theater. And concurrently in the Pacific Theater, the United States was engaged with the Imperial forces of Japan. In order to more truthfully understand the *"scale of the conflict"* and the nations involved one must familiarize themselves with an understanding of the scale of the players who were involved.

Japan: The events leading up to the war can be traced back to 1937 when Japan, seeking to extend her colonial realm and to secure vast raw material reserves and natural resources such as ores and petroleum, launched a full-scale invasion of mainland China. To force Japan to cease their hostility against China, in May 1939, President Franklin D. Roosevelt ordered an embargo of all exports to Japan. Angered over this maneuver and now severely lacking in critical resources to fuel its war effort, Japan turned its aggression on its southern neighbors.[318]

Cost In Money and Lives According to my Oxford Companion to WWII in strictly monetary terms here was the breakdown for the major players in their currencies: UK-Pounds Sterling 20,500,000,000: US-Dollar $306,000,000,000.00: Germany-Reich-marks 414,000,000,000: Japan-Yen 174,000,000,000: Italy-Lire 278,500,000,000: USSR-Ruble 582,000,000,000. I'm not sure if the US figure takes into account 50 billion in Lend lease aid that was given out.[319]

Read more: http://wiki.answers.com/Q/*How much did World War 2 cos*t # ixzz1ZBK11mHe

---

[318]   **This situation** is somewhat like the present. We are informed that an Aircraft Carrier squadron is being deployed to that area of the Pacific. Why? Have we not learned anything? Of course this will give the boys something to do.

[319]

Monetarily, in 1940 dollars, the estimated cost was *$288 Billion*. In 2007 dollars this would amount to approximately *$5 Trillion*. In addition, the effects of the war on the U.S. economy were that it decisively ended the depression and created what seemed to be a booming economic windfall, for a brief period.[320] Because the United States mainland was untouched by the war her economic wealth and prosperity soared as she became the world leader in manufacturing, technology, industry and agriculture.[321] Right now (2012) we are paying for that monetary fiasco: it was a fiasco and should never have happened *however the past cannot be changed in any way.* In terms of the costs in American lives lost the following list the final estimations:

Army—234,874	Coast Guard—574
Navy—36, 958	Merchant Marines—9,521
Marines—19,733	

Total American personnel killed in action: 295,790. **Why?**

When the War was raging we had our two-party System doing whatever was necessary to promote this stupendous farce: our Politicians and leaders were not the best of men. We should not have been involved in Europe or Asia: George Washington had it right he said, "Stay Home."

Keep in mind the two Parties are, in many ways, very much the same. Leaders (so called) in both parties tend toward a one-World Socialist type Government: they have very similar ideas about how the World should be run. Seemingly they are maintained for purely political reasons and are generally kept in a *"knowable balance"* thus to be quietly although effectively controlled by a moneyed Elite. The moneyed Elite, because of *SIN* because of *GREED* cause most of the problems. *Individuals die whereas money is maintained in different hands in future time however retains its power over humanity.* This behavior, in the West, has become almost as an art form in political maneuvering. There may be some minor problems however when the people have *"Bread and Circuses"* they are easily controlled: our population pays billions for distracting entertainment; everywhere apparent. Little is done for simple pleasure: instead there must be uniforms, teams and all of the *"stuff"* which is complementary for a professional team: so called. We are told this is good for the economy. If you view the labels carefully to see where this stuff is coming from; one wonders which economies are we *"helping"* with this nonsense? **We elect jackals,** to lead us and are led from one carcass to another. The stock market goes up and down as the jackals accumulate more and more.[322] This is why there is so much support for a

---

[320] **Note 5 cents:** .05 the price of a cup of coffee in 1940: $1.50 to $2.50 the price of the same cup of coffee in 2013. This is approximately a 150% to 250 % increase in 70 years: a bit more in some places.

[321] **This was simply** a short term gain for the United States. We are paying for this right now (2013) with a struggling economy. The United States will not be the controlling Superpower forever that it is right now: it will be replaced by others in the future. This is a certainty as it should be. Our Nation and its tin-man leadership will give way to others in Time: right now VANITY is obvious, VANITY is a mortal sin which will not be rewarded for long. Our leadership is obsessed with self praise and uses the LIE to further their personal interests.

[322] **The Stock Market** is an ideal way of turning notional profit into real wealth; all the trading and the going up and going down of prices is the giant elephant in the room. It does provide opportunity for some however the prices can be dropped at any moment and the short-sellers will have the proceeds. This is a

"high level" Democratic System. It is believed by some that 350 individuals (the jackals) control one half of the World's riches. If it is true, this is incredible! The stock market is a way to do this, to convert notional wealth into tangible value, a good trick if you understand.*: It is a trick. The trick involves the nature of Time:* Time is dependable and it is said Time is money. This is a confused and confusing Idea which is attendant to Time. *Time provides for a period in which the proper act can have great economic consequence.* A single move can earn more than a lifetime of patient, intelligent and honest endeavor. ***This, Is THE modern tragedy!*** Everyone wants to make that move: only the Specialist succeeds repeatedly. Thus Time, in such instance, is an enemy of most decent men, only the shysters and the thieves spend all of their time considering what they can gain in a couple of days as a profit. Most men are working creating something useful; they have not the time to speculate on one or another ways of earning an income. We identify such economic treachery as luck. However for the really big boys luck is just a word!

The Korean War has helped big money to grow even bigger. Until that War we were in not too bad shape financially, however mothers were working and not tending as much to their children. This has had various effects on the children some are very depressing involving rape, dope addiction, the child running away from home and murder to mention some important ones. And, the consequence, any consequence from the past, is carried forward in Time. We read and lament about this in the newspapers. The children are now fed on fast food take-outs and the children began to form in gangs for friendship and protection. Some gangs were probably decent however others began seeking money in various criminal activities. Mom and dad were both away from the home; often they were divorced or were never married. Mothers were left alone with their children; dad was just a passer-by. Dad was interested in the brief pleasure from an ejaculation with a new woman. **Wow!** Illegitimacy began to expand since another child meant an increase in welfare payments, however raising a family was a two-person job. One can easily understand where this is going.[323] War, work and raising a family all come into play one way or another.

It was December 1945. With the surrender of Japan some four months earlier World War II was finally over and, as with all wars, the victors assembled to negotiate the rules for divvying up their winnings. One such agreement, reached at the Moscow Conference of Foreign Ministers, called for dividing Korea in half at the 38th parallel. Furthermore, the United States and the Soviet Union would jointly occupy the country for four years, the Russians to the North, the Americans to the South.

North Invades South: On June 25, 1950, the North Koreans became the first to carry out their threat. Equipped with Soviet tanks, their Army crossed the 38th parallel and invaded the South. Outnumbered in manpower and all other military resources, the South Korean Army was unable to repel their new enemy.[324] When North Korea was on the verge of success, the United Nations approved a plan to assist South Korea in preventing a communist takeover of their country. Ironically, the approval of this resolution was made possible only because the Soviet Union was temporarily absent from the Security Council and therefore was unable to apply its veto.

---

wonderfully conceived way of stealing: and it works well. It is becoming apparent that some are taking much too much: when will it end?

[323] **See footnote285.**

[324] **This was very likely planned** in advance, by the unseen rulers.

Responding to the U.N. resolution, within days, President Harry S. Truman ordered the transfer of thousands of American troops stationed in Japan to South Korea. Also arriving on their shores were troops from a coalition of 15 other countries all under the auspices of the United Nations. The American troops were under the command of General Douglas McArthur.

Monetary Costs: For the United States, the cost for her involvement in the Korean War was an estimated *$67,000,000,000.00: 67 Billion (1953 dollars) or $535,000,000,000.00 Billion (2008 dollars)*. The numbers are approximate however they are reasonable estimates. The difference is an adjustment for an inflation that we are constantly told does not exist: Those who say *"that there is no inflation"* are conniving liars, if not they do not understand the function and reasons for using money as a medium of exchange. The admission is that it takes $7.9850 now so to buy what could have been purchased at that time for a single dollar. This is an increase of 798% in the aggregate. Divide this number by 60 and you will get 13.308% inflation per year. You are told inflation is negligible: something in the range of 3-5% per annum *(and you believe what you hear on the News).* One believes what they hear when they are not able or not interested enough to figure out the details. And no one wants to even consider Reality; most are too occupied with the meaningless trivia of the day. The News reporting is where you receive your information; many individuals are too tired to search out the truth on any issue. Is this a lie or not? Inflation is an accession to **GREED**: greed which is a **MORTAL SIN**. Who believes this? Those that are greedy must change their ways or the World is doomed to constant anxiety and turmoil as one gouges the other for a few pennies.

Human Costs: There were 33,600 American lives lost in this conflict. This was a useless expenditure of young and vital life. Never the less we are most interested in the monetary costs as this is written: it is understood that Human life cannot be replaced.

$67 billion at interest of 5% is $3.75 billion per year. This number may continue for years and will compound in favor of the lending banks. Don't worry there are ways to refinance and to extend a loan. Keep in mind a Bank's money is not like your money which has been earned through some reasonable effort and in the building of the economy. ***With our System the Bank simply creates the money as a form of indebtedness:*** *clever however not wise.* If such debt is allowed to ride for fifty years it becomes $187.5 billion dollars. That is $187,500,000,000.00 this is quite a bit for a simple book keeping adjustment. Today the situations are much worse; all of the subterfuges and make believe remedies have been utilized and there is little room left to negotiate: *and, it will get much worse in the near future.* After the Korean War we have been treated to several more Wars: all contrived for the effect they will have on a gullible and trusting population.

Cost of Vietnam War: The Vietnam War ended up costing the US around $584 billion according to the website: http://members.aol.com/usregistry/allwars.htm#cst. The real cost of Vietnam? For 58,000 Americans it cost them everything: one can observe the cost for fighting a War is increasing, from one war to the next.

From Wikipedia the free encyclopedia; Jump to: navigation, search.
This article is about the war that began in 2003. For other uses, see Iraq War (disambiguation).
Further information: 2003 invasion of Iraq and Post-invasion Iraq.

The **Iraq War** or **War in Iraq** began on March 20, 2003[48][49] with the invasion of Iraq by the United States under the administration of President George W. Bush and the United Kingdom under Prime Minister Tony Blair.[50] The war is also referred to as ***Operation Iraqi Freedom** and the **Second Gulf War.***

The true cost of the Iraq war: *$3,000,000,000,000,000.00. $3 trillion and beyond; and there is some threat this may escalate into a Nuclear War.* We are really making progress: Aren't We?

What follows immediately below was written by Joseph E. Stieglitz and Linda J. Bilmes
Sunday, September 5, 2010

> "Writing in these pages in early 2008, we put the total cost to the United States of the Iraq war at $3 trillion. This price tag dwarfed previous estimates, including the Bush administration's 2003 projections of a $50 billion to $60 billion war."

> "But today, as the United States ends combat in Iraq, it appears that our $3 trillion estimate (which accounted for both government expenses and the war's broader impact on the U.S. economy) was, if anything, too low."

> **"Prior to the invasion,** the governments of the United States and the United Kingdom asserted that the possibility *(note the word possibility)* of Iraq employing weapons of mass destruction (WMD) threatened their security and that of their coalition/regional allies."[51][52][53]

> **"Following the invasion,** the U.S.-led Iraq Survey Group concluded that Iraq had ended its nuclear, chemical, and biological programs in 1991 and had no active programs at the time of the invasion but that Iraq intended to resume production once sanctions were lifted. Although some degraded remnants of misplaced or abandoned chemical weapons from before 1991 were found, they were not the weapons which had been the main argument to justify the invasion."

> **"The War in Afghanistan** began on October 7, 2001,[30] as the armed forces of the United States of America and the United Kingdom, and the Afghan United Front (Northern Alliance), launched Operation Enduring Freedom, invading the country, in response to the September 11 attacks on the United States, with the stated goal of dismantling the Al-Qaeda terrorist organization and ending its use of Afghanistan as a base. The United States also said that it would remove the Taliban regime from power and create a viable democratic state."

Democracy is being ruled by unseen powers that are only apparent as intended by their somewhat Socialist minded leaders. Democracy will always deteriorate and become something else: with the consent of the people, of course. It will take Time but it will happen: (Fiedler).

The preludes to the war were the assassination of anti-Taliban leader Ahmad Shah Massoud on September 9, 2001, and the September 11 attacks on the United States, in which nearly 3000 civilians lost their lives in New York City, Washington D.C. and Pennsylvania.

The aim of the invasion was to find Osama bin Laden and other high-ranking Al-Qaeda members to be put on trial, to destroy the organization of Al-Qaeda, and to remove the Taliban regime which supported and gave safe harbor to it. The George W. Bush administration stated as policy it would not distinguish between terrorist organizations and nations or governments that harbored them.

War in Afghanistan: What follows in the next two paragraphs is the cost;
By Richard Wolf, USA TODAY

> "**WASHINGTON**—the monthly cost of the war in Afghanistan, driven by troop increases and fighting on difficult terrain, has topped Iraq costs for the first time since 2003 and shows no sign of letting up. Pentagon spending in February, the most recent month available, was $6,700,000,000.00: $6.7 billion in Afghanistan compared with $5.5 billion in Iraq. As recently as fiscal year 2008, Iraq was three times as expensive; in 2009, it was twice as costly."

> "**The shift is occurring** because the Pentagon is adding troops in Afghanistan and withdrawing them from Iraq. *And it's happening as the cumulative cost of the two wars surpasses $1 trillion,* $1,000,000,000,000.00 including spending for veterans and foreign aid. Those costs could put increased pressure on President Obama and Congress, given the nation's $12.9 trillion debt. During the time this writing has taken the debt has grown substantially. *The debt will continue to grow to accommodate inflationary pressure.*"

One can see the tremendous effect all war has on the lives of the people and the economy of the nations. One can try to understand what is happening and why it is happening; just remember *you are in a world of fantasy.* It's quite a simple procedure to add up the numbers as being objectively defined in human life and money. However what this means is not clear: not at all."

This is a function of Destiny which is relentless and unforgiving: I have written about Destiny in Chapter II. Once a moment is expended it can never be recaptured: only the effect remains and the effect is not generally understood:

Now, let us add up all the costs of these senseless wars.

The Spanish American War:	$ 250,000,000.00	3000 lives
First World War I	$ 22,625,253,000.00	
Second World War II	$ 288,000,000,000.00	
	$ 306,000,000,000.00	295,790 lives
Korean Was (in 2008 dollars)	$ 535,000,000,000.00	33,600 lives
Viet Nam	$ 584,000,000,000.00	58,000 lives

Iraq (cited as true cost of War: What is true?)

$ 5,500,000,000.00 (cost for one month x 12) $ 55,110,000,000.00 1 year estimate

Afghanistan

$ 6,700,000,000.00 (cost for one month x 12) $ 67,134,000,000.00 1 year estimate

$ 1,857,875,253,000.00

This is one trillion, eight hundred fifty seven billion, eight hundred seventy five million two hundred fifty three thousand dollars. Think how many lotto tickets one could buy for this. If just ten percent of this was spent on truthful books and education the World would be much improved. These numbers are assumed as being close to what was actually spent. You can check various sources to gain more information.

In addition the United States would now have to include the wars in Iraq and Afghanistan. **Joseph E. Stieglitz and Linda J. Bilmes** suggest three trillion for Iraq. They imagine this number to be $ 3,000,000,000,000.00 for the present total cost of this seemingly senseless War. *They also state they believe this amount is too low.*[325] As the government spends more, we as citizens will owe more. Additionally there are millions of illegal aliens in the System they are milking the decent people. These should be our great concerns. *WAKE UP!*

---

[325]   If one adds the cost of the war in Iraq (three trillion) and Afghanistan (three trillion +) the total begins to soar. It will approach eight trillion dollars and go beyond in the future; ($8,000,000,000,000.00). This is because we have no inflation? The compounding of interest on this amount will be tremendous! $8,000,000,000,000.00 at .05% interest is $400,000,000,000.00 Four hundred billion per year. Divide that by 300,000,000 and you will have a cost of $1,330.00 per year per person. This exemplifies the meaning of DEBT! The principle sum is great but in time the interest is greater and when it has been paid you will still have a remaining balance. All this we are spending so to bankrupt this Nation and ready it for a Marxist/Socialist becoming. There will be some sports however not much else.

Additionally it is said we have an existing national debt of 16 to 20 trillion, perhaps even more. That would add at least $2,660.00 to the $1,330.00 for a total of $3,990.00 for every man woman and child; just for what the government now owes. A family of four will owe $15,960.00. Can you afford this? Such numbers are not exact however they are close and do represent a real threat to the system.

Richard Wolff sets the war in Afghanistan is costing $ 6,700,000,000.00 per month. Multiply this number by 12 and you will have a yearly expense of $ 80,400,000,000.00 per year. That is eighty billion dollars per year. Divide this number by 300,000,000 (the approximate number of Americans) and you will have $ 268.00 per year cost; for every man, woman and child in this nation. *How many of our welfare recipients can afford to pay for this?* From this you will better understand where some (much) of your taxes are going.

What do all of these numbers mean? No one really knows what exactly or even closely what this spending is accomplishing. However this amount also helps to place our people in a position of extraordinary debt. Who is it that wants this to occur?

The above numbers are not exact however they are reasonable and do paint a quite gloomy picture. This is absolute waste: no recourse. The Wars we are fighting will bankrupt the nation: *this is a part of our Destiny.* The true cost of War in Iraq is over three-trillion dollars when one includes all of the details: many details are left out. *We will follow the Romanov's to the Grave.*

Consider that amount of wealth may be had in various forms.
What is wealth?

First there is **Tangible Wealth** based on what is real and may be useful. However such wealth may be kept from you or it can be stolen from you. Perhaps the most important of these is the grains and various food commodities. Everyone needs food just to exist so food is number one. There are large-scale Commodity Exchanges in nearly every country which handle and distribute the food for the people. These are problematic because of the ignorant fighting that goes on between the ill-advised and greedy men amongst the populations. In some areas fighting and inability to utilize the food will take about half of all food. This must be corrected if things are to be made better in the future however at present we have agitators stirring up revolution so to keep the people enslaved to the System. *The revolution's singular intent is to reduce the number of people and make way for a one-World government.*

Second in order is **Notional Wealth** which to a great extent is promoted as being the Financial Market. The Financial markets are corrupted by the same ignorance, *Vanity* and *Greed* as has ever existed at any time. *Here we have the workings of the Devil* encouraging some to take advantage of their brothers. We call this business and make excuses for the theft, lying and hypocrisy that is a part of the System: it is incorporated into the Law of the land. Those, who succeed in this arena, are the wealthy of the world, well connected and vain in their greedy and somewhat secret (conspiratorial) efforts. A few make it from the bottom to the very top however they are very rare. The most successful have made hundreds of millions by converting Notional Wealth into what is tangible. This is done as a paper transaction: some do lose. Notional Wealth can be evasive and appears and disappears like magic. Many derivatives are like this; their value is not even known to who holds the *"paper"*. Time is an important factor as prices go up and down, in Time, like a yo-yo. The clever position themselves to take advantage of this while others, just to exist from day to day or week to week, are working hoping to gain enough to pay for their families food. There should be no shortage of food except so much is lost to spoilage and War. And there are *big shots* stealing from the most destitute people. This is a tragedy.

The third form of wealth is **Virtual Wealth** which is of the mind: ideas and invention, also virtues such as temperance and patience may be important factors. This is what in truth drives the World to new forms of being and should be helpful to everyone. This is especially apparent in the past two-hundred years and is coincident with the becoming of the Modern Age.

The fourth form is personal and has to do with **good health and *is the most important of all; it provides an ideal Physiological basis for one's existence*.** It is the belief of some that today's somewhat poor health of the World population is, in the more wealthy countries from excessive living and in the poorer countries from starvation, disease neglect and injury inflicted because of War. Most of this can be corrected if people would endeavor to live peaceably and abandon all forms of War. If individuals cannot do this there is little hope for the future and ultimately millions perhaps billions will be annihilated because of this. **The understanding and practice of Christ's calling would provide the necessary method for improvement.**

—————

Sunday, September 5, 2010
Professor Emeritus; Robert Fiedler
Sept 18, 2012, Oct. 20, 2013.

CHAPTER XIII

LIBERTY

Concerning Liberty there is much ineptitude and Babble
Consider now; Personal volition and the meaning of Words

Present dialogue includes some of the understanding of Ron Paul for the meaning and extent of Liberty. He has made much of his assertion concerning the meaning of Liberty as a part of his bid for, the nomination for the Presidency of the United States. My understanding is that most who listen do not understand exactly what Congressman Paul is saying. **If they had understood him he would now be our President.** *The so-called liberals have scored heavily since he is not returning for another term. This is most unfortunate we have ended up with a much less desirable President: once again, Obama (who probably does not understand completely the truthful meaning of the word* **Liberty** *either) with his Socialist and Marxist "trained" background. In fact, given the broad definition of the word* **Liberty** *and the working of vested interests to corrupt any reasonable dialogue the world continues to flourish in spite of all the misunderstanding; it will continue in spite of misinformation and the thinking of Politicians.* [326]

---

[326] **1. Liberty;** State or fact of being a free person; *exemption from subjection to the will of another* claiming ownership of the person or services; freedom;—*opposite to slavery, serfdom, bondage,* etc.

2. Freedom from external restraint or compulsion; power to do as one pleases; also, with of and to, leave permission or opportunity; as the *liberty* of the air; *liberty* to come and go; large *liberty* of action.

3. Privilege; exemption; franchise; right or immunity enjoyed by prescription or grant; as the *liberties* of the commercial cities of Europe.

4. A place within which certain immunities are enjoyed or jurisdiction is exercised; specif., in certain British cities as London and Dublin, a district within which the exercise, privilege or franchise, of executing legal process was by royal grant, vested in one or more persons, exempting those from the jurisdiction of the sheriff.

5. The sum of the rights and immunities of all of the citizens of an organized civil community, concurrent with the guaranteed protection against interference with such rights and privileges **(civil liberty),** or the state of condition of those who are invested with the right effectually to share in framing and conducting the government under which they are politically organized **(political liberty),** or of those that are free from external restraint in the exercise of government to control **(individual liberty).** Individual liberty under Constitutional Governments in general involves freedom of the person in going and in coming **(personal liberty),** equality before the courts, security of private property, freedom of opinion and its expression and freedom of conscience.

Like all words Liberty can be misunderstood, misinterpreted or imagined to mean what it does not mean: today imaginations are running wild. This brings one to babbling about a subject with the wrong outcome as a consequence of the misunderstood communication; _we have too much meaningless communication._ As an aside it is possible that Obama is a committed narcissist: if this is true then it is certainly a problem in his being the President; now for a second term. Additionally, because of his background, he is not truthfully an American. There still remains the question: Where was Obama born. I have heard of a copy of a document that says he was born, Barry Soetoro, in Honolulu 4-8-1961: this was Indonesia, the address I have is Menteng Dalam R001? R003. He was accepted in the first grade on 1-1-1968 (January 1, 1968). The name of Obama's parents was Mr./Mrs. L. Soetoro. In any event this is certainly interesting; _with all of our laws and restrictions on the people how could he have become the President?_ In addition

---

6. A privilege or license in or as if in violation of the laws of strict etiquette or propriety; a freedom or familiarity; as, to permit or take, a _liberty;_ he would not venture so great a _liberty;_ to take _liberties_ with one's health.

7. A certain amount of freedom; permission to go freely within certain limits; also, the place or limits within which such freedom is exercised, as, the _liberty_ of the dungeon.

8. [_Cap._] A Liberty bond;—chiefly in _pl. Colloq._

9. A color, reddish—blue in hue, of very high saturation and low brilliance. Cf. COLOR.

10. _Jurisprudence._ A condition of legal non restraint of natural powers. See PRIVLEGE, n., 5c.

11. _Mane'ge._ An upward curve in a bit to accommodate the tongue; port; called also **liberty of the tongue. R.**

12. _Naut._ Permission for a sailor to go ashore: in the navy permission is granted listed men to leave the ship and return for the next working day or earlier, longer absences being granted as _leave._

13. _Philos._ This is the power of choice, freedom from necessity; freedom from compulsion or constraint of willing.

Syn.—see FREEDOM

At liberty; **a.** Unconfined; free; as they set the captive _at liberty._ **b.** A leisure, unoccupied. **c.** Free to (do something) as, he as at _liberty_ to say what he thinks **d.** _Slang._ He is out of employment.

At one's liberty. At one's will or choice. **Obs.**

Liberty (lib-er-ti) adj.

1. This designates a kind of thin, soft, satin-finished silk;—from the name of the inventor.

2. Having, granting, or having to do with liberty, or short leave; as a liberty man; a _liberty_ boat; a _liberty_ party.

Liberty /lib-er-ty n, pt -tie. _From the Merriam Webster Dictionary_ 1: FREEDOM /2: an action going beyond normal limits: _exp:_ FAMILIARITY 3: a short leave from naval duty. _(Merriam-Webster Dictionary)._ Given Liberty as part of a Political equation, this is an inadequate definition.

Liberty (Lib'er-ti), _n.; pl._ -TIES (-tiz). [ME. liberte, fr. OF. Liberte', fr. L. libertas, fr. Liber free. See LIBERAL].

This is taken from Webster's New International Dictionary, Second Edition, unabridged with reference history.

to this his grandmother says he was born in Africa. So who shall we believe? While people are trying to figure out just who this man is, he is ruining the nation. The damage he is inflicting will manifest in various ways in the future.

1.] Liberty is a state or fact of being a free person: the meaning is that _one is free of being dominated by the will of another._[327] Will, can manifest as an act of control or an expression of power. Given the scale of governments this is a difficult possibility since even in a Democracy elected officials, and some not elected, are given to make decisions for the total population.[328] Our elections are generally very close races therefore nearly half of the people have no confirmed representation. Additionally only about one half of the people will vote. This means that about a bit more than twenty five percent are represented. In any event our two Party systems, is in large part a fraud in spite of the valiant effort to keep it legitimate.

When a War is declared young men are conscripted and many are sent to their death, others are crippled physically and emotionally: at present we are fighting undeclared wars in different places, presumably to make the World safe for Democracy. This is a monumental tragedy that should be reconsidered and probably stopped. One man, Dr Ron Paul wants us to reconsider this dilemma and bring the troops back home to defend the United States of America. _We cannot expect the entire world to do as we would like them to do:_ we can certainly encourage them by example to do what is right however they must and should make their own decisions. In any event we should not supply them with armaments and means of killing each other. Their decisions will determine the success or failure of their nation. Our intervention may corrupt many of their decisions. The War on Terrorism, in many ways, seems to be contrived for the effect it will have on our population. _Those who are not like we are should be brought to realize right from wrong by persuasion and example: this may take a hundred years or longer._ There are many factors which bear upon this including language, habit manner and custom; also various religions see things differently; one cannot ignore Reality as presently exists. There are

---

[327] **The President** is not a King or a Czar: he is a citizen like any citizen elected by the people for a brief period of time. He must follow the dictates of the Constitution and all that entails. The Constitution is, at this time, about the best thinking on Government responsibility and freedom for the people. It is presumed that any President *will* understand this and will adhere to and enforce that document*; as it is written.* Whether he does or does not is for future-knowing,

[328] **Franklin (van) Roosevelt,** the President, lied us into the Second, World War, thus to promote the killing of millions of innocent white European victims. He was a very biased and bigoted man to have done what he did nevertheless he is still considered as a form of folk hero: this should not continue however with the present make-up of the news services it will be encouraged as long as possible (certainly, any particular understanding of Roosevelt has the influence of the thinker understanding depends on one's viewpoint and the information and understanding or misunderstanding that one has). Newsmen and movie makers have made millions promoting his form of intransigence. Hitler was evil however he was trying to do what we are now attempting under a different form of government. He wanted Europe to become more unified and he wanted to retrieve the lands which were taken from Germany after World War I. The entire Issue is confused over a dialogue that is only truthful in part; much has been fabricated and Time leaves many details in its wake. Interestingly Europe has since the Second World War become united in a form that at present (2012-2013) seems to be experiencing some economic problems.

important leaders that don't totally agree with our methods. A new One World Governmental organization is a poor Idea and will be a disaster.

2.] *Freedom from external restraint or compulsion* is also difficult to achieve in a large population: in some instances it may be somewhat possible. At present psychologists, who are at times misdirected in their efforts, or are not well understood, may cause problems to occur. For some the Idea of freedom is misunderstood, for many freedom stands to mean do anything that you would like to do: but freedom is not a license to do anything whether it is right or wrong. Such freedom is most destructive in the area of human relations for example involving sexual conduct. We have seen recently on Television that condoms are being given to youngsters as young as twelve. This is supposed to stop illegitimacy however the consequences are that such behavior is sinful and will make illegitimacy worse than it is at present.[329] Individuals today are encouraged to engage in illicit, improper and incendiary forms of coitus all of which can be and many of which are definitely debilitating. Forms of homosexuality and lesbianism are now considered legitimate means of self expression and are considered as being a *life style.* *Depending on one's sense and understanding of morality, one might consider that they are illicit and unnatural,* which in the minds of millions may or may not be true.[330] Such behavior was considered (by some) as a mental illness just a short time ago. Coincidentally: today we have same sex marriages which, in fact, defy the meaning of words which must be reconsidered and altered to accommodate an unfortunate misunderstanding: *it is a misunderstanding.* One's behavior is a personal issue and should not be used as a Political Ram to gain favors for some at the expense of others. And certainly the meaning of words should not be changed to accommodate one or another point of view. This encroaches on the meaning of Law and what is considered (by millions, perhaps billions of individuals) as being somewhat criminal.[331] This is a very complex Issue to deal with and, in fact, should not have come to be as it is. For two individuals of the same sex to pretend marriage is a farce and is ridiculous. Marriage implies by definition a man and a woman united for the purpose of raising a family. Those involved can have a relationship supported by Law however such relationship is not marriage. Marriage is considered by Catholic and some other Christians, to be a sacrament. Children are considered a gift from God; *a reward for decent and committed spousal behavior.*

There are no physiological or psychological issues that suggest homosexuality is a normal behavior: one way or another. In any event Sex is not a political or social issue that can be dealt with in terms relative to politics or widely promoted civic Ideas. ***Sex is a biological given, is definite, is permanent and requires only simple acts and gestures.*** Those that encourage a

---

[329]   **Illegitimacy** is a means of destroying the biological family unit. This is one of the goals of those that hope to create a one World Government; they hope to destroy the family. Bolshevik, Communists and Socialists aspire to destroy the biological family as such; they will impose a Statist form of relationship.

[330]   **See footnote number 281, page 164;** Truthful understanding of Religion.

[331]   **Homosexual behaviors** are supported by an imagined as more reasonably informed maturity which is undoubtedly contrary to much of what the rest of the World can tolerate. This **[is]** a very important issue. This issue must be more thoroughly and carefully considered; comments should be welcomed by objectively qualified and trained individuals. There is too much emotion and not enough thoughtful and honest inquiry. Many practitioners see homosexuality as a way of making money: there are medical fees and, of course, legal fees that can be considered, others as well.

change in what is biologically ordained and given to one or another as a gift are doing so often for a monetary reward. They are also faced with an Issue of *VANITY*, one of seven deadly Sins, they imagine they are brilliant in their endeavor; more likely they are simply foolish. They do not consider Sin, as being destructive on the person so involved. How one deals with sex, should be kept generally private: by that is meant it should not be made Public for an imagined reason. Sex change operations should be more *carefully and objectively* considered. This is easily understood however has been corrupted in the minds of millions by ignorance and an inability to accept *(The)* given reality. Eager Doctors may encourage unnatural forms of behavior. Many believe Homosexuality is a learned form of behavior: nothing more and nothing less. Sex is the manner for reproducing the species, it is pleasurable however should not be considered simply as being a form of entertainment. In a civilized community Sex includes bearing the burden of raising and nurturing children until they are mature. Truthfully this is what sex is all about. Much of the world is overlooking or under-valuing this function. We conscript young men in the armies of the World and wonder why they rape women that appear to be their imagined enemies. Young men should have and indeed require a decent wife, someone whom they can love who, in fact, returns that same love. Together they are the only hope for any decent form of Civilization. There is nothing in this world that equals the love and caring of a truthful mate. The marriage oath includes to "Love honor and obey till death do us part." Each is *"sworn"* to obey the other. This is a serious issue which is completely misunderstood by many.

3.] Privilege; Freedom allows for and encourages certain forms of privilege which augers for the best interests of all. Such privilege will be given where it is either necessary or simply wise. Individuals must be mature enough to accept that there are limited privileges which all do not enjoy. However if everyone is treated fairly this should not cause any problems from what could be deemed as discrimination: privileges are earned one way or another. What is required is better definition of one's understanding which will ultimately affect how one acts; how one lives.

4.] A place given to some forms of immunity *(see definition as cited above).*

5.] The sum of the rights and immunities, privileges **(civil liberty),** or the state of condition of those who are invested with the right effectually to share in framing and conducting the government under which they are politically organized **(political liberty),** or of those that are free from external restraint in the exercise of government to control **(individual liberty).** Individual liberty under Constitutional Governments in general involves freedom of the person in going and in coming **(personal liberty):** this concerns property rights, opinion and conscience. Expression of conscience may involve Issues upon which not all agree however, given a peaceful approach, one should be able to express an unpopular opinion without threat of being sued and bankrupted: in some instances there have been threats of death and some have been murdered. *Face it all men do not agree on every Issue.* Such as these may be subtle in their inclusion however are knowable. Especially is honesty a requirement in understanding what they mean.

The LIE is the greatest enemy of every Human Being.

6.] A privilege or license however not without a proper use of restraint on the personal liberty of another *(see definition as cited above).*

7. A certain amount of freedom; within strict parameters as for example in prison or on a ship. Individuals are allowed, for example, to move freely within a courtyard of a Prison for exercise and for relaxation. Also while at sea sailors are limited by the size of the ship however are allowed to venture about as is within certain confines established or existing for such purpose.

8.] [Cap.] A Liberty bond, chiefly in *pl. Colloq.*

9.] A color, reddish-blue in hue, of very high saturation and low brilliance. Cf. COLOR.

10.] Jurisprudence which concerns the legal non-restraint of natural powers. This is somewhat difficult to understand. This concerns knowledge of or skill in Law: also the science of Law. Following French law, the course of decision in the courts can be and is distinguished from legislation and doctrine. This can be considered as Law, or a system of laws, a department of Law. Nevertheless it is not justifiable to use jurisprudence as the equivalent of Law.

11.] Manage: A grouping of like-mined individuals.

12.] Naut. Permission for a sailor to go ashore: *(See definition as cited above).*

13.] Philosophy. Freedom to choose one thing or idea over another however such freedom may not impair the freedom of another or of others. In wartime this is a difficult assignment since one is obliged to kill a presumed enemy: <u>The enemy is almost always a *(Presumed Enemy)*. This is true because we are told by others, who negotiate the Politics, who is the enemy.</u> When you are placed in a position of being shot at or bombed you will realize times are tough: you revert to kill or be killed. <u>*Remember the men at the top who placed you there are Thieves, Fornicators and Liars who will always blame another for the Problem*</u>. A couple hundred years ago this was called war: now they call this International Politics. One can only wonder: what is such behavior doing to the Culture and the Civilization. Let's not forget the people those killed and maimed because of war: men, women and children. Why should any intelligent man or woman auger for War <u>which *is a blasphemy,*</u> an indecency it is the result of the Devil's control. The Devil is as an Idea spawning evil acts in the hearts and souls of millions. The Idea is incessant, continuous; *Ideas move from one individual to another.*

Almost always the victim in warfare is a *presumed and unknown* enemy and is probably without guilt. The presumption arises in the mind of another who is most generally far away from the killing. Indeed the man responsible might be enjoying a day on his yacht or at a party given in his honor. ***Nevertheless he is still a vain and uncaring fool.*** The men and some women who fall into this category are often liars and thieves. They may take unfair advantage of all the little people by means of stock and securities manipulation. We have created a System which guarantees that the Thieves will prevail. Ask yourself, what kind of information a man must have, to make a billion dollars on one deal: this happens in a very short time, a few days. During so short a time how might the average citizen be informed? The System is structured to provide such opportunities for just a few Thieves: they are Thieves. There are only a few of such gangsters however all the world is told how smart they must be. Another *(Decent Man)* works for a lifetime so to have enough to feed his family, pay for a humble place to live and finally a small plot where he will be buried. The thieves have beautiful monuments and people hold many of them in esteem; perhaps for centuries. At present people are talked into cremation which defies much of past Religious Belief: *but it is a bit cheaper.*[332] How can one address this Issue? Such behavior gives one to understand the complexity and intransigent nature of the World.

Keep in mind the World, generally, will not change very much and will continue on the same path until a major tragedy occurs which will destroy some, most or all of man's efforts. This is a certainty! When this may happen is unknown. Don't wait for it, enjoy the life you have:

Life is short;

———

Professor Emeritus; Robert Fiedler
January 12, 2013

---

[332] **In the past** it was considered inappropriate by a Catholic to be cremated. The body, it was believed by millions would be resurrected. It is understood that this was a bit metaphorical. Nevertheless who knows and understands the truth in an Issue such as this? To destroy one's body by cremation is an act of volition and would not be tolerated if one was a true and faithful Catholic Christian; consider that Christ came to save all of humanity not just a portion. In a newer scheme of things one's volition is altered, compromised by newness by what is happening now. Many have lost the meaning of history and what it means to be a Christian; this is unfortunate for the Christians however it is true. Of the really important issues, one being death, we have no way of gaining precise Knowledge the only way to know is to die. The reality is no one really wants to die rather they imagine they will live forever.

CHAPTER XIV

WHO IS GOD?

*Many individuals speak incessantly about God without any understanding
of who He is. Is there evidence of God on this earth?*

To begin imagine God as an Idea. The Idea has persisted for as long as can be imagined. Much thinking concerning God is driven by the imagination and what people hope will happen to them when they die; death is the one and absolutely known certainty. It is imagined that after death we face eternity, forever; we will be alone quiet in our grave? The only question is; when will one die? Much, perhaps most of what happens before death is of the imagination or as *"pieces of thought"* given by other persons[333]. The *"pieces of thought"* coalesce and become one in being with other thoughts of the receiving individual. Such *"pieces of thought"* will influence what an individual may, or will do in the future. Add to that, no one really knows precisely or even cursively what is the meaning of death. There are imaginings too about this issue as it does relate to who is God. It is imagined/believed that men have created religions and metaphors and have pondered this question concerning the meaning of death since they were reasonably able to think. Such thinking, knowingly or unknowingly, is always somewhat centered on a God being. **The Christian believes** *God is the Creator of all that is seen and unseen.* Thus, God is a progenitor! A man is a progenitor and is masculine **and produces from the past** a fluid, the seaman, the medium to stimulate the becoming of a new being. The new being will have an independent body and will manifest a spirit; this can be likened to the Soul. After the act of coitus the female's body will hold the seaman and the seaman will attach to an egg. At that existential moment a new life begins. The new life is unpredictable there are many possibilities. However the female controls the future as she will develop and produce a new person.[334] Many others understand and believe similarly. And keep in mind what is unseen has direct and pertinent effect on every Being. The outrageous behavior of many women will determine to an extent how the child will become; *illicit sex, drinking, poor thoughts and all other characteristics* will somehow influence the child. No one understands how and why many traits develop however one can be sure that the complex will produce some definite results.

---

[333] **Pieces of thought** are in fact, what enters into one's consciousness. Thoughts are in Streams and are continuously becoming in the conscious mind and only a part of any thought can be conveyed in a moment. The next moment may, or will involve another thought form. Thus thoughts are very difficult to follow and perhaps more difficult to understand and they are impossible to predict in advance.

[334] **This is a time-space factor.** The development of a new person takes place within the body of the mother. Therefore the mother controls the future.

God is thought to be omnipotent and outside of time as we understand time. God is thought to be infinite and to exist everywhere simultaneously.[335] God is thought to be apparent or perhaps missing in the face of every man. God is thought to be the judge of all men at death conferring blessings or tragedy on every single person. The Catholic or Christian believes if one finds favor with God this is the highest reward possible for any human. The reward is thought to be an existence into eternity and Heaven forever; Heaven is imagined as being a perfect place; certainly a pleasant, reward. Keep in mind forever may be as an *"infinite"* moment. If one is not favored by God and has become a slave to sin and to the Devil that person it is imagined, will be damned; destined to an *"infinite"* eternity in Hell. Who knows, what is Hell? There are beliefs, musings and metaphor concerning how hell would appear; such beliefs bring forth a strangely imagined and often childish imagery. What appearance might the Devil have? Who is Lucifer; how might he appear?

God has taken on various forms to suit the intellectual levels of who are thinking of him; beside there are all of the above mentioned elements. God's being is described in various languages some rather simple others more complex. The complexity of language will influence one's understanding of God. Some individuals are so confused in their thought content and patterns that they cannot understand or describe, any element truthfully concerning God. In fact few people can; they rely on repetition of what someone else has told them, has said or has written. Most individuals do not think without the help of others who do not have absolute truth.

With God are His Angels;[336] magnificent creatures they are imagined as being beautiful, destined only for goodness sake. Many imagine that Angels have wings and can soar in the

---

[335] **Presumably, Infinite Space** goes on forever. *There can be only one all* (a multiplicity) and one Infinite Space that contains it. The questions arriving from the awareness of an Infinite Space have puzzled man for centuries and continue to do so. Oswald Spengler considered this in his writing and posits the question how far does space extend to contain all things? *Space is one of God's profound Ideas.* What is truthfully profound is certainly very rare.

[336] The word "angel" actually comes from the Greek word *aggelos*, which means "**messenger**." The matching Hebrew word *mal'ak* has the same meaning

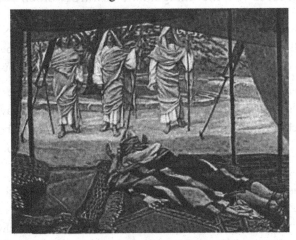

Abraham was visited by three heavenly messengers.

Heavens. Angels support God in his various endeavors and help in his meeting of men.[337] Angels are thought to be near infinite and it is believed by many that they can travel at the speed of light; even faster and will look after individuals as is necessary. Many speak of a guardian Angel, one who will take care of and protect an individual person. Most Angels are men however they are delicate creatures nevertheless very determined in their purpose.[338] No one knows if and how God communicates with His Angels however it is imagined that he does. There are twelve different classes of Angels serving different purpose. Some are Archangels, Cherubim and Seraphim; there are others. *(See the Internet under Angels).*

In fact the speed of light is not a constant. It has much to do with where the light is and what are the gravitational and other forces that affect it? There are presumably forces that affect the speed of light, forces beyond present human understanding. Such forces are imagined to be directed by the God of all creation. *Some Physicists believe the speed of light is three times faster than has been imagined.* In fact God being a simultaneous and Infinite Creature is all places at all times carried within the minds of Humanity. God may be as a cloud in the space covering all space; infinite space. He stands as a very persistent Idea. This is the most profound of all Ideas however humans do not agree and much hardship has been inflicted on both groups and individuals because of ignorance and misunderstanding. *The Idea of God cannot be abandoned; the Idea of God is a permanent part of our collective consciousness.* One proves himself a fool to deny this. One cannot exist independently outside from the nature of collective consciousness.

Can anyone imagine, what is the reason for light?
Is light that element or force that creates and maintains all manner of form?

God is a singularity a single, omnipotent Being. *There can only be one God because God is Omnipotent.* God is above all other creatures and things. Given a pyramid God is the apex the absolute top, the point at the top, He is the crown so to speak of Reality. Various peoples have given a physical identity to God. The Christian believes God is in every single person; this would make him a ***multiplicity*** as well as a ***singularity***. Such as this adds to the confusion and misunderstanding that surrounds this God figure. Presumably God can be what and who he wishes; such judging by his being omnipotent. If God is in every man he can be as anyone is. The Muslim has Allah as his God however Muslim thinking is not like that of a Christian. The Muslim thought process is quite antagonistic toward women. This is becoming more

---

[337] **The Bible makes it clear** that angels can only be in one place at a time. They must have some localized presence. It appears all angels were created at one time. No new angels are being added. Angels are not subject to death or any form of extinction; therefore they do not decrease in number.

[338] **When angels do appear,** they generally appear in the form of men. In Genesis 18, Abraham welcomed three angelic guests who appeared at first to be nothing more than some travelers. Angels in the Bible never appear as cute, chubby infants! They are always full-grown adults. When people in the Bible saw an angel, their typical response was to fall on their faces in fear and awe, not to reach out and tickle an adorable baby.

In Sodom they were assumed to be simply a pair of human visitors. With the possible exception of one debatable passage in Zechariah 5:9, angels always appear as males rather than females (Mark 16:5). Angels are essentially "ministering spirits," (Hebrews 1:14) and do not have physical bodies like humans. Jesus declared that "a spirit hath not flesh and bones, as ye see me have" (Luke 24:37-39

apparent at this present time with emphasis on equality. The emphasis on equality is not always correct; it is a part of man's imperfect thinking. The Muslim man expects his woman to do all of the menial tasks. The man imagines himself superior; *this is a profound and complex misunderstanding.* In fact women are superior as they hold the future of mankind in their bodies; men are representatives of the past in there semen which at any moment is from the past. An understanding of this aspect of reality is absolutely essential before the World can go forward.

Being a singularity and a multiplicity does not make of God more than one being. In fact it is believed that God is trip ret; three persons in one; Father, Son and Holy Ghost (Spirit). This is consistent with reality since children are, in many ways known and unknown, like the parent. These are profound understandings however they have grown with the presence of one believed to be God. The Father conveys the thought and understanding and is the progenitor of all that is seen and unseen. The Spirit can be everywhere at once which provides for the Infinite Being. The son became as a man for a short period so to gain a real presence in the minds of men. Because not all men understood this He was crucified, died and was buried later ascending to heaven. It is believed that the Son forever after will be seated at the right hand next to the Father. Some Primitive men may have had various understandings concerning God of which we are unaware. This is a subject for serious and sustained study by who might be interested. Those most interested have been Saints, often dying a terrible death for their belief, Priests, Rabbis, Nuns and various forms of holy people.

Some learned men have attempted to analyze God in terms of numbers. Certain numbers, believed by some, are God's numbers. The number three (3) is definitely indicative of the Trinity; Father, Son and Holy Ghost which appears obvious. There is the number seven (7) which appears to have somewhat magical characteristics; the lucky seven. Also there are Spaces which are believed to be Holy, they may be bounded in various ways using a number as a measure. The way they are bounded is given certain numbers. Thirty and sixty are considered as somehow being holy numbers.

The Gothic Cathedrals, especially in Europe, are believed by some to contain sacred Space. This is apparently projected in the dimensions of the buildings. This is a fact that breeds some contempt in a non-believer who may despise our God? The cruciform is paramount in the laying of the foundations for the great Cathedrals. Some of God's measurements are imagined as thirty (30) and (60) sixty feet (approximately) this may/will determine the height of the buttresses and the base of the central pointed arch. That is from the base to the beginning of the Point where the arch begins that are the ceiling arches of the Cathedrals.[339] There is some work being done in the preservation of these great structures as has been done in the past, so to maintain them for a bit longer. They will not last forever! Nevertheless the flying buttress was an ingenious almost magical solution to the problem of how the tensions and strains in these buildings have been contained. The flying buttress in fact was a stroke of genius!

---

[339] **See the Internet** "Gothic Cathedrals" for photos and some descriptions of Gothic Cathedrals. You can be well informed and you will be amazed by what you see.

These wonderful Cathedrals were constructed with outer walls largely made of beautifully stained and leaded glass. In many Gothic Cathedrals the Interior of the Church was imagined to be close to Heaven. The interiors were lit by beautiful colored light flowing through the stained glass; such light was believed to have been _light as coming straight from God's heaven_. Keep in mind when the great Gothic Cathedrals were built there was no electric; no artificial light except from a candle or an oil lamp. There were the intricacies in the stonework, the carved sculptures, the magnificent inlays on the floors, all attesting to the genius of creation. These forms expressed the wonderful talent of the builders; all this supported by their understanding of holiness. At present our Churches have been desecrated as so many seek to _destroy the Catholic Church and replace it with a hoard of talking fools._ Such replacement and destruction is encouraged by many politicians whom we have elected to lead the people. The Catholic Church was founded by Jesus Christ, believed to be the Son of God and is the real and universal church; **it is the Church for all humanity; all are welcome.** To repeat it is (**The Church**) for all of humanity.[340] Christ came to earth to redeem all of humanity however it is essential that you deserve to be redeemed. A virtuous life will make one most deserving.[341]

> ### You are under protection of the Catholic Church no matter what you believe. Christ came to earth to save all men!

The Cathedral builders were a population of dedicated and somewhat holy men. They were very proud of serving the Lord in this manner; building the highest and most regal structures known to man at that time. **They were not built to make a profit** they were built to praise the God of all creation. These were much different men than those that build for a profit; those that build for a profit, _are commercially driven however not very wise._ Today's buildings enclose vast space standing as a monument to the architect or design team that created the ugliness and vacuous spaces within them. The sculptures that stand in front or are a part of the new buildings are not nearly as great as the Art one observes in the great ancient Cathedrals. There are now not many stained and decorated windows that allow the light of creation to filter in upon a population beholden to what is _fine and holy and good_. Such windows are thought to be too expensive **rather we spend our money on some means of killing our presumed enemies.** Enemies are always presumed; someone else will tell you, who are your enemies. And the money lenders wait for their interest payments as a return on the investment in the commercial nonsense. This is what in large measure has built the great fortunes of Today. When the numbers are right the lenders will destroy the building and replace it with one that can show an increased monetary gain on what was torn down. This aspect in our lives adds greatly to the Inflation

---

[340] **Humanity,** as such, is a complex singularity. Viewed from space the earth and its people become as one, as a singularity.

[341] **Catholic Theology,** strictly speaking, demands that you be a baptized Catholic. This has raised much dissent and wondering amongst the various people who are not baptized Catholics. This is a question of Theology. Christ said to his Disciples and to mankind "_Follow Me_". The questions are centered on the correct meaning of what he said. The meaning is most significant however is not well understood by everyone. Baptism can be a volitional act, the giving of the self to the idea of a God being. In fact Baptism is more often from the positive volition of the parent who has the infant baptized. An adult beside the parent may also be responsible in some instances.

which is ruining the Civilization. The building will go into a land-fill or now be ground up for making road beds, destroyed to make room for "bigger" and more densely peopled buildings; this is what is foolishly imagined as progress.

The idea of creating greater density for greater profits is absurd and should be abandoned. Inflation guarantees that you must have more money to invest however the money as specie is worth much less; then the value of currency as money is in the imagination.[342] The buildings and their mortgages are in real time together with the over-crowding of our cities with slums and crime. We are told we are running out of space; however there exists many places suitable for construction beside prime farm land. Much land could be reclaimed for cities without destroying the most productive land in a nation. And, the World is a big place! Also land can be improved for farming and raising animals. All would benefit from such improvement. People should move to higher lands and away from the oceans whenever possible. Nevertheless the oceans hold a quiet mystery for millions; people enjoy living by and seeing an ocean. Who knows why?

Developing the land should be considered as a substitute for War.

For now the United States has been chosen by a corrupt few as that nation best able to assist in the desecration and destruction of Christianity and goodness, ***to capture the World for the money-lender,*** *the Marxist/Socialist types.* This is near to being a done deal however there is some understanding and a growing opposition to this monetary and intellectual take-over.[343] It has been known for a long time that money lending can control commerce and the people beholden to *Greed.* There exists a problem with China and India in this respect, since both nations have so many people and they are catching up commercially with the West and with the United States. China is right now number two in the World economy; *soon China will be number one.* This is inevitable the Chinese are smart people when given a chance. Check out our Chinese University students and the many Chinese in our fine orchestras. Check out the number of doctors and other Professionals that are Chinese. Economic factors will play an important part in this respect as the United States is becoming presumably less important than in the recent past. Oswald Spengler saw much of this one hundred years ago in his great writing.[344] Too bad more individuals did not comprehend, understand and act upon what he was saying. In truth he was a Philosopher; he was somewhat of a Prophet as well, today not many understand what that means.

Humanity should go back to building wonderful places of worship beautiful and exquisite structures and rid itself of the false needs of perpetual warfare. Money changers who have captured the World must be contained, than all people would be better off. However at present the United States is the World's leading maker of armaments made too often to kill innocent people: this is nothing to be proud of. We are spending our substance on what is trivial and evil

---

[342] **This illustrates** the inanity of promoting an elastic currency, one that is stretched to give more money which in fact is worth less. Eventually the money as currency will have no value at all; it will be simply paper.

[343] **Chang, Matthias,** *Future Fast Forward, The Zionist, Anglo-American Meltdown.* First American Editions, 2006, American Free Press, Washington D. C. 20063

[344] **Spengler, Oswald;** *The Decline of the West,* in two volumes.

all to kill another man's child imagining we are bringing the World closer to Democracy so to promote a secret conspiracy; to destroy this World and its people as we know them to be.[345] All the while we do this our population is attempting to save the starving babies and children all over the World; this is certainly a hypocrisy. With our money, and military hardware and armed forces the United States is providing a means for the concentration of the World's wealth in just a few deep pockets. This thought is most likely primary in the minds of the money lenders who are slowly accumulating the tangible things of this earth; they accumulate them and pay for them even as there is a declining value in the currency. What they own will not be encumbered by debt; *it will be free and clear.* Inflation is a perfect means for them. They will eventually own all that is worth owning including the lands and what they produce and they will have no debt. The debt is for the common man who will remain common as clay.

This may seem absurd but it is true. It is believed by some that there is a secret conspiracy attempting to control the World. This conspiracy has in the recent past used countries in Europe and the United States to further its objectives.[346] It has worked quite well *till now.* The question now arises: what shall happen to China and the rest of Asia? Are they in on the deal? Most people are good, probably most are decent except they are weak in spirit and cannot comprehend beyond what it is that they imagine they want; they are preyed upon by all the means available to the *Devil* and his *Evil.*

Two thousand years ago the World's people were divided into Good and Evil by Jesus Christ, who said *"Either you are with me or you are against me."* Jesus Christ was believed to be the only Son of God and was the Good. Satan the devil it was imagined was all that is Evil. This relates to the seven deadly Sins amongst which *Greed* is motivational with objects and economic transactions. And there are *Lust* and *Vanity* which have more to do with the function of the

---

[345] **In any event** a Democracy is not the best form of government for an entire World; a few then will control all. *Individual Nation States or well administered Monarchies would be better* (I have written about a nation state in Chapter X). Russia was ruled by two royal families for nearly a thousand years it was destroyed by the Socialist and Collectivist types in just a few years. Socialism is the Enemy of all mankind. What is required is unselfish humility and Christian decency. Even a responsible King would be better than a Dictator or an International Cartel or even an elected Official; if he did something wrong the King could be dismissed from office, poisoned, imprisoned or killed. How might one dismiss a Cartel or Corporate entity? The People are now controlled by a bloated Government. Presently those in control are aiming at a Communistic, Marxist, Collectivist and Socialistic form of Government, disguised as a Democracy, inspired in part by a narcissist like Karl Marx. *In fact Marx was a hired hand, so to speak, given an opportunity by those unseen however in control.* All the Politicians of temporary significance appear to be in favor of a one-world government which the few super rich hope to control. As an important part of this Conspiracy; many of the not so rich are not aware that they are pawns being used by the very wealthy who will implement their plan for dominating the World. This is an age-old expectation of a small elitist non-Christian minority. There payment is often in coins; just like Judas. *Nevertheless Judas did commit suicide.*

[346] **The French Revolution,** the American Civil War, The murder of the Romanovs and the more recent First and Second World Wars are all a part of this take-over and were attempts at consolidation.

body as a form for evil pleasure; sins of the flesh.[347] Each Sin has a special calling from Satan. Evil enjoys corrupting and destroying innocence somehow using the curiosity of youth as an important means. Youth are intelligent and curious however they are not wise. God is presumed to know all of this in his omnipotent being.

Greed and Vanity are the Sins that drive some individuals as wanting to rule over all others and are a fundamental cause of all war. ***Greed and Vanity underlie the feelings of a Will to Power.*** Greed is insatiable and demands more and more, even as the greedy have more than they will ever need or use. Some men use their excess wealth attempting to alter the Political Structure of the Nation and of the World. They hope to make it better for people like them. When they are wrong in their thinking the World suffers: they are almost always wrong. Many tend to be Socialists and they are not truthful Christians. They are hypocrites! To rule over all is a near impossible pipe dream however the greedy will spend and do whatever they believe is necessary to accomplish this foul purpose. Political structures form often in response to the urging of the greedy. The good man's best defense is that *"In the end we are all dead."* This includes all evil men and all the good ones too. Millions have been killed in the greedy attempt to gain control and perhaps billions more will die as the greedy move toward their nefarious objective. ***This is total War; the War of the Apocalypse,*** a few driven by greed hope to gain control of everything and at times they appear to be succeeding. Just before this page we attempt to explain how this is happening. Pay special attention to this. I will repeat it in part.

This thought is most likely primary in the minds of the money lenders who are slowly accumulating the tangible things of this earth; they accumulate them and pay for them even as there is a declining value in the currency. What they own will not be encumbered by debt; it will be free and clear. Inflation is a perfect means for them. They will eventually own all that is worth owning and they will have no debt. The debt is for the common man who will remain common as clay.

What is required to gain control is money, money as currency. The money factor is most significant in a world such as ours, driven by commerce. Most commerce is reasonable and honest however there are many that corrupt every deal they make and this in turn may corrupt even what appears as honest. The most serious problems lie in those Institutions that control and deal in money transactions, the International Investment Banks. We read in the newspapers and in some other places about this or that Bank *"going under"* as they say. You can check this out by yourself and find what you may. Generally one or two individuals seem responsible having absconded with the funds by one means or another. The International tenor of such situations combined with the scale make it difficult to follow. The average man or woman has absolutely no comprehension of the function and control enjoyed by these super-national banks. It is near impossible to get a criminal conviction because of the complexities involved in the Law. Court procedures can involve months or years during which time individuals forget, change emphasis or may even die. *Keep in mind that an omnipotent God may be watching.* Importantly Banks

---

[347] **Lust** is a personal form of Sin and often involves a man and a woman. There are many stories about a voluptuous woman seducing a frivolous and vainly curious man; such stories have caused untold damage. The stories are made into cheap movies which poison the Soul of the viewers. As such they become and are a part of the pieces of thought mentioned above.

have ways of disappearing and being resurrected in curious ways. The presumed loss of capital is often absorbed by the people as a tax; just a little bit from each one.

The compounding of interest on large scale Capital is awesome. Money can be doubled in this way over and over. This is what has made the *"Great Fortunes"* of this world;

The exponential growth of great sums of money is the means!

1x2 = 2; 2x2 = 4; 4x2 = 8; 8x2 = 16; 16 x 2 = 32; 32 x 2 = 64; 64 x 2 = 12 8; 128 x 2 =256.

From this point the doubling becomes astronomical. This is where the truly wealthy find them and the money flow never stops. They are the ones that own the Stock in all of the great Corporations; often tens of millions of shares.

Imagine if all the greedy monsters amongst us were thinking of building beautiful churches, like those from the Gothic Period, how much better the World could be. Instead our technologies and much of our money is squandered on armaments and ways of killing another man. The Gothic Cathedrals encouraged the development and use of highly developed skills of the hand so to create the beautiful elements found within and about them. The sculpture and ornamentation and the beautiful paintings and murals were all works from the hand. Interestingly little skill of the hand is required in a money transaction rather the elements are cleverness and often secrecy

Addendum: to Chapter XIV

The immediately following material was taken from the Internet. You can gain much more beyond this from the same source of information.

Then Jesus said to those Jews who believed Him, "If you abide in my word, you are my disciples indeed. And you shall know the truth, and the truth shall make you free.—John 8:31-32 (NKJV) The Bible classifies some angels as "elect" (1 Timothy 5:21) or "holy" (Matthew 25:31; Mark 8:38). All angels were originally holy, enjoying the presence of God (Matthew 18:10) and the environment of heaven (Mark 13:32). The belief is that other angels oppose God under the leadership of Satan (Matthew 25:41; 2 Peter 2:4; Jude 6; Ephesians 6:12). We often **call these "demons."**

- **They are stronger than man, but not omnipotent (Psalm 103:20; 2 Peter 2:11).**
- **Their knowledge is greater than man not omniscient (2 Samuel 14:20; Matthew 24:36).**
- **They are more noble than man, but not omnipresent (Daniel 9:21-23, 10:10-14).**

Kings 6:17)! No, angels are not glorified human beings. Matthew 22:30 explains that they do not marry or reproduce like humans, and Hebrews 12:22-23 says that when we get to the heavenly Jerusalem, we will be met by "myriads of angels" and "the spirits of righteous men made perfect"—two separate groups. Angels are a company or association, not a race descended from a common ancestor (Luke 20:34-36). We are called "sons of men," but angels are never called "sons of angels." You are of your father the devil, and the desires of your father you want to do. He was a murderer from the beginning, and does not stand in the truth, because there is no truth in him. When he speaks a lie, he speaks from his own resources, for he is a liar and the father of it. John (NKJV)

Professor Emeritus; Robert Fiedler
2013.

Does Space belong to God?

How does God relate to each and every Human?
The Christian understanding is that God is Primary, the First Cause:
The Creator is Infinite, Omnipotent and Eternal.

Physicists have discovered what they imagine to be a God-particle. It will take some time to follow the events of their discovery. My understanding is that God is all that is and is infinite and is perfect; what is works because it is of God's being. God is not in a single particle or a group of such particles, although he controls all particles, persons and galaxies; this is a big job, even for God. Of some importance is that all do not believe in God or they have differently formed Ideas of who is God. Nevertheless if he is omnipotent there can only be one God. *(This is a question of Linguistics, the meaning of words.)*

God is the Creator: Hundreds of millions believe He is the progenitor of all that is, has been and will become in the future. He formed the past through a word. This is the belief that true Christians hold at present: *however this belief is being slowly undermined and is becoming less politically effective as time passes.* The separation of Religion from Politics is a fatal mistake for Religion. Belief in God presents a defensible mechanism, especially for Catholicism. The questions arise concerning the timing of what has been done and what may be done in the future. ***How might a word create the Reality that we perceive as we enact life's doings?*** A word can be the embodiment of some thought content, as a container: then one will first ask what is contained. *An Idea is contained in a word, such as a noun, used to convey the meaning of an object or thought; a person, thing, action or quality. (This is semantics.)* This is true. Once a word is known and understood it is propagated from person to person and becomes a part of common knowing and understanding. Meaning becomes a part of the endless space as the word is uttered over and over by more and more individuals. The word works its way into common thought patterns, what I describe as *"thought clusters"*, and the word is interpreted and used for various reasons. The meaning may vary slightly which can cause confusion. The understanding expressed immediately above is known and exploited by those who wish to control the World.

Man is just now beginning to understand and to utilize the qualities and potential of the Space which surrounds us. Interestingly Space is "apparently" as nothing however there are unseen and unknown possibilities within the Space. Movement is an important condition within all space. Movement requires of space; there must be different places from which and to which the movement is ordered. This seems quite simple however is not so. Wireless communication is an example of an unseen possibility: more recently the computer and various functions such as the locks on your car being opened without a wire or a key. Things of this nature work because the *Space has the properties necessary to transmit a force,* to make certain implements work. This type force is a small part of God's infinite and eternal presence. There may be others yet undiscovered. Such properties as propel various occurrences emanate from the movement and progression of minute wave function. Many implements for war are driven by means of waves set up in space. The drone missiles are an example. Waves are fictional attributes within the Space. The average individual does not understand how this works however they will benefit or be destroyed by such: one way or another. Among other things Space is a plenum (Bearden, *Aides Biological Warfare*). *Also see the Internet on Wave function.*

Time is not an absolute as we imagine an absolute to be. An absolute time segment would be a matter of certainty. However when we consider a time certainty, wherein time cancels itself, then this is something quite different *(Bearden).* The space within the Universe is so vast that it confuses the imagination. And the space is a corollary of the Time: the two are inextricably combined in various ways. Conversely, the space within an atom is so small it also confuses the imagination. Nevertheless the greatest space and the smallest space have common properties: *a manner and form given to near-nothingness and to the All.* As mentioned in other parts of this book we are now told by some advanced thinkers that an atom is only one two-billionth part matter. How can one be certain of this? Presently, we are given to the understanding that all matter is one or another form of light. This is difficult to imagine: more difficult to understand. In fact understanding is what is lacking. In Genesis we are reminded that God is the "Light of the World." It is time to begin to reconsider the truthful meaning of this statement. What does this mean, to be the light of the World? Seemingly this is a simple question.

See my illustration of the head of Christ at the beginning of this book and try to understand the meaning of the brief text that accompanies the Image. Do some personal reflection on this image to help in your understanding of it. The Image is my imaginary understanding, given to the Image, of *the power of light in defining reality.* The short strokes are intended to convey the existence and path of photons moving in space. The head of Christ has the same coloration as the space around it and appears ether-like, if it existed in three dimensions. Use your imagination.

Both Time and Space are thought to be Infinite!

We are at this time just beginning to appreciate this fact of Reality and Existence. This understanding may have been a part of a former understanding that has been lost in the infinity of that same Time. We do not and cannot know all of what has occurred in the past. Reality as being our thought is quite different than the reality that we witness as object and event. The Ideas that we entertain originate and are derived from the space between the proximate neurons within the brain. The brain is a phenomenal human containment that is not completely understood by even the best of human minds. *When we die, what happens to the content held within our Brain? Where does it go? Does it become a part of the infinite space from which it came? Can it be used again? Is it simply extinguished? These are some questions that you can think about. Get started with your thinking! (Spend some quiet time just thinking).* Don't demand so much loud noise and movement be quiet and still. Loud noise and movement are distractions; they are childish.

"The brain appears to be man's link to infinity, *understanding and doing: whatever he may do. Interestingly the brain is a complex and finite concentration of electrically and chemically charged/organized water and is the substance that provides the physical means for all human activity and records in the memory; whatever one does. It provides a manner of recall that is both dependable and ephemeral simultaneously and is the driving force of the human person; mentally, physically spiritually and emotionally it controls the cells: many other aspects as well."* (Robert Fiedler Sr.)

"Memory is the power *to recall past incident and object; memory also provides a basis for envisioning the future: one way or another. This may even be considered as day-dreaming.*

Memory function is coincident: unfolding/enfolding with the present and mingles as it combines with the incoming elements from present moments. It is easy to understand that this creates a most complex circumstance that is ultimately lost to human understanding." (Robert Fiedler Sr.)

"Thought increments *combine in unpredictable ways and may be recalled in the future adding to the viability and certitude of thinking: thinking is transient and changes from moment to moment. Human presence allows for and provides the basis for trillions of functions every second for a lifetime: every cell functions every moment to do what must be done, this is an ultimate complexity with infinite possibilities. One's thinking can change from moment to moment: thoughts co-mingle and cancel some other thoughts that are "morphed into new configurations:" thereby creating a distinctively understood Reality: **absolutely** personal and unique. All understanding of Reality is both personal and unique. This is true for a variety of not well understood reasons. Millions of individuals might be dismissed from reality seeming to have little importance to the totality. Nevertheless they are important in ways which we do not and cannot quite understand. The human Race is profound in what is and did occur however not everyone is capable of understanding the nature of Human Being. Humanity is a difficult subject" (Robert Fiedler Sr.)*

Human Being is perhaps/probably the most profound of all forms of being.

"Experience *varies from person to person as does the transient thoughts in one's mind. With the millions of moments encoded in one's brain the possibilities for differences in interpretation are nothing less than phenomenal: they are awesome. This is the reason why we have so many forms of human being. Every person is absolutely distinct from all others. People can be and are grouped around certain thought forms which is undeniable and cannot be easily altered. Politicians try to alter and control such similarities and dissimilarities however cannot ever hope to form or force the becoming of a totality in respect to the consensus of the World's population. All demagogues are guilty of attempting to do this: they attempt what is "in fact" impossible." (Robert Fiedler Sr.)*

All understanding of Reality is unique and in a state of flux.

"This is an accommodative function *of the human brain. The brain must function this way or it could/would not function at all. The only way the human brain can do what it does is dependent upon this manner of function. The brain receives and transmits discreetly functional information and thought content simultaneously. The actual workings of the brain are of an ultimately complex nature and every brain is distinct. The brain relates to the physiology and complete structure of a particular humanness: there may be and probably are some small similarities in one brain with others."[348] (Robert Fiedler Sr.)*

---

[348] **Research on sex and psychology** investigates cognitive and behavioral differences between men and women. This research employs experimental tests of cognition, which take a variety of forms. Tests focus on possible differences in areas such as IQ, spatial reasoning, and emotion. IQ tests, regarded by psycho-Metricians as measures of intelligence, have shown that differences between men and women are minimal or negligible, but men are often overrepresented at extreme scores, both very high and very low. [1][2][3]

Recent research involving brain function has provided a means to attach the brain to an outside implement so to transmit impulses to and from the brain. This research is proving effective concerning individuals who have lost a limb. An artificial limb is able to function with motivation from the brain as interpreted by the transmitter. The artificial limb is made functional by the force of the implementation. This is not exactly or generally understood however the reader can pursue further understanding of this on his/her own.

Man's connection to God is the brain which is a phenomenal mechanism for entertaining thoughts and planning actions. And: the brain has remarkable abilities to consider and process thoughts, individually and in patterns. As mentioned earlier: To repeat, thoughts occur in the spaces between proximate neurons and are evasive. Thoughts interlock, that is they combine, and become functional in determining actions and future thoughts. This is not well understood except is partially understood by a few somewhat more professional individuals. With the distractions that have been imposed for making money and controlling Politics the average being, distracted beyond reason, has little understanding of just how the brain works. *Educations should focus more on this* and less on athletics which should be considered simply, as a pleasant physical exercise, a distraction.

In God's world *we* do not need Elementary School and Junior High School boys dressed in the latest gear for playing a sport; they are pretending to be men, which is ridiculous. Adults should allow the youngsters to play without all the unnecessary and misplaced attention on winning. Such attention may be responsible for ill feelings and the disrespect of the self. What is really happening is *they are being conditioned* to accept a brutal and, for some, a life threatening sport; and they are training at a too young age to play in some league. The coaches view these youngsters intently hoping to find an outstanding player. Some coaches become celebrities and in the professional sports they are paid millions for what they do. The recent $750,000,000.00

1. **Hedges, LV; Nowell,** A (1995). "Sex differences in mental test scores, variability, and numbers of high-scoring individuals". Science **269** (5220): 41-5. Bibcode 1995Sci . . . 269 . . . 41H. doi:10.1126/science.7604277. PMID 7604277. edit

2. **McKie, Robin** (November 6, 2005). "Who has the bigger brain?". The Guardian (London). http://www.guardian.co.uk/education/2005/nov/06/research.gender.

3. **Ali, MS; Suliman, MI; Kareem, A; Iqbal, M** (2009). "Comparison of gender performance on an intelligence test among medical students". *Journal of Ayub Medical College, Abbottabad : JAMC* **21** (3): 163-5. PMID 20929039. http://www.ayubmed.edu.pk/JAMC/PAST/21-3/Sohail.pdf. edit

   Because social and environmental factors affect brain activity and behavior, where differences are found, it can be difficult for researchers to assess whether or not the differences are innate. Studies on this topic explore the possibility of social influences on how both sexes perform in cognitive and behavioral tests. Stereotypes about differences between men and women have been shown to affect a person's behavior.[4][5] Common stereotypes characterize men as aggressive and angry, and characterize women as emotionally sensitive and irrational.

4. **Fine, Cordelia,** *Delusions of Gender: How Our Minds, Society, and Neuro-sexism Create Difference* 2010

5. **Gallagher Ann M.,** James C. Kaufman, *Gender differences in mathematics: an integrative psychological approach.* Cambridge University Press,

allotment for satisfying those hurt while playing the game should be indicative of this nonsense. Millions of people gather on the special occasions to watch the College and Professional games. They scream and gyrate like fools imagining they are having a good time. They have been taught by the example of others to act as a fool for enjoyment. At times they even have caused riots and a few have been killed because of this misplaced exuberance. Attendant to the games is much misbehavior which is overlooked for the benefit of the event. Many of the players have been deemed indecent for their extra activities. All manner of personal sins hide in the turmoil; foul language, drunkenness, immoral sex, rape and many related issues including abortion of those conceived under sinful circumstance. Abortion is murder and there are many others. The big game should be more carefully considered by a truthfully intelligent understanding.

Adults imagine, quite incorrectly that young children are unaware of reality. This is simply not true. Children learn fastest when they are youngest since the brain is virtually *"empty"*. As they experience life their brain becomes *"full of ideas"* and the incoming ideas and energies must compete, with what is there. Children learn quickly when they are given an opportunity to learn and they understand what they are taught. *If they are taught well their understanding will be decently formulated.* This is why the parents are so important; if the parents understand truthfully they will pass this understanding on to the child; this is how it should be. The reverse is also true in most instances and is why we have so many personal problems. This understanding is known by those who would indoctrinate or prepare a population for one or another manner of thinking. This understanding is always a part of propaganda.

More Adults, both father and mother must take more responsibility for the raising of their own children and should realize that the children, given Time for the phenomenal unfolding of events are more important than the parent. In a spiritual sense *the children are the future the parents are the past.* Children, require the competent and patient adult attention of both parents or they will grow up to be stupid and irresponsible: *many are this way at this time.* Their parents were chasing around thinking they were having a good time with drunkenness and adultery: especially this is true of the fathers. *We burden our children with toys that are money making frauds.* There is too much emphasis on team sports and not sufficient understanding or effort is placed on truthfully important Thoughts and Ideas: *generally speaking real learning is lacking in most individuals.* We load our children up with nonsense and then expect them to do well in college beside which we give them many poor examples of what a college student should be doing. The Hollywood productions about youth are often quite revolting. *This is an absurdity that is nearly incomprehensible.*

If more individuals, both men and women, understood what is written in the above paragraph, the World would be much improved in a short time. To learn requires time and attention of the learner and the teacher must be patient and available as is required.IN our public schools not enough attention is given to serious learning. Those who are inept are often responsible for keeping the learning too simple. This is fine for the inept however punishes the more intelligently inclined. For survival the Civilization is dependent upon the more intelligently-inclined. Many individuals are not able to learn at the highest levels because of physical and emotional malformations. We should not attempt to hide this under the rubrics of equality and fraternity. *We must acknowledge some individuals are simply to dumb to learn at the higher levels demanded by difficult or serious subject matter.*

212

We have placed too many obstacles in front of learning and too much emphasis has been placed on athletics and on team sports. This will sell uniforms and all of the junk that is believed to be necessary for success; having fun has been turned into a profitable business for a few. The remaining millions are merely spectators with enough to buy the tickets, the beer and the popcorn. The general level of ineptitude is increasing as more and more individuals are denied the proper nurturing in a two parent home.[349] Social problems arise as adults prey on children and youth: this is certainly sinful: this is a situation where the Devil has invaded the mind of an uncaring and unknowing adult. Ephemeral Politics has eclipsed important subject matter study. Importantly the best minds are often subverted by the Lie or they are omitted from the dialogue.

<u>In many instances Fools captivated by incorrect understandings</u>
<u>are chosen to rule the population.</u>
Many of such Fools have somehow gained an enormous Monetary and Political advantage.

The collectively formed mind of the majority can be altered by manipulation and deceit.
This is a fundamental misfortune of Democracy. The majority is not always right!

This is [THE] Modern tragedy.

This country, and other countries, will be destroyed from the inside.
There are too many bold faced Liars and far too many Lies.
There is too much stealing and too many Thieves.
Too many people are simply not interested.
Too many are looking the other way.

───────

Professor Emeritus, Robert Fiedler
July 20, 2011. October 21, 2013.

---

[349] **Pendell, Elmer PH. D**. *Sex Versus Civilization.* Noontide Press, P. O. Box 76062, Los Angeles, CA, 90005. © 1967 Dr. **Elmer Pendell** (1894-1982) was an American sociologist. In the tradition of Malthus,[1] he focused on population issues. He was a eugenicist and a social Darwinist, holding the hypothesis that as civilization advances the less intelligent members tend inevitably to numerically outbreed the more intelligent.[2]. He was associated with the Population Reference Bureau and with "Directors of Birthright, Inc." [3] He was once fired from the University of Nevada for circulating among his students a paper about sex and birth control.[4] In his work, he weighed different theoretical approaches to inducing a higher average IQ in the population particularly of the United States and Europe. He was also concerned about population growth in the Oriental and Northern African countries.[5] In addition to points surrounding licensing marriage, he suggested limits to migration from countries that fail to maintain population control measures.[6] He also believed that banning abortion would be harmful to both population numbers and societal problems.[7] Dr. Pendell edited a textbook for undergraduates, *An Introduction to* Sociology, about which a reviewer stated that "Each chapter is excellent covers a wealth of material . . ."

Consider

Who is our God?

God is the Infinite Power of Presence
God is the Infinite Power of now and then
His is The Existential And all enduring Reality

God is trip ret present in all places at all times
Also keep in mind; He is as, the enduring Idea:
God, created all that is, was and will be
He will create whatever else may be
He is idea and the consequence
He is the will and reason
He is all THAT IS

God is supreme
God is absolute
And, God is Omnipotent
He is first amongst all things
And also, Whatever else may ever be
Nothing is beyond nothing is above him

His was and is the word

Professor Emeritus; Robert Fiedler
January 14, 2013

CHAPTER XV

TODAY IS THE VESTIBULE OF ETERNITY

Today contains and holds all the knowledge from the past:

We call This Tradition!

All past occurrence exists as TRUTH. Truth is what is occurring and has occurred in the past. Whatever, in fact is occurring is as TRUTH: and truth must be known rather than falsehood. Men make-up clever stories in order to further their selfish, short-sighted objectives. Some individuals have been known to hide the truth and propagate falsehoods. This become as a metaphor or a contrived abstraction of reality. Those are some of the worst enemies of humanity.

Man's greatest enemy is the LIE

A Lie is a consequence of some menial objective having captured the Soul and being of a man. The LIE is the work of the Devil. Who is the **DEVIL**? The Devil may not be a person rather the Devil may be an *Idea* however, when the Devil captures a Soul the Soul will then do the Devil's work. The Devil's work is always mischievous. Some masons fit into this picture.[350] Some individuals believe the Devil is a person; they seek a form, for such being: however many believe the Devil is a Spirit and is formless existing in the space all around. The Devil is absolutely contrary to the Holy Spirit which is one part of the Trinity: God the Father, Son and Holy Ghost comprise the three Persons of the Trinity.[351] This should be easy to understand: however most people have only a quite vague notion of what this means: what does it mean to exist as a tri-parity, what is an omnipotent singularity?

These are difficult Issues to contemplate since self-interest and ignorance are always part of any thinking. Self-interest cannot be denied since every being is a biological, physiological

---

[350] **Dr. Wardner, the real God** is antithetical to the false god of the Masons: a world-wide subversive organization (determined to rule the World and its people with a One-World Government). **As inferred** by Dr. Wardner Masonic worship was and perhaps is, phallic worship; Dr. Wardner says it is a Phallic Cult. Do you want such as those to rule the World? Freemasonry began in about 1700 with Albert Mackey and Albert Pike.

[351] **God is imagined as being a perfect Being:** all good, all knowing, all understanding and is everywhere in the same instant: God is, among other things, *the omnipotent epitome of simultaneity.* This is related to what we understand as time-space phenomenon and is an issue considered presently by contemporary physics. It relates to what is understood as a time-surround where time cancels itself. See: **Bearden, T. E., Col.,** *and Aids, Biological Warfare,* Tesla Book Co. P. O. Box 1649, Greenville, TX 75401. ISBN # 0-914119-04-4.

and neurological center of his own reality.[352] Ignorance is always a part of any thinking: man's knowledge is **always** imperfect. _Probably Political knowledge is the most unreliable of all knowledge_. Political knowledge is time-based and changes from day to day; meaning may be altered in the process. Consider perfect-knowledge to be God's knowledge: yet we are, one and all, not certain of who is God. Not knowing exactly who God is, we meet with the most profound questions. To call one Ignorant is not an accusation: rather given Time and Space limitations imperfect knowledge is all that any Man will or can have. This is a consequence of time-space relationships combined with the fact that man, as man, is a temporary being and he can only be in one place at any given time: therefore he has a very limited-understanding of the total Reality that surrounds him. The numbers of people are increasing and this too adds to the confusion.

For a more complete understanding of Space wrapped in Time, See Thomas Bearden's "Aids, Biological Warfare," Tesla Book Co., P. O. Box 1649, Greenville, TX 75401. ISBN # 0-914119-04-4.

The Sphere of existence

The Sphere of existence. Imagine this as being a sphere, project the elements.

This is a two-dimensional sketch of how the person relates to the surroundings. There are no numbers. The Drawing is the basis for the understanding. The person is in the center: words explain the meaning of the lines. One must imagine a sphere to complete the picture.

---

[352] **I have written** about this is other places especially so in my book _"The Eve of Annihilation."_ There is an attendant diagram obviating as it defines what is meant by this: The self, provides the physiology, the ordered form, for one or another means of knowing and doing. **See the diagram which appears immediately below.**

The totality will exist in the mind's eye;
Thereby bringing one closer to an understanding of the concept.

What is known for certain about all men?
All men are not the same:

Man's habits, manners and customs have evolved in different locations and at different points in time therefore there are distinct differences in character and meaning: never the less it is the belief of millions that all men are made somehow in God's (infinite) image. *If God has an infinite image this is certainly possible.* Men have devised Systems, which are not properly or truthfully ordered in every instance: especially this is true if one considers our absurd preparations for War. Such Systems provide for and allow certain forms, of behavior which, in time, becomes as a manner of Habit, Custom or Law. Clever men create and then imagine that they understand a System and work to exploit what the System provides as opportunity for them and others like themselves. *Systems are understood to mean certain acts are tolerated so to achieve one purpose or another.* They become as a way of doing business, so to speak and provide the guiding principles for acts of volition. *At this point we sense the possibility of the comingling of human thought with the thought of the **Devil** and his ideas,* which captivate and eventually may possess an individual.[353] *Such co-mingling of evil within the thought cluster changes the "nature" of the thought cluster.* It cannot be known in advance what the consequence will be. Such grouping of Ideas can be termed as a neurosis however becomes more acute when it drives the individual to outrageous behavior.[354] As a neurosis, it may be treated as a form of mental disorder, drugs are prescribed to *"fix the problem"* which is generally not well understood. Outrageous behavior may be encouraged by occult, perverted or some other deviate form of understanding, which at present has come to a position of authority or control.[355]

Every one of the individuals named below *(footnote 357)* imagined they did the right things: they had high opinions of themselves; in a word they were **Vain**. Christ admonished that all men are **Vain**. *In fact the men listed below were all foolish* one way or another and worked from a limited and destructive understanding of what life is. Additionally they all caused monumental damage to the Civilization and those people who were unfortunate enough to be influenced by them. Because of their ignorance and aggressive-personalities many who were influenced by them found an early grave? One need not labor the point. The informed reader will understand and those that hope to better understand have mountains of research touching upon the thinking

---

[353] **To be possessed** is to be under the continual influence of another.

[354] **To give pertinence** to the above assertion I will mention a few individuals that I believe have shared in this manner of being: most are now dead: *Napoleon Bonaparte* (an aggressive general); *Amschel Rothschild* (an eager money-grubber); *Adolf Hitler* (a would-be leader of the German people); *Josef Stalin* (an ignorant tyrant); *Jacob Schiff* (a cowardly sneak); *Winston Churchill* (a presumed leader of the British people), *Franklin Roosevelt* (a verbose hypocrite); *Pol Pott* (a monstrous fiend), *George Soros* (a clever exploiter); *Barack Obama* (a make-believe President) and finally we can include *Harry Reid and Nancy Pelosi* (two simple-minded Politicians); you can add to the list on your own. There are many others just like them as well: the reader can find many for his list.

[355] **Wardner, James, Ph.D.** *Communist Infiltration of the Catholic Church.* Video produced by, Most Holy Family Monastery, 4425 Schneider Road, Fillmore, NY 14735.

and consequence of the being of such *"important"* people. [356] The unknowing must better inform themselves truthfully about what is Reality. How is Reality structured and just who and what are, in fact, responsible for the structuring?

The LIE works its way into all systems of thought. Sometimes this is intentional however it is probably most often a case of having only a small part of the necessary understanding of a situation. Keep in mind although they may be very intelligent in many ways and have some good ideas, Politicians are not generally of the genius type. A genius is a man like St. Thomas, Leonardo da Vinci, Oswald Spengler, and a few others. Mechanical genius is not critical thinking in the same Idiom. Most situations are complex: there are causes and the expected effects are not always clear nevertheless they do influence the thought process and the general tenor and direction of any Idea. [357] *The spoken language, because it may be piece-meal, seems incapable of conveying information correctly*: with the understanding of ideas and generally the substance of any situation. When committed to writing, the thinking is often obscured by the extent of certain contrived explanations. Explanation often is plagued by the prior knowledge and experience of the speaker or writer. Therefore, thousands of pages are written which few read and fewer still might or could possibly understand the *nature or meaning* of what is written. [358] *In such dialogues the lies are often carefully woven with the truth to make the lie more acceptable.* [359] This is especially true in questions involving finance, big money and War: especially War which provides outrageous opportunity for profits tendered to *Greed:* here we find reasons for theft. We the People do have reporting of various issues however we are often distracted during the reporting for various Commercial Messages and only get the portion that will fit in a certain *time-frame.* This is unfortunate however we therefore have only a part of the thinking concerning any Issue. Let us consider a few special issues at this time.

Napoleon Bonaparte is considered a great general by many. Apparently he was somewhat bound by conceit and suffered the consequence of this affliction. He was a rather small man physically just 5 foot 7 inches tall. He was married (1810-1821) to the Duchess of Parma; they

---

[356] **Harry Reid and Nancy Pelosi** may be included not for their monumental importance however rather as two individuals that will cause some unknown damage to the Civilization and Culture. This is difficult to understand and more difficult to prove. Such type of individual sees only the part of the picture that they are looking at and often they have self-interest as a main driving force: Self-interest alone is always incomplete and is therefore always limited: this is a subject for another book!

[357] **The direction of a thought** depends upon *time-space orientation:* the when, where and how it is known. Also who knows what is known is an important factor: since some individuals have more influence on circumstance than others: one's social position and wealth are in large measure responsible for this factor. Thought content and meaning can move upward toward the higher classes or downward toward the common and vulgar in a society.

[358] **Such Verbosity** is often employed in political writing so to confuse the reader. To create confusion is often the object of such writing. And it has become a standard in the legal profession confusing all who participate.

[375] **Some truth** is always included along with the lie. The lie thereby becomes more believable and is somewhat disguised. It is important that the lie is believed so to serve some deviate purpose.

[359]

had three children; (See internet for complete information). Napoleon was a studious youth and became and was considered one of the World's brilliant generals. He entered Russia with a Grand Army of 400,000 men: most were killed others froze to death in a winter they had not anticipated: some certainly deserted for the love of a Russian peasant girl, only about 10,000 returned home to France. Imagine the genetic damage done to France as a nation from his "*brilliance*" as a general? Those who spoke of his brilliance as a general somehow overlooked the genetic damage that was inflicted on the nation. Many still suffer from the misunderstanding and ignorance which surrounded his being and doing. This has been followed by a general breakdown of French Catholicism since the French Revolution. Was this the working of the Devil? *The French Revolution was a monument to ignorance* and to man's inhumanity toward his fellow man: with beheadings and cannibalism. Nevertheless the misunderstanding is promoted, even now, for commercial and societal endeavors that one might certainly question. Much of what is promoted has elements of grandeur and beauty none of which had anything to do with Napoleon and the death of hundreds of thousands.

Adolph Hitler's coming and going is quite complicated. Following is an abbreviated concept of what happened. *The deal was a set-up* determined to destroy the Economy of the German Nation and the German People for the good of England (of course this was not mentioned in our mass communications prior to or during the War: perhaps it may have been mentioned co-incidentally). Hitler was the man who would do the job. *The money interests from England and especially the United States played an important role.* The Jewish question was used as a stimulus for the level of barbarity. There are few that are certain if the numbers reported were accurate or if they were contrived for the effect that they did have? During a four year War many of all races and most nations died of natural causes, for example old age; certainly some Jews starved to death as did many others, including the Germans, disease took the lives of others. Many thousands of English were killed and millions of Germans and others involved in that nonsense: we have named this nonsense World War II.[360] We are still stupefied by Television reruns of the Great War; we sit with beer in hand watching how we beat the Nazis: the Hun.[361]

---

[360] **Approximately 65,000** English were killed, in England, **during four years** of War from the Blitzkrieg. About **250,000 Germans** were killed during the raids on Dresden, **in two days** when the War, in fact, had already been won by the Allies. Who knows the exact death toll in Dresden, this is an estimate. *Who was the real Villain? Who was the real Hero?* Keep in mind Roosevelt and Churchill would not accept a German surrender until the country was totally destroyed. The genetic damage done is incalculable especially since Germany has led the way in many areas of intellectual ability and accomplishment and in philosophy and understanding in general.

[361] **Blurb from David Meyer's August 2007 Last Trumpet Newsletter:**

I'm not certain that what follows is true however it is interesting.

"Angela Merkel was born in the D.D.R., the Communist portion of Germany in 1954. Her biography says she was born on July 17, 1954, and that she is the daughter of a Lutheran minister from an East German-controlled church. Recently, however, Soviet KJB archive files reveal an entirely different story. Stasi GDR files indicate that she was born on April 20th, 1954, and details of her birth were included in the records of the German Dr. Karl Klauberg, who was one of the Nazi "death doctors" convicted by Soviet courts and imprisoned. When he later was recognized as a brilliant scientist, he was released after seven years and was recognized as *the father of artificial insemination.* The Soviets were even more

Germanic people added much to Western Civilization: music, art, literature and various forms of technology. There elite thinking combines Reality with Metaphor and what is Existential. They remain the most prosperous and diligent people on Europe. However they have been constantly insulted for a century.[362] The German people are not the same as the people who

---

intrigued when they discovered Dr. Klauberg had preserved frozen samples of the sperm of Adolf Hitler. The forces of darkness in high places decided to try to produce a child from Hitler's sperm, obviously for occult and illuminist purposes. Dr. Klauberg then brought the youngest sister of Eva Braun (Hitler's wife), whose name was Gretl, to Eastern Germany, and the result of the experiment produced not a biological son of Hitler, but rather a daughter. Amazingly, Adolf Hitler was born on April 20th, 1889, and Angela Merkel was born on April 20th, 1954. *(April 20th is 11 days before the witches' high sabat of Beltaine.)* Angela became a custodian of the Catholic Church through its connections with the East German Lutheran Church. Once a German Pope would take the Roman throne, Angela Merkel was to also take her biological father's position as German Chancellor. On April 20th, 2005, the Nazi Joseph Ratzinger became Pope Benedict XVI, (16th), precisely on the 116th birthday of Adolf Hitler. Then on November 22nd, 2005, Hitler's biological daughter, Angela Merkel was elected Chancellor of Ger. The day of that election, Nov. 22nd, was the anniversary of the publication of Charles Darwin's Origin of the Species, which is antichrist publication denying the Creator of the universe.

If the Soviet record is true, and the evidence is strong, it opens up some amazing possibilities. The undeniable fact is that Angela Merkel came from obscurity to triumph-viral power as German Chancellor, President of the European Union, and head of the powerful G-8 economic cartel. When I began to do further research on this, I discovered that Hitler's father, who took the name Hitler, was *the illegitimate son of a Rothschild mistress* whose last name was Schicklgruber. The etymology of the name Hitler reveals that the name means a shepherd who lives in a hut. The name Adolf from Old High German means noble wolf. Thus, his combined name indicates that he was the Shepherd Wolf, or false shepherd. Strangely enough, former Pope Ratzinger, or Benedict XVI, also has the title of Shepherd of the Church, and since he took office, the Roman Catholic Church has had a German shepherd. Incidentally, that breed of dog resembles a wolf. We also know that Adolf Hitler nicknamed himself Herr Wolf. His East Prussian headquarters was called Wolfsschanze; his headquarters in France was called Wolfsschlucht, and his headquarters in the Ukraine was called Werwolf. Will the powerful European Union become the New World Order and Fourth Reich? Only God knows.

One more interesting point is that Chancellor Angela Merkel has an unusual obsession with the works of the occult composer Richard Wagner, who was a Satanist. She made her obsession known in an interview with the newspaper Frankfurter Allgemeine Zeitung in July 2005. Wagner wrote the infamous composition called Parsifal, which is purely occult and demonic. Parsifal was a favorite of Hitler as well, and Hitler stated that the music of Wagner occupied his mind. Angela Merkel, like Adolf Hitler, is deeply fascinated with Wagner's Ride of the Valkyries. The Valkyries were minor female deities that would ride through every battle to gather the most valiant of the slain and carry them off to a place called Valhalla where they would wait to join the army of Odin in the last battle at the end of the world.

Is this woman, Angela Merkel, being used of Satan to marshal the forces for the last battle called Armageddon? It is also interesting to note that Chancellor Merkel has exactly the same eyes as Chancellor Hitler, and she bears a striking resemblance to him except for the little moustache, of course." *You do not have to believe this however do consider it in your thinking.*

[362] **This to a great extent is because of America:** lied into both the first and second World Wars, by Wilson and Roosevelt, and now doing the work of the International English and Zionist money-grubbers, who

have led them and deceived them, ***much as we in America are being led and deceived.*** Some Germans may have disliked some Jews however all Germans did not hate all Jews. *Some Germans risked their life to save a Jew.* People celebrate each and every year overjoyed that as a Nation we killed millions of innocent German people: the young, the old and the ailing. *Hitler* was a tyrant however *Roosevelt* and *Churchill* were no better: *they were all psychopathic and they were all liars as well however for different reasons.* Both Roosevelt and Churchill are held in high esteem by an uninformed and distracted people: the real enemies of mankind, the money-lenders are rarely mentioned, they go unpunished they were and are secret in their doing: found living quietly in palatial accommodations they continue to amass wealth beyond reason. And many of them are Jewish. Christ warned that all in this world is Vanity, why can so few understand what this means? This subject requires the examination of a more completely elaborated set of issues.

Financial dealings are often shaded with nuance so to sell a product or a fiduciary instrument. This helps to amass great fortunes for those fortunate few that control circumstance. Keep in mind *"Secret knowledge is the key to winning in any Political endeavor."* Secret knowledge also helps in Economic affairs; some individuals make millions because of this. Our financial Systems must be restructured so to make them serve all participants not just a few Specialists in the transaction Type: (as is presently the case.)[363] We must abolish the Federal Reserve and place the issuance of currency back in the hands of the congress as was intended by our Constitution. The men who framed our Constitution did indeed recognize what is lawful money as "Specie". Money must remain stable, unchanging inviolate; it's quite simple. Nothing else will work![364]

---

have combined with the banking system to conquer and exploit all of the world's riches. Someone should convey what is happening, truthfully, so that circumstance could be corrected. We believe this will not happen, except co-incidentally and temporarily. It may be cause for another World War III. This is one aspect of Evil: the Devil working against the Divine power of goodness: the divine power that we call God.

[363] **The present means** of turning imagined wealth into real wealth must be better understood. This is an abstraction that makes possible the wealth of (for example), George Soros and others of his kind. In fact it is theft: take a little from the unknowing and give the profits to those in a position to *know and control the knowledge and implementation of some of the greatest forms of financial treachery.*

[364] **Pay attention** to what is here mentioned and check out Jubilee Year on the Internet. This is one of the smart things that you can do right now. You must be informed that our Federal Reserve, so called is not Federal and it has no reserves. It places the people in debt who are then required to pay off the debt with the added interest. This is why there are so many amongst the poor: *simply stated they are being robbed.*

1. Pass this Bill on a State Level. It Can Be Done State By State. **2.** By Law, Require That The Federal Reserve Buy Back All Outstanding Government Debt. **3.** In A Single Step, Audit and then Close Down The Federal Reserve, Place It and Its Member Banks Under Permanent Control Of The United States Congress (Article 1, Section 8 of the U.S. Constitution), Change The Letters On Top Of Our Money To Read: "UNITED STATES CURRENCY" instead of "FEDERAL RESERVE NOTE" and Outlaw The Practice Of the Central Bank Created Debt Money.

Step 1 will introduce wealth based money into every single State, directly fund a "Value Added Infrastructure," nearly eliminate unemployment, repair our crumbling infrastructure, restore our economy and make the U.S. Dollar the strongest currency in the World. **Step 2** will pay our creditors and

Amschel Rothschild (an eager money-grubber) was a very smart and clever man however he was not philosophically wise. He imagined loaning money to the Kings and Rulers of Nations would net, a better profit than loaning to a farmer or small businessman. He was a Jew and a usurer, a loan shark: however he loaned to gentiles that were killing each other for some arcane reason:[365] both Jew (Shylock) and Gentile (Goyim) were wrong in their endeavors. The words Shylock and Goyim are used because they are pertinent in this instance. The Political control of language must not be allowed. To do so is a mistake; one cannot alter the real and truthful meaning of words; except this can be done temporarily.

When the confusion cleared the enemies became friends however the *Rothschild's* kept the profits from the Gentile's involvement in any conflict, the profits were generally considerable. He did do well for his clients, no doubt. By 1850 it is believed that the *Rothschild's* were worth a billion dollars: $1,000,000,000.00 not too bad for the family of a poor boy. At that time a working man made perhaps $30.00 a month; *that's $360.00 a year.* *Rothschild's* five sons followed in his footsteps; soon all of the nations in Europe owed money to the Rothschild's.[366] Their presence, in one or another form, is still an important factor in World finance. It is understood that by the year 2000 the Rothschild's and the variety of associated entities were worth just about nine trillion dollars: a lot of money even for a rich man.[367] The assets are in various properties, land, mining interests and about ten percent in cash. We are not certain how this number came to be however one can presume great numbers of successful transactions along with a somewhat tainted past: a condition in many instances. One can imagine a ***perverted consistency*** in auguring toward such achievement.

A financier of notable importance was *Jacob Schiff,* a sneaky hypocrite. It is believed that he spent $20,000,000.00 in financing the elimination of the Russian Monarchy. What he did was illegal,[368] *making him a felon* and unconscionable, making him a notoriously evil man as well. Nevertheless he was respected by some for his brilliance in finance and money manipulation. In fact he was an opportunist and a fraud, and a deceitful thief beside. As they say: in Russia he was in on the ground floor: ***a liar, a thief and an unmitigated hypocrite***. His hands were clean but his heart had a stink that will never go away. Schiff imagined himself to be somehow

---

eliminate the national debt. **Step 3** will stop the *fraud and theft by deception* carried out by the Federal Reserve Bank: and return the U.S. to constitutionally sound Wealth Based Money.

[365] **The arcane reasoning** goes back hundreds of years and is impossible to understand clearly. Nevertheless it is influential on the present moments.

[366] **Corti, Count Egon Caesar,** *The Rise of the House of Rothschild.* Western Islands, Publisher, Belmont, Massachusetts, 02178. © 1928 The Cosmopolitan Book Corporation,

[367] **Compare these numbers** with those outlined in Chapter XII concerning the value of the Russian Nobility's holdings when the Czar and his family were butchered.

[368] **At the time he did this** it was against the Law to do business with Russia. His money and Prestige (?) allowed him to ignore the Law. This is what he did! Many financiers, money men, are known to have done this: many continue to do so today. Often they associate their activities with being clever or just smart: Are they? The point is, many businesses can be run profitably within the confines of the Law however the criminal types are not satisfied with a fair profit: they want more than is reasonable from their involvement. They are not honest: they are thieves.

brilliant, a real doer. Certainly ignorant fools were hired to pull the trigger so to destroy the persons who were the <u>rightful rulers of Russia; truthful monarchs.</u> To repeat the Czar was murdered, also his wife and five innocent children and some of his faithful servants. Why? Who in fact would perpetrate such a blasphemy on five innocent children: and their mother as well. Interestingly at present there is a movement in Russia to restore the Monarchy: big money will prevent that this would happen at the present time. The One World Order is almost in place and it will probably prevent the existence of a real monarchy: however there are a few problems.[369]

Still another financier of a manner of importance, Gyorgy Schwartz, known by the World as *George Soros* has amassed a fortune, it is alleged to be in the billions.[370] He is a thief and an opportunist of the worst kind. He imagines, himself to be a smart businessman working with the *LIE* and the fear of those that have much less than he. The *LIE* involves the workings of the techniques of trading securities, which is tied to time and space functions: 24 hour trading of securities is not a good idea. Twenty four hour trading is made a bit easier when given an International venue; the big money wants this to happen. It benefits most those who are Specialists and a few traders that control the market while others are sleeping preparing to do some honest work. Not many understand how fortunes are made however it helps to know for certain *when the victim is sleeping.*[371]

Our current President, *Barack Obama* is an opportunistic and a scene-shifter: it is believed or imagined by many that he is a liar and a hypocrite as well: to our disadvantage he is also somewhat intelligent. He is no genius however he is a clever manipulator.[372] He has denied the workings of our Constitution and seems to be a sociopathic and vain zealot that will do anything to drive his opinions to their desired conclusion; apparently he ignores the wishes of the people and their elected representatives. He has been elected to a second term; we must wait to see what will happen. He uses various appointed socialist types to do his bidding. *He should never have been elected the President of this or any Nation.* Are his opinions his own? As an attorney he did not do well: his license was taken away, coincidentally so too was the license of his wife. We wonder why? President Obama is a very dangerous man. He is somewhat a psychopath

---

369 See **Chang, Matthias,** *Future Fast Forward, the Zionist, Anglo-American Meltdown.* First American Editions, 2006, American Free Press, Washington D. C. 20063, This book suggests, at least, that there may be some problems in the future development if a One World government. We certainly hope so.

370 **Glen Beck:** from interview with George Soros (60 Minutes). "What we have in Soros is a multi-billionaire atheist, with skewed moral values, and a sociopath's lack of conscience. He's anti-God, anti-family, anti-American and anti-good."

371 **Admittedly,** a few lucky and often dishonest players make money, some make a lot of money however most lose most or make relatively little.

372 "**Obama** the man thinks and speaks in the hoariest of clichés, and that's when he has his Teleprompters in front of him; when the prompter is absent he can barely think or speak at all. Not one original idea has ever issued from his mouth—it's all warmed-over Marxism of the kind that has failed over and over again for 100 years." This quote is taken from: "Marilynn Sortino" <jsortino@fea.net>Subject: Fw: Washington Post Hits Obama!

and it is believed by some that he is a Marxist Communist.[373] He seems to be pro-Islam and is planning the future of the World made over in his outdated and incorrect image: which is the same as any foolish Collectivist. All Collectivists play the same tune: they want everyone to be subservient; to themselves. Those then, the confused and mistakenly inspired will lead the band? He is seemingly working from a perverted imagination and has a poorly formed idea of Reality except as he would have it. How he was elected is a classic in political manipulation; and now for a second term. It is alleged that he was favored by non-other than George Soros, the Hungarian born (presumably) billionaire: an immigrant who had come to the United States in 1956: and, who himself is an Opportunist and a Thief. If Mr. Soros was a good and decent man he would go back to Hungary and help his own people.

Finally we find the names of two seemingly innocuous participants, *Harry Reid* and *Nancy Pelosi;* they are like performers, in what appears to be the destruction of America. <u>*Why they would want to harm America is unclear*</u> however one can imagine that they are working from self-interest and they are driven by somewhat psychopathic tendencies, including that they hope to be important somehow. It seems apparent they don't understand what freedom is. Actually they are <u>*merely servants of those with the big money*</u> and the real influence. In fact they might be considered somewhat as ***traitors***. In War time (and we certainly are at War, an undeclared War) a traitor, in the past was hung by a rope until dead. We are too Christian to do that however it was a well considered option at one time. Hanging is considered unchristian and cannot be tolerated by the more sophisticated of those involved: they have developed other ways to mesmerize the world. Considering other situations; is it alright to kill millions of innocent people women and children in a contrived manner of Warfare? Who is the hypocrite?

Both Harry and Nancy will be replaced by other amenable types of Socialist, Communists or Collectivist Creatures, talking heads; life will go on. The damage they do will be difficult to assess and they will be given much of the necessary cover for their participation in this tragedy. Nancy Pelosi though intelligent and appears quite well is, no doubt, suffering from her role as a leader of men. She is attempting to be what she is not. There is room for women in Politics even at the top however they should not pattern themselves after the fools that hold many of our highest elected offices. This is a subject of its own, with a basis in the study of deviant psychology. The problem is that no competent psychologist will be given any opportunity or support in informing the population what is wrong.

---

[373] **Years from now,** historians may regard the 2008 election of Barack Obama as an inscrutable and disturbing phenomenon, the result of a baffling breed of mass hysteria akin perhaps to the witch craze of the Middle Ages. "How, they will wonder, did a man so devoid of professional accomplishment beguile so many into thinking he could manage the world's largest economy, direct the world's most powerful military, execute the world's most consequential job? Imagine a future historian examining Obama's pre-presidential life: ushered into and through the Ivy League despite unremarkable grades and test scores along the way; a cushy non-job as "community organizer"; a brief career as a state legislator devoid of legislative achievement (and in fact nearly devoid of his attention, so often did he vote "present"); and finally an unaccomplished single term in the United States Senate, the entirety of which was devoted to his presidential ambitions." From: "Marilynn Sortino" <jsortino@fea.net>

Subject: Fw: Washington Post Hits Obama!

The two-party system provides a somewhat meaningless pair of political adversaries. Such structure gives the people an opportunity to influence government; this is what they are told and this is what they believe. At the present time there appears to be debate and argumentation over some issues; abortion and immigration for example. Such as this is an apparent difference which gives foolish people something to argue about? However generally the parties are nearly the same in most respects: the elected ones, especially as individuals, have no ideas or influence of their own. *They march in lock step, just like the Nazis did and those who march with Obama condone many of the same sordid intentions.* Most are pretenders, somewhat Socialist, they are hypocrites hoping and trying to make a fortune for them.

Many of our elected leaders suffer from an inability to do what must/should be done *because of their friendships and allegiance to each other.* There are certainly personality problems beneath the political structure of the situation. Keep in mind that many of our Politicians are Masons of the thirty second and thirty third degree, thus they do not divulge their secrets to other people.

Tradition is built and structured on the doings of men. What is presented above is a brief period showing just a few of the various players and suggesting their influence on reality. All is related to a religious dictum which harbors an understanding of who and what is God: this author writes from a Catholic, meaning a universally acknowledged and implied perspective. Keep in mind Catholicism is the primary Christian Faith of Western Civilization, coming directly from Christ, believed to be the Son of God first in order and it is uncontestable. Physicists are just now beginning to see the relationship between God and Reality which he has created. Unfortunately I don't have much time left to make observations.

—⁓◦⊶⊶⊷⊶⊶⊶◦⁓—

Professor emeritus, Robert Fiedler, July 26, 2013.

CHAPTER XVI

WE WILL END ON MUSIC

Everyone thought the Pied Piper was a Character in a Story,
However, the Pied Piper is alive and He is very well, right in America.
He has more influence on the Children, of this Nation, than the parents do.
The Moral Order is being certainly subverted by the Music of this same Character.

The Music Industry generates Billions as it Distracts, Incites and Profanes our Children

The music of now is symptomatic, of some of us having fallen to depths of degradation; all because of an incessant noise considered as music. Many of these sounds are liken to the sounds of the Savage; what does this mean? Many philosophers and wise men from the past have been wary of music; we have been warned. Music incites the emotions and is a strong motivation for mindless movement, gyrations, sexually explicit innuendo and orgiastic behaviors. Recently the "new dancing" has many signs of sexual intercourse. This type nonsense is promoted as the "way to go" for the young and the unwary amongst the middle aged. This form is all done as part of today's entertainment and recreation. Each year is more explicit than the past. This has been known for centuries however man is very slow to learn. Man's inability to understand and control the sounds of madness, which are typically found in the recent forms of what is called rap music suggest that *the culture and the civilization are in a terminal phase, soon to be submerged.* Our technologies will not help indeed those have made all of this possible. Technology is the driving force of our "Music of Madness;" **we are mad however we do not recognize this as being madness in our own person.** We imagine that the primitive urges and gyrations, indeed the movements and behavior of a savage, which we have accepted have no effect on our sub-conscious being, *nevertheless such urges destroy our sense of self-restraint and civilized composure.* Keep in mind the subconscious is always working somehow and will have some effects. All of the effects are not evil however many is certainly just that.

To be Civilized requires the discipline that will encourage self-restraint.
This must be coupled with a higher level of intelligent behavior.
We should have a truthful and decent respect for all others.

The salesmen for the music industry have taken an unreasonable amount of liberty in the promotion of their products. It is a very conspicuous presence, which it is impossible to deny. The Icons of our music are everywhere on billboards, magazine covers, T-shirts and embedded in the minds of the entire population, excepting perhaps just a few. Music is present in athletic spectacles, adding a feeling of belonging so to enliven the *"Vicarious Participation"* of the **Watchers,** *those who imagine to be somehow participating in the events.* Music will *"free one* *up"* so to be a better participant or customer and to spend more money, of course. This is the object of the salesman's approach, to have the clients spend more money, and this is why he will work so hard on such endeavor: ***Greed***, quietly underlies this; it is behind any and every economic motivation. We accept that **Greed** is a mortal **Sin one of seven deadly sins.**

Great Music, at one time, had form and structure and was given to an intelligent appreciation of adults. Composers studied and attempted to fulfill valid and high level expectation. Music had a structure and a form, often combined with meaningful verbal content. Composers studied past great music and attempted to arrange meaningfully contemplated forms and verse. There was also a form of folk music that was considered common and was for the socially lower standing citizens. Neither one had the technology that is present today. It was mostly about love and romance and much was in fact was quite tender. There were many simple songs that people could sing and of course there were Troubadours that roamed and sang and played to make a living. Today we are hearing the products of children ill-educated and mostly ignorant. They create all the stuff on the airways and the tapes and disks, for sale to other children for a few dollars. All the youthful practitioners are trying to be different: to demand attention. This is a wonderful opportunity for the salesman and the kids that perform to become millionaire celebrities selling millions of copies; *all that noise and very little comprehensive understanding.*

Our intention is not to simply discuss music per se, however to bring into mind some interrelationships which (it would seem) are important considerations concerning our present moment in time. Others are better qualified to discuss music, nevertheless music is so powerful one might consider ways in which music is both positively good and negatively evil in respect to some profound implications. *Music is wonderful and because this is true when music is used subversively, as at times presumably it has been used, it is a powerfully destructive force.* Furthermore, such destruction as does occur is difficult to recognize. The human mind is complex, one is not always (if ever) able to draw a proper and correct inference from any occurrence or genre of comprehension. We can depend that the human mind will assist in correcting some of the damage: *some*! Thus we attempt to deal with a difficult topic, difficult because music has captivated the spirit of the Time and is dear to the hearts of millions, one way or another. Nevertheless, critical insights might be brought to bear, which may yield an altered understanding in the minds of any willing to digress from the popular and sensation driven mind-set. If one is a movie buff and/or enjoys gambling in Las Vegas or other *chancy places*, one may find some of the assertions difficult to handle. Be that as it may. Keep an open mind if you can.

For all of known history, sound has been a part of important ceremonial occasions and sounds were organized into some manner of Music. Presently at the dawn of the Third Millennium, the advent of the twenty-first Century, *rhythm as the important element in music*, has been given to the expression of musical innovation as never before imagined. The sounds given to Rhythm as are being introduced into the Soul of the Civilization **reverberate, over and over as they find their way repeatedly to the depths of individual consciousness.** This is an invasion of the individual psyche and also of the collective soul. Music fills a space and is acceptable to the ear however it is not the space; Space has its own properties. Sound *travels* however *goes nowhere* except that it may be received within a conscious being, perhaps as noise, perhaps as music, which has a reasoned structure relating to the *harmonic nature* of blended tonalities. Thus sound fills and is an audible extension within a given space, however to repeat it is not the space.[374]

The reign of Music as Master of the Soul has an origin beginning with the Symphony Orchestra and the great Music of the seventeenth through the first half of the twentieth Century. Presently, popular music has been nearly conquered by the invention of electrified music, having emphasis on the guitar, the sound of which can be and often is ***aggressive, insidious, insistent and profane.*** In fairness one must admit it is possible to achieve the most sensitive and beautiful sounds on a stringed instrument, however they are not always acknowledged by the masses. *The masses, it would seem, prefer sounds, which are vulgar, insidious, aggressive and leavened with popular lyrics concerning simple-minded pleasures involving an adolescent notion of love and sex.*[375] And the listeners enjoy jumping up and down and gyrating like a simple minded fool. Certainly there are exceptions however youth is especially captivated by dissonance and screaming for attention, as is evident in the amplification to deafening levels. Beyond this many Television programs and many commercial messages are *"backed up"* by noise we call music.

A wide array of musical innovation competes for prominence. Modern practitioners bring forward in time every sound ever made by human ingenuity. Movement within the cities creates noises and is likened to a form of abstract or non-structured Music. *Such sounds function as a continuo underlying the activities within the city.* Certainly this has been true in the past as well, however not to the extent **"Or"** with the force of the present example of the great Metropolis. This is due in part to the great numbers of people that are gathered together in a great city. The intervention of a mechanically determined noise, the freeway being most in evidence, is a constant and important part of what this world is about, at the present moment and may have psychological consequence, which we can only imagine. To repeat the consistent imposition of mechanical noise is much like a continuo in a musical composition, against which all other musical elements are in contrapuntal accord. Some musicals attempt to incorporate the sound or pulse of the city into the fabric of a musical score and succeed quite admirably.[376] The Musicals are very powerful in promoting the emotional tensions found in living and the composers are to be complimented on their perception.

Nevertheless, the consequence may, at this moment, be evident in the way, which individuals behave toward one another, especially concerning the relationship between some men and women and how they respond in an emotional situation involving love and what it means to

---

[374] **Spengler,** Oswald, *the Decline of the West, Vol. I, Form and Actuality,* (Alfred A. Knopf, NY Pub. Nov. 1928) pg. 168. "Everything extends itself, but it is not yet "space" not something established within itself but a self-extension continued from the moving here to the moving there."

[375] **An adolescent notion of love** and sex is also responsible for many misfortunes including unwanted pregnancies, divorce, wife swapping, child beating, child desertion and even at times murder.

[376] **American in Paris or West Side Story** for example: When one views and hears the presentation one is made to feel a part of the pathos of the youthful participants in Westside Story. Such as this, is used by Social Engineers to "*steer*" the public to a favorable feeling about, for example, immigration and inter-racial marriage. Both immigration and inter-racial marriage are fraught with problems however these are caused to be overlooked by the tempo and nature of the music. This is a great Issue which we can only touch upon at this writing.

be loved. The consequence of a pleasant distraction is perhaps already evident; however most do not see it because they do not understand what it is they are looking for. We can be more certain of the effect that music is having when we consider the influence of celebrity type singers and musicians, who influence the habits, manners and customs of the World's children and some adults as well. Through the medium of music and the accompanying Lyrics children are assaulted and assuaged, for various reasons. However, _no one understands truthfully what might be the consequence of an addiction to sounds accompanied by insinuating narrative_. One can imagine that both good and evil consequences are certain, however it would be impossible to predict that goodness will triumph in any circumstance, dominated by Rock and Roll and Rap Music, both of which are often structured as an attack on goodness, decency and modest personal behavior. The evidence is that theatrics and the accompanying acid sounds are corrupting millions, victimized by millionaire pipers, with a foul mouth and an itching crotch! Country music panders to immature feelings of love and silly situations for effect. There are some good ones amongst the mix; this gives cover to the vulgarity and nonsense straight from the ghetto. Some religious programs use music reasonably well however others are about the same as the junk. Certainly there is not much of the Gregorian chant which is quite beautiful. Music and various other forms of addiction go hand and hand: many musicians, so called, are addicted to some illegal drug. Some musicians believe that their music is enhanced when they are in a somewhat hypnotic or stupefied trance because of the use of dope. _This is an absurd excuse promoted by ignorance._ The peddlers sell millions of copies of the inane babbling of adolescent ignorance and the performers pocket fortunes for the noise they make.

Music and Noise can be imagined as primary constants, which assault as they distract young and old. The distraction may be pleasant or invigorating, soul wrenching or spiritually uplifting, however it is in the form of a complex imposition that music will force entry into the Soul of the individual and the Civilization. Especially, because of lyrics and insinuation, attitude and repetition, Music is responsible for much of what youth may imagine and ultimately will **act out.** The term **"Spaced Out"** is one symptom of this phenomenon. The profits generated from the music business are monumental and are responsible for quite a large slice of the gross national product, or the GNP. This alone guarantees that no restraint will be imposed upon those who create whatever is happening, regardless of any consequence, real or imagined. The gyrations, the noise and the encouragement toward obscenity are all tolerated for the billions that are involved. Profit appeals to **Greed**, a Cardinal Sin, which sits quietly and is resting patiently on the shelf of history. However, the consequence of Greed and other forms of Sin as well is apparent all around in manners, habits and customs of the general population. **When there is so much money to be made adults are happy corrupting the children;** and there exist _billions for the taking_, given all the forms and implementations given to this industry. Admittedly most people are good _"most of the time"_ however even the good ones will fall into this pit and even the good one's may not have the comprehension which permits truthful understanding of the Issues which are being considered.

The music Industry provides a salesman's dream came true. New songs are issued nearly every day and the number of vain performers is endless, beside which the kids can watch the slick VCR's and will pay a handsome price for the latest release. Kids are curious, therefore a little bit of T and A can be thrown in, thus to make the performance more appealing. Never mind many VCR's are as soft-porno or blatantly sinful. When kids are having fun whom is the wise man that might interfere and stop them. Mom and dad have many problems of their own; most Parents present little (if any) mindful and/or constructive imposition and encourage little restraint.

Many Parents simply don't understand the dynamics of why their families disintegrate as the kids become Pubescent, then Adolescents, daughters shack up with some nincompoop, and the daughter becomes pregnant only to kill the little "bastard" rather than face an adult and profound lifelong responsibility which she didn't intend to assume. In reality, children are not ready for what they may presume is their right. Maybe mom and dad did the same things themselves, without considering the consequences. Some of the serious consequence may be attributed to the pied pipers and their sinful songs, no doubt. Not to forget sluttish and vain young women wiggle their body parts as they scream or coo. Lasciviously contrived costuming and movements when combined with almost any form of nonsense will hit the jackpot, earning big bucks, almost every time. As manners, habits and customs are modified the *clever man* will make a business out of every detail, no matter what form it has taken which can be given to and promoted by a manner of salesmanship. Have you noticed how many ladies have different colors of hair and nails and now tattoos; these are symptoms. The young ladies are given many choices in over-priced cosmetics to make them beautiful. Actually such beauty is an imposition on one's looks and is mostly in the imagination; beside beauty is in the eye of the beholder. This is very significant where truthful love is involved. Beside, beauty treatments are only temporary. We admit discreetly applied cosmetic surgery may be necessary in some instances; this is understandable. This really doesn't work very well for the intended purpose. Recently the ladies allow their bodies to be disfigured with some abysmal tattoo; they do this as an expression of the self imagining they are somewhat different. In reality they are all about the same. What they imagine is that they are free to do as they choose; to live their own life. This is true however they should choose more wisely.

Coincidentally, mostly imported from other parts of the world, the amount of Junk generated in support of silly Ideas is staggering. Music is used to pitch everything, which can be sold. The sound is all around: surround sound (at a price) distracting as it comforts, perhaps annoys shoppers, plying the isles in the Mall. To the sound of music youth are taught to hug trees and imagine they are *somehow* making a difference in this big wide, confused and pleasantly distracted (although mostly misinformed) world. Nevertheless, most kids appear to be happy as a bird. Imported plastic Stuff, of various kinds, in wild and atrocious colors, lines the homes of an entire Civilization. In the mean time Politicians bemoan the fact that there is so much garbage.[377] There are always new styles and innovations, introduced with music or some fanfare, so as to make obsolete whatever one might have acquired in the past; as recently as three months ago. Not to worry, the plastic card allows that one can *replace what is imagined to be obsolete* made so deliberately as part of the deal. To make this work, the kids are given access to instant credit at eighteen, after which age they are suddenly assumed mature, responsible dependable and

---

[377] **The Oceans are being flooded** with plastic garbage. Some say it will take a few centuries for this stuff to be broken down. In the meantime what will happen to the marine life, which must live in the oceans. In some areas fishermen are complaining that the numbers of fish being caught is insufficient to make a living. They too imagine living must include all of the commercial nonsense that is available.

truthfully informed voters, ready to steer a nation in rocky straits. This presents a quite absurd understanding especially when one considers the lack of truthfully significant learning that emanates from many perhaps most public schools. Children actually imagine that those know just about everything and many misinformed adults are looking forward to when the kids will vote. Those are imagined as being able to understand what to do with the politics of this nation. They don't realize that learning requires time and that most learning is part of what one does after they are released from the formal educational process. Even in the Professions experience is an excellent teacher; then all the portions begin to fit together. One "lives and learns". Keep in mind many have not been properly (*"educated") in our great schools?* The schools are too concerned with equality and making sure that all are included in every program. How might one accomplish such as this; lower the level of the instruction. Just watch the Jerry Springer Show and you will get the picture; if what is above is not convincing.[378]

Politically, the *nature* of much music provides a useful and effective motivational tool, as a means to win the acceptance and adoption of new ways of thinking, accompanied by a feel-good mentality. Political Conventions are Carnivals, which entertain as they induce the Voter's acceptance of programs, with a hope for impossible results driven by ignorant expectation, the consequence of which none can foresee excepting in respect to costs involved. Many view the political convention somewhat as a vacation or a diversion from their routine tasks. Politically motivated expectation is assuaged by transient friendship and a sense of satisfaction gained from participation in a *seemingly* important event. Everyone feels especially involved when they play the Star Spangled Banner. As they sing, each individual imagines they are a *very important part of something;* however few realize what that **something** really is.[379] Actually every person is very important however few understand how this is truthfully expressed.

Music has been and is used to *encourage the boys* to kill another man's children. In more barbaric times, like the twentieth century the rewards included the savaging of another man's wife or daughter. All this is happening to the sound of the beat, largely the beat of the modern machine and the buzzing of the city's traffic, or the rumble of a sixty-ton tank. The Picture is especially vivid, when made especially for entertainment, accompanied by an academy winning movie score, for a film designed as propaganda. Such War Movies appear frequently to be accompanied by music scored for effect. One might consider that *"The Effect is never Art"!* *Young men and some older were stupid enough to fight wars in the past, however at present*

---

[378] **Jerry Springer** was a talk show host in about 2000, the turn of the millennium. His programs were very informative and showed what many individuals are like: drunken, degenerate slobs. Much was done for effect however the picture emerged as being quite clear. Jerry Springer is a clever man; he still moderates his own show.

[379] **Generally speaking,** in a political sense that *"Something"* is a move toward the left: toward a Socialist and perhaps Marxist, certainly collectivist existence for the masses. The collectivist wants all people to be the same thus they can be controlled more easily. The Directors or masters will live in a mansion until some other Master replaces them. ***This is as the repeat performance:*** new faces, old Ideas. The Old Ideas are endemic to the System which has been crafted by money grubbing fools. *What is missing is Virtue: decency, honesty, fairness and a noble sense of being.* Many of the Big-shots spend much of their time with whores, one kind or another or with other men of like mind and attitude. Together, this group makes up the talking heads that we hear about.

we are becoming more enlightened, encouraging our daughters to be as mindless as our sons. And we have succeeded; the girls will now have the opportunity right in the front lines with gun in hand. Some will be killed, wounded and disfigured for the cause; without understanding why they are fighting in the first place. For their death the family will receive a folded flag and neighbors and friends will cry some crocodile tears. We wonder, where the crocodiles are. We are not certain how the family of an enemy may be treated when their son or daughter is killed. The feelings of family and friends which accompany such event are perhaps much the same.

Modern music is often an intrusion on Tradition. Tradition supportive of present reality is abandoned, in a futile pursuit of present satisfaction, based upon how one is feeling, rather than upon one's Intelligence, as a function in support of Reason, in service of Intellect. As the Pied Piper plays, Truth as embodied tacitly in Tradition gives way to imagination, metaphor and misunderstood notions of reality engendered, in part, by sound. The sounds are orchestrated with masterful imagination, thus to create a false sense of person-hood, which may be quite confused and perhaps is not understood for what it really is. Many individuals harbor a misunderstood notion of reality, as a consequence of having abandoned Tradition, which *in fact* defines all of what is and much of what will happen, even before an event. Music can be evil as it is lulling or bludgeoning the world to sleep just when so much that is good has been awakening. This is a mortal conflict, no doubt, in which music plays a major role, perhaps it will be the decisive one.

Most often today's music is accompanied by an imagery, created for effect, which captivates a somewhat vacant mind-space, typical of many within our population *especially youth*, bored with what they consider a mundane and uninteresting circumstance, created for them by those in pursuit of money and power.[380] Those with money and power often work together or they work in secret. Every Idea is given to some form of business and neither Politics nor Religion is excluded from the Businessman's sight. The world, at present, is driven by a Salesman's mentality. The sales men are not always wise and are mostly self-interested. Money and power are an important part of any Political-agenda; money makes elections possible, power derives from those who are elected.

---

[380] **Video productions,** which can be viewed almost any time on Television, are examples of prurient nonsense as entertainment, which *perhaps inadvertently in some instances* undermines the Tradition of the Western Soul. Within brief periods of time, various Segments of our population *especially porno queens and rock stars* gnaw away at the roots of all that is in support of who they imagine they are. *This is a consequence of an irreligious attitude prevalent amongst millions of youth.* Vulgar utterance punctuates almost every sentence, as language and manners are profaned by savage behavior, suggesting a return to the jungle. Much is profaned as well in the form and content of the silly, anti-Christian Comedian, who makes a fortune with smut, vulgarity and their assault on decency. Recently women are being added to the assailants; we must consider everyone as being equal. Furthermore, stupid talk shows parade on television, appearing one after another like bats flying from a cave. All these events are punctuated with the sound of music and the noise of the city. The events are interspersed with silly and vulgar commercial messages to sell something; anything from thumbtacks to luxury mobile homes.

Abstract thinking, is based upon certain knowledge acquired over Centuries in Time.
Abstract thinking, is being subverted in deference to a Hollywood type Imagery
Such Imagery given in film is an atavistic and unholy form of imagery.
All this supported by aggressive sound and excessive movement.
It is also often unholy, appealing to evil and to Satan.
This will mesmerize one into a Feeling of ecstasy.
The feeling of ecstasy will be short lived. [381]

Professor Emeritus, Robert Fiedler
May 13, 2013/July 28, 2013/October 15,20013

---

[381]   *Don't Trust your Kids to Disney;* Article.

ADDENDUM A

INSANITY

This is no ordinary discussion on insanity; it is rather a dissection of the culture and people responsible for this, our present condition. I am not a Medical Doctor nor do I have any patients, which I am treating. As an artist and Professor of Art, for over fifty years, I view the world quite differently than most people do. I am also a rational man, a quiet man with a definite curiosity concerning life. I judge my rationality as being that quality, which prevents overly emotional-judgment. My judgment is generally the result of careful and thoughtful consideration of the Issues involved. I am a father and I view immorality as being among other things primarily

Sinful Behavior.

I had been married for fifty-three years to my High School Sweetheart, *the only woman with whom I have ever slept.* She died recently of Cancer. It was the greatest loss I have ever known. I was never interested in sowing wild oats, which may and does lead to many unfortunate results. I certainly never even considered an affair with another woman in violation of a <u>sacred and most holy oath</u>, the marriage vow. This is not, nor has it ever been considered as prudery, rather this is considered by millions as self-control and simply stated: *Decency.* How could any man cheat his wife, mother of his children, for a moment of foul and obscene pleasure? One reads much in the papers and magazines about all of the sleaze-bags that are lecherous however not so much about the good men. Why is *Sin* so interesting whilst *Virtue* is generally unnoticed? There are stories, about children and stray dogs that are compelling; but little about who are good men.

Nonsense is given too much notoriety by the media which consider this to be *cool* rather than what it is: *sinful.* Nonsense will destroy our society and our culture. Sin should be considered and discussed in school beginning in kindergarten. Some of the movie stars have made sin seem acceptable with their multiple partners and carousing. There are certainly decent movie stars as well to who I give my respect and admiration. I have known moronic Types that have bedded down a number of sluttish women. Men who boast of their conquests are *retarded and adolescent* in their lecherous behavior. *Women that oblige them are no better.* Some boastful athletes have made a business of "screwing for obscene pleasure." Everyone is reminded of this by our nitwit Television. Many men secretly wish they could be doing the same. This corrupts the collective consciousness of a group within the totality. Many are somewhat informed of all the indecency and sin as those athletes, wallow through their sinful lives. Why? This is certainly the opposite of goodness.

Pablo Picasso and **Earnest Hemingway,** both considered by millions as being celebrities, were also lechers of the most brutal and insensitive, vain, ignorant and mundane Type. Nevertheless those received praise for their work, which was not any better than the work of many others. Anyone that would pay millions for a Picasso is a Vain Fool. They imagine this will bring them a form of notoriety. *It might do that but so what.* May it have been a way to cover some illicit funds? Much, of Picasso's work was derived others were pirated from other artists. Much of it was vulgar and much was simply nonsense. Some of his art, so called, was disgusting pornography. He is said by some hangers on to have hated and loved women with the greatest passion. In fact he was a demented moron with just a little talent for art. He had great publicity and this is what the people are fed. Much of Hemingway's writing was largely simple-minded. Neither could compare with the "Great Art" from the distant past; Leonardo Da Vinci, Bernini, Michelangelo, St. Thomas, Raphael and many others.

The reputations of both Picasso and Hemingway were products of pumped up mass-market promotion: glitzy and overdone. They were pumped up for a profit to the promoters. The Promoter's were very successful in their selling some bad imagery or a mundane idea. Neither, Picasso or Hemingway, were men of genius. There are many just like them which are why our art forms and literature are often so bad; in fairness there are many good things as well.

Unfortunately many man and women do like to be included in various forms of tainted pleasure. They imagine this will give them status and respect amongst the better informed. *Why is this so?*

Vain and stupid individuals have paid millions for the trash they have been sold as Art. And millions of dollars have been paid for the books authored by small minds. Can one imagine what this has done to the collective psyche of the human race? Fortunately for humanity Picasso and Hemingway are deceased and will create no more nonsense for the kids.

There are many antique shops (so-called) and many other resale and junk shops all over the country. The prices paid for some of this stuff are unbelievable. Nevertheless an excellent cabinet maker of craftsman will have trouble selling his work. The imported stuff is much cheaper so one can have excellence, many imagine for a third of the price or less. The imported stuff is often stapled together but the finishes often appear quite good. The finish is what shows.

Sex is the principal driving force for Humanity and for Civilization as well. One's behavior in respect to sex is a determining factor in regard to reality and the tenor of the Times. Decently inspired, sex is both motivational and satisfying for body and soul. Lustfully inspired sex is debilitating and destructive to the mind and to the body and, most importantly, to the soul.[382] Rape, the extreme sexual and lustful expression, is emotionally and psychologically destructive

---

[382] **The existence of the Soul** must be considered. No one knows exactly what is a Soul however the Idea is prominent. *The Soul it is believed will last beyond the body extending to infinity.* The Soul is a spiritual concept and can sustain in the space moving forward with the eventualities of time. The Soul will exist in part as a portion of any individual's knowing when the person of the soul is known. It is my understanding that this relates although abstractly to the Idea of Father, Son and Spirit: that is the trinity as defined in the Catholic (universal) faith.

as it places the woman in a completely submissive posture against her will; some of this is motivated by narcotics. In consideration of the sexual act, tender tolerance is required of both man and woman; and privacy. Any act so personal is demanding for such attitude and mutual consideration. Youth has not been taught properly and adulthood is full of the blemishes of the poor instruction, which is what we have, generally, in our Public Schools. Thus our schools are no help and they encourage rather than discourage premature and meaningless copulation, this is considered as being simple recreation. Many of our teachers do not understand the truthful meaning of sexual expression and many will/may do more harm than good to a youngster. Some teachers are a bit perverted and this is passed down to the children. Much has been made recently of same sex marriage. This idea is absurd however the Idea has the backing of much of the political establishment. This is unfortunate however true. It is also true that those who prefer a partner of the same sex can do so without deforming the truthful meaning and reason for marriage. Marriage is the meaning of lawful parenthood; the population must be reproduced. The questions concerning birth have to do with the health and quality of the newborn; for many this raises serious questions. *The lower classes generally and some from the upper classes as well, have accepted much of moronic behavior as being O. K.*

What is your opinion?

There are essentially four forms of Insanity that we shall mention briefly; there are a variety of types which we cannot deal with. Below are the four Types which we will mention briefly. This writer is not a Psychiatrist and has little precise information about the forms of what may be considered as a mental disease. What is considered are generalities which are determined by common experience in the observation of various Individuals?

The first consideration is for the individual person: how does he or she respond to reality? Personalities which comprise very common human traits are difficult to judge therefore one must be cautious in the pursuit of any remedial or curative procedures. Given the complexities in the forming of various personalities the possibilities are endless. In some instances youth have been beaten or sexually molested and threatened in ways that must and will work into the formation and/or deformation of the personality. As such they will be carried until death and because of this the individual may become dangerous to himself/herself and to those in close proximity.[383] Any mental illness is difficult to treat and to determine what treatments should be applied, if any.

---

[383] **Prisons are full** of individuals who have been abused and become abusive in response to their treatment. Here is an example of learning from one's own experience: this is what we do. One will learn from what has happened to the self. In fact this should be easy to understand. With our illegitimacy and recreation, certain individuals are given and have all of the most incorrect understandings that are attainable. With women working outside from the home not allowing sufficient time to teach their children so to make them happy and feel loved: *we are damning youth to a lifetime of sorrow.* Many diseases contracted in older adults are no doubt from some form of aggressive behavior or threats during ones youth. Some imagine with a New World Order everything will be just fine. However many will acquire a mental illness of some sort as a response to a too imposing and relentless government or as a cover up for what they have missed.

What treatments might in fact work? There are drugs that can be used for various individual cases however here too there are problems in choosing and applying correct measures. Drugs can only be used in consultation with a clinically informed Doctor, preferably an MD. In addition drugs can be dangerous to one's health in some instances drugs have been fatal. If children are treated with the respect due them from birth they will generally do well and have a wholesome outlook on life and on other individuals. One should work with diligence to make children happy, glad to be alive. It is our belief that this is the best medicine and that happy people are more likely to be successful no matter what they might have to do to earn a living.[384] A few studies have shown that happy people live longer and are more successful in their endeavor. It is quite well known that happy people can withstand tragedy and various negative type personal experiences which can be or are detrimental for the unhappy or improperly informed individual. We have placed too much emphasis on occupations and not enough on the Soul and happiness of the Individual. Happiness can be motivated by others, especially the parents and will row with the maturing person.

Almost any individual will respond to whatever opportunity is placed before him. Thus any response will include and be modified by a shadow from the influence of all the happenings from the past; from early childhood, remembered and forgotten. The brain (somehow) stores as a shadow all past personal incidents for the individual who is involved. Dreams often include situations from a distant past reinforcing the fact that this is true. Such influence cannot be judged accurately and will therefore have an unforeseen and unknown consequence. Presumably such influence will be negative or positive depending upon the nature of the prior experience. Thought clusters will emerge which are a combination of past/present occurrence. Some individuals have horrific experiences in childhood and those will very likely be important in forming the adult's manner of thinking and also their behavior. The results might be damaging however there may be at times a positive consequence from what appeared to be damaging.

The second group is the gang: a group of youngsters with not much to do. _Many of these youth are from broken homes or they do not know who their father is:_ many of the mothers are on welfare and some engage in prostitution. They are often not working and many of them have bad personal habits. Admittedly many are decent and do the best they can which is commendable. Some women have birthed many children: in Detroit one woman is said to have given birth to twenty four (24) children: all of this on welfare; there were different men involved in the inceptions.[385] One such as this should be sterilized so as not to have so many children, _which she cannot possibly support without "stealing" from the decent and more respectable citizens_ in the

---

[384] **Happiness must be gained** one day at a time from birth forward. Adversities are best dealt with by individuals that are happy. This may seem a bit naive however it is true.

[385] **Consider in 1810** there were 1,377,808 black folks in the United States. This number grew to 9,827,763 by 1910 an increase of 7.1328973 times. By 2010 there were 42,020,743 and increase of 4.27757179 times over the population in 1910 and an increase of 30.498257 times over the number given for 1810. Using these numbers as a basis for a calculation there will be 1,262,600,000.00 black folks in the United States by the year 2210; that is one billion, two hundred sixty-two million, six hundred thousand in total. This statement is not meant to be derogatory it is a simple fact and must be considered as part of the population equation.

community including some of her neighbors and friends.[386] It is quite likely that one or more of her children will become a part of some criminal type gang. The child will not have the proper attention as he/she is growing up; this is a cause for many problems. In such instance we are reminded of God and that he has given her so many children and she is so blessed. *She will hide behind a religion which she does not understand and will refuse to give up on the disgusting and illicit sex which she obviously enjoys.* For her the children represent an increase in salary: so why not have more? In fact she is simply stupid and unwise beside which she is a Slut: the worst kind. Who will have the guts to tell her what she is?

Many gang members live in constant fear from others in the gang. There are antagonisms brought about by the inclusion of the sluttish young women, runaways that can be exploited as prostitutes and do favors for the gang members. The favors may be disgusting abominations which subdue the young ladies to perpetual abuse. The young ladies are often doped up and moved from place to place not realizing what is happening to them. The young ladies are told that they like being abused and should therefore continue accepting such abuse. The pretty young ladies are often in more danger than those not so pretty. Some do go straight with the encouragement of a friend or a caring individual: they are the lucky ones. The others wallow until they are allowed to leave the Gang bangers and start a new life. Some die from an overdose or venereal disease, some commit suicide as a last resort, others hang in there and become part of the problem for younger women who become trapped in a life of shame and sin.

Gangs have been exploited by the mass media to sell tickets so as to show the general population the *"other side"* of existence. Such presentations are advertised relentlessly so to encourage viewing: *it doesn't occur to the promoters that they, the promoters, are a great part of our problem.* Why not show decent materials that encourage correct behavioral patterns rather than those, that are debilitating and degenerative. Once again we are advised that America is a free country and many people enjoy such showings of Evil and sinful behaviors. Some enjoy raunchy entertainment because they don't know any better; they have not been properly educated to appreciate what is decent, refined and good. How many do they imagine prefer such junk and the nonsense that is displayed to sell near worthless tickets? There are probably millions who should be properly entertained rather than brutalized for the effect: and it is getting worse if one considers the present content in respect to what was forty or fifty years ago. Beside this even the junk is interrupted for the commercial nonsense played just before an interesting or dramatic portion of a presentation.

We are given all forms of brutality and too much nonsense presumed as entertainment. The Government is quietly building ways to intimidate the honest and decent citizens who may not agree with the Socialistic and Marxist principles that are overcoming much of the world. They encourage alteration of behavior *(they encourage behavioral modification)* with a relentless program, designed to infect everyone.[387] And the government is working so to confuse the Ideas

---

[386] **This type of individual** encourages researchers like Cloward and Piven to develop outrageous schemes to deal with the problem. Our leaders will base some of their thinking on the Cloward and Piven strategy. This will corrupt their thinking because they have been misled.

[387] **Behavioral Modification** consists of intruding on a person's specific behavior and replacing it with the behavior *suitable for the group or for a nation of suppliant citizens*: presumed as being happy for their very small portion.

ROBERT R. FIEDLER

attendant to Christianity. In the meanwhile we are told of the new weapons designed to kill our supposed (imagined) enemies. We are supposed to feel secure and well protected. This is a fact however we have a large country isolated from the rest of the world which will help to keep us secure; for now. Even our President Obama with little experience does not understand the problems or the solutions.[388] We are told by our President Obama that we are not a Christian Nation and should allow all forms of Religion to flourish in the *"land or the free, home of the brave."* This proves he does not understand what Religion is; or does he? Various populations are being moved into the country under Religious pretense which in fact in time will destroy what Christianity has built over four or five centuries of patient and deliberate effort.[389] Freedom will go with our Christianity as we have understood freedom to be.

The third category is the mob at a sporting event or some public happening. Once again individuals learn from each other and youth sees the old folks acting like fools so they do the same in keeping with the tenor of the occasion. Some of such mobs may become vicious when their team is losing and they trample individuals to their death in a showing of blatant ignorance: *certainly all for good clean fun!* What is the difference who wins a game? It is supposed to be a sport for pleasure irrespective of who might win it is rather a show of skill and perhaps bravery. That's all that any game is supposed to be. Games should not be played with the idea that one must win: *games are not warfare although they have been advertised as though this is the case.* At this point one must question the nature and intent of the advertising: millions are made by this means so it is important to understand what one is paying for. The whole Idea of team spirit is made corrupt by the advertising and promotion *"to rake in the bucks"*, **to make money**, the more money the better. Sportsmanship, be damned! And the advertising is often offensive and distracting from the event: the whole conglomerate is corrupt in very subtle ways: however it is

---

[388] **Of the 44 US Presidents:** Obama rated as 5th best president ever! The Democratic Party publicity release said," . . . after a little more than four years, Americans have rated President Obama the 5th best president ever."

* The details according to White House Publicists read like this. **In fact Obama came in as #42!**

* Reagan, Lincoln, and 8 others tied for first. * 15 presidents tied for second.

* 17 other presidents tied for third.* Jimmy Carter came in 4th.* Obama came in fifth.

In fact Obama was rated as number 42. Check out the numbers immediately above!

[389] **Populations** cannot be mixed indiscriminately. Such mixing must be natural and will require several centuries at least if it is to work well. Common sense informs one on how to deal with the various antagonisms that has been acted out on the News. In Europe and Africa, some other places as well, the various groups are at continual conflict encouraged by the weapons gotten from the *(more civilized)* Free World. To solve the problems a few years ago, we had sent Madeleine Albright, a Jewess, who stated that killing five hundred thousand Iranian children might be considered as collateral damage. What do you imagine the Iranian mothers and fathers thought of that? More recently we have sent Hillary Clinton who is attempting to do what most of our populations object to: a one World Government where we give up our sovereignty and gun control. She can't seem to understand that a gun is one's last means of protection from people like her and her husband Bill and, yes, the government. *She also doesn't quite understand that in a few years she will be dead.* Whatever she does will be subordinated to what new fools will do. In Switzerland they require that each citizen has a gun and they instruct them how to use it. They have virtually no crime: the exceptionally wealthy people live there for protection.

240

corrupt. Perhaps the athletes do not understand this. They only hope to be given higher salaries so they can enjoy the comforts of luxury. Many are paid tens of millions for their efforts and performance. This is a subject for a book which I leave to another. Especially minorities are praised for their physical ability; they are heroes in their communities. The bedlam is assisted by the beer: now even the ladies are shown drinking beer from a bottle or a can just like the men; they imagine they are equal. One is told this is freedom to do what one likes: many women some surmise would like to be men they have lost their self respect as a woman.[390]

We the people comprise the fourth category. This is the nation composed of perhaps millions of individuals that are manipulated and therefore act in harmony. They are told this is a good thing and they are very patriotic and willful in their compliance. In time they can be convinced of almost anything; who are their enemies and who are their friends. Friends and enemies change from generation to generation. The youth are dressed in a uniform and sent to kill the imagined enemies even as it is certain that they could never have known them. This is called Patriotism which is a wonderful thing given the correct understanding. The word Patriot should not be used as a cover for murder and brutality. *War is murder and brutality.*

The death penalty is certainly a deterrent however it is rarely used: *this is because we imagine ourselves to be a Christian Nation*. Some of the new prisons are like a country club in appearance and the inmates are given all manner of life support: games, good food, computers, gymnasiums and many other amenities: the food is prepared for them and is better than they might obtain on their own. The death penalty is certainly brutal however it is also quite effective in deterring criminals: it would certainly reduce the costs of keeping someone like Ed Guine (deceased) and Charles Monson's (still living) in jail until death; this could be twenty or perhaps seventy years. Instead of the death penalty we provide the criminals with computers, decent living conditions and allow them to study law: some day they may even free themselves with their knowledge. They will become more adept in the Law than their captors. There are many good men in law enforcement risking their lives to protect the citizens however our life and death equation seems to favor the ill doer as it in fact punishes the good guy who may have killed a criminal; *a menace to everyone on the street.* All of this is witnessed by youth who learn best from examples. We are in a state of wonderment. We cannot execute a known killer or brutal rapist nevertheless we send armies to kill tens of thousands of women and children in other nations. What in fact does this mean? How and why are the circumstances formed as they are? Who determines if we should fight or be a bit patient? Who is making the most money on all of

---

[390] **Humanity could not exist without women.** They are the stronger of the sexes and give birth to the next generation. Women control the future by giving birth; this should be easily understood. Some wealthy women have given the idea of gestation to a surrogate mother who is implanted with the fertilized egg. This of course is as absurd as it can get however they don't want to spoil their shape, that can be done by eating the wrong foods and drinking too much liquor: and there is partying and excessive and illegitimate sex that will help to do this. Some women at present are showing off their enlarged abdomen at parties and various affairs: modesty seems not to be a consideration that's only for the prudes as one can imagine. And of course many of the *"now generation"* don't bother to marry they just shack up for convenience and a naughty thrill. They don't understand that marriage is a very civilized state especially when it continues until death that lovers are parted. We realize this is judgmental however it is imagined that history should teach one something.

our recent wars? We imagined and are taught by the hypocrite that killing is wrong: it matters who is being killed. All of this ties in with and relates to the "Will to Power" and to the idea and belief that some individual or groups are superior to all others.

What is this telling us? Do we listen? Do we understand?

Immoral behavior, by Christian standards, is observed by some youth from babyhood on: they learn from adults and from there parent. There is much talk about Racism however no one really wants to face the issue publicly rather they keep their thoughts to themselves. One can imagine that everyone is a bit Racist: they are proud of who they are as well they should or might be. However the issue has taken on *Political meaning that is mostly bad* in spite of the hypocritical gestures that are somehow related to the issue. If one does speak up he\she is *"branded"* as being a racist and shamed before their peers. Eustice Mullins (now deceased) was one of the brightest and most perceptive men of this century. He was considered a racist because he spoke the truth on many issues.[391] The shame is really artificial, although not recognized or admitted as such. It is manufactured, by a liberal elite making a living off a System; it is *"a System gone mad"*. Common sense can deduce that such as this "System" is the cause of much of our illegal behavior and many of our vicious crimes. Many of our Politicians and law makers are *"in It"* for the money that can be made on each deal and they are attempting to acquire a name for themselves. With a big name they might charge a bit more. Do they *"give a damn"* about the Laws; many do not; they exploit them for their own vain and often immoral purpose.

One can inquire on the broad subject of insanity on their own. There are thousands of examples that one can consider; one need only be interested to do so. Such study will be very illuminating and it might surprise even the most stubborn of individuals.

---

[391] **Mullins, Eustice;** The World Order, Our Secret Rulers. (Ezra Pound Inst, Staunton, VA. 24401, 2nd. Ed. 1992).

ADDENDUM B

GOD THE INFINITE POWER OF PRESENCE. WHAT DOES INFINITE MEAN?

Consider, once again

Who is our God?

God is the Infinite Power of Presence
God is the Infinite Power of now and then
His is The Existential And all enduring Reality

God is trip ret present in all places at all times
Also keep in mind; He is as, the enduring Idea:
God, created all that is, was and will be
He will create whatever else may be
He is the idea and the consequence
He is the will and reason
He is all THAT IS

God is supreme
God is absolute
And, God is Omnipotent
He is first amongst all things
And also Whatever else, may ever be
Nothing is beyond nothing is above him

His was and is the word

Emeritus Professor, Robert Fiedler
January 14, 2013

ADDENDUM C

EIGHT MARKS OF FASCIST POLICY

John T. Flynn, like other members of the Old Right, was disgusted by the irony that what he saw, almost everyone else chose to ignore. In the fight against authoritarian regimes abroad, he noted, the "United States had adopted those forms of government at home, complete with price controls, rationing, censorship, executive dictatorship, and even concentration camps for whole groups considered to be unreliable in their loyalties to the state." (Lew Rockwell).

After reviewing this long history, John T. Flynn proceeds to sum up with a list of eight points he considers to be the main marks of the fascist state. Seven of the points, are listed hereunder.

(I include this only for the reader's information and for his/her careful consideration. One need not agree with everything written however it is certainly interesting and compelling of careful and deliberate thought. The elements fall within certain "thought clusters" which I have mentioned in this writing. Reality is so complex that it is difficult to understand in respect to both reason and objectives. Often the objectives remain obscure; only those on the cleverly guarded inside understand the real meaning and significance of what happens.)

Remember, we're in somewhat of a "Disneyland"; that is the Land of make-believe.

Point 1. The government is totalitarian; it acknowledges no restraint on its powers. It suggests that *the US political system can be described as totalitarian.* This is a shocking remark that most people would reject. But they can reject this characterization only so long as they happen not to be directly ensnared in the state's web. If they become so, they will quickly discover that *there are indeed no limits to what the state can do.*" This can happen boarding a flight, driving around in your hometown, or having your business run afoul of some government agency. In the end, you must obey or be caged like an animal or killed. In this way, no matter how much you may believe that you are free, all of us today are but one step away from being completely controlled.

As recently as the 1990s, Clinton seemed to suggest that there were some things that his administration could not do. Today I cannot recall any government official pleading the constraints of law or the constraints of reality to what can and cannot be done. All of healthcare is regulated, but so is every bit of our food, transportation, clothing, household products, and even private relationships. There are hundreds of regulations.

Mussolini himself put his principle this way: *"All within the State, nothing outside the State, nothing against the State.* He also said: "The keystone of the Fascist doctrine is its conception of the State, of its essence, its functions, and its aims. For Fascism the State is absolute, individuals and groups relative. *I submit to you this is the prevailing ideology in the U. S.*

Point 2. Government is in fact a de facto dictatorship based on the leadership principle.

I wouldn't say that we truly have a dictatorship of one man in this country, but *we do have a form of dictatorship of one sector of government over the entire country*. The executive branch has spread dramatically and over the last century it has become somewhat of a joke to speak of checks and balances. What the kids learn in their civics class has nothing to do with any real and truthful understanding of reality.

Point 3. Omitted

Point 4. Producers are organized into cartels which in the way may be considered as syndicalism. Syndicalism is not usually how we think of our current economic structure. But remember syndicalism means economic control by the producers. Capitalism is different. It places by virtue of market structures control in the hands of the consumers. The only question for syndicalism is which producers are going to enjoy political privilege; one or another.

In the case of the United States, *in the last three years, we've seen giant banks, pharmaceutical firms, insurers, car companies, Wall Street banks and brokerage houses, and quasi-private mortgage companies enjoying vast privileges at our expense; at the expense of the governed of "we the people".*

They have all joined with the state in living a parasitical existence at our expense.

This is also an expression of the Syndicalism idea, and it has cost the US economy untold trillions and sustained an economic depression by preventing the post-boom adjustment that markets would otherwise dictate.

Point 5. Economic planning is based on the principle of autarky. Autarky is the name given to an idea of economic self-sufficiency. Mostly this refers to the economic self-determination of the nation-state. The nation-state must be geographically huge in order to support rapid economic growth for a large and growing population. This was and is the basis for fascist expansionism. Without expansion, the state dies. *(I mention this in my writing in a plea for a smaller and less powerful State. When the State is kept small it is controllable however when it expands further expansion always seems necessary. Ultimately the State is the only compelling player; one then will have a **Dictatorship**.*

Point 6. Government sustains economic life through spending and borrowing.

This point requires no elaboration because it is no longer hidden. There was stimulus 1 and stimulus 2, both of which are so discredited that stimulus 3 will have to adopt a new name: call it the American Jobs Act.

With a prime-time speech, Obama argued in favor of this program with some asinine economic analysis. He mused about how is it that people are unemployed at a time when schools, bridges, and infrastructure need repairing. He ordered that supply and demand come Hello? The schools, bridges, and infrastructure that Obama refers to are all built and maintained by the state. That's why they are falling apart. And the reason that people don't have jobs is because the state has made it too expensive to hire them. This is not complicated.

Point 7. Militarism is a mainstay of government spending. Have you ever noticed that the military budget is never seriously discussed in policy debates? _The United States spends more than most of the rest of the world combined._ And yet to hear our leaders talk, the United States is just a tiny commercial republic that wants peace but is constantly under some threat from the other side of the world. They would have us believe that we all stand naked and vulnerable. ***The whole thing is a ghastly lie. The United States is a global military empire and the main threat to peace around the world today.***

To visualize US military spending as compared with other countries is truly shocking. One bar chart you can easily look up shows the US trillion-dollar-plus military budget as a skyscraper surrounded by tiny huts. As for the next highest spender, _China spends 1/10th as much as we do._

Point 8. Military spending may have imperialist aims. Ronald Reagan used to claim that his military buildup was essential to keeping the peace. The history of US foreign policy just since the 1980s has shown that this is wrong. We've had one war after another, waged by the United States against noncompliant countries; with creation of more client states and colonies.

US military strength has led not to peace but the opposite. It has caused most people in the world to regard the United States as a threat, and it has led to unconscionable wars on many countries. Wars of aggression were defined at Nuremberg as crimes against humanity.

Obama was supposed to end this. He never promised to do so, but his supporters all believed that he would. Instead, he has done the opposite. He has increased troop levels, entrenched wars, and started new ones. In reality, he has presided over a warfare state just as vicious as any in history. The difference this time is that the Left is no longer criticizing the US role in the world. In that sense, Obama is the best thing ever to happen to the warmongers and the military-industrial-complex.

———

Professor Emeritus, Robert Fiedler
July 12, 2013

ADDENDUM D

BRIEF HISTORY

The following information is taken from the Internet: This is an addendum which deals with the soul and what it is. There is also some history in evidence given the various countries listed.

Each country/culture has a different understanding however there are similarities one to another and some to our own. By immortality is ordinarily understood the doctrine that the human soul will survive death, continuing in the possession of an endless conscious existence.

Together with the question of the existence of God, it forms the most momentous issue with which philosophy has to deal. It belongs primarily to rational or metaphysical psychology and the philosophy of religion, though it comes also into contact with other branches of philosophy and some of the natural sciences.

Following is a brief outline of some of the main Religious beliefs. There appears to be somewhat of a progression involved. There are many religions and one is given free will and may decide which one is proper and most effective.

Egypt: (3050 to about 300 BC) "Offerings of provisions of all sorts to the spirits of the departed, elaborate funeral ceremonies, and the wonderfully skilful mummification of the bodies of the deceased, all bear witness to the strength of the Egyptians' convictions of the reality of the next life."

China: "In China worship of ancestors is evidence of belief."

Japan: "Similarly in Japan, whatever may be the genuine logical theory of the soul in the religion of Shintoism."

Judaism: "That early Jewish history shows that the Hebrew nation did not believe in a future life is sometimes stated."

Greece: "The Greeks seem to have been among the first to attempt systematic philosophical treatment of the question of immortality."

Christianity: "With the birth of the Christian religion the doctrine of immortality took up quite a new position in the world."

"Modern thought has not added much to the philosophy of immortality. Descartes" conception of the soul would lend itself to some of the Platonic arguments."

"Justification for immortality: As we have already observed, the immortality of the human soul is one of the most fundamental tenets of the Christian Religion."[392]

---

[392] **For a more complete understanding** with expanded references see the Internet.

1. ***Referring to the Bible*** *we are informed that there will be a last day. This is a difficult question to ponder for all that do not believe in the Bible. Nevertheless, every single living being will come to his last day as a human person: the day of death. There is much dissent and doubt on the part of many regarding exactly what does this mean. When we die what happens afterward? Is the content of our mind and being extinguished? Present understanding suggests that there is an infinite space and that our thought content and Spirit will become one with the Infinite Space. No one knows exactly what this means; there are many Ideas about this. If God is as all space than after death the presumption is we might become one in being with the Father.*

2. ***Brown, Walt:*** *Creation: in the Beginning: Compelling Evidence for Creation and the Flood. This belief will find great criticism from some other Christians. There have been many heretics, some of which have deserted the Catholic Faith and began a new religion. Martin Luther is prominent among such dissidents. Nevertheless most Lutherans are very decent individuals and they most certainly are Christians in most every way. (**See the Internet** under heresies).*

3. ***a Summation*** *is understood to be a complex mixture of all past incidents, a complex combination, which is very difficult to understand. This is especially true since no person knows for certain what the important elements are and why they must be considered. <u>Almost all rhetorical considerations meet with this problem sooner or later.</u> When individuals move from one continent to another they maintain their thinking which will thereafter be affected differently as their mind and manners develop. After a period of time they will have a distinctive past-present formed individuality. Each individual will be unique: it can be no other way.*

———————————————

Professor Emeritus, Robert Fiedler
July 12, 2013

ADDENDUM E

HOW DOES ONE FORM HIS/HER BELIEFS?

Where does a Belief come from?

Beliefs are very significant in the acts of any individual. Some men will kill others over what they believe. This understanding in fact lies beneath all forms of conflict, including ultimately War. Belief is difficult to trace and more difficult to understand. There are many elements that make up any system of beliefs; *beliefs exist as a part of a system of thought.* The individual may not even be aware of his own *"Thought System".* All elements are somehow related however not well understood in their peculiar relationships; the peculiarity is a matter of individual thinking and thought patterns or what I call *thought clusters.* When a prominent or powerful individual has a strong belief this may affect the lives and activities of millions of individuals. If the belief is decent the results will be good. If the belief is evil or perverted the results will follow evil or perversion. It can be no other way. *This is precisely why giant scale is generally wrong; better one should deal with smaller entities to keep things more nearly in order.* What is smaller is more easily understood and controlled because it is easier to assess all of the elements.

The imagination is an important element in the forming of a Belief. The imagination may be the most important component in the structures of thought that are developed and continue throughout one's life. In some other places I have referred to *"pieces of thought"* since thoughts form as a continuum within the mind; they are divided in time by various intrusive elements. *The intrusive elements vary widely and are introduced as singularities however they combine with the existing mind's content forming more unique and personal ways.* The result is a complex array. Within the matrix of entering elements are light, sound, movement and images of whatever is apparent to sight and mental *"wanderings"* which are elements from the existing minds content. Such images are difficult to understand. Again, some of such imagery may turn up in a dream. *All of these factors add up to making the individual's mind content absolutely unique* and whatever acts follow will be especially unique; as acts they are absolute. This is what we understand as life being what it should be. This fact refutes that there are no absolutes; *every individual is an absolute and singular being.* Individuals inhabit different bodies, are born at different times and are found in various places. There are superficial similarities however they are of less importance than time and place.

The number of elements, affecting individual human existence and belief is countless. They are also limited in duration and accepted in various ways by the receiving individual. How they are accepted will determine the effect that they will have on the individual who accepts them and on others who are in contact with her/him. One's personality is an important factor in determining how any fact or idea will function. We have all known of or heard of temper tantrums, such as this are a consequence of how information is received. One can learn to control this and indeed must do so, for his own good and the good of others. A temper tantrum is related to impatience and one's feeling for himself. Impatience shows lack of Humility; **_Humility_** is a cardinal Virtue. A temper tantrum may also have nutritional origins in that the wrong food is being eaten.[393]

A feeling of self respect is an important element in any personality. At present we witness many elements that work against this understanding and the feeling of self respect.[394] That feeling of self respect which may be apparent is often gained for the wrong reasons. Also familial love is important; love of both mother and father for their child and the love of the children for their parents are very significant. This may be difficult to assess. One should also love others truthfully. The result of such truthful love or lack of it will last for one's lifetime. _Real and devoted love is absolutely essential to the human race,_ fundamental in the development of the personality which is so important throughout one's life. People who love and are loved seem to develop the most positively natural personality.

Parents should be the source of correct information and knowledge for their children; this is how it should be. By this means a culture and Civilization is able to continue and to develop. _This is one factor why Tradition is so important;_ Tradition can be and is generally understood. Each child can add something to the total and have an important place in the scheme of things. When one cares for and is teaching his children what is appropriate and correct the child will grow to a reasonable maturity without all of _"the hang-ups"_ that are obvious at this time. At present the Television programming that is encouraged works against the child's being able to understand the truthful meaning of love; the _"hang-ups"_ are often justified or made to appear as humor. A book, perhaps many can be written on the hang-ups; I leave this as a call to others. What is learned in the home in the first one to seven years will be carried as part of one's beliefs and understandings for a lifetime.

---

[393] Many years ago I read an interesting tract on food and nutrition, I do not remember the source however I do remember the message. He Idea was it is best that one should eat only what is grown within one hundred miles of where one was born. This thought bears against all of our present habits, beliefs manners and customs. Some ancient people were very healthy; perhaps this is why. And our foods are processed too much and have too much sugar and various forms of fillers to give them shelf life, weight and bulk and to make them pretty. Food is best right from the plant however we have made too much of food preparation as a national and international means of making a profit. The profit is too often the only reason for making the alterations in the food.

[394] Young women especially are often placed in positions which encourage the loss of self-respect and the forced acceptance of some moronic man. They are led to be prostitutes and worse; many are murdered as a consequence of their misunderstanding of the meaning of sex. One can view the news reports on TV for better understanding.

252

There is a conflict between decent reality and presumed or imagined Reality which is the hall mark of advertising and various forms of *money-grubbing.* Some of our movies are destructive in that they teach youth how to be EVIL. The fantastic movies with strange large creatures that devour people and other creatures are seemingly destructive on the spirit and tenor of Time. They are unwise productions. They glorify what is not real and this is given as entertainment. Many individuals with a strange and demented Idea present this to all who might watch. *One wonders how many mass murders are related to what is seen as entertainment that is debilitating and destructive.* One cannot dismiss the possible consequences of such material on the mind of the individual or on the community. Beside this many movie stars often set the worst possible personal example for youth, adults as well, with their graphic showings of sex, violence and immorality. Beside which many are addicted to drugs and other somewhat suspect activities. And the actors rake in millions for their often very sleazy efforts. It is believed by many that the movies, comic books and pornography are detrimental for millions. All of this nonsense finds its way into the minds of millions and is part of the collective form of psychic space and of what may be called a *"collective-neurosis".* The *"collective-neurosis"* is a psychic phenomena and spills out on everyone; who is somehow aware of what may be happening. The awareness is not logical and is more inadvertent than truthfully known and understood.

Armies and warfare have placed millions of young men in a bad situation. They are sent to other countries and have no opportunity to meet there kind, a decent and loving woman to marry and with whom to have a family. Many children are born without the father, the father may have been killed or the father may be a stranger. The men, some not all, are destined to use the *"prostitute"* for what is more natural, healthy and beneficial to the married man and woman. During the Second World War it is said that about ten percent of the American men suffered from a venereal disease. One need not wonder what the origin of such disease was. The women were often placed in the most unfortunate situation and prostitution was seemingly a reasonable alternative; a prostitute could always earn a bit of moneyy. During a War one can imagine that those involved did not have proper sanitation or medical care. Prostitution is always sinful however it is easy to understand; this is Reality.

An inadvertent knowing is what allows or provides for the making of a group; one way or another. This is an important understanding given the gang violence and screaming at an athletic event. It is important in the forming of an attitude which condones fighting as a means to solve a problem. When men are stupid they will revert, refer to a primitive type solution, to solve what are certainly insoluble problems.[395] We call this War. No war is intelligent however those who invent the JUNK used for fighting Wars are very intelligent. They are now making millions for their efforts. It should be obvious to everyone that this is *"the wrong way to go"* for any nation or any people. Much of the World Economy depends on the use and sale of this weaponry. The Bankers love the Wars from which they profit immensely. It is sad to say however given the information I have America seems to be leading the pack. It is alleged that the United States

---

[395] This brings to the fore the role of the Politician, and near-endless contemplation concerning the most basic and often mundane thoughts.

spends ten times as much on developing its fighting force than China which has five times the number of people. We are not certain that this is true; what is truth? Ultimately such hardware may destroy the World; the fools imagine they will be somehow spared. Thus what is written in the several paragraphs above should be taken very seriously.

—⁓∾◦◠◠◠◦∾⁓—

Professor Emeritus, Robert Fiedler
May 17, 2013/July 28, 2013.

Consider this book to be included in your library.

Some other books written by this author

Money Murder Madness; Copyright 2006
ISBN # 13:978-0-595-41500-7 (pbk)
ISBN # 13-978-0-595-85849-7 (ebk)

Musings I; Copyright 2008
Greed Love and Indignation
ISBN: # 978-0-595-42901-1 (pbk)
ISBN: # 978-0-595-87238-1 (ebk)

In Honor of Geri, Musings II; Copyright 2010
ISBN: 978-1-4502-3009-4 (pbk)
ISBN: 978-1-4502-3010-0 (ebk)

The Eve of Annihilation; Date released 9-15-2011
ISBN:978-1-4620-3112-2-SC
ISBN-978-1-4620-3113-6-OE

Apocalypse in Paradise; 2012
(Soon to be published)

The books can be purchased at Barnes and Noble World-wide
Or directly from the Publishers i*Universe 1663 Liberty Drive,
Bloomington, IN 47403 www.iuniverse.com*
_Or_
The Destruction of America; Copyright 2009
LC # 2009903271
ISBN # 978-1-4415-2629-8 Hard cover
ISBN # 978-1-4415-2628-1 Soft cover

The book can be purchased from
Xlibris, 1-888-795-4274 w*ww.Xlibris.com*
Orders @ Xlibris.com

Fantastic Sketch Book 2013
Printer, Image Plus
Telephone # 1 424-727-5200

BIBLIOGRAPHY

Adler, Mortimer. Ten Philosophical Mistakes, Mac Millan Pub., NewYork, Collier Macmillan, London. ISBN # 0-02-500330-5.

Alexander, Anthony F. Rev. _College Apologetics,_ Henry Regnery Co., Chicago, ©1954. _Nihil Obstat._ Very Rev. Edward L. Hughes, O. P. Censor Librorum. Imprimatur, Samuel Cardinal Stritch, D. D. Archiepiscopus Chicagiensis, Oct. 13, 1953.

Allen, Gary, _NoneDare Call It Conspiracy._ Publication Date: December 1, **1971** | ISBN-10: 0945001290 | ISBN-13: 978-0945001294.

Aquinas, Thomas, Saint., _Summa Theologica_ 1, 14, 13, ad. 1, Trans, Anton C. Pegis (New York, Random House, 1944), Vol. One.

Architectural Digest, Oct. 2002. _One Central Park Tower, N. Y._

Barabanov, Evgeny, _From Under the Rubble,_ (Little Brown & Co., Boston, Toronto, 1975).

Barzun, Jacques, _The House of Intellect._ January 1, 1959.

Barzun, Jacques, _From Dawn to Decadence, 1500 to the Present_. Harper Collins Publishers Inc., 10 East 53rd Street. New York, NY 10022. ISBN 0-06-017586-9.

Bearden, T. E., Col., _Aids, Biological Warfare,_ Tesla Book Co., P. O. Box 1649, Greenville, TX 75401. ISBN # 0-914119-04-4.

Beaty, John Ph. D. _The Iron Curtain over America_. Chestnut Mountain Books, Barboursville, Virginia, 1968. © 1951, John Beaty. First Printing 1951.

Benson, Ivor, _The Zionist Factor._ Millennium Edition, GSG Associates, P. O. Box 590. San Pedro, CA 90733. USA. ISBN: 0-945001-63-0. Pp. 25-26-27.

Blumfield, Samuel, _Is Public Education Necessary._ Barnes and Noble, 1981 edition.

Bondi, Herman, _The Universe at Large._ Publisher: Garden City, N.Y., Anchor Books. Language: English Butler, _**The Lives of the Saints.**_ **Benziger Brothers Ed.** Also note: **Butler's Lives of the Saints (4 Volume Set)** by Herbert J. Thurston and Donald Attwater (Jan 2, 1956)

Carlson, Elof Alex, _Human Genetics,_ (D. C. Heath and Company, U. S. A., 1984, Ch. 6, Mendel's Laws and Genetic Disorders).

Carpenter, Lynn, Editor, _The Fleet Street Letter,_ Vol. 67, Issue 7, Special Forecast Issue 2004. P. O. Box 925, Frederick, MD 21705-9913.

Cathey, Bruce _The Bridge to Infinity._ Quark Enterprises LTD, 1983, 158 Shaw Road, and Brookfield Press, P. O. Box 1201, Auckland, New Zealand. ISBN 0-86467-024-9.

Chang, Matthias, _Future Fast Forward, The Zionist, Anglo-American Meltdown._ First American Editions, 2006, American Free Press, Washington D. C. 20063.

Clark, Hulda Regehr, Ph. D., N. D. _The Cure for All Cancers._ The New Century Press, 1055 Bay Blvd., Suite C, Chula Vista, CA 91911.

The New Century Press, 1055 Bay Blvd., Suite C, Chula Vista, CA 91911. ISBN# 1-890035-01-7.

Clement, Marcel, _Christ and Revolution._ Transated by Alice von Hildebrand. Arlington House, Publishers, New Rochelle, New York. Copyright © 1974, Arlington House. ISBN # 0-87000-233-

Collison, Joseph, Writer and Director, Office of Pro Life Activities, Norwich, CN. *Abortion in America: Legal and Unsafe.* The New Oxford Review Magazine, June 2000. Pp. 33-35.

Coughlin, Charles E. Rev. *Money, Questions and Answers.* Pub. The Radio League of the Little Flower, Royal Oak, MI. © 1937, The Radio League of the Little Flower,

Corti, Count Egon Caesar, *The Rise of the House of Rothschild.* Western Islands, Publisher, Belmont, Massachusetts, 02178. © 1828 The Cosmopolitan Book Corporation.

Cusa, Nicholus, *On the Quadrature of the Circle.* Fidelio, Magazine, Vol. X, #2, Summer 2001. Publisher, Schiller Inst., Inc., P. O. Box 20244, Wash., D C., 20041-0244. Ed. Wm F. Wirtz, Jr.

Dall, Curtis, *My Exploited Father in Law.*

Diamond, Michael, Bro., *Creation and Miracles.* Most Holy Family Monastery, 4425 Schneider Road. Fillmore, NY 14735.

Disraeli, Benjamin, later Lord Beaconsfield,

Dillon, George E., Mgr. DD., *Grand Orient, Freemasonry Unmasked.* Dublin, M. H. Gill & Son, Upper Sackville Street. London and New York: Burns and Oates, 1885. The Brother's Publishing Society, London, July 27, 1950. GSG & Associates, 2000, P. O. Box 6448, Rancho Palos Verdes, CA 90734.

Dodd, Bella V. *School of Darkness. The record of a life and of a conflict between two faiths.* The Devin Adaire Co., 23 E. 26th. Street, New York, N. Y. LC # 54-10204.

Douglas, William Campbell II, M. D., *Aids, The End of Civilization.*

Engle, Randy, *Sex Education, the Final Plague.* Publisher, Human Life International, 7845-E Airpark Road, Gaithersburg, Maryland, November 1989. ISBN # 1-55922-025-2.

Eugene IV, Pope *The Council of Florence.*

Fahey, Dennis, Rev., C.S.Sp., D.D., D.Ph., *The Kingship of Christ and Organized Naturalism.* Christian Book Club of America, P.O Box 900566, first published June 1943. Reprint October 1993, Palmdale, CA 93590.

Fahey, Dennis, Rev., C.S.Sp., D.D., D.Ph., *The Mystical Body of Christ in the Modern World,* Third Ed.

Fahey, Dennis, Rev., C.S.Sp., D.D., D.Ph. *Secret Societies and the Kingship of Christ,* Christian Book Club of America. Pub. 1928, republished 1994.

Flynn, John T., *The Roosevelt Myth,* (The Devin-Adair Company, New York, Copyright, July 1948, eighteenth Ed., July, 1953).

Freeman, Richard & Tucker, Arthur, *Wal-mart Is Not a Business, It's an Economic Disease.* From, Executive Intelligence Review. Nov. 14, 2003, Vol. 30 No. 44.

Freeman, Richard, *Reverse the 35 Year Devastation of America's Industry and Labor Force,* Executive Intelligence Review, March 21. 2003, Vol. 30 #11.

Frost, S. E.Jr. Ph. D. (Then) Assistant Professor of Education, Brooklyn College. *Great Philosophers.* Barnes and Noble. © 1942, Doubleday and Company, Inc., Sixth Printing

Gerber, Richard, MD., *Vibrational Medicine, The # 1 Handbook of Subtle-Energy Therapies.* Third Edition. ©2001, Richard Gerber. ISBN 1-879181-58-4. Bear and Company, Rochester, Vermont, 05767.

Gregory XVI, Pope

Grand Prix, Don, Col. USA Ret. *Barbarians Inside the Gates, The Black Book of Bolshevism.* GSG & Assoc. Publishers. P. O. Box 590, San Pedro, California. ISBN # 0-945001-79-7. First Printing 2000.

Hackett, Ken, Executive Director, Catholic Relief Services. *Letter of appeal, dared October 2002.*

Hadrian I, **Pope,** *Second Council of Nicaea, 787:*

Haksell, Grace, *Prophacy and Politics, Militant Evangelists on the Road to Nuclear War.* First Published, Lawrence Hill and Co. USA, 1986. Second Printing by Veritas Publishing Comany, Pty. Ltd. P. O. Box 20, Bullsbrook, Western Australia. Distributed by GSG Assoc., P. O. Box 590, San Pedro, CA 90733. ISBN # 0-945001-98-3.

Heilbron, J. L. *The Sun in The Church, Cathedrals as Solar Observatories.* Harvard University Press, Cambridge, Massachusetts, London, England. ©1999, by the President and Fellows of Harvard Col. ISBN # 0-674-85433-0.

Hoppe, Donald J., *How to Invest in Gold Stocks and avoid the Pitfalls.* ©1972 Arlington House, New Rochelle, NY. LC # 72-77641. ISBN 0-87000 178-7.

Intelligence Publications, *Who Rules America, Nature and Power of Conspiracy.* Extract: On Target 10-24 March 2001 issue. Donald A. Martin, Editor. Published by intelligence pub, 26 Meadow Lane, Sudbury, Suffolk, England.

Johnson, Paul, *Intellectuals.* Harper and Rowe Publishers. 10 E. 53rd. Street, New York, NY 10022. © 1988, Paul Johnson. ISBN # 0-06-016050-0. LC# 88-45518.

Jones, Michael, **Ph. D**. *Fidelity Magazine* (Issue,? #, date)

Jones, Michael, Ph. D. *Degenerate Moderns, Modernity as Rationalized Sexual Misbehavior,* © 1993, Ignatius Press, San Francisco. ISBN 0-89870-447-2. Lc # 92-75406.

Jones, Michael, Ph. D. *Monsters from the Id, Part III., The Monster travels from Germany to America,* (Spence Pub., Co., Dallas, Texas 75207.

Jones, E. Michael Ph. D. *Libido Dominandi, Sexual Liberation and Political Control.* St. Augustine's Press, South Bend, Indiana. © 2000 E. Michael Jones. ISBN # 1-890318-37-x.

Jones, E. Michael, Ph. D. *Philadelphia Delenda Est:The Republican Convention and the Reality Tour.* Culture Wars Magazine. Sept. 2000, Vol. 19, No. 9. Pp. 28-41.

Kaufman, Walter, *Nietzsche, Philosopher, Psycologist, Antichrist.* Meridian Books, Inc. New York. First Published 1956. Fourth Printing December 1959. USA. LC # 56-6572.

Knupffer, George, *The Struggle for World Power, Revolution and Counter Revolution*. 4th ed./, 1986. ISBN # 0-85172-703-4.

Knuth, E. C. *The Empire of the City, The Jekyll/Hyde Nature of the British Government,* 1983 Edition, The Noontide Press, P. O. Box 1248, Torrance, California 90505.

Koestler, Arthur, *The Thirteenth Tribe.* Khazar Empire and its Heritage, Pub. Macmillan. September 9, 1977.
Paperback 224 pages. English.ISBN-10: 0330250698. ISBN-13: 978-0330250696.

Kramer, Father Paul, B. Ph., S. T. B., M. Div., S. T. L. (Cand.) *The Mystery of Iniquity,* Unmasking Iniquity Assoc., Liberty Lake, Washington, U. S. A. St. Catherines, Ontario, Canada.

Kuehnelt-Leddihn, Erik Maria, Ritter von, *Leftism, From de Sade and Marx to Hitler and Marcuse.* Arlington House 1974. ISBN #0-87000-143-4.

LaRouche, Lyndon H., *What is God, That Man Is In His Image?* (Fidelio Magazine, March 18,1995).

LaRouche, Lyndon, *Dope Inc.* Publication Date: **June 1992** | ISBN-10: **0943235022** | ISBN-13: **978-0943235028** | Edition: **3**rd

LaRouche, Lyndon, *The Essential Fraud of Leo Strauss,* Executive Intelligence Rev. Mar. 21, 03, Vol. 30 No. 11.

Larson, Martin Ph. D. *The Federal Reserve & Our Manipulated Dollar.* The Devin-Adair Co., Old Greenwich, CONN, 1975.

Lonergan, Bernard, *Method in Theology,* The Seabury Press. Winston press, Inc. 430 Oak Grove, Minneapolis, Minnesota. LC #78-68581. ISBN 0-8164-2204-4.

Lucaks, George, *The Remembered Past.* On History. Released March 31, 2005: Paperback. ISBN-13 9781932236286 / 978-1-932236-28-6: ISBN 932236287 / 932236-28-7

Mailer, Norman, *Picasso, Portrait of Picasso as a young man. An Interpretive Biography,* Warner Books Ed., Copyright 1995 by Norman Mailer, Warner Books, Inc., 1271 Avenue of the Americas, New York 10020. ISBN # 0-446-67266-1.

Malthuse, Robert Thomas. *Principles of Political Economy, Considered.* 1821, 431 pages 1836, 516 pages. Original documents, Oxford University, England.

Manifold, Didirae, *Karl Marx, a Prophet of Our Times.* G. S. G. & Associates, Publishers. P. O. Box 6448, Eastview Station, Rancho Palos Verdes, CA 90734. ISBN# 0-945001-00-2.

Markoe, John P., Rev., S. J., *The Triumph of the Church, accompanied by an Historical Chart., 21 st. Edition.* (A Catholic Viewpoint Pub., Scafati Printing Co., Inc., 1205 Whitlock Ave.,. Bronx, NY. 10459).

McMasters, R. E., *the Reaper, Newsletter.*

Mechizedek, Drunvaldo, *The Ancient Secret of the Flower of Life, Vol.II.* Light Technologies Publishing, P. O. Box 3540, Flagstaff, AZ 86336. ISBN # 1-1891824-21-X.

Mendelsoh, Robert, MD., *How to Raise Healthy Children in Spite of Your Doctor.* Contemporary Books, Inc. 180 N. Michigan Avenue, Chicago, IL 60601. Copyright ©1984. ISBN 0-8092-5808-0.

Meyerowitz, Steve, *Wheat Grass, Natures Finest Medicine, The complete Guide to Using Grasses to Revitalize Your Health.* (Sproutman Publications, Great Barrington, Mass., 01230).

Michili, Vincent, DD. SJ. *The Antichrist,* Roman Catholic Books, P. O. Box 225, Harrison, N. Y., Jan. 24, 1981.

Mitchell, Richard, *The Leaning Tower of Babel, and other affronts from the Underground Grammarian.* Little, Brown & Com. Boston, Toronto. Richard Mitchell ©1984. ISBN # 0-316-57509-7.

Morgan, Dan. *Merchants of Grain, The Power and Profits of the five Giant Companies at the Center of the World's Food Supply.* The Viking Press, 625 Madison Avenue, NY, 10022. July 1979, 2nd. Printing. ISBN# 0-670-47150-X. **Most Holy Family Monastery,** *A Voice Crying in the Wilderness,* Issues 1-2-3-4. 4425 Schneider Rod, Fillmore, N. Y. 14735.

Mullins Eustice, *The World Order, Our Secret Rulers.* (Ezra Pound Inst, Staunton, VA. 24401, 2nd. Ed. 1992).

Mumford, Lewis, *The City in History;* Its Origins, Its Transformations, and Its Prospects.

Nietzsche, Friedrich, (1844-1900) was a German philosopher of the late 19th century who challenged the foundations of Christianity and traditional morality.

New Age Humanism. Dominion Press, 7112 Burns St., Fort Worth, TX 76118. ©1986, Gary North. ISBN # 0-930-462-02-5.

Orwell, George, *Nineteen Eighy-four.* Paperback: 304 pages. Publisher: Plume; 60th Anniv. Edition, April 1, 1983: English. ISBN-10: 0452262933: ISBN-13: 978-0452262935.

O'Grady, Olivia Marie, *The Beasts of the Apocalypse,* First Amendment Press, Copyright © 2001. Printed in the United States of America. ISBN 0-945001-66-5.

Packard, Vance, *The Hidden Persuaders,* 1957. ISBN # 0-671-52149-2.

Parker, LLD, *Imperium.* The Noontide Press, ©1962, Sausalito, CA. LC # 62-53156.

Pendell, Elmer PH. D. _Sex Versus Civilization._ Noontide Press, P. O. Box 76062, Los Angeles, CA, 90005. © 1967 Dr. Elmer Pendell.

Pierce, William L., Ph. D. Editor, National Vanguard Books, Cat. #14, December 1992. Reprint in the _Committee to Restore the Constitution_, P. O. Box 986. Ft. Collins, CO 80522. Bulletin #376, May 1993.

Paul III, Pope _Council of Trent,_ Session 6, Chap. 3

Pius IX, Pope, Dec. 8, 1864, _The Encyclical Quanta Cura_ and_The Syllabus of Errors,_ Reprinted by The Remnant, 2539 Morrison Ave., St. Paul, MN 55117.

Pius X, Pope _The Encyclical Quanta Cura and the Syllabus of Errors._ Issued in 1864. Reprinted by the Remnant, 2539 Morrison Avenue, St. Paul, MN 55117.

PiusXI, Pope Encyclical Letter, _Mortalium Animos,_ Gregorian Press, Berlin, NJ.

Pius XI, Pope, Encyclical Letter, _On Fostering True Religious Unity,_ Gregorian Press, Berlin, N.J.

Pius XI, Pope, Encyclical Letter, _Ubi Arcano Die, On the Peace of Christ._

Pius XII, Pope, Encyclical Letter, _Humani Generis,_ Daughters of St. Paul Press, N. C. W. C. Translation. **Podhoretz, Norman** _Breaking Ranks, a Political Memoir,_ NY, Harper and Row, 1979.

Privetera, James MD., & Stang, Alan, Pursley, Leo A., DD, _The Apostolic Digest,_ Our Lady of Victory Publications, Ed., Kieth E. Gillette, P. O. Box 80363, San Marino, California 91008.

Quigley, Carroll, Ph. D., _Tragedy and Hope.A History of the World in our Time._ Chapter V.

Rafferty, Max, _Suffer Little Children,_ (The Devan Adair Co., NY).

Ratzinger, Joseph Cardinal, _Theologische Prinzipienlehre._ 1982 Erich Wewel Verlag, Munich. Translation by: McCarthy, SDN., Principals of Catholic Theology, 1987 Ignatius Press, San Francisco, CA.

Roberts, Craig, Economist, _Middle America News._ Middle American Institute, Inc., P. O. Box 20608, Raleigh, North Carolina 27619. Sept 2007, _"Return of the Robber Barons"_ Pg' 19., January 2008, _"Impending Destruction of the U. S. Economy,"_ Pg, 19., February 2008, _"Self-serving Lies Destroyed the American Dream,"_ Pg. 23.

Rueff, Jacques, _The Monetary Sin of the West._ Translated by Roger Glemet. Macmillan Inc., NY {1972}.

Ruppert, Michael C., _Crossing the Rubicon, the Decline of the American Empire at the end of the Age of Oil._ Ed., James Hecht. New Society Pub. Copyright © Michael C. Ruppert, 2004. ISBN # 0-86571-540-8.

Rutler, George W., DD. _The Fatherhood of God._ (Homiletic and Pastoral Review, June 1993).

Schlossberg, Herbert, _Idols for Destruction._ Thomas Nelson Pub., Fourth Printing, 1983. ISBN # 0-8407-5828-2 & 0-8407-5832-4**Schmidt, Austin G., S. J., and Perkins, Joseph A., A. M.** _Faith and Reason._ (Loyola University Press, Chicago, IL., 1937).

Schulze, Richard MD. _Understanding Your Immune System,_ Get Well, November 2002. Natural Healing Publications.

Schulze, Richard, MD. _The Ultimate Get Well Newsletter Collection,_ (Natural Healing Pub. Jan. 2002).

Sears, Alan E., President and General Council, Alliance Defense Fund, Scottsdale, AZ., _(Memorandum to Concerned Christians.)._

Skousen, W. Cleon, *The Naked Capitalist.* Private Edition Publication. 2197 Berkeley Street, Sault Lake City, Utah. Sixth printing 1970. A review and commentary on Dr. Caroll Quigley's book *Tragedy and Hope.*

Solzhenitsyn, Alexander. *Lenin in Zurich.* Farrah, Straus and Giroux, New York, 1976.

Spannaus, Edward, *Shock and Awe': Terror Bombing, From Wells and Russell to Cheney.* Executive Intelligence Review, Oct. 31, 2003.

Spengler, Oswald, *The Decline of the West, Vol. I. Form and Actuality,* Authorized Translation with notes by Charles Francis Atkinson. Alfred A. Knopf, Publisher, NY.

Spengler, Oswald, *The Decline of the West, Vol. II. Perspectives of World History.* Authorized Translation with notes by Charles Francis Atkinson. Alfred A. Knopf, Publisher, NY.

Stormer, John A. *None Dare Call it Treason.* "Treason doth never prosper, what's the reason? For if it prosper, none dare call it treason."

Struve, Otto, *The Universe,* The Massachusetts Institute of Technology. ©1962. LC 3 62-16928.

Sutton, Antony C. Ph. D. *Wall Street and the Bolshevik Revolution.,* Arlington House-Publishers, New Rochelle, New York, Copyright © 1974, Arlington House. ISBN o-87000-276-7.

Sutton, Anthony, Ph.D. *The Secret Cult of the Order.* Research Publications, Inc., Phoenix, AZ. 1984 © ISBN # 0-914981-09-9.

Sutton, Antony C. Ph. D. *Wall Street and FDR.* Arlington House, Pub., [1975], New Rochelle, N. Y.

Sutton, Anthony C. *How the Order Controls Education,* Research Publications, Inc., P. O. Box 39850, Phoenix, Arizona, 1983. ISBN 0-914981-00-5.

Thielicke, Helmut. *Nehilism:Its Origins and Nature with a Christian Answer.* Trans. John W. Doberstein, Schocken Books, NY., 1969 [1961].

Tolstoy, Leo, Count Von. ***War and Peace.* (Vintage Classics) Paperback**
Richard Pevear (Translator), Larissa Volokhonsky (Translator).

Varghese, Abraham, Ed. *Intellectuals Speak Out About God,* (Regnery Gateway, Chicago, Ill., 1984).

Verange, Ulick, LLD. *Imperium.* The Noontide Press, ©1962, Sausalito, CA. LC # 62-53156.

Vitz, Paul C., Professor. *The Intellectuals Speak Out About God,* Edited by Roy Abraham Varghese. © 1984, Pub. by Regnery, Gateway, Inc., 360 W. Superior St. Chicago IL, 60610. ISBN 3 0-89526-827-2.

Von Meises, Ludwig, *Human Action.* Political economy. Publication dates 1949, 1998, 2010. Yale University Press, Ludwig von Mises Institute. English, United States. Print, Hardback and Paperback; 881 pages. ISBN 9780865976313.

Von Kuenhelt-Leddihn, Erik. *Leftism, From de Sade and Marx to Hitler and Marchse,* Arlington House-Publishers, New Rochelle, New York, Copyright © 1974, ISBN 0-87000-143-4,

Wardner, Names, Ph.D. *Communist Infiltration of the Catholic Church.* Video produced by, Most Holy Family Monastery, 4425 Schneider Road, Fillmore, NY 14735.

Webster, Nesta. *World Revolution, The Plot Against Civilization,* Veritas Publishing Company, 7th. Ed., 1994, Cranbrook. Western Australia 6321,

Webster, Nesta, *The French Revolution, a Study in Democracy.* First Published 1919, Republished 1969.Second Edition, The Christian Book Club of America, Hawthorne, CA 90250

West, Samuel C. D.N. N. D. *The Golden Seven Plus One.* 1981 © Samuel Publishing Co. Orem, Utah. 84059 LC # 81-86099. 18th. Edition.

Wheeler, Richard S. *Pagans in the Pulpit,* Arlington House Publisher, New Rochelle, NY. © 1974 Richard S. Wheeler. ISBN 0-87000-264-3

Wickliffe, Vennard B., Sr., *The Federal Reserve Hoax, The Age of Deception.* Meador Publishing Co. 324 Newbury Street, Boston 15, MA. Seventh Ed. Pp. 14-70.

Wilton, Robert, *The Last of the Romanovs, How Tsar Nicholas II and Russia's Imperial Family were Murdered.* Copyright © 1993, *The Institute for Historical Review. First British Edition, pub. 1920 in London by T. Butterworth. First U. S. Edition* published 1920, in New York by George H. Dorn. French Edition, pub. Paris 1921. Russian language edition, pub. Berlin 1923. ISBN # 0-939484-1.

Wood, Garth M. D. *The Myth of Neurosis, Overcoming the Illness Excuse.* Harper and Row, Pub. New York, *Cambridgte, Philadelphia, San Francisco, London, Mexico City, Sao Paulo, Singapore, Sydney.* © 1983 by Dr. Garth Wood. ISBN # 0-06-015488-S.

Wormser, Rene A., *Foundations, Their Power and Influence,* (Covenant House Books, 1993, P. O. Box # 4690, Sevierville, TN 37864, ISBN 0-925591-28-9).

Yockey, Francis Parker, *Imperium: The Philosophy of History and Politics* by Ulick Varange (Francis Parker Yockey) (1969)